MATABELE

MATABELE

The War of 1893
and the 1896 Rebellion

Chris Ash

Also by Chris Ash:

The If Man: Dr Leander Starr Jameson: The Inspiration for Kipling's Masterpiece

Kruger, Kommandos & Kak: Debunking the Myths of The Boer War

Published in 2016 by:

30° South Publishers (Pty) Ltd
16 Ivy Road
Pinetown, 3610
South Africa
www.30degreessouth.co.za

Cover design by Anthony Cuerden / ant@flyingant.co.za
www.flyingantdesigns.co.za

Typeset by Blair Couper
Maps by Phil Wright

Printed in South Africa by Pinetown Printers

ISBN: 978-1-928211-89-1

Contents

Introduction

Shortly after the publication of my first book, I was asked to talk to the Johannesburg chapter of the South African Military History Society and spoke (probably very badly) on the subject of Dr Jim and the Matabele War. When my lecture finally spluttered to a close, one of those who had managed to stay awake throughout asked me if I could recommend a book which covered both the Matabele War of 1893—on which I had just spoken—and the rebellions of 1896/7. Despite having a library full of books on the subject, or on southern African history in general, this question made me realize that (as far as I knew) there was not a single volume that dealt with the Matabele Wars in their entirety and I decided to do my best to rectify this situation. While there are other—sometimes very dry and dusty—accounts that cover specific events of one or other conflict (often in mind-numbingly tedious detail) I am ever conscious of the fact that most people find history 'boring' these days. It was thus never my intention to cover every single aspect or nuance of the wars but rather to give an accessible, readable, and accurate account. Indeed, I have made every effort to deal in historical fact rather than to give a politically-correct 21st century reinterpretation of it and I make no apologies for being blunt. If anyone feels the need to be 'offended' I would suggest they have deeper psychological issues to deal with.

Though any mistakes and/or controversial outbursts herein are all mine, I would like to thank those who have helped me with this project. First and foremost, special thanks to Phil Wright, cartographer extraordinaire and all round good egg. A 'planning meeting' at my house in Johannesburg turned into a splendidly drunken evening and I shall never forget the story of the pubic hair which was called to stand in for a framed butterfly's missing antenna. Noted historian, Ken Gillings, who is always keen to discuss matters at great length, has been as helpful as ever, while Gerry van Tonder provided some fascinating insights and shared his copious research material freely. I am greatly indebted to all these fine gentlemen. Chris Cocks and Aulette Goliath of 30° South Publishers have been supportive and enthusiastic throughout, and I greatly appreciate their help.

§

The fact that no one has previously covered both conflicts in a single volume is surprising when one thinks about how many books there are on the 1879 Zulu War. It would be fair to say that few colonial wars have the appeal, or perhaps the 'glamour' of that conflict. The clash of stalwart redcoats against hordes of fanatically brave warriors was mirrored by various other campaigns, but none continue to capture the public imagination in quite the same way. Maybe Cy Endfield's[i] wildly ahistorical 1964 classic, Zulu, is to blame for the war's enduring appeal, and no doubt the 'humiliation'[ii] suffered by the British at Isandlwana appeals those who are, for some reason, terribly ashamed of the empire...but the conflict's allure extends well beyond the hand-wringing of today's liberals: 'Zulu' company of 45 Commando, Royal Marines, for example, advanced into battle in the Falklands War chanting their battle cry, 'Zulu! Zulu!'

Rather as the magnetism of soccer threatens to overshadow every other sport, however, the problem is that it tends to put other, equally fascinating, colonial wars in the shade as authors overlook them in the rush to churn out more and more books on the Zulu War.

Whatever the reason, the Matabele Wars of the 1890s have received relatively little attention and I hope this book will go some way towards filling the gap.

There is no denying that the Matabele Wars are a lot less romantic and photogenic than the Zulu War. The 1893 war, and the rebellions of a few years later, would not make for colourful Hollywood blockbusters, the British army having by then swapped their splendid red coats for rather more sensible khaki uniforms (although precious few imperial troops served in Matabeleland in any case). The wonky, unreliable Gatlings and (frankly) ludicrous rocket batteries of the Zulu War had given way, and highly effective Maxim guns were seeing major action for the first time. Nevertheless, the Matabele warriors showed every bit as much heroism, determination and selflessness as their distant kinsmen had in the Zulu War.

There were also some remarkable characters involved: old school savage tyrant Chief Lobengula, the ambitious and ever-scheming Cecil Rhodes, and the rascally Dr Jameson of course...but also men like Captain Lendy, one of very few men in history to have died from putting a shot, Frederick Selous the archetypal great white hunter, and Kagubi the infamous witch-doctor who whipped up so much trouble during the rebellion.

Baden-Powell, who would later defy the Boers in his defence of Mafeking and famously go on to found the Boy Scouts, cut his teeth in Matabeleland. So did Plumer, who would also serve against the Boers and later command the British 2nd Army in the Great War, finishing his career as a Field Marshall. The dashing and redoubtable Maurice

---

i Cy Endfield was 'exposed' as a communist by the House Un-American Activities Committee, and blacklisted in Hollywood as a result–something to bear in mind when considering how his film portrays the British Empire.

ii The reader will note that every British defeat of the colonial era is mindlessly described as a 'humiliation' in certain circles.

Gifford served in both Matabele Wars and lost his arm in the second–an inconvenience he did not consider sufficient to prevent him giving the empire yet more sterling service during the Boer War.

Another veteran of the Matabele Wars with links to the Boy Scouts was Major Burnham, an American frontiersman and tracker who sparked Baden-Powell's love of field craft. Despite his obvious courage and skill, Burnham was also a colourful fantasist of a man who claimed to have killed a rebel god during the rebellion, and had the distinct advantage of having written his own account of his exploits in the conflict. Equally extraordinary was 'Maori' Hamilton-Browne, a man whose far-fetched tales of derring-do were enough to earn him a senior appointment in the rebellion. Indeed, the characters are probably the most fascinating part of the tale: adventurous young Anglo-Saxons from every corner of the empire, and a few old Indian fighters from the American West, who all found themselves thousands of miles from home facing a brave and terrifying enemy.

Unlike the Zulu War, the later Sudan Campaign, or the Boer War, the First Matabele War was fought on a shoestring by troops raised and funded by Cecil Rhodes' British South Africa Company, not the famous old regiments of the British army. There are also endless intrigues, controversies and far-fetched conspiracy theories surrounding the origins of the conflict. As we shall see, today's usual suspects ignore the murderous rampages of the Matabele and instead heap all the blame on Rhodes and his men–something which we shall show to be politically-correct tedium. Similarly, and though somewhat pathetically dismissed as 'mercenaries' by squeamish liberals today, the reader will see that there was no shortage of dash and pluck on the side of the company men either. Indeed, the valour and gallantry of Major Wilson's men at the Shangani Patrol's last stand was equal in every way to that of the redcoats who won eleven Victoria Crosses at Rorke's Drift.[iii]

With oft-claimed links to the infamous Jameson Raid, the origins of the second Matabele War are as fascinating and controversial as those of the first, and it was a dirty, hard-fought guerrilla war, more akin to the African bush wars of the 1960s and 70s than those waged at the height of the colonial period. The brutal murders of women and children committed by the insurgents and the widespread use of dynamite to entomb rebels in their subterranean hiding places both sparked fury and condemnation at the time, but aside from the butchery, actions such as the Mazoe Patrol were as heroic as anything of the age.

---

iii Seven were won by soldiers of the 2nd Battalion, 24th (2nd Warwickshire) Regiment of Foot, and one each by servicemen of the Army Medical Department, the Royal Engineers, the Commissariat and Transport Department and the Natal Native Contingent.

But before we crack on with the action let us take a moment to explain how it was that a renegade offshoot of the Zulu tribe came to be at war with men employed by a company started by a sickly clergyman's son from Bishop's Stortford.

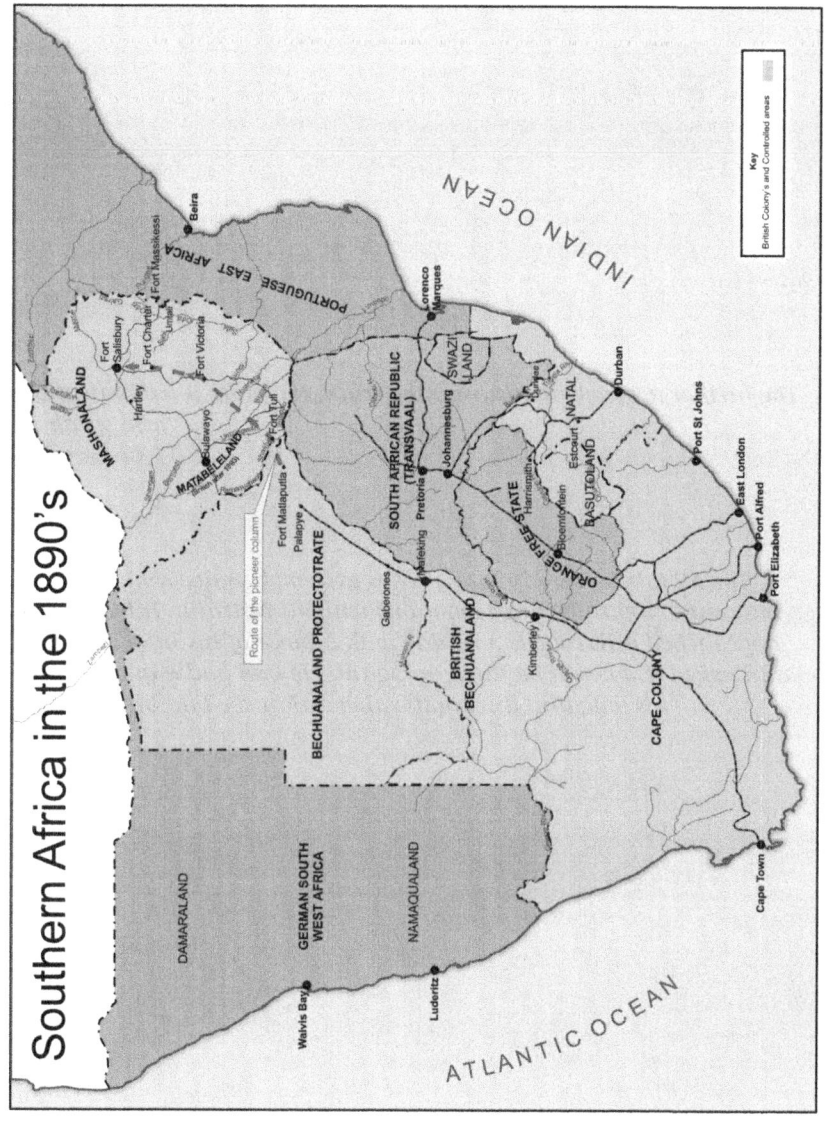

Southern Africa in the 1890's

'The further a society drifts from the truth, the more it will hate those who speak it.'
– George Orwell

'The Matabele were in many ways extremely naïve and childlike, giving vent to their primitive emotions without restraint. A black man approached a European one day with a piece of his nose on a leaf, and asked if it could be stuck on again. He had had a quarrel with his wife and during the altercation she had bitten it off.'[1]

Chapter 1
Background

Unfortunately, and as we have already mentioned, the insidious spread of political correctness impacts any attempt to discuss African history rationally. By daring not to toe the 'all black Africans good, all white settlers bad' party line, one risks the usual tiresome squeals of 'racist!' from shrieking liberals. Any rational discussion about the rights and wrongs of the Matabele War can therefore be guaranteed to provoke a knee jerk reaction along the lines of, 'well, the whites shouldn't have been there in the first place'.

This oft-squawked mantra is trotted out to excuse absolutely anything the Matabele did, as though they had some sort of God-given right to be there while the white settlers did not, and can therefore be exonerated for murder, pillage, slave raiding and, well, just about anything else.

Like most things that go down well with the Islington dinner party set however, there is very little logic to this. In truth, the Matabele were also recent settlers in the area so it is bizarre that their warlike and savage colonization is perfectly acceptable to the modern-day left whereas—and in stark contrast—the relatively peaceful and law-abiding settlement of the Mashonaland pioneers is regarded as, horror of horrors, 'evil, rapacious, exploitative imperialism'. Unfortunately, this sort of mindless nonsense permeates every discussion about the colonial period, so let us nip it in the bud before we go any further.

The earliest known inhabitants of southern Africa were the copper-skinned Bushmen and lighter Hottentots–not the blacks from the Bantu tribes that originated in west and central Africa. The names for these earliest southern Africans were (and still are) often used interchangeably, which is perhaps understandable given that it was several years before the Dutch settlers at the Cape recognized them as distinct ethnic groups.[i] Indeed, there was a great deal of inter-breeding between the two so the boundaries are certainly blurred and a collective term for the two groups, 'Khoisan', is currently in vogue.

The closest thing southern Africa has to an 'aboriginal' race would be the Bushmen, a people described as 'little sallow folk, barely five feet high, their heads adorned with peppercorn tufts of hair and lobeless ears, their triangular fox-like faces almost innocent of beards'.[2] The

---

i   These two groups are currently referred to as 'the San People' and 'the Khoikhoi' but I have elected to retain contemporary names/terms throughout this book. This is not intended to cause offence, though those who delight in taking offence at such things will no doubt do so.

Hottentots—who are thought, either to be an offshoot of the Bushmen or else to have arrived in the region somewhat later—largely displaced the Bushmen in places. They were:

> '...of slight build with backs as hollow and hands and feet as small as the Bushmen's; their eyes were far apart, their cheeks sunken and their chins pointed, their skins a dingy olive-yellow.'[3]

An early British visitor to the Cape described them as:

> '...a race of men distinct from both negroes and European whites, for their hair is woolly, short, and frizzled, their noses flat, and their lips thick, but their skin is naturally as white as ours.'[4]

Though roughly similar in appearance, the Hottentots, who worked copper and tended herds of cattle, were hundreds of years ahead of the Bushmen in terms of development. In contrast, the Bushmen were essentially Stone Age hunters,[5] so it is hardly surprising that the pastoral Hottentots were able to marginalize and effectively replace them.

In earlier times it would seem, scattered parties of both these groups had ranged over much of southern Africa before being driven into the extreme south by the black Bantu tribes as they started spreading out from central Africa. Around 915 AD, the Muslim explorer, Massoudi of Baghdad, wrote of having encountered Bushmen (known as Wak-Waks) as far north as modern-day Dar es Salaam–an area he described as being just 'south of the black man's land'.[6] Even then, he recorded how encroaching Bantus hunted down and killed the poor Wak-Waks 'as though they were baboons'.

The steady march of Bantu expansion continued inexorably over the following centuries, pushing ever southwards and driving both Bushmen and Hottentots before them. They settled the land in a way which, had they been European colonists, would have had modern-day liberals up in arms. Needless to say, anything done by non-white settlers is viewed in a completely different light for some unspecified reason. Though there are vastly varying theories, it would seem certain that by the 1400s (some claim hundreds of years earlier and no one knows for sure) the various groups of Bantu settlers which would later become known as the Mashona[ii] had arrived in what today is known as

---

ii Rather than a tribe in itself per se, the word 'Mashona' was first employed by the Matabele to describe a large number of different tribal groups in the modern-day Zimbabwe area, all of which shared a common language. There are various theories as to what the word originally meant, none of which are terribly complimentary. In contemporary works, names like Makalaka, Baduma, and Wahungwe pop up to describe various sub-divisions of what we now generally term 'the Mashona' but we will avoid undue complications by using the generic term throughout, as this book is not intended to be an anthropological study of Africa.

Zimbabwe, and the northern areas of modern-day Mozambique.[7] Other Bantu groups continued the push southwards and over the Limpopo into what is South Africa today.

Despite the modern-day view, the Mashona (and their various sub-groups and offshoots) were by no means the 'indigenous people' or 'original inhabitants' of what would later become Zimbabwe. By the time the 'Scramble for Africa' took place in the late Victorian era, the Mashona could at least claim to have lived there for a few hundred years or more.[iii] However, their neighbours to the west, the Matabele,[iv] could not even make this assertion as they had been a much more recent arrival.

The Matabele were an offshoot of the Zulu tribe which emerged when the Bantu advance south made it as far as modern-day Natal. Around 1817, after an especially successful raid on a neighbouring tribe, avarice got the better of the minor Zulu chieftain, Mzilikazi.[v] Such was the vast amount of plunder in the shape of cattle taken[8] that Mzilikazi was not keen to return to Zululand and hand the requisite amount of his loot over to King Shaka. Instead, he chose to lead his people north, away from Zululand towards the area around where Pretoria now stands,[9] thus creating the Matabele tribe.

Mzilikazi's warriors rampaged, ravaged and looted their way northwards, slaughtering or enslaving anyone who stood in their path, and established a Matabele kingdom in what later became known as the Transvaal where they dominated, in Zulu-style, the tribes they found there.[10] The ten-year-long orgy of mass-murder they inflicted on the region contributed to the 'Mfecane' (the 'scattering' or 'crushing')–a period of general chaos and massacre in which various Bantu tribes fought one another over a large part of southern Africa. No one will ever know how many were slaughtered in this poorly documented bloodbath, but it is widely accepted[vi] that the Transvaal was all but 'ethnically cleansed' as a result. One of the period's leading historians, Donald Morris, claims, 'At least a million people, and more likely two, died in a decade.'[11]

The Matabele raided in every direction, practically annihilating whole tribes of Bechuana.[12] The massacres only ended in 1837 when

---

iii Portuguese and Dutch settlers could have made similar claims in the parts of Africa they had colonized.

iv The word 'Matabele' is thought to originate from the phrase 'sank out of sight' as Mzilikazi's warriors would disappear behind their large shields when facing attack.

v Mzilikazi (c.1790–1868) sometimes written as Umziligazi, rather charmingly translates as: 'the spiller of blood'.

vi Other than by those who, without offering any real evidence to support their claims, declare the whole thing was some sort of vast apartheid-era fiction. For more details, please read Carolyn Hamilton's The Mfecane Aftermath.

Hendrik Potgieter's Boer Voortrekkers[vii] arrived in the area and clashed with the Matabele. Faced with the Voortrekkers' muskets and horsemen, Mzilikazi fled northwards once more, leading his people to happier hunting grounds across the Limpopo. Killing or driving out the Mashona they found in their new kingdom,[viii] the Matabele founded their capital, Kwa Bulawayo, in the west of modern-day Zimbabwe. The name 'Kwa Bulawayo' translates to 'place of slaughter' which gives some insight to the mindset of the Matabele.

Luckily for the Matabele, their new neighbours to the east— those they dubbed the Mashona, some of whom they had chased out when they established their domain—were a comparatively peaceful, disorganized and timorous people. This effective power vacuum made it possible for the Matabele to quickly establish themselves as the pre-eminent force in the region and they soon started sending raiding parties hither and thither to loot for cattle, women, and slaves. Though they did not directly rule Mashonaland— indeed, many Mashonas had never seen a Matabele—the Matabele quickly decided that Mashonaland, nevertheless, belonged to them and demanded regular tributes from a number of Mashona chiefs. The Matabele also raided Bechuanaland[ix] to their west regularly; in fact, along with the never-ending land grabs by Transvaal Boers, it was the constant attentions of the Matabele which later prompted King Khama of the Bechuana to ask that his people be shielded by a British Protectorate.[13]

Always keen for more cattle and loot, at some point during the 1860s, Mzilikazi personally led an impi north across the Zambezi to wage war against Chief Sebitoane's people. When he failed to return after several months, a group of his indunas[x] decided, not unreasonably, that he must have fallen off his perch, and placed a fellow called Nkulumana[xi] (one of Mzilikazi's various sons by one of his various brides) on the throne in his father's place. Unfortunately for all concerned however, rumours of Mzilikazi's death proved to be an exaggeration and when he returned to Bulawayo shortly thereafter, he did not see the funny side of this.

Over-reacting somewhat, the blood-thirsty brute had the responsible indunas thrown down a precipice to their deaths. To

---

vii White, mainly Dutch-speaking residents from the Cape Colony who packed up and headed north in response to the Cape having come under British rule and slavery thus having been abolished. One of the Voortrekker leaders, Andries Hendrik Potgieter (1792–1852) would later serve as head of state for the tiny republics of Potchefstroom and Zoutpansberg.

viii The survivors fled to join their kinsmen in what became known as Mashonaland.

ix Modern-day Botswana

x Subordinate chiefs

xi Sometimes written as 'Kuruman'

ensure that there would be no such troublesome misunderstandings in future, Mzilikazi then ordered the execution of all his sons.[14]

Third in line to the throne was Lobengula,[xii] Mzilikazi's son by one of his inferior wives. This remarkably fortunate youngster survived the whirlwind of butchery by grace of the fact that he had been hidden in a remote part of Matabeleland and only returned to Bulawayo in 1868. Luckily for Lobengula, the aging Mzilikazi's wrath had subsided by then. With his blood lust sated for a while, Mzilikazi rather sportingly named Lobengula his rightful successor just before he died but even this was not straightforward or devoid of the requisite slaughter. Various factions of Matabele clashed in a decade-long civil war for succession[15] which only ended when Lobengula's forces finally defeated the rival Zwangendaba clan[16] after many thousands had perished.

Lobengula was a large fellow–some say as tall as 6'2". His insatiable love of beer and semi-raw red meat combined to make him enormously fat and unhealthy as a result of which, he was plagued by gout and not terribly mobile.[17] One witness reckoned, 'His weight measurement must be about 300 pounds, and his chest measurement 55-60 inches. His walk is most majestically imposing; he treads the ground in a manner that shows that he is conscious of his absolute power.'[18] But if anyone had been naïve enough to hope that the crowning of this epicurean heavy-weight would usher in a rather more peaceful and benevolent regime they were to be sorely disappointed. Life in Lobengula's court was just as cheap as it had been in his father's and anyone who even mildly annoyed the new king risked being put to death in imaginative and horrific ways.[19]

One long-term visitor to Bulawayo, Francis 'Matabele' Thompson, recounted numerous grisly tales of Lobengula's savagery. Anyone who attracted too much attention risked being dispatched by a 'tap from a knobkerrie at the back of the head' and the 'victim's wife and children, and all his relatives within reach, were killed and their goods confiscated':

'I have passed over the bodies of men and women in their last agony. I have seen a child aged only days lying near its murdered mother, like a new-born kitten, dying by inches.'[20]

Thompson recorded an especially horrific episode after a man had foolishly taken a drink of the king's beer:

'The poor wretch was brought before the king. He was horribly afraid. His eyes stuck out of his head, and his knees knocked

---

xii Lobengula (translated as 'driven by the wind') Khumalo (c.1845–1894) ruled as king of the Matabele from 1868 to1894.

together as he tried to make obeisance. The king bade them hold him fast, then he said, looking the culprit up and down, "You have a nose and a mouth, and two ears, and two eyes. You have used your nose to smell the king's beer—(turning to attendants)—cut off his nose!" They cut off the man's nose. "You have used your mouth to drink the king's beer; cut off his mouth!" They cut off the man's lips. He was a horrid sight. Lo Bengula waited a moment. Then he said deliberately, "You have heard that it is not good to drink the king's beer; but your ears are no good to you." Off went the poor wretch's ears. He looked at the king with a look dreadful to see. "Your eyes–cover up his eyes!" shouted the king, "Put his forehead over his eyes that he may not see the king's beer!" and they cut the forehead of the man and turned down the flap of skin as a surgeon might turn it, so that it hung over his eyes. Then the king looked at the man for a few minutes, and the man grovelled before him in the dung; until suddenly the king fell into a rage— perhaps he was ashamed of himself—and bade them beat the man with logs of wood. They beat him within an inch of his life. Last, the poor wretch mustered strength to crawl away, like a broken snake, along the ground; and he went and lay under a wagon until nightfall. Then he crept down to the stream to bathe his wounds.'[21]

Long before the modern obsession with political correctness would have prevented such honesty, the missionary, J.S. Moffat, was able to describe the sheer savagery of Lobengula's highly unpleasant regime:

'The Matabele are a miserable people, and have made myriads of other people miserable too. One daughter of [Lobengula's] hung herself last week; this makes three of his children who have committed suicide. Another also tried to do so last week, but was prevented in time. One of the old wives of the late chief Mosilikatze [Mzilikazi] cut her throat a month ago. The induna of a kraal near Hope Fountain died lately. Two of the wives are daily expecting to be murdered on the charge of having bewitched him. These things are what may be called the upper circle. Meanwhile, the common people are awfully oppressed and there is no court of appeal for them–not in this world at least.'[22]

Lobengula's punishment for a wagon driver who had lost a heavily-laden wagon in a swollen river, was to order him bound, hand and foot, and thrown in after his load to be torn apart by crocodiles. Had the white witnesses of this horrific event not managed to hide the wagoner's newly widowed wife and children there is little doubt they would have suffered the same fate.[23]

Despite his barbarous streak, Lobengula bizarrely seemed to have had something of a soft spot for white visitors to his court,[xiii] and most were welcomed and treated kindly.[24] Many such visitors described Lobengula as a highly intelligent man with a natural talent for politics and all were impressed by his gift for public speaking, but he lacked his father's steely leadership as well as the deep respect afforded to Mzilikazi for his impressive military achievements. Indeed, Lobengula was never to enjoy quite the same iron fisted control over his tribe as Mzilikazi had.

For all his obvious intelligence, Lobengula was also a deeply superstitious man and put great faith in the lunatic ramblings of his gaggle of witch-doctors. The annual great dance, which was held to celebrate the appearance of the new moon at harvest time, was the highlight of the witch-doctors' calendar. Enormous numbers of Matabele congregated at Lobengula's kraal in Bulawayo for several days of eating, dancing, drinking, and killing. At some point in the festivities, Lobengula himself would haul his corpulent body onto its feet and stagger about doing a bit of jig for a while. Then he would fling an assegai into the air.[25] When the spear clattered to the ground, it indicated the direction in which the Matabele raiding parties would set off to loot, kill, and plunder in the coming year.

Lobengula did not only inflict this murder on his neighbours though–his fellow Matabele also stood a fair chance of being hacked apart during the dance. As soon as the assegai had pointed the way, Lobengula would unleash his witch-doctors, who would 'smell out' victims from the drunken mob. In an unrestrained orgy of slaughter which would continue for the remaining days of the festivity, the poor devils would then be dragged out of the crowd and murdered.[26]

The raids that Lobengula's assegai-flinging dance unleashed were the mainstay of the Matabele economy, and the Matabele quite simply, could not have existed without them. In 1888, the deputy commissioner of Bechuanaland, Sir Sidney Shippard, travelled to Matabeleland and described the way in which Lobengula's people lived off their neighbours:

'He described the ruins of a Mashona village destroyed this year, the burned huts, the little patches of garden ground fenced in and carefully cultivated by the industrious Mashona, none of whom have lived to reap the fruits of their labour. Every man, woman and infant in these villages had been killed by the spear or "stabbing assegai" of the Matabele matjaka,[xiv] except the old women who are

---

xiii Exceptions were the murders of Captain R. Patterson, Mr J. Sergeant, and Mr Thomas, who Henry Rider Haggard stated were all killed in September 1878 on Lobengula's orders.

xiv A matjaka/matjaha was a young, unmarried Matabele warrior.

used as carriers as long as they are wanted, and then tied to trees, round which dry grass is heaped up and then set on fire, such holocausts of old Mashona women being regarded as a capital joke by the Matabele matjaka.

Of the children and girls who are driven here [Bulawayo] as slaves, those who survive the journey are afterwards fairly well treated. Lobengula allows the slave boys nothing but beef to eat, however great their craving for farinaceous food; the result being that all the weaker boys soon die of dysentery, while the survivors become very strong, and consequently fit to be incorporated, in due time, into a regiment of matjakas of the requisite ferocity. I see great numbers of these slave boys here.'[27]

A single such raid over the Zambezi in 1889 netted, '…15,000 head of cattle, much loot and many captive children and girls. The atrocities committed were frightful.'[28]

The fair-minded reader will agree that far from being 'the original inhabitants' of the area, by 1890, the Matabele had only been there for a couple of generations. Indeed, Lobengula was only the tribe's second chief, and the first to gain power since they had fled north into modern-day Zimbabwe. What is more, the Matabele settlers—for that is exactly what they were—made no effort to develop and enhance the area. Instead they existed entirely by seizing whatever they wanted in raids against their neighbours and using their military muscle to intimidate weaker tribes into handing over cattle, women and slaves.

The historian Peter Baxter gives an excellent description of how the Matabele economy worked:

'It was based on the husbandry of cattle and the parallel husbandry of any unfortunate neighbours less warlike than themselves. The striking difference between the two systems of stock management was the cattle were nurtured and humanely treated while human prey was used and butchered in the most cynical and inhumane manner imaginable.'[29]

The way in which the infinitely more benign and benevolent British Empire is loathed and shrieked about by modern day liberals is truly bizarre when one considers that the same lefties—with characteristically shameless hypocrisy—fully support the much more violent colonialism and imperialist exploitation practiced by the Matabele. The reader will have to make up his own mind about why this is the case.

§

    While we leave the latter-day apologists to dream up some sort of reason why they should still maintain that the Matabele are the 'goodies' in our story, let us turn our attention to the other newcomers on the scene: a pioneering young band of settlers organized and funded by British diamond magnate and devoted imperialist, Cecil John Rhodes.[xv]

    By the late 1880s, a number of European powers were thinking of Mashonaland as the next logical place for settlement. Germany had come late to the Scramble for Africa but desperate to catch up, they had established their presence in modern-day Namibia away to the west, and modern-day Tanzania up in the north by the mid-1880s. To the east, the Portuguese had retained fairly modest coastal stations in modern day Mozambique for hundreds of years. In 1887, however, the Portuguese foreign ministry produced what became known as the 'Rose-Coloured Map', a remarkable document which laid claim to roughly all of modern-day Mozambique and Angola, and more importantly—with commendable ambition—absolutely everything in between, including Matabeleland and Mashonaland.[30] To the south, the short-lived British annexation of the Boer Transvaal had been embarrassingly ended by defeat in the First Boer War and the newly-independent-again republic was demonstrating a truly voracious appetite for expansion in pretty much every direction. The Transvaal Boers had earlier championed a pretender to Lobengula's throne,[xvi] the idea being to put him in power and then expand the borders of their ever-land hungry republic accordingly.[31] As previously noted, it was the territorial expansion of the Transvaal (and the raids of the Matabele) which in 1885, finally prompted the British to reluctantly establish a protectorate over Bechuanaland, immediately to the west of Matabeleland.

    It was in this heady environment that various concession seekers were sniffing about Bulawayo, while delegations from Germany, Portugal, and the Transvaal all vied for the chance to prospect in Lobengula's kingdom and his vassal state, Mashonaland.[32] Pricked into action by this interest, the British sent their man, the Rev. John Smith Moffat, Assistant Commissioner of the Bechuanaland Protectorate, to secure an agreement of their own.[33] Moffat's father, the Reverend Robert Moffat of the London Missionary Society, had been a close confidant of Mzilikazi's and this family connection undoubtedly played a part in prompting Lobengula to sign The Moffat Treaty in February 1888.

    The Treaty stated that Lobengula would, 'refrain from entering into any correspondence or treaty with any foreign state or power to

---

xv Cecil John Rhodes PC, DCL (1853–1902) was one of seven brothers and two sisters. Four of his brothers were commissioned into the British Army, one of which, Frank, became the Colonel of the 1st (Royal) Dragoons and would be intimately involved in the Jameson Raid.

xvi This was the Transvaal's preferred method of territorial expansion and was used to push out their borders to the determinant of their black neighbours on numerous occasions.

sell, or cede, or permit, or countenance any sale, alienation or cession of the whole or any part of the said Amandebele country under his chieftainship or upon any other subject, without the previous sanction of Her Majesty's high commissioner for South Africa'. At a stroke, Lobengula had entered the very loose and ill-defined British 'sphere of influence' in the region by effectively giving Her Majesty's government 'first refusal' on both Matabeleland and Mashonaland, and this would thwart the ambitions of London's rivals for the time being. Perhaps—rather like the other southern African British protectorates of Basutoland and Bechuanaland—the area would have remained in this loose, fairly 'hands-off' state of limbo had unfettered private enterprise in the shape of Cecil John Rhodes not intervened.

The son of a Church of England vicar, Rhodes was born in the pleasant Hertfordshire town of Bishop's Stortford in 1853. A weak, sickly child, young Rhodes was sent out to Natal in 1870 in the rather far-fetched hope that the climate would somehow improve his health. After a brief flirtation with cotton farming in Natal, Rhodes decided to try his luck at the nascent Kimberley diamond fields and moved there with his older brother, Herbert[xvii] the following year.[34] Though the tall, lanky, and rather awkward youngster might have been something of a figure of fun when he arrived at the diggings, the astute and Machiavellian Rhodes soon started buying out his competition. Made possible by funding secured from the famous Rothschild family, this feverish consolidation continued apace over the following years and Rhodes quickly became the main player in the industry. In 1888, Rhodes and his last competitor in Kimberley, Barney Barnato,[xviii] 'a Jewish digger, half-prize fighter, half music-hall artiste,'[35] established a virtual monopoly by merging their companies to form De Beers Consolidated Mines.[xix]

A man of matchless energy and ambition, Rhodes dreamed of painting a great swathe of British pink[xx] across the map of Africa, a

---

xvii Herbert was destined to die in spectacular fashion a few years later while elephant hunting in Nyasaland. Boozing heavily in his tent one night, he drunkenly lunged towards another bottle of gin, clumsily knocked over a paraffin lamp and was burned alive in the resultant blaze.

xviii Barney Barnato (c.1851–1897). Born Barnet Isaacs in London, Barnato's birthdate is the subject of some conjecture as he always claimed it to be different to the one on his birth certificate. One time prize fighter and music-hall act, Barnato arrived at the Kimberley diamond rush in 1873 and initially made his money selling cigars. Before long he began buying up claims and went on to set up The Barnato Diamond Mining Company with his brothers.

xix De Beers was named after a farm which became an especially profitable diamond mine. In 1927, a controlling stake would be bought by Ernest Oppenheimer's Anglo American Corporation. The Oppenheimers sold their remaining family stake in De Beers to Anglo American in 2011, the result being that at the time of writing, De Beers is 85% owned by Anglo American plc, and 15% by the Government of Botswana.

xx The colour associated with Britain was actually red, but printers compromised by using pink so that letters printed in black over the base colour would still be legible.

vast, unbroken belt of imperial territory from Cape to Cairo.[36] Rhodes' ambition literally knew no bounds–he once claimed that he would annex the planets if he could. He had no time for the dithering, sloth-like pace of the British Colonial Office, and constantly railed against what he mockingly decried as 'the imperial factor' for not sharing his grand vision for Africa. Ever fearful that the expansion of rival powers would block the route to 'his north', Rhodes snatched at the opportunity presented by the Moffat Treaty and quickly dispatched his own delegation to formalize a prospecting concession in Mashonaland; a treaty which would, he hoped, also finally checkmate any plans being made in Germany, Portugal or the Transvaal.

It took Rhodes' agents months of wrangling, but the lure of gold sovereigns and the 1,000 Martini Henry rifles on offer proved too much for Lobengula's greed. The Chief finally consented and signed 'the fly blown paper'[37] that was the Rudd Concession.[xxi] In exchange for the rifles, 100,000 rounds of ammunition, a payment of £100 each lunar month, and—somewhat peculiarly—a 'steam boat with guns suitable for defensive purposes' (this sweetener was one of Rhodes' ideas but it was never delivered) the Rudd Concession secured 'complete and exclusive charge over all the metals and minerals situated and contained in [Lobengula's] kingdom, principalities and dominions, together with full power to do all things [deemed] necessary to win and procure the same'.[38]

Armed with the priceless Rudd Concession, Rhodes travelled to London to secure permission to establish a chartered company to develop Mashonaland. The concept was nothing new: Her Majesty's government had long used chartered companies as a way of getting private enterprise, rather than the long-suffering tax-payer, to fund the expansion of the British Empire–and, just as importantly, to shoulder all the risk. The East India Company and Hudson Bay Company had been granted royal charters as early as the 1600s and more recently, in the 1880s, charters had been granted to the British North Borneo Company and the Royal Niger Company.

Some, like famed big game hunter, Frederick Selous,[xxii] raised the awkward question of whether Lobengula had any right to sign treaties relating to Mashonaland in any case. Selous was quickly brought into Rhodes' orbit, however, and no doubt realized that the Mashona— for whom he had a great fondness—would be much better off under company rule than Lobengula's tyranny. Indeed, Rhodes' money and highly placed connections smoothed over any and all such concerns

---

xxi   Named after the lead negotiator, Charles Dunell Rudd (1844–1916).

xxii Frederick Courtney Selous DSO, (1851–1917). Selous' remarkable life would inspire the Henry Rider Haggard character, Allan Quatermain, and he would go on to die a hero's death, cut down by machine gun fire while serving in German East Africa as a sprightly 65 year old subaltern.

which surfaced in London, and the charter was duly awarded to his British South Africa Company.[xxiii]

Like other royal charters, it was a far-reaching document that applied to a huge chunk of Africa, an area hazily defined as being 'the region of South Africa lying immediately to the north of British Bechuanaland and to the north and west of the South African Republic and to the west of the Portuguese Dominions'. Rather tellingly, and no doubt to Rhodes' great delight, no northern boundary was mentioned. Within this vast tract of land, the chartered company could 'make treaties, promulgate laws, preserve the peace, maintain a police force and acquire new concessions... make roads, railways, harbours, or undertake other public works, own or charter ships, engage in mining or any other industry, establish banks, make land grants, and carry on any lawful commerce, trade, pursuit or business'.[39] Though the charter confirmed that the colonial secretary still retained ultimate supervision and there were a few caveats in respect to native rights and the stamping out of any existing slave trade, it was nevertheless a remarkably unrestrained licence.[40]

The full text of the document can be read in Appendix 1.

In July 1890, the first batch of Rhodes' settlers—the famous pioneer column—set off from Fort Tuli on the border of Bechuanaland. Guided by Frederick Selous himself, the column skirted the south of Matabeleland proper and then pushed north into Mashonaland. Recruited from all over South Africa and commanded by 23 year old Major Frank Johnson,[xxiv] the pioneers consisted of about 200 young men, overwhelmingly of British stock,[41] who possessed a suitably wide range of skills and trades for building a new nation from scratch. Around 2,000 oxen dragged well over one hundred carts laden with 40 tons of Boer meal and several tons each of tea, sugar, salt, jam, and pickled vegetables. 250 cattle and 300 sheep were also driven along to provide fresh meat.[42] In addition, the pioneers carted vast quantities of ammunition, mining equipment, explosives, medical supplies, building materials and countless other essentials. Deemed equally essential to the sports-mad Victorians, were crates of cricket and lawn tennis equipment, and all the requisite costumes, scenery, and other paraphernalia sufficient to establish a theatre.[43]

---

xxiii Established in 1889 with a charter initially valid for 25 years, the British South Africa Company merged with the Central Mining & Investment Corporation Ltd and The Consolidated Mines Selection Company Ltd in 1965 to form a mining and industrial company known as Charter Consolidated Ltd, a large chunk of which was owned by Anglo American plc. After various name changes and different owners, it exists today as the London-based engineering company, Charter International, part of the American Colfax Group.

xxiv Lt Colonel Sir Frank William Frederick Johnson DSO (1866–1943). Born in Norfolk, Johnson arrived in Cape Town as a 16 year old with just £5 to his name and served as a Quarter Master Sergeant in the Bechuanaland Border Police.

Though they were a formidable paramilitary force in their own right, the pioneers also enjoyed the additional protection of 650 troopers from the recently-raised British South Africa Company Police– the fore-runner of the famed BSAP.

With the help of a few hundred levies loaned by King Khama of the Bechuana, these plucky young fellows literally hacked a path through the bush for months, working under the very real prospect of an overwhelming attack from Lobengula's impis. Though tensions with the Matabele were palpable, the Mashona they encountered on the march were understandably overjoyed by their arrival and happily traded with them, no doubt hoping that their presence would mean the end of Lobengula's reign of terror. Writing home in October 1890, Frederick Selous reported that the Mashona were 'few and scattered and a very harmless and peaceful lot' who all seemed 'delighted' to see the pioneers, and made use of such expressions as, "Now the white men have come into the country we shall be able to sleep," meaning that they would no longer live in perpetual fear of the Matabele.

In Bulawayo, the march of the pioneers stirred fury in Lobengula's court. The company's man there, Johann Colenbrander, recorded in his diary:

'I heard numbers of headmen asking the king for permission to attack the white men. The king said, "How will you attack them?" They said, "With guns and assegais." The king then said, "The assegai is the only thing you can depend on, the weapon your fathers had before you, but, if I get killed, can you bring me back to life again? Do you really speak as men that you wish to attack these people?" They said, "Yes, King, we mean what we say, and also that we do not mean them to come in."… Men were urging the king to fight and telling him that they were not afraid of horsemen or the white man's guns. "We will send one shower of assegais into them and finish them."'[44]

Fully expecting Lobengula's hordes to descend at any time, the pioneers established small forts along the way, the last of which, Fort Salisbury, was declared the capital of the nascent colony in September 1890. By any standards, the pioneers had performed a notable feat. Pushing forward at an average of about 10 miles a day, they had cut a road through 400 miles of dense bush, crossed numerous rivers and streams, built a string of forts and founded a colony a thousand miles away from the nearest railhead. With only hand axes, ox-power, brute strength, and Anglo-Saxon dynamism, and always under the risk of attack by overwhelming numbers of Matabele—a threat which never materialized—they had done this without a single shot being fired in anger or the loss of a single man. Perhaps Howard Hensman best sums up the pioneers' achievement in his 1900 work, History of Rhodesia:

> 'This march of the Mashonaland pioneers was a monument to British pluck and tenacity of purpose, and the annals of Britain's colonial history, replete as they are with brilliant feats, can show nothing finer than this.'[45]

Brilliant though it undoubtedly was, the arrival of the pioneers—and the many hundreds of other white settlers that soon followed in their wake—also altered the situation in Mashonaland completely. Where previously, Lobengula's raiding parties could cheerfully roam into the territory at will, grabbing slaves and demanding tribute as they wished, the sudden appearance of white-owned farms, mines and towns changed all this.

Regardless of the fact that these raids were overwhelmingly directed towards the Mashona rather than the whites, there was simply no way that the Matabele could be allowed to continue rampaging across the border to murder their neighbours and take whatever they wanted. The growing white settlements, mines, and other business interests in Mashonaland needed a reliable supply of labour, stability, and law-and-order to flourish and attract investment. Less tangible (but something Victorian imperialists always fretted about) was the potential 'loss of prestige' that they would suffer in the eyes of the Mashona if they sat on their hands and allowed the Matabele to continue their murderous incursions unchecked–how could the settlers risk being perceived as too scared to take on the Matabele?

Sooner or later something had to give: unless the Matabele changed their whole way of life or the white settlers packed up, threw away their investments, and headed south again, a clash was always inevitable. It was only ever a question of when.

End Notes
[1] Kane, The World's View: The Story of Southern Rhodesia, p.43
[2] Walker, A History of Southern Africa, p.33
[3] Walker, A History of Southern Africa, p.35
[4] Walker, A History of Southern Africa, p.35
[5] Theal, Ethnography and Condition of South Africa before 1505, p.28
[6] Walker, A History of Southern Africa, p.6
[7] Walker, A History of Southern Africa, p.109
[8] Wills and Collingridge, The Downfall of Lobengula, p.16
[9] Gale, One Man's Vision; the story of Rhodesia, p.19
[10] Morris, The Washing of the Spears, p.66
[11] Morris, The Washing of the Spears, p.60
[12] Wills and Collingridge, The Downfall of Lobengula, p.17
[13] Mathers, Zambesia: England's El Dorado in Africa, p.114
[14] Hole, Lobengula, p.63
[15] Rouillard, Matabele Thompson, p.110
[16] Kane, The World's View: The Story of Southern Rhodesia, p.33
[17] Wills and Collingridge, The Downfall of Lobengula, p.23
[18] Kane, The World's View: The Story of Southern Rhodesia, p.33
[19] Rouillard, Matabele Thompson, p.112
[20] Rouillard, Matabele Thompson, p.111
[21] Mathers, Zambesia: England's El Dorado in Africa, p.114
[22] Hanna, The Story of the Rhodesias and Nyasaland, p.74
[23] Kane, The World's View: The Story of Southern Rhodesia, p.42
[24] Wills and Collingridge, The Downfall of Lobengula, p.22
[25] Gale, One Man's Vision; the story of Rhodesia, p.21
[26] Mathers, Zambesia: England's El Dorado in Africa, p.114
[27] Mathers, Zambesia: England's El Dorado in Africa, p.88
[28] Mathers, Zambesia: England's El Dorado in Africa, p.197
[29] Baxter, Rhodesia: Last Outpost of the British Empire, 1890-1980, p.29
[30] Warhurst, Anglo-Portuguese Relations in South Central Africa, 1890–1900, p.11
[31] Mathers, Zambesia: England's El Dorado in Africa, p.93
[32] Johnson, Great Days, p.40
[33] Laurie, Every Man Has His Price: The Story of Collusion and Corruption in the Scramble for Rhodesia, p.35
[34] Le Sueur, Cecil Rhodes, p.7
[35] Le Sueur, Cecil Rhodes, p.9
[36] Imperialist, Cecil Rhodes: A Biography and an Appreciation, p.392
[37] Rouillard, Matabele Thompson, p.130
[38] Rouillard, Matabele Thompson, p.259
[39] Cary, Charter Royal, p.35
[40] Hanna, The Story of the Rhodesias and Nyasaland, p.83
[41] Brown, On the South African Frontier, p.49
[42] Kane, The World's View: The Story of Southern Rhodesia, p.52
[43] Mathers, Zambesia: England's El Dorado in Africa, p.339
[44] Jones, Rhodesian Genesis, p.27
[45] Hensman, A History of Rhodesia, p.55

'No one could seriously dispute that almost all of sub-Saharan Africa, all of North Africa except Morocco, all of the Middle East except Israel and Jordan and most of the oil-rich states, and the entire former British Indian Empire were better governed by Europeans.'
– Conrad Black

'The English sent all their bores abroad, and acquired the empire as a punishment.'
– Edward Bond

Chapter 2
The Gathering Storm

Read any recent history of Rhodesia or southern Africa, and you will see that the author falls over himself to convince you that no sooner had the pioneers settled in Mashonaland, than naughty old Rhodes was busily scheming and plotting to engineer a war with Lobengula so that he could get his grasping hands on Matabeleland itself. The truly God-awful BBC mini-series, Rhodes, even went so far as to portray the embryonic white settlements in Mashonaland as 'starving to death', thus forcing Rhodes to dream up an excuse to attack their neighbours and steal their land. Indeed, this tale—or increasingly fanciful versions of it—has been peddled so often that it is now trotted out as 'fact' by those who enjoy blaming the wicked English-speaking settlers of southern Africa for absolutely everything that happened in the region.[i] So though claims that Rhodes' agents concocted an excuse for war against the Matabele are gleefully—and unthinkingly—lapped up by modern day critics, is there really any truth behind them?

There were undeniably some settlers, and even highly placed company men, who had started viewing Matabeleland with a covetous eye. Indeed, in a musing telegram, Rhodes' right hand man, Dr Leander Starr Jameson,[ii] pondered whether 'opening up' Matabeleland would give the company's share price a boost.[1] The rainy season of 1890/91 had been very tough on the Mashonaland pioneers and gold had not been found in the quantities many had hoped for, but these hardy souls had weathered the storm and progress was gradually being made. Mashonaland's first administrator, Mr Archibald Colquhoun[iii] had proven himself ineffective and unpopular but the dynamic, decisive and well-liked Jameson—commonly known as 'the Doctor'— had quickly side-lined and then replaced him.[2] In his description of the differences between the first two administrators, Major Frank

---

i   Highly popular but equally ludicrous tales blame the British for being entirely responsible for starting the Boer War. Please read Kruger, Kommandos & Kak for a less rabidly pro-Kruger take on the issue.

ii   The Rt. Hon. Sir Leander Starr Jameson, 1st Baronet, KCMG, CB, PC (1853–1917). Hero, patriot, rogue, rascal or rotter depending on your point of view, Jameson led a truly remarkable life, the most famous episode of which was his eponymous raid on the Transvaal in 1896. Jameson inspired Rudyard Kipling's famous ode to stoicism, 'If...'

iii   Archibald Ross Colquhoun (1848–1914) had previously served as an imperial administrator in the Far East, but had muddled up two letters and inadvertently sent the wrong one to his boss, prompting his resignation shortly thereafter. For reasons known only to himself, this story greatly appealed to Rhodes and he offered Colquhoun the chance to be the company's first administrator for Mashonaland.

Johnson mentioned that Jameson had never been one for bureaucracy and 'red-tapism':

> 'Colquhoun, the first administrator of Mashonaland, was a failure–being an old Indian civil servant, he was obsessed with rules and regulations. But Jameson, who followed him, was excellent, simply because he governed the country with a common—if 'horse'—sense elasticity and justice, even though some of his decisions were certainly of the 'rough-and-ready', un-orthodox type.'[3]

Though the company's share price was still not strong,[4] the new colony had grown steadily under Jameson's common-sense stewardship and the notion that the settlers were 'starving' is nothing but sheer modern-day leftist fantasy. The company police foiled an attempted invasion from the Transvaal in June 1891,[5] and by the end of that year, the ban on female settlers had been lifted. Many wives (and a piano) arrived after the rains in early 1892, and that August, the Salisbury's Hatfield Hotel hosted the capital's first ball.

Mashonaland continued to attract new settlers and investment each month. Though much more modest than the vast deposits in the Transvaal, reefs around Mazoe and Fort Victoria were being worked and gold was being found. Wagon loads of settlers were making new homes in Mashonaland and farmers were reporting excellent harvests. Farms established around Fort Salisbury were growing cabbages, cauliflowers, onions, oats and mealies, irrigated by a dam that had been built to control water supplies. Salisbury was expanding and boasted a synagogue, a school, an Anglican church, a Masonic Hotel, a newspaper, regular race meetings, a cricket club, and a branch of Standard Bank. The telegraph had quickly reached Fort Salisbury and a railway was being built. There was a regular and efficient postal service and even a daily milk delivery service. In May 1893 the Salisbury Club was opened by Jameson (who was invited to serve as its vice president) and the settlement held its first 'white wedding' the following month. Other tastes in social activities were served by a brick-built billiard saloon, a lawn tennis club and a flourishing agricultural society.[6] One contemporary visitor recorded the steady progress:

> 'Owing to the severity of the rainy season [in 1890/1]... great hardships were experienced by everyone, all round, and the opening of the country was much retarded in consequence. However, sufficient has been done since then, not only to prove that the great portion of the country is fit for agricultural pursuits, but also that it is rich in gold-bearing reefs, and possesses, besides, many other deposits of valuable minerals, notably iron and cobalt.

Silver, copper, tin, antimony, arsenic, and lead have also been discovered.'[7]

So the notion that Mashonaland was a failed colony teetering on the edge of famine in 1893 can safely be dismissed.

But what of the other oft trotted-out claim that Rhodes and Jameson were plotting and scheming to provoke a war with Lobengula?

Based entirely on a report which appeared in the Cape Times in September 1930—i.e. over 40 years later—many modern writers maintain that Rhodes had planned to topple Lobengula by force as early as 1889. The claim in the report, made by none other than an elderly Frank Johnson, was absolutely riddled with inaccuracies, contradictions, and impossible timings. Moreover the alleged events were omitted from his memoirs which were published a few years later.

The thrust of Johnson's allegation was that, rather than wasting time with the pioneer column, Rhodes had simply contracted him to raise a force of 500 men and invade Matabeleland. Quite why Rhodes would have done this after having spent months negotiating to obtain the Rudd Concession and 'squaring' half of London to get his royal charter (not to mention the fact that his agents had just sent hundreds of Martini Henry rifles to Lobengula as per the agreement) was never explained–nor probably ever could be. Nevertheless, Johnson claimed that the contract had been signed in Kimberly on 7 December 1899 and alleged that he had immediately started recruiting forces and sending them up to a forward base at Shoshong, near the border of Matabeleland. He further stated that a local missionary—the Reverend Hepburn—had grown concerned about the build-up of troops, and written a letter of warning to Sir Sydney Shippard, the administrator of Bechuanaland, after one of Johnson's officers drunkenly spilled the beans. Upon receiving the letter, Shippard travelled to Cape Town to raise the alarm.

All very damning at first glance, but Johnson never produced the signed contract which he claimed (somewhat conveniently) to have left at his home in the Channel Islands when he fled just before the German invasion in 1940.[iv] An unsigned draft certainly existed, but Johnson admitted (also somewhat conveniently) to having typed this up himself as 'Rhodes did not want any lawyers involved'.

Aside from the 'unfortunate' loss of the contract, Johnson's claim is so packed with inaccuracies as to be utterly nonsensical. He wrote, for example, that Rhodes had been the prime minister when he was 'summoned in frantic haste to Rhodes' office' when the plot began to

---

iv Had such a document fallen into the covetous hands of the Nazi invaders, it would have been a huge propaganda coup for Herr Goebbels and his ilk. Needless to say, nothing ever surfaced.

unravel[8]– but Rhodes did not become the prime minister of the Cape Colony until the following year. Even more significantly, Johnson's timings are all absolutely impossible too. By Johnson's own admission, he and Rhodes were both in Kimberley at breakfast time on 22 December 1889–the day the famous pioneer column was agreed upon. Based on this, and Johnson's claim that he and Rhodes had signed the contract for the 'invasion' in Kimberley on the 7th, Johnson would have had to recruit a large enough force to make the Reverend Hepburn suspicious—and somehow transport them up through the bush to the Shashi River—in the two weeks between the 7th and the 22nd (some of which Johnson admits to having spent in Cape Town). One should bear in mind that the supposed base at Shoshong was about a three week trek from Kimberley and that it took about 6 months to recruit the men for the pioneer column. The Reverend Hepburn's letter would also have had to make its way through the bush to reach Sir Sidney Shippard, who in turn, would have had to make his way by mule-cart to Kimberley and thence by train to the Cape–a service which only ran every second day, and a journey which itself took two days.

On top of all that, after supposedly having been summoned to Cape Town to get their knuckles (very quickly) rapped by the high commissioner (an implausibly lenient punishment for having masterminded such a scheme) Johnson claims that his reason for being in Kimberly on the 22nd was that he was waiting for a train to Cape Town to see his family for Christmas, having just arrived 'by post cart from the interior'[9]– a remarkably blasé course of action for a man who had just been exposed for plotting such a dastardly scheme.

Even if Johnson's recollections had been a few days—or weeks— out, there is simply no way that this myriad of activities could have occurred within this approximate time frame. If his tale about the 'plot to invade Matabeleland' is to be believed, Johnson must somehow have made his way to Kimberley by train from Cape Town and travelled up country and back by post cart at lightning speed with a plan to return to the Cape in time to enjoy his Christmas turkey.

In short, this bizarre catalogue of events is so clearly ludicrous that it can safely be dismissed.[10]

Despite the implausibility of all this and the fact that Johnson produced absolutely no hard evidence to back up his remarkable tale, it is noteworthy that critics of Rhodes and Rhodesia nevertheless, still accept this single newspaper report as gospel and unthinkingly adopt it to 'prove' that there was always a plan to invade Matabeleland.

While any reasonable reader will agree there is no evidence of any such plan having existed in late 1889, is it possible that one was hatched as soon as the settlers had established themselves in Mashonaland? Many modern-day writers claim this was the case, but never feel the need to substantiate their statements–no doubt because all the evidence is entirely to the contrary.

Most tellingly of all, upon taking over the reins of the colony from Colquhoun, one of the first things Jameson did was to slash the company police to cut costs. The chartered company had been established with capital of £1,000,000, and maintaining the BSACP was costing £150,000 a year. Had Rhodes had a dastardly scheme to invade Matabeleland in mind, he could have bank-rolled the regiment with his vast personal fortune. Instead, he insisted that the company run at a profit, and so, in late 1891 (and to howls of protest and anguish from the settlers) Jameson cut the only standing military force in the colony, the 650-strong BSACP, down to just 150 men– leaving a force sufficient only to maintain law and order and to man the field guns and Maxims.[11] To placate the colonial office, a body of volunteers called the Mashonaland Horse was raised, though this was little more than a 'paper regiment', and parades were generally neglected by all except officers and NCOs.[12] Had Rhodes and Jameson harboured any plans whatsoever to provoke a war with the Matabele, why on earth would they have cut the company police so drastically? This fact alone should convince the reader that no such devious plot existed.

Though there is no reason to believe that Rhodes was keen to provoke a war with Lobengula, conflict between the chartered company and the Matabele was inevitable–not because of some bizarre and unexplained lust for war on the part of the settlers, but because of the actions of the Matabele.

§

Lobengula's court was not a happy one in the early 1890s. The signing of the Rudd Concession had not been well received by many of the king's indunas, and especially not by the more volatile younger ones who considered Lobengula to have 'sold them out' to the white men. Feeling the heat, Lobengula tried to back out of the agreement, citing the age-old excuse that he had been tricked into signing it. That a man as highly intelligent as Lobengula could have been 'duped' despite the negotiations having taken many months is scarcely credible, and the historian Alexander Hanna offers a much more plausible explanation– that Lobengula had simply been unable to resist temptation:

'Why did the salmon swallow the hook? Not because, poor fish, he could not see it, nor yet because the wicked British chameleon thrust it down his throat, but quite simply because he could not resist the bait. He did not like concession-hunters, and dreaded

the consequences of yielding to their entreaties–but he did like
their presents.'

The growing power struggle in Bulawayo had been reported as
early as 1888, when Sir Sidney Shippard visited Lobengula's court. Sir
Sidney noted that the king's power to restrain some of his indunas had
been, 'greatly diminished within the last few years':

'The older indunas, the companions of his boyhood, are said to
still be devoted to their chief, but the younger regiments, many
of which can boast of no Zulu blood, and consist entirely of
maghole, i.e. slave boys or captives taken in war, and trained up
to become matjaha, are said to be anything but loyal to Lobengula.
It is impossible to forecast the future in such a country as this. A
matjaha rebellion, attempted revolution, and civil war, appear to
me not unlikely… some of the older Matabele indunas and indolas
are confessedly sick of carnage, and desire nothing so much
as a peaceful government with a security for life and property,
not to be obtained under the present regime; but the restless
and bloodthirsty matjaha are perpetually craving for the fresh
slaughter of helpless victims… Lobengula dare not withstand the
importunity of his troops, even if he would. The insatiable vanity
and almost incredible conceit of the Matabele matjaha seem to
have much to do with the continuance of the raid system.'[13]

The outrage over the fact that he had signed the Rudd Concession
left Lobengula increasingly desperate to divert the attention of the
most hot-headed indunas ,[14] and he shamelessly offered up a suitable
scapegoat in the form of Lotjie, one of his closest advisors. Lotjie was
a wise and well respected old chief who the British referred to as
'the Beaconsfield of Matabeleland', and who had counselled Lobengula
to sign the Rudd Concession. Lobengula had Lotjie killed and then
slaughtered his entire extended family for good measure. One of
Rhodes' agents witnessed the execution:

'He was taken outside the council kraal, and on kneeling down
he said, "Do as you think fit with me. I am the king's chattel." One
blow from the executioner's stick sufficed… That night was spent
by the Matabeli in putting to death the men, women and children
of Lotjie's family… three hundred men, women and children were
killed.'[15]

Despite the savagery of this butchery, all Lobengula achieved was
to buy some time. He failed to divert criticism from himself entirely

and as the months went by, the increasingly beleaguered king was to prove less and less able to restrain his more aggressive underlings.

Seemingly in an attempt to undermine the Rudd Concession, Lobengula and a rival group of European prospectors signed a contradictory agreement (the Lippert Concession) in April 1891. Perhaps unable to resist the offer of £1,000 up front and £500 annually thereafter, Lobengula granted the holder of this concession (a Hamburg based financier, Eduard Lippert) the exclusive right to establish banks, mint money, and conduct trade in the chartered company's territory. Much more controversially, and in direct contradiction to the Rudd Concession, the Lippert Concession also permitted the holder exclusive right to make grants of land to Europeans throughout Lobengula's dominions for the next hundred years.[16]

Whether it was Lobengula's cunning intent that the Lippert Concession would essentially nullify the Rudd Concession, or if he was simply blinded by the prospect of more trinkets and presents will never be known. He was out-manoeuvred in any event: Rhodes simply purchased the Lippert Concession late in 1891. Ironically, Lobengula's devious, if clumsy, attempts at intrigue—or perhaps his insatiable avarice—handed the company much greater rights than the Rudd Concession alone would ever have given. Though it is currently fashionable to present Lobengula as a poor, innocent victim, the reality is that he is undeserving of much pity. His own greed—and love of intrigue—contributed in no small part to his downfall.

For as long as he had been administrator, Jameson had fastidiously urged the settlers to respect the 'border' between Mashonaland and Matabeleland, and informed Lobengula that he would not permit settlers and prospectors to operate west of the Umniati[v] and Shashe[vi] rivers. Despite latter-day claims that Jameson simply invented the border, he and Lobengula had made reference to it in their communications as early as November 1891[17] and the Doctor was firm about making the settlers respect this frontier. When a Mr J.G. McDonald and his companion were accosted and roughed-up by an impi of some 400 Matabele on the wrong side of the border, Jameson showed no sympathy whatsoever, and stated, "You had no right to be beyond the Shashe River; you will both be in trouble with me if you are again."[18]

Jameson made sure that his respect for the border was communicated to Lobengula, and wrote to the company's agent in Bulawayo in May 1893 to remind him:

'All the white people in Mashonaland have strict orders not to enter his country... my police and magistrates in each district have strict

---

v   Renamed the 'Munyati River' in 1983

vi Often referred to as the 'Shashi River'

orders to prevent any white people going beyond our recognized line... I am determined not to have trouble between the king's people and ourselves through the recklessness of individuals and they should be punished in each case.'[19]

The not-unreasonable quid pro quo for this was the Doctor's request that Lobengula forbid his raiding parties from rampaging across this boundary. From the communications between them, and the fact that there was a brief hiatus in raiding, Lobengula seems to have grudgingly acknowledged that there was now some sort of de facto boundary between his lands and those of the Rhodesians. Whether he liked it or not, or felt the need to continue respecting it, or, indeed, could have done anything to force his more warlike indunas to respect it, were different issues altogether.[20] The whole Matabele way of life was built on raiding Mashonaland–there was simply no way that Lobengula, even if he had been so inclined, could completely have restructured the economy of Matabeleland at a stroke, especially given the volatile and bellicose mood in his court at the time. As Philip Mason, a member of the Institute of Race Relations, conceded in The Birth of a Dilemma:

'Lobengula's state was founded on annual raids on the Mashona. To have given them up would have involved a complete change of direction in the spirit of his people, a complete economic reorganization. He was not big enough for that; even if such an idea appealed to him, he could not have carried it through. And the idea did not appeal to him; he had made up his mind not to give away any element of sovereignty; he had no intention of reforming his kingdom on lines that would fit into the new world. His raids then would go eastward, as they always had done, not only because he must raid somewhere, but to assert his authority over the Mashona.'[21]

Sure enough, the lull in raiding did not last long. Towards the end of 1891, a Mashona chief called Lomaghundi refused to pay the normal tribute to his Matabele 'overlords', prompting a furious reaction from Lobengula. An impi was despatched into Mashonaland to raid Lomaghundi's kraal which was located about 70 miles to the north-west of Fort Salisbury in an area where gold fields were being worked by the pioneers. Due to this distance, there was a delay of a few days before panic-stricken Mashona messengers arrived at Fort Salisbury to report that Matabele raiders had murdered Lomaghundi and three of his indunas.

Despite the fantasies of his modern-day critics, Jameson had no wish to provoke Lobengula and spark a war. He downplayed the attack and informed the Matabele king that the company would help enforce payments so as to prevent further killing, should any other Mashona chiefs refuse to pay tribute. On 2 December 1891, a distinctly unwarlike Jameson wrote to one of the bosses of the chartered company, explaining what had happened and concluding, 'This is of course unfortunate, but in accordance to Lobengula's laws and customs.'[22]

Perhaps emboldened by Jameson's rather feeble reaction, more Matabele raids soon followed, though they were primarily directed towards the area around Fort Victoria rather than Salisbury; indeed, after the raid on Lomaghundi's kraal, the rest of the attacks were all directed south of Fort Charter. On 27 August 1892, The Rhodesian Chronicle reported that a 200-strong Matabele impi had crossed the border to capture slaves. An unfortunate settler called Mr Hill had been caught up in the fray, and recorded that the raiders had made off with 'a large force of Makalaka women taken from the kraals where they had been raiding'. Though Mr Hill escaped unharmed, the raiders stole his rifles and 'bonsellas of tea and coffee'.

§

While these constant raids put pressure on Jameson to act, he was not the only one taking strain: over in Bulawayo, the influence of the 'war party' in Lobengula's court was growing every month. In echoes of the massacre of Lotjie's family, Lobengula sought to placate the young-bloods by having another of his most senior chiefs, Mhlaba, put to death in June 1892. The fact that Mhlaba had been Lobengula's closest advisor ever since he had succeeded Mzilikazi, and was even designated to act as regent if anything happened to the king,[23] was not enough to save him. His brothers and their wives and sons were also slaughtered in the outrage, and an impi was despatched to capture all their cattle and slaves and even stone their dogs to death.[24]

The ostensible reason for this latest whirlwind of butchery was that Mhlaba had been 'smelled out' for practicing witchcraft, and somehow using his magic skills to drug and rape Lobengula's various Queens.[25] His real 'crime'—just like Lotjie's—had actually been to support the signing of the Rudd Concession. That, and the fact that he was a wise old 'dove' in a court increasingly dominated by bloodthirsty young 'hawks'. Colenbrander, the company's man in Bulawayo, described the prelude to the slaughter, stating, 'The best man in the country, and I should say the most harmless, was smelled out by these devils.'[26] Some of Mhlaba's family managed to escape the carnage, fleeing to the safety of the white settlements in Mashonaland. They would fight for the company—Rhodes' 'wicked white imperialists'— in the coming war.

Not surprisingly, the ongoing raids and increasingly bloody power struggle in Bulawayo made tensions rise in Mashonaland's pioneer community and there was growing demand for a solution. Reacting to this feeling of unease among the settlers, The Rhodesian Chronicle's lead article on 17 September 1892, was entitled: 'The Matabele Raids' and declared:

> 'The traveller cannot consider himself free from the chance of a possible meeting with the Matabele... the question arises, are the authorities doing their best to protect these settlers from raids of the Matabele? ...The manner in which wandering impis of Matabeles have recently treated travellers has been the cause of some alarm and uneasiness in the country... The ostensible object of these impis... is to collect tribute from the Mashonas and Makalakas, or, in other words, to rob them of every grain of corn and every head of cattle. It is, we contend, a disgrace to the chartered company to allow these raids on natives whom they have taken under their protection... unless the BSA Company changes its present policy of... cringing to the powerful, they will not be able to avert trouble with the Matabele.'[27]

Shortly thereafter, a Matabele impi attacked a company post cart near Fort Charter, overwhelming the two-man escort. The brother of one these out-riders was Percy Fitzpatrick[vii] who would go on to be knighted and gain fame as the creator of Jock of the Bushveld. The following year, when certain disapproving elements suggested that Jameson had been seeking any excuse to start a war with the Matabele, Percy Fitzpatrick wrote a thundering letter to the London Times, describing the incident and the company's feeble response to it at the time:

> 'They [the Matabele raiders] surprised and overpowered the escort... robbed them of their food, clothing, rifles and ammunition, broached and plundered the mails and, after taunting, harassing and insulting the two men, left them to proceed on as best they could. The incident was reported at headquarters and the company's officials, after compensating the men for their horses, provided them with free passes by post cart out of the country! In reply to the demands of the people that Captain Lendy should be sent to Bulawayo and exact reparation, the company stated that, as the two men had left the country, it would be impossible to identify the offending Matabele! Is this the conduct of men

---

vii Sir James Percy Fitzpatrick, KCMG (1862–1931) was one of the leading Johannesburg reformers, a group that campaigned for a fair franchise for the English-speaking residents of the Transvaal.

hungering for an excuse? Dr Jameson, the patient, tactful, and courageous administrator, has often enough borne censures for his extreme forbearance.'[28]

Despite Jameson's toothless protests, the raids continued unabated. In November 1892, a 600-strong impi was sent to punish another Mashona chief, Chibi Mazorodze, who had dared refuse to pay tribute to Lobengula. Lobengula's warriors captured the unfortunate fellow as he returned from consulting his witch-doctor, transported him to Bulawayo, and skinned the poor devil alive.[29]

Mr (later, Sir) Phillip Bourchier Wrey,[viii] consulting engineer for the chartered company, detailed yet another incursion into the area around Fort Victoria:

'A large impi passed through the camp of the Mashonaland Agency, situated about fourteen miles from Victoria, at the time they were employing about 150 natives; these were absolutely paralysed with fear and announced their intention of leaving directly. It was only with great trouble and persuasion that they were induced to remain, and our position was a most false one; for, as the natives very plainly said, "When you white men came into Mashonaland, you promised that if we worked for you, you would prevent the Matabeli from raiding us. Here we are working for you, and there are the Matabeli killing our wives and children, and raiding our homes." Doctor Jameson, still desirous of maintaining peaceful relations, contented himself with again merely remonstrating.'[30]

So, far from Jameson grabbing at the first excuse he could find to start a war, he was actually so wedded to a policy of pacifism that he was coming in for criticism, not only from the Rhodesian press, but even from the poor Mashona. What is astounding is that many modern writers simply choose to ignore this on-going raiding, murder, and pillaging as well as the head-in-the-sand Rhodesian response to it. None of this is ever mentioned in the rush to blame Jameson and Rhodes for starting the war. In truth, the Rhodesians actually showed incredible reluctance to react to these constant provocations but could not be expected to keep turning the other cheek indefinitely.

Similarly, today's leftist historians who unthinkingly spout the story that 'Lobengula did everything he could to prevent the war,' can only be living in an alternative universe. Though he was undoubtedly losing control of some of his more blood-thirsty indunas by then, the reality is that, time and time again, Matabele impis were being

viii   Sir Philip Bourchier Sherard Wrey (1858–1936).

sent across the border into Mashonaland with the express purpose
of raiding, looting, murdering, exacting tribute and capturing slaves.
How existing entirely by such rampaging savagery and mass murder
can possibly be considered 'doing everything he could to prevent war'
is anyone's guess. That certain modern day writers give the notion any
credence at all tells one a lot about their motivations–it is clear that
dealing in historical reality is not one of them.

End Notes
[1] Baxter, Rhodesia: Last Outpost of the British Empire, 1890-1980, p.86
[2] Colvin, The Life of Jameson, Vol.1, p.173
[3] Johnson, Great Days, p.103
[4] Baxter, Rhodesia: Last Outpost of the British Empire, 1890-1980, p.85
[5] Gibbs, The History of the BSAP, Vol.1, p.89
[6] Tanser, A Scantling of Time: The Story of Salisbury, Rhodesia, 1890-1900, p.115
[7] Norris-Newman, Matabeleland and How We Got It, p.68
[8] Cary, Charter Royal, p.56
[9] Johnson, Great Days, p.94
[10] Blake, A History of Rhodesia, p.66
[11] Tanser, A Scantling of Time: The Story of Salisbury, Rhodesia, 1890-1900, p.87
[12] Keppel-Jones, Rhodes and Rhodesia, p.325
[13] Mathers, Zambesia: England's El Dorado in Africa, p.91
[14] Hanna, The Story of the Rhodesias and Nyasaland, p.83
[15] Rouillard, Matabele Thompson, p.178
[16] Mason, The Birth of a Dilemma, p.161
[17] Glass, The Matabele War, p.32
[18] Glass, The Matabele War, p.33
[19] Glass, The Matabele War, p.35
[20] Hanna, The Story of the Rhodesias and Nyasaland, p.90
[21] Mason, The Birth of a Dilemma, p.163
[22] Glass, The Matabele War, p.52
[23] Keppel-Jones, Rhodes and Rhodesia, p.25
[24] Keppel-Jones, Rhodes and Rhodesia, p.229
[25] Keppel-Jones, Rhodes and Rhodesia, p.230
[26] Keppel-Jones, Rhodes and Rhodesia, p.231
[27] Glass, The Matabele War, p.52
[28] A.H. Duminy, Fitzpatrick: South African Politician: Selected Papers, 1888-1906, p.16
[29] Glass, The Matabele War, p.57
[30] Wills and Collingridge, The Downfall of Lobengula, p.58

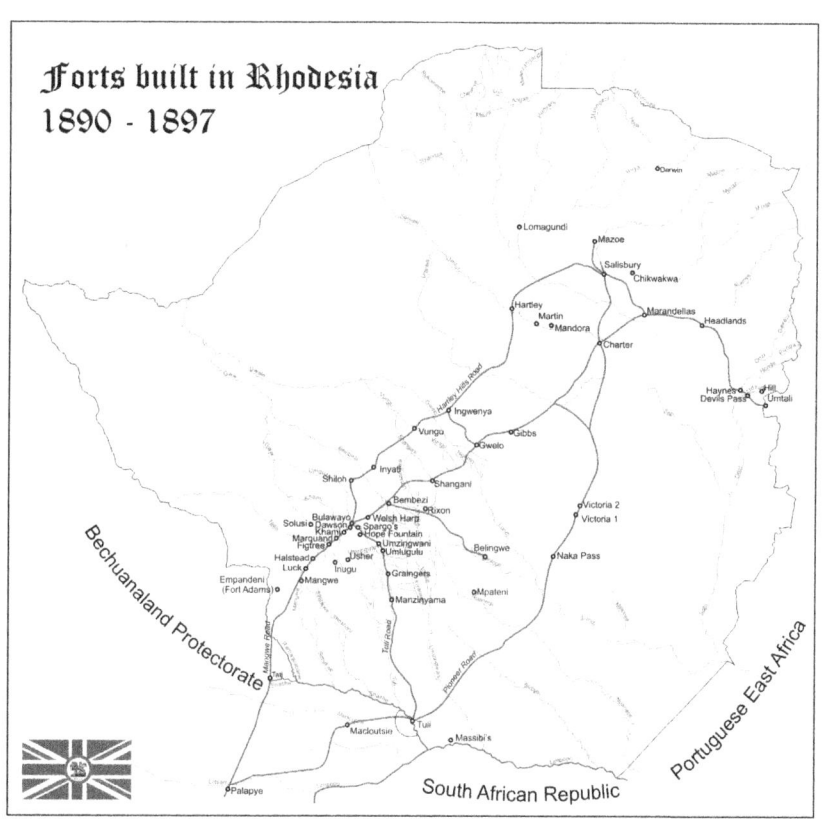

*'The same dispute between civilized European and African savage
would have raged even if the Africans had been flaxen-haired
blonds. All cats are grey at night, as many a prurient white man
has conceded; what made the African native unacceptable to him in
broad daylight was his unfortunate behaviour.'[1]*

– Peter Gibbs

'An empire founded by war has to maintain itself by war.'

– Charles de Montesquieu

Chapter 3
Incidents at Fort Victoria

As 1892 drew to a close, the atmosphere around Fort Victoria remained tense. When, in December that year, a section of telegraph wire was stolen from near the settlement, it was not unreasonably thought that another of Lobengula's raiding parties had pilfered it. Jameson's reaction was to send one of his officers, a Captain Lendy, to Bulawayo to address this with the Matabele chief face-to-face. Lendy carried a letter from the Doctor with him, a communiqué in which Jameson stressed his desire to maintain friendly relations with Lobengula and his people. He went on to explain the 'injury' to the telegraph wire and asked Lobengula to keep his warriors under control. He then reminded the king that, due to the number of whites in Mashonaland increasing weekly, it was now more important than ever that his people remain within the lines that had been lain out.[2]

Despite later claims that he had never even heard of the boundary line, Lobengula made no comment about the repeated references to it in Jameson's letter–indeed, the king appeared interested only in complaining to Captain Lendy about white hunters shooting hippopotami.[3]

This incident ended peacefully when the true culprits turned out to be some local Makalakas,[i] and not Matabele raiders after all. Captain Lendy conveyed this message and an apology to Lobengula and all seemed calm. Perhaps in recognition of the diplomatic way in which Lendy had handled the incident, Jameson promoted him to resident magistrate for the Fort Victoria district.

A few months later in May 1893, another 500 yards of telegraph wire were stolen, this time between Fort Tuli and Fort Victoria. A BSACP investigation swiftly traced the missing wire to a nearby Mashona village and the headman, Gomalla, was informed that he had either to hand over the culprits, or pay a fine of cattle. Gomalla immediately elected to pay the fine and cheerfully gave the requisite number of cattle to the BSACP patrol. What he failed to tell anyone, however, was that the cattle he had handed over with such alacrity actually belonged to the Matabele royal herd–his people had merely been tending them. The mischievous Gomalla then fired a message off to Lobengula telling him that the dastardly Dr Jameson had stolen the king's cattle.

Unsurprisingly, Lobengula was not amused and sent a message to Jameson demanding to know what on earth was going on. Far from

---

i A sub-division of the Mashona people

seeking confrontation, however, the Doctor responded, 'Now that I find the cattle belong to the King, of course they shall be returned to him.'[4] It is often claimed that the theft of the telegraph wire was gleefully seized upon by the warmongering Jameson, delighted to have been presented with an 'excuse' to start a war with the Matabele–but this was certainly not the case. Indeed, both incidents ended peacefully and on both occasions, the chartered company displayed an almost craven determination not to provoke Lobengula. Though the theft of the wire did nothing to lessen the increasingly fraught atmosphere along the border, it actually had little to do with the war that would soon inevitably follow.

The following month, a 70-strong Matabele raiding party attacked the kraal of the Mashona chief Bere some 10 miles from Fort Victoria. When a panic-stricken Mashona lad ran into the town to raise the alarm, Captain Lendy, in his new role as magistrate of the district, boldly rode out with just three other policemen to investigate. Lendy's diminutive patrol arrived at the scene to find that the Matabele marauders had left after torching Bere's village and granary, murdering several Mashona men, and seizing all the women, children and cattle. Lendy and his tiny force gallantly gave chase and caught up to the impi, at which point, the Captain reported, 'They fled in all directions, dropping whatever they might be carrying and shouting that they had only come to punish the Mashonas.' Bere's crime had apparently been to steal 30 head of cattle from Lobengula[5]– a somewhat tenuous reason to burn down his village and murder and enslave his people.

Despite being variously described as 'notorious', 'psychopathic', and 'violent' by his modern-day armchair critics, Captain Lendy handled this incident with almost excessive lenience. Though he reminded the Matabele raiders of Jameson's request that they respect the border, he took no action against any of them and described the attack as an 'inter-tribal dispute' in his report[6] Lendy ensured that the raiders departed with their tails between their legs and freed the women and children they had enslaved, but the Captain and his three police troopers took no action to prevent the theft of all Bere's cattle. Nevertheless, Jameson approvingly described the extreme restraint that Lendy had demonstrated towards the murderous marauders as 'judicious action'.

Giving the lie to the oft-squawked claims that Rhodes was desperate for war with Lobengula, company agents delivered the last of the Rudd Concession's Martini Henrys to Bulawayo that same month– June 1893.[7] Needless to say, if—as many latter day commentators like to claim—Rhodes and Jameson had been plotting some sort of devious attack, it would have been completely ludicrous to hand hundreds of modern rifles over to Lobengula just weeks beforehand.

§

Though no doubt infuriating for the white settlers and the long-suffering Mashona alike, the Doctor's reluctance to even consider going 'toe-to-toc' with the Matabele is understandable when one considers the forces at his disposal. As we have seen, the cuts Jameson himself had recently made to the BSACP left a force of just 150 officers to police the whole company territory. The part-time volunteers of the 'Mashonaland Horse' seemed to view their unit as something of a jolly social club[8] and it was by no stretch of the imagination a like-for-like replacement for the disciplined, well-drilled, professional regiment that had been the BSACP. Worse still, it was reckoned that, in July 1893, there were barely 100 cavalry horses in the whole colony[9] and only 38 of those were in the 'front line' district of Fort Victoria.[10] The reader might have been surprised to read that Captain Lendy headed out against a 70-strong raiding party with just three officers at his back—but the fact is that Lendy's patrol represented 50% of all BSACP strength in the area in the wake of Jameson's cuts.

It is abundantly obvious, therefore, that the last thing Jameson wanted—or was ready for—was a war with the Matabele. Though it is difficult to believe that a man as astute as the Doctor was simply living in the hope that the Matabele attacks would somehow simply stop, Jameson was a born optimist and it is possible that he was indeed simply trusting his legendary luck. Perhaps he was hoping that his 'softly-softly' approach would give Lobengula time to reassert his authority over his more belligerent underlings, or even that sooner or later, the rival elements of the king's court would plunge the Matabele into a power-shattering civil war. Whatever Jameson might have hoped, events quickly overtook him in any case.

§

No sooner had the 70-strong raiding party arrived back in Bulawayo than Lobengula unleashed another, far larger and much more murderous attack into Mashonaland. On 9 July, 3,500 of his warriors fell upon the outlying settlements around Fort Victoria, gorging themselves on a spree of looting, murder and carnage. There was nothing the white farmers and miners could do as the Matabele drove their cattle off and murdered their workers right in front of them. Many of these settlers fled to Fort Victoria, leaving their houses and possessions to be smashed, looted or torched by the Matabele raiding parties.

The Anglican minister at Fort Victoria, the Rev. A.D. Sylvester, described the scene in a letter written shortly after the raid:

'One Sunday, July 9th, at about 3 o'clock in the afternoon, whilst I was holding my Sunday school, I found my church and parsonage surrounded by an impi of Matabele, who were on all sides massacring the Mashonas without mercy, simply out of thirst for blood... To Europeans who know little of the situation it would be a sickening sight to see the number of human beings lying dead on all sides, mutilated by the Matabele... No Christian people can simply fold their hands and allow hundreds of their fellow creatures to be murdered wholesale.'[11]

Realizing that this raid was of a completely different scale to all the previous ones, Captain Lendy ordered all the settlers from outlying areas to take refuge in Fort Victoria. Many of the townspeople left their houses to gather at the small police fort itself and the small settlement readied itself for an attack. Most of the Mashona opted for their traditional hiding places, fleeing into kopjes and caves and leaving their kraals to be looted and burned by the raiders. A few, however, made their way into Fort Victoria and begged Lendy to offer them sanctuary within the walls of the police fort. Lendy agreed to this, prompting a furious reaction from the Matabele who demanded that he hand over the refugees. When the Captain refused, the raiders attempted to persuade him, sportingly promising that the poor wretches would be murdered well away from the town so as not to contaminate the water supply. Captain Lendy was having none of this and the Matabele mob skulked off empty handed. Though he had saved the refugees at the fort, there was little Lendy could do to prevent the wholesale butchery and slaughter that was raging all around the beleaguered town and he sent an urgent telegram to Jameson who was up in Fort Salisbury, 190 miles away.

Jameson's rather less-than-warlike response to this outrage was to send a stiff letter of complaint to his agent in Lobengula's court:

'His impis are not allowed to cross the border agreed upon between us. He not being there, they are not under control, and Captain Lendy informs me that some of them have actually been into the town of Victoria, burning kraals within a few miles, and killing Mashonas who are the servants of the white men; also, they have captured some cattle of the government and of other white men. I am now instructing Captain Lendy to see the head induna, tell him that those cattle must all be returned at once, and his impi must retire beyond our agreed border, otherwise Captain Lendy is to take his police and at once expel them, however many they are.'[12]

Responding to Lendy, Jameson sent a reply on the evening of the 9th, saying, '...you have authority to use extreme measures if necessary, but I trust to your tact to get rid of the Matabele without any actual collision.'[13] Far from the tedious claims about Jameson having elatedly used the raid to whip up support for a war, Lendy was further instructed to 'prevent any exaggerated press reports'.

Ever fearful of the financial implications of such bad news, the Doctor also fired off telegrams to the chartered company's offices in Kimberley and Cape Town, downplaying the severity of the raid: 'The Victoria people have got the jumps,' he assured Rhodes, adding, 'I hope to get rid of the Matabele without trouble,'[14] and further counselling, 'Lendy's description of burning kraals and Mashonas killed, of course, very harrowing, but this was at first blush and after sundown... will wire you in the morning when I hear from Lendy that they have all cleared.' Jameson went on to ask the company's people to contradict any 'exaggerated reports about Matabele near Victoria'.[15]

Rather incredibly, Jameson's very measured response—indeed, some would say, lack of response—to this latest savage attack was enough to have him branded a war-monger by the usual modern-day critics. Giving no evidence to support the claim, Lawrence James, in his The Rise and Fall of the British Empire, asserts that the raid was 'just what Jameson wanted and gave him the excuse for war'[16]–a statement which, needless to say, is utterly irreconcilable with the Doctor's reaction. Martin Meredith, wearisome critic of the British Empire in general and Rhodesia in particular, also shows complete disregard for reality, stating, 'When he had the choice between peace and war, Jameson chose war.'[17] This is completely at odds with Jameson's actual reaction after having heard what was happening, and entirely ignores the salient fact that several thousand Matabele warriors were rampaging about on a killing spree at the time. Meredith also inadvertently reveals how desperate Jameson was to avoid conflict, by quoting one of the Doctor's telegrams to Lendy, in which he specifically warned against provoking a war which, 'from a financial point of view would throw this country back to God knows when'.[18] So all the evidence—even that presented by his most blinkered critics—shows that Jameson was the one doing everything he could to avoid a clash.

Another who demonstrated no knowledge of what had actually happened, but who quickly made up his mind that the chartered company nevertheless had to have been entirely and solely responsible, was contemporary critic of Empire, Henry Labouchère[ii] who used his

---

ii Henry Du Pré Labouchère (1831–1912). Virulent critic of the British Empire and especially of Cecil Rhodes, Labouchère was a disreputable and deeply unpleasant radical politician and media tycoon. His biggest 'contribution' to British society was the Labouchère Amendment which outlawed all male homosexual activity. It was also widely thought that Labouchère was involved in the practice of share-rigging, using his Truth magazine to run unfavourable reports on companies after having advised shareholders to dispose of stocks. When the share prices fell as a result, he would buy them up at a low price.

inappropriately named Truth magazine to give voice to his irrational vendetta. So out of touch with what was actually happening at Fort Victoria was Labouchère, however, that he even referred to the raid as 'the occurrences at Fort Salisbury'.[19] Labouchère's near-hysterical rantings in Truth continued throughout the subsequent war, but their accuracy never improved.

§

The Matabele raiders showed no inclination to leave the area, and the killing and looting continued over the following days. Despite this, it was not until the 12th—after having been positively bombarded by telegrams from Captain Lendy—that Jameson decided the situation was serious enough to warrant travelling down from Salisbury. Jameson was suffering from terrible piles at the time but gritting his teeth against the pain, the Doctor finally set off on horseback the following day and arrived in Fort Charter on the 14th where he stopped off to send some telegrams–and presumably tend to his backside. Judging by the typically upbeat and reassuring telegram he fired off to Sir Henry Loch,[iii] the British High Commissioner in Cape Town, it would seem that even then, Jameson remained unable, or perhaps unwilling, to accept the true severity of the situation around Fort Victoria: 'This is merely a raid against Makalakas round Victoria, and not against whites... I hope to get rid of them without trouble.'[20]

The doctor, complete with aching piles, finally arrived at Fort Victoria on the 17th and can only have been astounded at what he saw on his way into the settlement. The Matabele raid was still in full swing and mobs of Lobengula's warriors were roaming about with impunity, searching for more victims to butcher. Other groups were driving stolen mules laden with booty back towards Matabeleland.

Jameson's party passed Mashona kraals and out-lying white-owned farms which had been set ablaze, while mutilated corpses lay all about. The damage inflicted on a farm belonging to a Mr Napier might serve as an example of the havoc wrought:

'The raiders completely wrecked his homestead, destroying everything in his house. The throats of all his fowls were cut, and the dead birds left lying on the ground. All his goats were killed and skinned and the carcasses left, while all his cattle were driven off, and three cattle herds murdered. Altogether between three

iii Henry Brougham Loch, 1st Baron Loch GCB, GCMG (1827–1900). A Scotsman who left the Royal Navy to join a cavalry regiment in the British East India Company's army. After serving in the Crimean War and the Opium Wars, he joined the colonial office and was appointed Governor of the Cape Colony and High Commissioner for Southern Africa in 1889.

and four hundred head of cattle belonging to white men were driven off by the Matabeli.'[21]

Though no whites were killed in the raid, it was reckoned that some 400 Mashona had been slaughtered in the ten day orgy of violence, so one can only imagine the scale of the carnage witnessed by the Doctor.

Jameson entered Fort Victoria to find the settlement in a state of siege with sentries posted and all the townspeople holed up in the police fort. The fort itself was a rectangular red-brick structure surrounded by a belt of barbed wire about ten yards deep. Though Jameson's cuts to the BSACP meant that there had only been seven police officers based there when the raid began, Captain Lendy had quickly formed a 400-strong militia of volunteers from among the townsmen. There was a terrible paucity of suitable horses though, meaning that these volunteers could only be deployed as infantry–which was fine for defending the Fort and the town, but no good for driving the fleet-footed Matabele away, or facing them out in the open. Indeed, there was such a shortage of horses that none whatsoever could be spared for the artillery and the few field pieces and machine guns available had to be pulled about by the gunners themselves. If, as their liberal critics perversely and illogically suggest, Jameson and Rhodes had harboured a secret, wicked desire to provoke a war with Lobengula, their forces were certainly in no condition to fight it.

The doctor immediately despatched a police patrol to summon the Matabele indunas and a meeting was held in the fort at midday on the 18th. Jameson lounged back on a kitchen chair with the sobering sight of two Maxims and a Gatling gun up on the battlements behind him. The large Matabele delegation included Manyao, who was nominally in charge of the raid, and his much younger second-in-command, Umgandan. The latter was a fine-looking unmarried warrior, variously described in contemporary accounts as rude, insolent, ill-tempered and hot-headed.

The doctor quickly laid down the law for Manyao, demanding to know why he had permitted his warriors to commit such atrocities and cause such devastation. Jameson then asked Manyao if he had lost control of some of his men, and the Matabele chief admitted that this was indeed the case. Umgandan tried to shout Jameson down, but the Doctor gave him short shrift, telling him to shut up and informing him that he only spoke with men, not boys.[22]

The meeting was wrapped up in under 20 minutes and ended with Jameson telling Manyao to set off for the border with the warriors he could still control. He was given one hour to start this movement, and Mr Napier, Jameson's interpreter, clearly demonstrated the time scale to

Manyao using the movement of the sun. Manyao himself claimed that the Doctor's parting words to him were, 'Now go—or I will drive you across.' Manyao left quietly, but his hot-tempered second in charge, young Umgandan, defiantly shouted back at Jameson, 'Very well—we will be driven across!'

Once the Matabele delegation had departed, Jameson and Captain Lendy assembled all the available horses, and a mounted troop was readied for Lendy to lead out if needed. About 38–40 strong, this force comprised the handful of policemen available and was filled out by volunteers, of whom there was no shortage. The tough colonials and Boer frontiersmen were not the sort of men to shrink from such a duty.

Once more, there was no indication that Jameson wanted to provoke a fight and the patrol was kept in Fort Victoria well beyond the allotted hour. Indeed, it was only after the horsemen had enjoyed their lunch that Lendy called his troop together. Jameson sent the patrol on their way with the following orders to Captain Lendy:

> 'You have heard what I told the Matabele. I want you to carry this out. I do not want them to think this is merely a threat. They have had a week of threats already, and with very bad results. Ride out in the direction they have gone to Magomoli's kraal. If you find they are not moving off, drive them as you heard me tell Manyao I would, and if they resist, and attack you, shoot them.'[23]

One witness, an Afrikaans doctor called Hans Sauer, claimed it was not until 16h00 that Lendy's troops trotted out of Fort Victoria[24]– about two-and-a-half hours after the time limit had expired. Sauer was certainly no apologist for Jameson, having locked horns with him years before over the small pox outbreak in Kimberley, and having been left penniless after the Doctor had beaten his four kings with a straight flush in an epic game of poker.[25]

Lendy led his 40-odd troopers out against 3,500 and the mounted men soon caught up with the Matabele raiders. Most of Manyao's warriors had heeded his orders and set off for the border, but as Lendy's patrol approached the kraals of two Mashona chiefs, Magomoli and Makoombi, they started encountering scattered parties of Matabele just a few miles from Fort Victoria (reports of exactly how far vary from 'three miles' to 'one hour', none of which suggests that these warriors intended to comply with Jameson's demand).

These elements were under the command of young Umgandan, the arrogant braggart who earlier, had dared Jameson to drive his men over the border; nevertheless, had they simply been stragglers attempting to make their way for the frontier when Lendy's men caught them, there would probably have been no bloodshed. As it was, however, some of Umgandan's men were still actively attacking Magomoli's kraal, while others were driving captured company cattle off at spear-point even as the mounted patrol approached. At the later inquiry, Manyao himself claimed that these warriors had ignored him when he ordered them to head for the border immediately.

Either way, with the Matabele still busily attacking the Mashona kraal, Lendy's men had ridden into an ongoing skirmish and the Captain reacted in the only way he really could have, shaking his men out into a skirmish line and ordering them to dismount. Lendy's men fired a few warning shots[26] and put a few volleys into the raiders, and it was all over. The highly unpleasant young Umgandan, conspicuously resplendent in his white ostrich feathers, was one of the first of the Matabele shot down. The Mashona Chief Makoombi, who also testified at the inquiry, confirmed that his kraal had been under siege since the raids began, and, that afternoon, hours after the indaba at Fort Victoria, Umgandan's thugs had been taunting, and shouting, 'Come out, we want to kill you.' The Chief also claimed, 'They ran away as soon as the white men fired the shots.'[27]

No sooner had the firing begun than Lendy ordered his trumpeter to sound the 'cease fire' and the rest of the raiders fled. Matabele witnesses who were interviewed in the 1930s claimed that Lendy's men had only shot down two or three of their number, including Umgandan. One witness, Mpagama, testified, 'Only two people were killed by the white people, but a lot of people were killed by the Mashonas. The Mashonas waited for them in a narrow defile in the hills, and they shot them as they passed through.'[28]

The Mashona also mutilated Umgandan's body after the clash, hacking off his head-ring,[iv] genitals and other body parts–though one can hardly blame them for being delighted that this murderous brute had got his comeuppance.

Fearing he would be drawn into an ambush, Lendy did not pursue the fleeing Matabele. By any standards, it had been a short, sharp and highly effective engagement.

Though Lendy's action might ruffle the feathers of today's liberal critics, the bravery and resolve of the patrol was greatly appreciated at the time, and not just by the white residents in the area. One volunteer who took part recalled their return journey to Fort Victoria:

'We passed several places where the Mashonas in their strongholds amongst the kopjes had held out against the Matabele, several of whom were lying about dead, showing that the Mashonas had made good use of their old muzzle loading rifles... after repeated

---

iv   A Matabele warrior who had proven himself in battle was allowed to 'plait' his hair into a piece of fibre which formed a 'ring' around his head.

calls first one head appeared over the top, then another, until about 400 [Mashona] men, women and children were in view, no doubt feeling greatly relieved when they were told the Matabele had been driven across the border.'[29]

Another volunteer, Mr Herbert Stokes, stated, 'It never occurred to me that I had been engaged in an action which would be the subject of anything but favourable remark.'

The effect on the Matabele raiders was dramatic, and they hurried back to Bulawayo. Indeed, one warrior who had been separated from the rest made it to Lobengula's capital first, '...spreading the report at every kraal that he was the only one left alive out of the impi, and that the white men on horses were following close behind him. This created consternation throughout the country and for a hundred miles inland natives fled in all directions with their stock and possessions. On arrival at Bulawayo the warrior reported the matter to the king, who promptly ordered him to be put to death as a bearer of evil news.'[30]

The inquiry held into the skirmish the following year found that Lendy's men had fired first,[31] contradicting the report Lendy had filed immediately after the action, which stated that his patrol had come under fire and replied. The Captain was unable to defend himself though. Shortly after the war that followed the skirmish, he died in a splendidly unusual fashion by rupturing his intestines while 'putting the shot' with a little too much gusto.[32] Whether Lendy's men came under fire first or not would seem completely irrelevant in any case: no one denied that Umgandan's raiders had cheerfully been attacking Magomoli's kraal at the time, or could claim they had shown any interest in complying with Jameson's ultimatum. Jameson and Lendy's decisive action had finally ended the Matabele's 10-day rampage of killing and looting.

§

Needless to say, the safe return of Captain Lendy's patrol was very well received by the townspeople at Fort Victoria, but one who was there recalled:

'Feeling in Victoria was running very high at this time, for everyone felt if no further action was to be taken, Lobengula would again make excuses and promises, and the following year, if not sooner, things would be much worse. Capitalists openly spoke of withdrawing capital. Farmers and traders threatened to trek out of the country, and a very strongly worded address was presented to

Dr Jameson, with a request that it might be forwarded to the high commissioner, to the effect that, unless the company settled this question once and for all, in the only way it could be done, namely by breaking up the Matabeli power, they were determined to do one of two things: leave the country, or undertake the settlement of the question themselves.'[33]

One traveller met a group who had already decided enough was enough, and were fleeing Fort Victoria:

'A woman told my wife that the Matabele were about to attack the town; that all women would be killed in a horrible manner; that they could cut out the tongue of our little boy, and other details of like cheerful nature. She advised us to turn south while yet there was time.'[34]

Critics of the war, both then and now, simply overlook the pressure that the settlers were putting on Dr Jameson. It was easy to say that Jameson should have 'turned the other cheek' when lecturing from the safety of faraway London, and it is easy to do so now, looking back over a hundred years later, but to the townspeople of Fort Victoria in 1890, it was quite literally a matter of life and death. Luckily for them, the Doctor had had more than enough of appeasement, and quickly made up his mind to deal with the matter once and for all.

Dr Hans Sauer, the Afrikaner who the Doctor knew from his days at the Kimberley diamond fields, recalled:

'After dinner, Jameson asked me to go and find out what was the opinion of my Boer countrymen as to the strength of the military force that would be required for the conquest of Matabeleland. I spent about two hours in interviewing various groups of Boers around their camp fire, and found that the almost unanimous view was that a mounted force of from eight hundred to a thousand men would suffice... I reported the opinion of my countrymen to Jameson, who seemed pleased that the Boer estimate... was so modest.'[35]

It is little wonder that Jameson was pleased: most British army sources suggested that a force of 7,000 would be needed to take on Lobengula's 25,000 strong army. Buoyed by this news, and back to his decisive, self-confident best, the Doctor immediately replied, 'I'll do it.'

However, Jameson still had to convince both Rhodes and Sir Henry Loch that war was necessary and he spent the evening of the 18th cranking out telegrams to plead his case:

'That night, I had a long conversation by telegraph with the high commissioner and Mr Rhodes. Described everything which had occurred and discussed future proceedings.'[36]

In 1899, Jameson wrote the foreword of a biography on Rhodes in which he rather glosses over all this to give an example of his boss' leadership style:

'Five words from Mr Rhodes and eight words from myself decided the question of our action in the first Matabele war... what a man of action and not words Mr Rhodes is... observe too, Mr Rhodes left the decision to the man on the spot, myself, who might be supposed to be the best judge of the conditions.'[37]

This is eloquently exemplified in the telegram exchange between Rhodes and Jameson in which Rhodes, the clergyman's son, takes the ecclesiastical route to caution the Doctor against biting off more than he could chew:
'Read Luke 14:31.'
Jameson called for a bible and read the following passage:
'Or what king, going to make war against another king, sitteth not down first, and consulteth whether he be able with 10,000 to meet him that cometh against him with 20,000?'
Despite knowing that the odds would be nearer to just 1,000 meeting 20,000, the Doctor replied simply, 'All right. Have read Luke 14:31.'
Ever dubious about wasting money, and showing no enthusiasm whatsoever for conflict with Lobengula, Rhodes tried a different tack, reminding Jameson that the chartered company simply could not afford a war. The company had invested heavily in building the telegraph line and there was little money to pay for Jameson's military adventure—however justified it might have been. The doctor bluntly demanded that the money be found from somewhere and finally gained Rhodes' approval.
Unsurprisingly, and with mind-numbing predictability, the decision made by Jameson and Rhodes to deploy military force to resolve the issue is today criticized by the usual suspects; all of whom conveniently forget that it was not the 'wicked' settlers who caused the war at all–it was the constant, and increasingly murderous, Matabele with their raids into Mashonaland.
Consider, for example, a scenario in which, for several years, France regularly sends huge raiding parties over the border into Italy, murdering, looting and pillaging as they see fit. Finally, they launch a brigade sized attack, lay siege to the border for 10 days, butcher 400

Italian civilians, burn numerous towns and only retreat when they are finally driven off by the Italian army.

Would any right-thinking person really consider it 'wrong' of Italy to retaliate? Would anyone automatically assume that the French were somehow the 'goodies' in this scenario, and start squawking about how the evil Italians had only reacted because they had always wanted to invade France? Would anyone instantly presume that the Italians must have had some vast and unexplained octopus-like Machiavellian scheme which caused them to gleefully seize upon all these murderous raids to give them a casus belli against their poor, innocent neighbours?

Of course not–everyone would accept that Italy had a perfectly valid reason—indeed, an obligation to their people—to take military action.

So why is it somehow 'different' in the case of the Matabele attacks into Mashonaland? The usual response, 'the whites shouldn't have been there in the first place', is clearly ridiculous as the Matabele were also very recent arrivals, who equally 'shouldn't have been there in the first place'. Indeed, what gave the Matabele more right to invade an area and exist by raiding and killing their neighbours, than the white settlers had to move into the adjoining area and live peacefully and develop it? Furthermore, if this bizarre response comes down to some sort of 'reverse racism', any action the Rhodesians took to shatter the military power of the Matabele massively benefitted the Mashona and Bechuana, the people who had suffered most at their hands and who for decades had lived in abject terror of their raids. In fact, the idea appealed so strongly to the Mashona and the Bechuana that they provided contingents to support the Rhodesians in the war that followed.

Those on the ground certainly thought Rhodes and Jameson were perfectly justified in responding as they did. Dr Hans Sauer, who, as we know, was no friend of Jameson's, wrote:

'I consider Jameson was right in the action he took, for, however strong the Matabele case may have been, from the practical point of view it was clearly impossible that the white men resident in Mashonaland should tolerate the yearly over-running of the country by Matabele impis, with the consequent killing of harmless Mashonas living under the protection of the chartered company. The estimation of the white man would have dropped to zero if the chartered company had allowed the Matabele king to continue his raids.'[38]

Another resident of Fort Victoria expressed the mood of the townspeople in a candid letter to his father:

'When it comes to [the Matabele raiders] killing our own native servants in the precincts of the town, even we, who take our pleasures sadly and our cheek soberly, had to rise in our wrath, and chastise our dusky brethren. Of course, according to the gospels of 'St. Labby' [Mr Labouchère] and Exeter Hall, we should not have done this, but let them gang their ain gait until the wet season had properly set in–those of us who had not the sense or means to go down country, being all the more or less down with fever, the full rivers forbidding relief column or more provisions; and then they would have swooped down in their tens of thousands, and butchered man, woman and child. This is the programme Exeter Hall would have liked us to follow, rather than injure a few of their petted heathen, who, by-the-bye, would have as much pleasure in slitting a few of the above-named trageophilists, as those of their Mashona vassals. Being, however, men who live among the black devils, and know their ways, we are taking the bull by the horns and are going to make a bold push for Bulawayo, the head-quarters of this savage potentate. Remember I am no servant of the British South Africa Company, and in many ways I have despised their ways and policy, so that you may regard me as a perfectly unbiased witness in the matter. That being so, I say, without the slightest fear of contradiction, that the company has been forced into any action they have taken by Lobengula himself; for at the time the disturbance took place they had neither the means nor inclination to commence what may eventuate into a big war. As to the innuendos in several of the English papers about a hankering after Matabeliland by the company, that's all bosh; but what would have happened had they not taken the stand they have done, would have been a slaughter of almost every white person in Mashonaland, and the company would have lost what they have already got, and paid so dear for–Mashonaland. Had the affairs been in less capable hands than those of our administrator, Dr Jameson, I dread to think what would have happened; but on the occasion there arose a man to cope with it; and if the expedition is successful, as it must be, the chartered company ought to recognize that in Dr Jameson, they have a man second in ability to Cecil Rhodes himself.'[39]

The company's man in Bulawayo, Colenbrander, was probably better placed than anyone—certainly better placed than those bleating from the safety of London—to comment on the need to lance the boil. A frontiersman who had lived among the Matabele for many years and knew both their customs and the prevailing mood in Lobengula's court, Colenbrander reported, 'The whole country [Matabeleland] is in arms and anxious for the fray,' and 'The amajaka are clamouring for war.'[40] He later telegrammed to say, 'Should you succeed in patching up some peace for the present, the same raiding would be repeated and neither the lives of the Mashonas or the white men would be safe.'[41]

Confirming Colenbrander's view, and even as Lobengula was protesting his innocence, another large Matabele raiding force was rampaging through Barotseland.[v] According to Barotse Chief Lewanika, this 6,000 strong impi, '...scoured Batokaland for three months, destroying property and killing many of my people in the most revolting manner. Women were ripped open and impaled, men and children were made targets of and roasted alive like meat. Nothing, not a dog, escaped where they passed.'[42]

One missionary reported having seen the bodies of forty babies and toddlers hung upside down from their heels, slowly roasting to death over a long fire while Matabele warriors sat around watching.[43] With war with the Rhodesians looming, Lobengula despatched runners to summon these murderous marauders back to Bulawayo. As one observer, Colonel Stevenson-Hamilton, put it at the time, 'Ignorant people at home cried out at our 'brutality' in conquering these fiends of hell.'[44]

§

So those modern-day critics who like to declare that, 'when he had the choice between peace and war, Jameson chose war',[45] are being as unrealistic as they are disingenuous. Jameson's patient attempts to live peacefully alongside the Matabele had failed, through no fault of his, or of the settlers. They had shown restraint and tolerance for longer than most, but when push came to shove, the Rhodesians were left with a stark choice either to pack up and abandon the new colony (and thereby also leave the Mashona to their fate) or tackle the murderous attentions of Lobengula's impis once and for all.

By 1893, the Matabele way of life was a complete anachronism in what was rapidly becoming the modern world. They were a savage, highly militarized and aggressive warrior society which existed by killing, dominating, enslaving and pillaging from their neighbours. European nations would not have been expected to turn a blind eye if, instead of joining the modern world, the Vikings had still been launching raids against them in the 1890s; it is every bit as farcical to suggest that the settlers of Mashonaland should simply have tolerated hordes of Matabele warriors swarming over the border whenever the fancy took them.

---

v   Barotseland is in the west of modern-day Zambia

End Notes

1 Gibbs, A Flag for the Matabele, p.143
2 Glass, The Matabele War, p.61
3 Glass, The Matabele War, p.62
4 Mason, The Birth of a Dilemma, p.165
5 Glass, The Matabele War, p.66
6 Glass, The Matabele War, p.67
7 Keppel-Jones, Rhodes and Rhodesia, p.252
8 Tanser, A Scantling of Time: The Story of Salisbury, Rhodesia, 1890-1900, p.88
9 Mason, The Birth of a Dilemma, p.164
10 Wills and Collingridge, The Downfall of Lobengula, p.4
11 Glass, The Matabele War, p.76
12 Glass, The Matabele War, p.86
13 Michell, The Life and Times of the Right Honourable Cecil John Rhodes 1853-1902, p.87
14 Hanna, The Story of the Rhodesias and Nyasaland, p.91
15 Glass, The Matabele War, p.86
16 James, The Rise and Fall of the British Empire, p.261
17 Meredith, Diamonds, Gold and War, p.280
18 Meredith, Diamonds, Gold and War, p.284
19 Rhodesiana, December, 1967, p.20
20 Glass, The Matabele War, p.87
21 Wills and Collingridge, The Downfall of Lobengula, p.7
22 Colvin, The Life of Jameson, Vol.1, p.254
23 Wills and Collingridge, The Downfall of Lobengula, p.96
24 Sauer, Ex Africa, p.222
25 Sauer, Ex Africa, p.67
26 Keppel-Jones, Rhodes and Rhodesia, p.243
27 Colvin, The Life of Jameson, Vol.1, p.257
28 Keppel-Jones, Rhodes and Rhodesia, p.243
29 Jones, Rhodesian Genesis, p.76
30 Jones, Rhodesian Genesis, p.77
31 Glass, The Matabele War, p.121
32 Gibbs, The History of the BSAP, Vol.1, p.109
33 Wills and Collingridge, The Downfall of Lobengula, p.62
34 Burnham, Scouting on Two Continents, p.119
35 Sauer, Ex Africa, p.224
36 Glass, The Matabele War, p.97
37 Imperialist, Cecil Rhodes: A Biography and an Appreciation, p.401
38 Sauer, Ex Africa, p.224
39 Wills and Collingridge, The Downfall of Lobengula, p.247
40 Keppel-Jones, Rhodes and Rhodesia, p.251
41 Glass, The Matabele War, p.154
42 Keppel-Jones, Rhodes and Rhodesia, p.251
43 Hanna, The Story of the Rhodesias and Nyasaland, p.95
44 Barotseland Journal, p.99 (found in Hanna's The Story of the Rhodesias and Nyasaland)
45 Meredith, Diamonds, Gold and War, p.280

"Instinctively the Englishman is no missionary, no conqueror. He prefers the country to the town, and home to foreign parts. He is rather glad and relieved if only natives will remain natives and strangers strangers, and at a comfortable distance from himself. Yet outwardly he is most hospitable and accepts almost anybody for the time being; he travels and conquers without a settled design, because he has the instinct of exploration. His adventures are all external; they change him so little that he is not afraid of them. He carries his English weather in his heart wherever he goes, and it becomes a cool spot in the desert, and a steady and sane oracle amongst all the deliriums of mankind. Never since the heroic days of Greece has the world had such a sweet, just, boyish master. It will be a black day for the human race when scientific blackguards, conspirators, churls, and fanatics manage to supplant him"

- American / Spanish philosopher, essayist and man of letters,
George Santayana, on the British Empire

'If it was the blacks that were cruel first, and the whites that retaliated, it was the whites who had robbed the blacks of the country in the first place.'[2]

– In his determination to excuse them of all wrong,
Professor Keppel-Jones conveniently ignores that the
Matabele themselves had 'robbed other tribes
of the country' just a couple of generations earlier.

Chapter 4
The Coalition of the Willing

In spite of all the evidence to the contrary, there are still some who claim that the conniving Rhodesians had been plotting the war all along, and were delighted when their schemes came to fruition. Though a pleasing notion for those of a virulently anti-imperial persuasion, those who blindly accept it are never able to explain one salient point: the fact that in July 1893, the Rhodesians did not have an army. Any logical observer might find cause to stop at this juncture, and consider how ludicrous it is to suggest that the settlers would have gone out of their way to provoke a war when they had no means to fight one.

Jameson had to spend months building a suitable force. This created a delay which threatened to derail the whole thing as it gave Lobengula time to present himself as the innocent victim of the piece–a truly nonsensical claim, eagerly lapped up by the ghastly Labouchère and his radical gang in London. The greater the time lag between the atrocities committed by the Matabele around Fort Victoria and the Rhodesian response, the more risk the company ran of being accused of embarking on an 'unprovoked war of conquest'–despite how utterly irrational that accusation might have been.

Always a firm believer that the end justified the means, the Doctor did what he could to keep the pot boiling and was 'somewhat economical' with the truth in the reports he sent down to the company bosses in Kimberley and Cape Town. There was always a chance that, under pressure from Labouchère and the Exeter Hall mob, the colonial office might get cold feet and block the invasion before the Rhodesians could assemble their forces.

Jameson had no intention of letting Lobengula wriggle off the hook once he had decided that war was the only possible way to deal with the threat. This was not some sort of dastardly desire for bloodshed; it was the certain knowledge that, if not dealt with once and for all, the Matabele would pop up a few months later and unleash yet more murderous raids on Mashonaland. In the months of 'phony war' between the raid on Fort Victoria and eventual Rhodesian retaliation, the Doctor admitted, 'I cable carefully, send the truth occasionally and Cape Town does the same.'[3]

He had little choice: the simple fact was that no invasion would be launched without a go-ahead from Sir Henry Loch, the high commissioner down in Cape Town. It was vital that Loch be kept on side and given no excuse to take the easy way out by ruling that Lobengula be given another chance.

With the BSACP slashed to the bone and Rhodes grumbling about pennies, it would be a war fought on the cheap. One initial plan was to recruit five hundred Transvaal Boers under the command of a Colonel Ferriera who had, himself, been faced down by Jameson a couple of years earlier while in charge of the Boer commando that attempted to invade Mashonaland. Nevertheless, Jameson seems to have thought he was the man for the job.

Not surprisingly, this proposal never got off the ground. Indeed, the very notion that the settlers themselves should launch a cheap-and-cheerful, Boer-style invasion made up of unsupported mounted infantry prompted a furious fall out among the Rhodesians. Many argued that it would be suicidal to launch the invasion without a considerable wagon train to cart supplies, machine guns and plentiful ammunition stocks for the artillery and, most importantly, to make it possible for defensive laagers (circles of wagons rather like those in old cowboy films) to be formed. Major Frank Johnson, who had commanded the pioneer column three years earlier, had been appointed to command the invasion and was particularly agitated about the plan to go in without wagons. He had a blazing row with Jameson[4] and even offered to provide half of the wagons himself, if the company agreed to match this.[5] However, neither man was the sort to back down publically and thus, a furious Johnson resigned his position as the commanding officer, and refused to have any part in what he felt would end in a massacre. When all Johnson's officers openly supported his stance over the need for a wagon train, Jameson summoned him and demanded that he leave the country so as to forestall a mutiny. Common sense quickly prevailed, however, and though Johnson would play no part in the war,[i] the concept of an all-mounted, flying-column style invasion force was quietly dropped. Jameson was certainly conscious of the need to keep costs down, but he was pragmatic enough to know when to change his plans. Ultimately, the company's forces went in with even more wagons than what Johnson had demanded.[6]

Johnson's replacement was Major Patrick Forbes[ii]–a man Johnson rather unkindly dismissed as 'a typical British bulldog, with about as much brains'. A 32 year old imperial officer and a product of Rugby and Sandhurst RMA, Forbes had been serving as the magistrate at

---

i Astoundingly, this fact did not prevent the BBC from having depicted Johnson murdering wounded Matabele warriors after a battle in their mini-series, Rhodes. The use of utterly baseless propaganda to blacken the history of the British Empire knows no bounds, it would seem.

ii Patrick William Forbes (1861–1918), was commissioned to the 6th (Inniskilling) Dragoons and joined as 2nd in command of the BSCAP when the regiment was formed in 1889. After the 1893 Matabele War, Forbes would go on to serve as commissioner of the BSAC territory in north-western Rhodesia (now Zambia), from 1895 to 1897.

Salisbury since 1890, and had already seen active service with the company during their undeclared war with Portugal a couple of years earlier.[7] The early Rhodesians were a highly idiosyncratic bunch,[8] and Forbes was blessed with far more chiefs than Indians. Two of his subordinate officers dropped out at the last moment over continuing squabbles about how the campaign would be run.[9] Other mavericks were keen to join the invasion, but weren't interested in being stuck in a unit. A scouting section was formed so that these individualistic fellows could also go along.

§

Once the squabbling was finally over, the company forces would consist of three columns: one raised at Salisbury, another at Fort Victoria, and a third in Johannesburg–that the latter town happened to be in the Republic of the Transvaal did not seem to trouble anybody.[10]

Commanded by Forbes himself, the Salisbury Horse struggled to muster their allotment of 250 whites, so a 60-strong unit of 'colonial natives and coolies'[iii] was authorized to supplement them:

'The coolies were armed with combination guns, one barrel carrying M.H. [Martini Henry] ammunition, the other twelve-bore cartridges loaded with loupers.'[11]

In addition, there were 55 Mashona—drivers, servants, cooks and bottle-washers—and 242 horses.[12]

This contingent also boasted two Maxims, two other machine guns (a Nordenfelt and a Gardner) and a single 7-pdr field gun.[13] Supplies and ammunition were carried on 16 ox-wagons which would also serve as a defensive laager each night. The bishop of Mashonaland, Bishop Knight-Bruce, served as the unit's padre, travelling in his own purpose-built carriage[14] (please see appendix 2 for more details).

The unit raised at Fort Victoria (the Victoria Rangers) was significantly larger, consisting of 414 whites commanded by the dashing Major Allan Wilson,[iv] a man who was every inch the sort of heroic alpha male one finds in every Wilbur Smith book. According to a contemporary, he was '...always popular and loved by everyone who knew him. In those days of hard drinking he could join in with the crowd visiting the different hotel bars, and he was the noisiest of

---

iii A 'coolie' was a gentleman of Indian extraction–the term has since fallen out of favour.

iv Major Allan Wilson (1856–1893) emigrated from his native Scotland to the Cape Colony where he joined the Cape Mounted Rifles and saw service in the Zulu War and First Boer War before being commissioned into the Basuto Police. In 1893, Wilson was working for the Bechuanaland Exploration Company in Fort Victoria and immediately volunteered for service in the invasion.

the lot, but he never took anything stronger than ginger ale. He was always a man among men, tall, square-shouldered, and fine looking with a heavy moustache.'[15]

40 Mashona drivers manned the Victorians' 18 ox-wagons which were laden with plentiful stocks of ammunition and provisions for two months. Despite scouring southern Africa and even having requisitioned some from within company territory, Jameson's agents were unable to find enough horses. The shortage meant that only about 170 of the Victoria men could be mounted–a far cry from the initial plan to muster an all-mounted force. An artillery troop (commanded by our friend Captain Lendy) comprised three Maxims, a 7-pdr, and a 2-pdr quick-firing Hotchkiss gun.[v] A force of around 400 Mashona warrior allies marched with the Victoria column[16] under the command of Lieutenant Brabant,[vi] but—according to the practice of the time—did not laager with them (for full details, please see Appendix 3).

Doctor Jameson might be criticized for 'starting' the war, but at least he showed a lot more courage than today's politicians. There was never any doubt that he would ride in with the invading force, thus running just as much risk as the men he was pitching into the conflict. Though Jameson was to have no real say in the military aspects of the campaign, he would still be in charge as the administrator over-all. Sir John Willoughby[vii]—who was the adjutant of the BSACP and a good friend of Jameson's—would serve as the Doctor's 'military advisor' throughout the campaign.[17]

The troopers were equipped with .577 calibre, single shot Martini-Henry rifles, the same tried and trusted rifles the British army had used in the Zulu War. Though the regular British Army had by then started re-equipping with .303 magazine rifles, the Martini-Henry was still a formidable man-stopper and would remain in service until after the Boer War. Many of the men also received revolvers and Victoria Rangers' large dismounted contingent were given sword bayonets in anticipation of fierce hand-to-hand combat. Copious numbers of entrenching tools were taken, along with signal rockets and some magnesium lights which a friend of Major Forbes' had developed for shooting lions at night.[18] Forbes had toyed with the idea of sourcing

---

v   Built by the French armament firm, Hotchkiss (established in France by American gunsmith, Benjamin Hotchkiss) this was a very light (116lbs) 42mm field piece with a range of around 1500 yards.

vi   Later Major-General Sir Edward Yewd Brabant, KCB, CMG (1839–1914), a veteran of the Cape Frontier Wars (also known as the Xhosa Wars, or—less commonly these days—the Kaffir Wars) Brabant would go on to raise Brabant's Horse and command the Colonial Division in the Boer War. His son was killed in the Boer War, while serving in the Imperial Light Horse.

vii   Captain Sir John Willoughby (1859–1918) of the Royal Horse Guards, who served in the 1882 Egyptian Campaign, charging at Kassassin and fighting at the Battle of Tel-el-Kebir three days later. Willoughby would later take an active part in the Jameson Raid.

fifty sabres so that a troop could be equipped as cavalry (distinct from mounted infantry) stating, 'I knew from my experience in Zululand what a horror the natives had of mounted men who could gallop them down.'[19] It appears he was unable to lay his hands on this cold steel.

Indeed, as the company had been completely unprepared for war, there were not even sufficient uniforms for all, and many men had little choice other than to sling their bandoliers over their everyday attire. Saddlery and other accoutrements where also in short supply, despite the company having bought up as many of these as possible.[20] Khaki jackets, corduroy riding breeches and slouch hats[21] were issued to some but, unlike the pioneers, who three years earlier, had been very smartly turned out, the company's invasion force must have looked a very rough and ready crew. Not surprisingly, a great number of the 1890 pioneers served in the Matabele War—indeed, the company took a huge gamble by taking so many of the colony's menfolk out of Mashonaland. If Major Forbes' men were massacred, or even if the Matabele managed to side-step them and slip past into Mashonaland, the company's territory would lie virtually defenceless before them.[viii] One settler, John Meikle, describes the risibly puny forces which were left behind to defend Mashonaland:

'The handful of men left behind had to be organized into some sort of defence force. A friend of mine was appointed captain and I was lieutenant and adjutant. Most of the men had never fired a gun before. They were taken down to the range for rifle practice. One, a Jew Kaffir-store keeper, made a bull at 500 yards. On inspecting the sighting of his gun, it was found to stand at 100 yards. I am afraid that, if the Matabele had come, there would have been little hope for any of us that were left behind.'[22]

Even by Jameson's gung-ho standards, the invasion was an all-or-nothing gamble of the first order.

Though the fellows who joined the Salisbury Horse and the Victoria Rangers seem to have been of 'the right sort' in the main, the unit raised down in Johannesburg quickly gained a rather less enviable reputation. Unable to attract enough men of the right calibre, Captain Raaff[ix]—who would be in command—was forced to recruit from the seedier parts of Johannesburg and plenty of the dregs who had been

---

viii The company left several artillery pieces at Fort Salisbury for defensive purposes: one 7-pdr, one Maxim, two Nordenfelts, and a 2-pdr Hotchkiss–the last three had been captured from the Portuguese in 1891.

ix Capt. Pieter Johannes Raaff (1849–1893) was an Afrikaner born in Bloemfontein, who served with the imperial forces in the Basuto War, the Zulu War and the First Boer War in 1881. Raaff died of enteritis shortly after the Matabele War.

drawn to the gold rush ended up in the unit. Officially named 'Raaff's Rangers', the regiment quickly gained the nickname 'Raaff's Riff-Raff', and some in Johannesburg rather unkindly claimed that the company had done the town a great service by getting rid of these decidedly dodgy characters. The anti-Rhodes newspaper, The Standard and Digger's News, ran several stories about the boisterous behaviour of these recruits. The editor openly declared, 'The Rand is being purged of its riff-raff,' and went on to relate tales of how they had looted canteens and committed other such drunken misdemeanours.[23]

Though probably the work of a few bad apples, the Raaff's Rangers' lack of discipline as they moved forward through the Transvaal, prompted the republic's state secretary to send a telegraph to the high commissioner, Sir Henry Loch, complaining of 'stealing and looting along the road' and, not unreasonably, stating that the Transvaal would not permit 'further trekking of such persons through this state'.[24]

Forbes' initial plan was for the three units each to be self-sufficient and to proceed towards Bulawayo independently. Once more, however, the somewhat chaotic command structure of the company's forces intervened and the Victoria Rangers insisted on linking with the Salisbury Column so they could march in together.[25] Dr Jameson backed this strategy, over-ruling Forbes–but even this logical adjustment to the plan would later cause more bickering. Everyone accepted that Forbes would be in charge of the united columns, but Captain Lendy, who was in command of the Victoria Artillery Troop, would later cause a fuss, demanding that his unit remain independent of Wilson's Victoria Rangers as it had 'been raised independently'.[26] Forbes did not stand for this nonsense though, and gave Wilson and Lendy ten minutes to amalgamate their commands or return home. They amalgamated.

§

Paying a conventional wage to all these hundreds of men presented a problem to the ever cash-conscious British South Africa Company and an alternative scheme was thus adopted. In lieu of cash payment, it was decided that the recruits would instead receive various 'rewards' if the invasion was successful. These points were formalized by a committee and set out in each man's conditions of service. Every volunteer would receive the right to mark out a 3,000 morgen (6,000 acre) farm in Matabeleland–these had to be marked out within 4 months of the end of hostilities. Each volunteer was also entitled to a total of 20 gold claims, with the stipulation that a 30-foot shaft within 6 months, or a 60-foot shaft within a year, had to have been sunk on reef claims.

Clause 7 of the terms of service dealt with Lobengula's cattle–
the undiplomatically named 'loot'. It stated, 'The loot shall be divided,
one half to the British South Africa Company, and the remainder to
the officers and men in equal shares,'[27] and was destined to become
the most controversial clause in the conditions. Those who got their
knickers in a twist over it conveniently overlooked the fact that the
Matabele had themselves built up this herd by seizing cattle from their
neighbours, and that, in any case, only the vast herd belonging to
Lobengula himself, not the private property of the Matabele people,
would be commandeered.[28] In the 1960's, Rhodesia historian, Robert
Cary, explained:

'In its present-day connotation, 'loot' conjures up visions of faceless
men stealing goods from bombed-out tobacconist shops; but in 1893
it meant nothing more than the relatively respectable word 'spoils'.
For many decades in southern Africa volunteers had expected to be
rewarded for their efforts with a share of the spoils… Critics might
argue that this entitled them to the label of 'mercenaries', but to
apply this pejorative term in the context of border warfare in 19th
century Africa is as meaningless as to condemn Lobengula for not
operating a system of universal adult suffrage.'[29]

Interestingly, Captain Donovan of the Victoria Rangers wrote that
the dismounted men recruited in Johannesburg were instead enlisted
at five shillings a day plus clothing and rations. Donovan also recorded
that the Victoria Rangers were offered the chance to change their terms
of enlistment before they set off:

'Few did so, except where two 'pals' decided to go halves in farms
and claims, in which case one took the farm and claims, the other
taking the five shillings per day. But not more than half a dozen
did so.'[30]

The reader should not form the impression that the company
troopers made millions from this loot. Jack Carruthers,[x] who had been
one of the 1890 pioneers and fought in the 1893 war, noted that,
after the fall of Bulawayo, 'farm rights were being sold for ten pounds
each and loot rights were fetching twelve pounds'.[31] To put this into
perspective, a stage coach service was established to link Bulawayo to
Fort Salisbury shortly after the war: the three day journey cost £25.[32]

---

x Jack Carruthers (1863–1951) was born in Grahamstown and went on to serve as interpreter and
guide to Cecil Rhodes. Carruthers acted as an intelligence agent for the 1890 pioneers, and travelled
independently, meeting the column at the Shashi River. He would later earn a living as a prospector,
making his last prospecting trip at the ripe old age of 85.

Whatever the rights and wrongs of it, the concept of 'loot' was, predictably enough, instantly seized upon by the Labouchère set at the time (and critics ever since). We shall return to this thorny subject in Chapter 11.

§

While the company forces were assembling up in Mashonaland, the 'imperial factor' was also preparing for war with the Matabele. With tensions rising, Sir Henry Loch ordered that the Bechuanaland Border Police (BBP) be expanded in case trouble spilled over into the protectorate. The regiment was brought up to full strength and then authorized to raise an additional troop, bringing it up to 450 strong. 225 of these played an active part in the invasion, forming part of the Southern Column which would march from Fort Tuli under the command of Lt. Colonel Goold-Adams[xi] of the BBP.[33] Raaff's Rangers— the 'riff-raff' recruited in Johannesburg—would march in with the BBP contingent and numbered 225 officers and men with 191 horses, a maxim gun, and eleven wagons. Though rarely mentioned by critics of the invasion, King Khama of the Bechuana was not going to miss the chance to rid himself of his volatile and violent neighbours, and placed a large number of his warriors at Sir Henry's disposal–these would also enter Matabeleland with Goold-Adams' Southern Column. Indeed, the Bechuana contingent was by far the largest component of the whole force: '130 mounted men, and between 1,700 and 1,800 dismounted men, about half of whom were armed with Martini-Henry rifles.'

When one considers the 400-strong Mashona contingent, the modern-day portrayal of the invasion of Matabeleland as some sort of white supremacist crusade seems rather ridiculous. Lobengula's antics had made him plenty of enemies over the years and it is little wonder his neighbours showed such enthusiasm about breaking his power.

§

Over in Matabeleland, there was not a great deal Lobengula could do, other than hope that Jameson and the company would, once again, let him off with no more than a warning. Suddenly playing the part of the victim, the king busily fired off messages, to anyone who would listen, demanding to know 'what great wrong' he had done. Presumably the butchery his men had indulged in around Fort Victoria

---

xi Lt. Colonel Sir Hamilton John Goold-Adams, GCMG, CB (1858–1920) an Irishman who was commissioned into the Royal Scots and then joined the newly-raised Bechuanaland Border Police. After service in the Matabele War, Goold-Adams fought in the Boer War before serving as the Lieutenant-Governor of the Orange River Colony and, later, Governor of Queensland.

did not figure in his thinking–or, for that matter, that of his past and present apologists. When he heard about the troops mustering on his borders, Lobengula must have realized that he had gone too far during the July raid, and that his previously docile new neighbours finally meant business. His survival was now in the hands of his formidable army, deemed to have been somewhere around 15,000 strong.

It was reckoned that the Matabele army comprised about 20 regiments,[34] or impis, divided into age groups in the Zulu style. By 1893, however, many of these were no longer made up of 'pure' Matabele/Zulu stock. In the years prior to the war, the Matabele army had increasingly relied on the man-power provided by boys captured in slave raids and raised in Matabeleland–one regiment contained only a single veteran from Mzilikazi's time. The large numbers of women-folk seized from neighbouring tribes had spawned offspring that didn't have 'the dash of the old Zulu warriors' and the army lacked discipline.[35] The 'proper' Matabele derisively dismissed these as 'maholis'.[xii]

Standards throughout the army certainly seemed to have slipped: Previously, regiments had fought long and hard for the honour of being permitted to marry but this had become very easy during Lobengula's reign. Under Mzilikazi, warriors had only counted kills against 'Zulus, Griquas, or Dutchmen', while in Lobengula's army, regiments were rewarded for kills against 'old men, women and children of the once despised Makalakas, Mashonas and Tauani'. Worse still, Lobengula had once permitted an entire regiment to marry because they had—in spite of tradition—knocked up several hundred girls:

'…it was therefore considered inexpedient to put so many breeders of soldiers to death, the usual penalty for frailty before marriage. In Mzilikazi's time, they would certainly have been massacred.'[36]

As we saw in the previous chapter, Lobengula had summoned a 6,000-strong force which was plundering their way through Barotseland on their way to Bulawayo in preparation for the coming war. To add to the king's woes, however, these returning marauders brought smallpox back with them–poetic justice, perhaps. On 22 September, a company agent in Bulawayo reported, 'The people who belong to the impi are dying daily, but so far as we have heard, no others have caught the infection; the admitted deaths amount to a great many hundreds.'[37]

Despite the erosion of discipline over the years and the setback of the smallpox outbreak, the Matabele could be forgiven for feeling confident. They enjoyed a huge numerical advantage, they would be fighting on home soil, and their way of war, based on cunning

---

xii Serf class or subjugated tribes

and stalking, was tried and tested. The impis would approach their enemies stealthily, crawling forward on their bellies until ready to leap up, scream a blood-curdling battle cry, and then surge forward for the slaughter.[38] Many Matabele warriors carried firearms of some sort, but the famous assegais and large cow-hide shields were still the mainstay of their arsenal.

These weapons and tactics had worked well enough against their poorly armed and disorganized black neighbours over the years. Whether they would win the day against the breech-loaders and Maxims of the Rhodesians, Bechuana Border Police and King Khama's warriors was a different matter altogether.

End Notes

[1] Wills and Collingridge, The Downfall of Lobengula, p.21
[2] Keppel-Jones, Rhodes and Rhodesia, p.440
[3] Glass, The Matabele War, p.14
[4] Johnson, Great Days, p.222
[5] Johnson, Great Days, p.223
[6] Johnson, Great Days, p.224
[7] O'Reilly, Pursuit of the King, p.9
[8] Bulpin, To the Banks of the Zambezi, p.325
[9] Wills and Collingridge, The Downfall of Lobengula, p.67
[10] Glass, The Matabele War, p.146
[11] Wills and Collingridge, The Downfall of Lobengula, p.69
[12] Wills and Collingridge, The Downfall of Lobengula, p.77
[13] Wills and Collingridge, The Downfall of Lobengula, p.79
[14] Wills and Collingridge, The Downfall of Lobengula, p.77
[15] Jones, Rhodesian Genesis, p.82
[16] Wills and Collingridge, The Downfall of Lobengula, p.93
[17] O'Reilly, Pursuit of the King, p.9
[18] Wills and Collingridge, The Downfall of Lobengula, p.79
[19] O'Reilly, Pursuit of the King, p.11
[20] Wills and Collingridge, The Downfall of Lobengula, p.69
[21] Wills and Collingridge, The Downfall of Lobengula, p.69
[22] Jones, Rhodesian Genesis, p.84
[23] Glass, The Matabele War, p.147
[24] Glass, The Matabele War, p.148
[25] O'Reilly, Pursuit of the King, p.11
[26] O'Reilly, Pursuit of the King, p.12
[27] Glass, The Matabele War, p.149
[28] Mason, The Birth of a Dilemma, p.186
[29] Cary, A Time to Die, p.25
[30] Donovan, With Wilson in Matabeleland, p.203
[31] Jones, Rhodesian Genesis, p.113
[32] Jones, Rhodesian Genesis, p.114
[33] Wills and Collingridge, The Downfall of Lobengula, p.217
[34] Mathers, Zambesia: England's El Dorado in Africa, p.195
[35] Mathers, Zambesia: England's El Dorado in Africa, p.197
[36] Mathers, Zambesia: England's El Dorado in Africa, p.195
[37] Keppel-Jones, Rhodes and Rhodesia, p.251
[38] Mathers, Zambesia: England's El Dorado in Africa, p.196

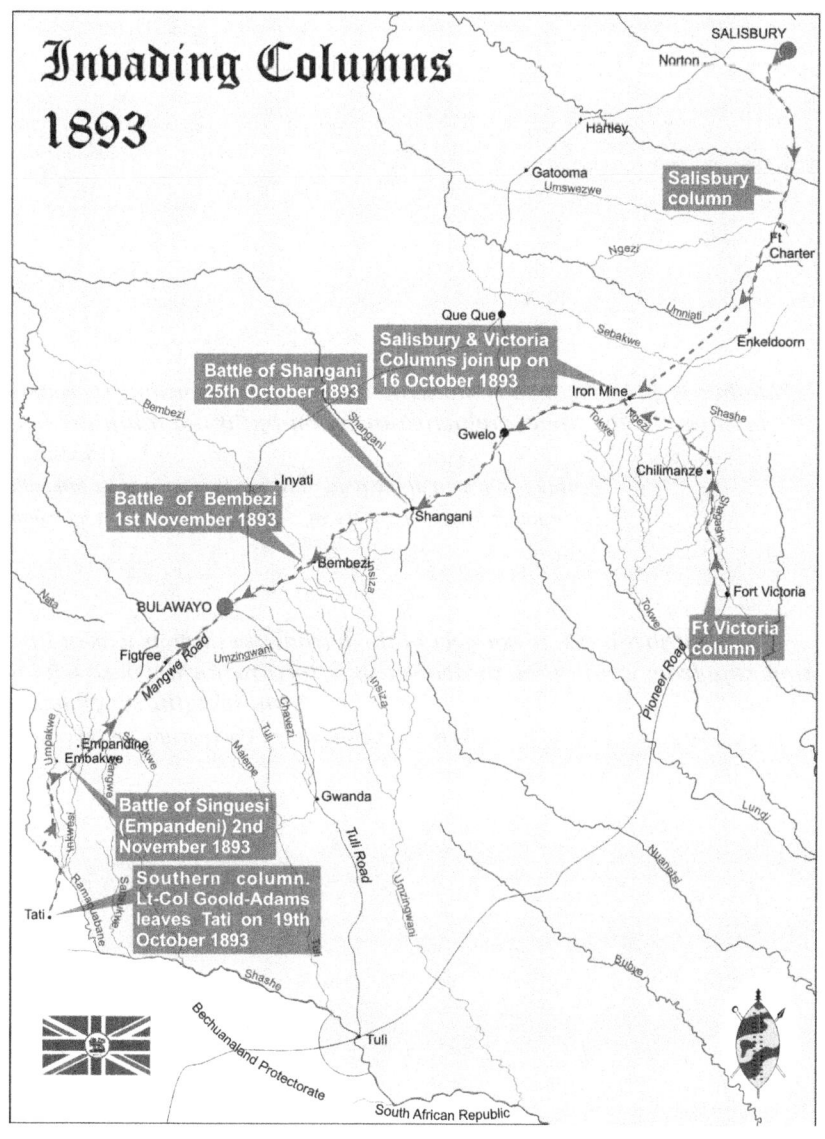

'Mother is quite right in comparing the Doctor to Gordon. He seems to have just the same magnetic attraction but is not a lunatic like Gordon.'[1]
– Writing to a friend at the time, W.A. Jarvis compares Dr Jameson of another great hero of the age, General Gordon of Khartoum

'...in Matabeliland, no subject of the barbarian despots was at any time safe from mutilation, or death under torture, for the most trivial and imaginary offences.'
– Wills and Collingridge, The Downfall of Lobengula

Chapter 5
Opening Shots

By mid-September, the company was ready. The Salisbury Horse had moved to a forward base at Fort Charter and both they and the Victoria Rangers were poised–ready to advance into Matabeleland independently and then unite as a single force once they were over the border. Down at Fort Tuli, Goold-Adams' Southern Column—made up of the Bechuanaland Border Police contingent, Raaff's Rangers, and a sizable force of Bechuana warriors—was also waiting for the word to advance. Before Dr Jameson could unleash his forces though, he needed permission from Sir Henry Loch, the British High Commissioner down in Cape Town. Jameson's luck at the poker table was already legendary, but his remarkable good fortune in gaining the justification to start his invasion at exactly the right time was enough to raise more than a few eyebrows.

As the prospect of war loomed large, Sir Henry seemed to be getting cold feet. On 26 September 1893, he sent a telegram to the Doctor, instructing him to send small patrols to the border. If these found no evidence of Matabele impis, Sir Henry stated, '…all necessity for aggressive operations would be obviated.'[2] Needless to say, this was the last thing Jameson wanted to hear. Cancelling the invasion would not prevent a war–that would come sooner or later whatever Jameson did. One can hardly blame the Doctor for wanting to fight while the company's forces were prepared and mustered rather than letting the crisis subside, only for Lobengula's impis to pour into Mashonaland at a time of their choosing. Some, writing from the safety of the 1960s, disapprovingly described the Doctor as a 'warmonger' for his resolve–but it is unlikely that anyone in Mashonaland or Bechuanaland viewed him that way.

Jameson only received the telegram on the 28th and replied immediately, insisting that there were Matabele impis on the border, 'not in small parties, but in regiments,' and requested permission to have the area 'thoroughly patrolled'.[3] Sir Henry agreed to this in his reply of that same day.

Two days later on the 30th, a Matabele impi attacked one of these scouting parties about 25 miles to the north-west of Fort Victoria. The small patrol returned fire and withdrew. The officer commanding, Captain the Honourable C.J. White, further reported that his men had found spoor which suggested that there were 6,000–7,000 Matabele in the area, and that friendly natives had confirmed the presence of

significant numbers of Lobengula's men.[4] This minor clash became
known as the First Border Incident and its timing was so suspiciously
convenient that many assume it to have been a total fabrication.

Jameson was made aware of this skirmish on 2 October, and did
his best to use it to convince Sir Henry to unleash the company's
forces. In a telegram describing the incident, the Doctor concluded by
asking for the high commissioner's permission to start the invasion.[5]
Sir Henry was not persuaded, however, and sent a lengthy reply,
conceding that '...evidence of the large impi in the vicinity of Victoria
and within striking distance of that settlement, justifies you in at once
adopting measures necessary to ensure the safety of that position...'
but he also made it clear that the skirmish didn't give him enough
reason to grant permission for an 'aggressive advance on Bulawayo'
and requested that additional patrols provide proof of this same large
impi in the border area.[6] On 4 October, Jameson sent another telegram
to Sir Henry, this time to report that patrols had confirmed the presence
of '...some 7,000–8,000 Matabele. Captain White and Mr. Brabant were
both satisfied that these were massed in three bodies.' This time, the
report was enough for the high commissioner, who finally sent the
mail the Doctor had been hoping for:

> 'Whatever your plans are with regard to the advance of the
> columns from Fort Charter and from Fort Victoria, they had better
> now be carried out.'[7]

The company forces were not alone in reporting such things. On 5
October, Lt. Colonel Goold-Adams, the imperial commanding officer of
the Bechuanaland Border Police, telegrammed the high commissioner
to relate a similar incident:

> 'A patrol of mine, consisting of a non-commissioned officer and
> two men, reports by heliograph from my post between here and
> the Shashi, that whilst patrolling this morning on the bank of the
> Shashi River, they were fired upon by, as far as they could gather,
> about thirty Matabeli.'[8]

This became known as the Second Border Incident and—in stark
contrast to his reaction to the first—Sir Henry immediately used it to
justify ordering the Southern Column to join the invasion. Sir Henry
then telegrammed the colonial secretary, the First Marquis of Ripon,[i]

---

i   George Frederick Samuel Robinson, 1st marquis of Ripon KG, GCSI, CIE, VD, PC (1827–1909).
A long serving liberal politician variously known as Viscount Goderich, the Earl of Ripon, and the
Earl de Grey and Ripon at different stages of his life. He was secretary of state for the colonies from
1892 to 1895.

declaring that the Second Border Incident was proof that the Matabele were 'taking the offensive' and that '...the impis have got out of hand and intend to force a war.'[9]

Unsurprisingly, most critics of Rhodesia and the Empire take it as read that all these incidents were fabricated. The timings were certainly suspiciously convenient, but that is not reason enough to assume that they were made up. In his history of the 1893 war, Stafford Glass claims that a telegram sent by the company's Cape Town secretary, Dr Rutherfoord Harris,[ii] shows 'strange foreknowledge of what the patrols were to report', a 'foreknowledge' which is only understandable, apparently, 'if we remember that plans had long since been laid'.[10] This is all terribly damning at first glance, but the telegram (sent on 29 September) does not actually support Glass' conspiracy theory at all. The only thing Rutherfoord Harris said, was that he believed that by 3 October, the additional company patrols would have returned and '... informed you of the numbers and menacing character of the Matabele impis on your borders and close to us... should this be the case there is little doubt whatever as to what he [Sir Henry] will wire you.'[11]

One can scoff and say it is 'naïve' not to realize that there was a devious plot, and perhaps this is the case–but it is equally incorrect to say that Rutherfoord Harris' telegram in any way proves it.

Goold-Adams' men certainly had no reason to fabricate reports of border clashes and indeed, the Colonel did not take the Second Border Incident especially seriously.[12] Some time later, a member of 'Raaff's riff-raff' made a very strange claim—that they had been the ones who had fired on the Bechuanaland Border Police patrol—though quite how professional imperial policemen would have mistaken them for 'about thirty Matabeli' is not explained.[13] There is little reason, therefore, to doubt that the Bechuanaland Border Police patrol did indeed come under fire from the Matabele on 5 October, in which case there is equally little reason to doubt that the company patrol also came under attack on 30 September. Indeed, it stands to reason that parties of Matabele would have been patrolling the border so there really is no compelling reason to doubt that these border clashes took place. The reports of spoor showing 'thousands of warriors' are a little more dubious, however, and it is not unreasonable to suggest that they might have been exaggerations.

Others have also suggested that Sir Henry Loch was not keen to give Jameson permission to move until Goold-Adams was ready. The theory goes that if the Southern Column captured Bulawayo first,

---

ii   Dr Rutherfoord Harris (1856–1920), a medical doctor who fell into Rhodes' orbit in around 1882. A legendary windbag, Harris was dismissed by Jameson as a 'muddling ass'. Despite being heavily involved in the Jameson Raid, he managed to survive the fall-out and went on to serve as a Conservative MP–a role perhaps well suited for a windbag and muddling ass.

Matabeleland would become crown territory, rather than that of the company, though it is not clear how a mere three day delay from the 2nd to the 5th of October can have made a significant impact–especially as Goold-Adams' Southern Column did not move until the 11th in any case. This theory also disregards the fact that the 450-strong Bechuanaland Border Police was a standing imperial force that could easily have been ready months earlier than the company's forces which had to be recruited and equipped. There was also no need for the Southern Column to wait for Raaff's Rangers to be formed and ready to march with them: the Bechuanaland Border Police could also have been reinforced by other imperial units like the Cape Mounted Rifles relatively quickly had the high commissioner harboured a secret plan to gain Matabeleland for the crown. In any event, there was no reason whatsoever why the colonial office could not simply have declared Matabeleland a crown colony whichever forces captured Bulawayo.

It would seem that this notion is based on a couple of secret telegrams between Sir Henry Loch, the high commissioner in Cape Town, and the Marquis of Ripon up in London. Sir Henry had raised his concerns: '...the executive of a country should not be personally interested in the acquisition of the lands and properties of those they are called upon to govern,' but he also conceded that, '...unless Her Majesty's Government are prepared to assist the company with men and money and accept all the responsibilities that now attach to the company, I do not see how HMG can exercise the right of interfering with the company's freedom of action.'[14] In the same secret despatch, Sir Henry did raise the possibility of declaring imperial responsibility over both Mashonaland and Matabeleland, but only until the company was established enough to take control–so this would only ever have been a temporary solution, no matter which column got to Bulawayo first. Of course, Rhodes and Jameson probably didn't know about any of this, so their determination to make Lobengula's capital fall to company troops is understandable.

§

Whatever the reality regarding border clashes, imperial master plans and other Machiavellian schemes, war was more-or-less formally declared on 6 October, when a very gracious Sir Henry Loch wrote to Lobengula, saying:

'My Friend: it has been reported to me that your impis are collected in considerable strength near to the white settlements in Mashonaland. It is with deep personal regret that I inform you the present state of feeling which has grown up between your people and the white people renders it impossible that large impis can be permitted to remain in such near proximity to the white people as to be a source of constant danger of collisions arising between them.

I have already informed you of a recent occasion when your people fired upon a small party of white men in the vicinity of Victoria. The state of uneasiness which exists between your people and the white people is due to several causes. The most serious one is the practice of raiding the Mashonas with your impis. To levy taxes legally due to you as king is right, but to accompany levying taxes with taking from the Mashonas all their property, and killing indiscriminately men, women, and children, and taking those who escape death to be your slaves is what the English will not permit in any country in which they reside.

Your people have further, without any provocation, fired yesterday morning upon Her Majesty's Bechuanaland Border Police near Macloutsie. These acts, together with the barbarous customs to which I have alluded, cause the white people to live in daily apprehension as to the safety of their lives and property. This state of things cannot be allowed to continue.

In Khama's country, the white men and black men live side by side as friends. You may ask, How is this? My answer is, because Khama rules his people with justice, and protects all who come into his country. That is why the English people are friends of Khama and his people. They respect and honour him for his fair dealing as between man and man, and because he protects the lives and property of his people.

When the present sad time is past I trust you will have learned to treat your people with kindness. Rule through their hearts, and not through their fears, and we may then again be friends and be able to trust you and your people.'[15]

It would seem that Sir Henry shared Sir Winston Churchill's belief: 'When you have to kill a man, it costs nothing to be polite'. Interestingly, Loch's letter only reached Lobengula in Bulawayo on 15 October, three days after his own people informed him that the various invading columns had started moving–which rather suggests he did indeed have some sort of force screening his borders.

British colonial wars are often (and perhaps reasonably) stereotyped as having followed a very predictable pattern: war would be joined by whatever unprepared imperial forces and over-confident commanders happened to be close at hand. There would then be the almighty cock-up—a glorious defeat—and everyone would start taking things a little more seriously. More troops would then be rushed to the theatre, logistics belatedly sorted out, professional commanders brought in, and the cock-up would be avenged by a string of victories thus bringing the war to a satisfactory conclusion. Other than the end result, the First Matabele War would prove to be almost the exact opposite.

The two company columns and the Southern Column were soon on the move. There was little or no interaction between the two sets of forces, so we shall deal with them one after the other, starting with the company's men.

The Victoria Column was first to move, with the advance elements setting off from Fort Victoria on 6 October and heading for a rendezvous with the Salisbury Column at Iron Mine Hill–about 90 miles north-west of Fort Victoria, 65 miles south-west of Fort Charter and well inside Matabeleland.[16] Dr Jameson and his military advisor, Sir John Willoughby, moved out of Fort Victoria on the 8th, together with the artillery and the last of the dismounted men, and caught up with the rest of the unit the following day.[17] One of the American scouts, Major Burnham,[iii] reported a Matabele impi within 5 miles as soon as they crossed the border and this prompted the column to quickly form a laager and stand to until patrols confirmed a false alarm.[18] If nothing else, this suggests that there was a genuine belief that Lobengula's warriors had been massing on the frontier.

In the days that followed, the column pushed on, skirting the most broken terrain, and advanced towards the kraals of two chiefs Chilimanzi and Ndema, who, though Mashonas, were believed to be loyal to Lobengula. In the event, both proved to be friendly, and sent presents of oxen and offered contingents.[19] Other native kraals proved equally friendly and Brabant's unit of Mashona allies proved invaluable, both in scouting and in liaising with these villagers.

At midday on the 13th, the column stopped for lunch and were informed by friendly local natives that the Salisbury Column had already arrived at the Iron Mine Hill rendezvous (which proved to be untrue) and, rather more worryingly, that there were two Matabele impis between the Victoria men and their Salisbury comrades. On the 14th, scouts reported five impis in the vicinity.[20] Whether or not Jameson stage-managed, or, at the very least, exaggerated the border clashes, there is no doubt that there were plenty of reports of Matabele forces in the area.

The following day, the 15th, some of the Victoria Column scouts clashed with Matabele cattle guards in a small action which became known as 'The Fight at Indaima's kraal'.[21] Major Burnham was in

---

iii   Major Frederick Russell Burnham (1861–1947). American frontiersman and Indian fighter who served as a scout in both Matabele Wars and the Boer War. Burnham introduced Baden-Powell to tracking and field craft and is one of the founding fathers of the Boy Scouts.

charge of the group of five scouts which, through the night of the 14th, had been tracking an impi driving a massive herd of cattle. They caught up with them at first light on the 15th, and looked down from high ground:

> 'Half a mile in advance of the herd of cattle were about one hundred savages; we could see their guns and shields. About the same number brought up the rear a mile and a half behind; while in the middle was a guard of about forty driving the cattle up the valley into the mountains.'[22]

Major Burnham sent a galloper back to the main column for reinforcements, but then, fearing that his quarry would escape before aid came, he rather sportingly decided to attack anyway. The odds of four against about 240 did not seem to concern the Rhodesians and they rode down off high ground to engage the rear guard:

> 'The savages were armed with the same kind of rifles we carry and evidently did not think it possible that four men would attack them. We rode straight at them until within five hundred yards– then turned and went up the valley like a flash, and before the cattle guard realized what was up, we were upon them. We killed twelve in less than five minutes. We hardly missed a shot, while they were so excited that their bullets went wild. We rushed the animals out of the valley but were attacked by the advance guard. These we fought for some time, but they recovered about two hundred of the five hundred head of cattle. We got clear with the remaining three hundred and turned them over to our column.
> Then, reinforced by ten more scouts, we returned to the attack and fought the advance guard until they suddenly brought up more than a thousand warriors over the mountain, who gave us volley after volley... the situation was getting serious, however, and we were forced to retire.'[23]

Despite the outrageous disparity in numbers, the scouts came off much the better, claiming 22 Matabele dead in addition to the captured cattle. The thousand warriors who came to the aid of the cattle guards were from a 7,000-strong impi in the area.[24]

Though this is not how the war is viewed today, it would be fair to say that most who encountered the Victoria Column viewed them as liberators rather than conquerors. One officer recorded:

> 'Every day witnessed the passage of vast numbers of natives going forward 'to the war'. They passed our camp in hundreds, a big

ragged mob of dusky savages, singing, dancing, and flourishing their guns, assegais, and bows-and-arrows, and threatening the total annihilation of the Matabele race. Some thousands must have thus gone by: but a few days later we met an equal number returning! They never showed up at any of the fights, with the exception of those commanded by Messrs Quested and Brabant. The native contingents raised by these gentlemen did much valuable service.'[25]

§

The Salisbury Column set off from Fort Charter on 7 October and, unlike the Victoria force, arrived at Iron Mine Hill on the 14th without any drama. As the Salisbury men waited for their Victoria comrades to come in, some Mashona headmen approached to pay their respects and to welcome them. Major Forbes reported that these fellows were '...delighted to see us, and hoped that we would be successful in exterminating their ruthless enemies.'[26] The Rhodesians then traded with them for food and grain.

One feature of the war's early stages, was on-going skirmishes over cattle, which pitted mounted Rhodesian patrols against similarly sized Matabele parties. No sooner had Forbes arrived at the Iron Mine Hill rendezvous than he was leading one such operation himself. Acting on information from local Mashonas, Forbes determined to bring in a large herd of Lobengula's cattle which were being grazed nearby, tended by Mashonas and guarded by elements of the Insukameni impi.[27]

In the early hours of 15 October, Forbes led the sixty-strong fighting patrol out of the laager with Jameson and Willoughby, who had ridden on ahead of the Victoria Column, and arrived just in time to tag along for the jaunt. Well after day break, they came across a herd of around 250 cattle, which Forbes described as 'all fine cattle, but very wild'. Leaving the bulk of his patrol to drive these tempestuous beasts back to the laager, Forbes, his staff, and a small escort pushed on to interview a nearby Mashona induna.

While this was happening, however, the troopers who were driving the cattle in, came under fire from Matabele riflemen hidden behind some rocks. Captain Campbell[iv] was shot from his horse, but his comrades bravely rode back to recover him under fire and brought him into the camp that afternoon. Dr Jameson assisted in the operation to save him, but it was to no avail. Captain Campbell was the first

---

iv   Captain John Alexander Livingstone Campbell (1856–1893) was commissioned into the Royal Artillery in 1876. On leaving the army, Campbell arrived in South Africa in 1892 and joined the British South Africa Company as a magistrate in Mashonaland. Campbell volunteered to join the Salisbury Horse as the ordnance store officer.

Rhodesian fatality of the war and was buried with full military honours by the Rt. Rev Knight Bruce, Bishop of Mashonaland.[28]

On the morning of the 16th, the Victoria Column—nearly 1,000-strong all told—arrived at the rendezvous and the two units united with Major Forbes in overall command. Though the two columns would remain distinct units, Captain the Honourable White was placed in command of all the scouts, and Captain Lendy in command of the combined artillery trains.[29] Lobengula had missed the opportunity to attack either column before they could meet up, thus throwing away his chance of smashing them separately. The combined columns made for a considerably tougher nut to crack. Though no major units of Matabele were encountered in the first week, there had been enough reports of impis shadowing the Victoria Column to keep everyone on their toes.

Departing Iron Mine Hill the following morning, the united columns pushed on, where possible advancing 300 yards apart, each in a double column of wagons. The generous infantry component of the Victoria force marched beside their wagons while the few dismounted Salisbury men did likewise beside theirs. The native contingents of both columns led the way, cutting roads and digging drifts.[30] The following day, the 18th, yet another report of an impi hovering nearby forced the Rhodesians to form laagers and run out their machine guns. No attack came, but there were definitely Matabele in the area as the alarm had been prompted by the butchering of a group of local Mashona who had made the mistake of trying to bring a gift of grain to the Rhodesians.[31]

The next couple of days saw the Rhodesians pressing on and sending fighting patrols hither and thither to torch Matabele kraals. We shall leave Forbes and the company forces pushing forward, and turn our attention to Goold-Adams and the Southern Column.

§

As we know, Goold-Adams only began his advance on 11 October, crossing the Shashi River and arriving at Tati on the 18th. His rather disparate force was made up of the professional police troopers of the Bechuanaland Border Police, the rough-and-ready 'riff-raff' of Raaff's Rangers, and a substantial number of Bechuana allies. All in all, the column numbered 440 whites, about 2,000 blacks, 520 horses and about 2,000 oxen.[32] Before the Southern Column could push on from Tati, however, there was time for another spot of intrigue.

The day after Goold-Adams' men pulled into the settlement, James Dawson, a white trader based in Bulawayo, also arrived in the company of three Matabele envoys. Lobengula had sent this delegation down with a response to Sir Henry's 'declaration of war' and the indunas were surprised to see such large numbers of white troops. Dismounting in the Tati Concession Company's yard where Goold-Adams was speaking to the manager, Dawson introduced himself to the Colonel, but did not explain who the three Matabele with him were. Instead, he asked the Tati Concession Company's foreman to look after the indunas while he went off to get a cold drink.

Due to this unfortunate mix-up, Goold-Adams, not unreasonably, placed the indunas under guard, explaining that no harm would come to them, but if they attempted to run, they would be shot. For some reason, the Matabele got it into their heads to attack their guards; one of them snatched a bayonet from one trooper's frog and stabbed another with it. Unsurprisingly, this rather brainless act resulted in one of the Matabele messengers being shot and another having his head smashed in by a rifle butt. Both were dead within an hour.[33] The third emissary was restrained by the Bechuanaland Border Police's RSM. Dawson and the surviving envoy were allowed to continue the following day.

To make matters worse, that day—the 19th of October—another prisoner was also shot by a sentry after ignoring a warning and breaking into a run. His attempt to escape prompted two other prisoners to run as well and both were shot down by guards. Two of these three were killed and the third was wounded. Though tragic, this incident seems to be entirely the fault of the man who decided to run away while under armed guard–never an especially sensible thing to do.[34] Needless to say, despite an enquiry which exonerated all those involved,[35] and even though both incidents involved professionals from the Bechuanaland Border Police—an imperial police force—rather than Jameson's men, they were quickly seized upon as 'evidence' of Rhodesian wickedness by enemies of the company. Despite being accidents, they also shattered what little trust remained between Lobengula and the chartered company, and were to have an impact at the end of the war.

End Notes

[1] Ranger, Revolt in Southern Rhodesia, 1896-7, p.125
[2] C 7196, p.71
[3] Glass, The Matabele War, p.167
[4] Glass, The Matabele War, p.173
[5] Wills and Collingridge, The Downfall of Lobengula, p.195
[6] Glass, The Matabele War, p.174
[7] Glass, The Matabele War, p.176
[8] Wills and Collingridge, The Downfall of Lobengula, p.195
[9] C 7196, p.47
[10] Glass, The Matabele War, p.167
[11] C.T. 1/14/1/2, Harris to Jameson, 29 September 1893
[12] Glass, The Matabele War, p.178
[13] Glass, The Matabele War, p.181
[14] Mason, The Birth of a Dilemma, p.184
[15] C 7196, p.91
[16] Norris-Newman, Matabeleland and How We Got It, p.90
[17] Wills and Collingridge, The Downfall of Lobengula, p.199
[18] Burnham, Scouting on Two Continents, p.134
[19] Wills and Collingridge, The Downfall of Lobengula, p.201
[20] Donovan, With Wilson in Matabeleland, p.209
[21] Glass, The Matabele War, p.193
[22] Burnham, Scouting on Two Continents, p.134
[23] Burnham, Scouting on Two Continents, p.135
[24] Wills and Collingridge, The Downfall of Lobengula, p.92
[25] Donovan, With Wilson in Matabeleland, p.210
[26] Wills and Collingridge, The Downfall of Lobengula, p.88
[27] Wills and Collingridge, The Downfall of Lobengula, p.89
[28] Donovan, With Wilson in Matabeleland, p.208
[29] Norris-Newman, Matabeleland and How We Got It, p.90
[30] Wills and Collingridge, The Downfall of Lobengula, p.97
[31] Wills and Collingridge, The Downfall of Lobengula, p.99
[32] Wills and Collingridge, The Downfall of Lobengula, p.218
[33] Glass, The Matabele War, p.200
[34] Glass, The Matabele War, p.202
[35] Wills and Collingridge, The Downfall of Lobengula, p.217

Tell the wretched natives, sinful are their hearts,
Turn their heathen temples into spirit marts.
And if to your teaching they will not succumb,
Give them another sermon with the Maxim gun...
– To the tune of 'Onward Christian soldiers', this is a verse from a satirical poem
penned by an outraged British liberal about the Matabele War, and subsequently
adopted by the Rhodesian troopers themselves–with tongues firmly in cheek.

'Bishop Knight-Bruce came up with a billy of water. By posing as a
dying man, I managed to get a drink out of him of real whiskey. He
was not very free with what he had, and for years afterwards the
chaps said I should have received the VC for getting as much liquor
out him as I did.' [1]
– A wounded trooper proudly recalls conning the
Bishop of Mashonaland out of a drink of Scotch.

Chapter 6
The Battle of Shangani

On 22 October, the company column reached the Somabula Forest. There was no way to form laagers in this strip of thick brush and progress through called for a path to be hacked. It was a near-perfect ambush site, and had been identified as such by the Matabele: a 5,000 strong force lay waiting in the woods, ready to pounce while the company's troops were strung out, cutting their way through the obstacle.[2]

At this point, however, a dense fog rolled in, an event which added to the anxieties of the Rhodesians but in reality, proved to be their saving grace. It was claimed that the ambushers panicked, thinking this mysterious fog to be proof of Dr Jameson's all-powerful magic[3] and the column got through the forest and onto more open ground long before an ambush could be sprung. The importance of having come through these woods unscathed was not lost on the invaders. That night, the Honourable Maurice Gifford[i] wrote, 'We are now on the high veld and don't care a cuss for the Matabele nation.'[4]

For all Gifford's bravado, the skill in getting 5,000 men so close to the Rhodesians without having been spotted should not be under-estimated, and the Matabele commander, Mjaan, continued to shadow Forbes' invasion force secretly, waiting for another chance to pounce.

§

On the 23rd, not long after the Rhodesians had started moving, another dense bank of fog rolled in and, with Matabele scouts having been spotted, Forbes took the precaution of re-forming his laagers–a feat achieved by the company men in just 6 minutes.[5] The Victoria Rangers and Salisbury Horse each formed their own laagers about 200 yards apart while the Mashona allies made their own plans. Further contingents of these had joined the invasion, taking their numbers up to around 900 by this point.[6] In addition, the 'wicked invaders' had rescued some thirty Mashona women and children from slavery and these newly liberated non-combatants camped with their kinsmen.[7]

---

i Hon. Maurice Raymond Gifford, CMG (1859–1910), served in Egypt in 1882 and in Canada's Red River Rebellion. Gifford went on to serve in the 1896 Matabele War and lost his arm in that conflict– an injury which did not prevent him going on to fight in the Boer War. After surviving several wars, he died in a bizarrely brilliant fashion: he decided to have a cigarette shortly after having cleaned his clothes with petrol–with predictable results.

The Rhodesians stood to and waited for the fog to clear before moving at around 09h00. Progress was very slow and when a galloper rode in to report that a scouting party had come under fire and Mr Burnett[ii] had been shot, all thoughts of pressing on were abandoned for the day. Forbes ordered Captain Spreckley[iii] to ride back with the galloper at the head of a twenty-strong fighting patrol. Instead, a heady and rather disorganized over-enthusiasm seems to have over-taken the Rhodesians. Rather than waiting a few minutes for Spreckley's patrol to form up, Dr Jameson, Willoughby, Dr Edgelow, and the galloper took it upon themselves to ride off and help Burnett immediately. In a comedy of errors, the galloper got lost and was unable to find the scouts. Spreckley's patrol, which rode out shortly afterwards, desperately tried to follow their spoor but also lost their way and came under fire from another group of Matabele.

By the time both Jameson's group and Spreckley's patrol got back to the company laagers very late that evening, the rest of the scouting party had already returned, bringing Burnett's body with them. Though it is impossible not to admire the spirit of the company men, small parties randomly galloping about the veld in some sort of chaotic Keystone Cops episode was not part of the plan, and Forbes really should have taken control of the situation. Though the irregular company forces could not have been expected to exhibit the same discipline as British regulars and there was no shortage of virtually unmanageable mavericks and alpha males—Dr Jameson probably being the worst offender—the Rhodesians were lucky that this farcical free-for-all was not severely punished.

§

One of the more useful Matabele dissidents who served with the Rhodesians was a rather bizarre fellow called Man-yéze. Always clad in a French Army great-coat (no one seems to know where he obtained this garb) this rather eccentric old man had been an induna in Lobengula's court. Perhaps fearing him as a potential rival, the king had ordered Man-yéze and his entire clan slaughtered–a massacre which Man-yéze

---

ii Mr Albert Edward Burnett was born in East London and served in the Warren Expedition and the Bechuanaland Border Police. He entered Mashonaland as one of the 1890 pioneers and volunteered as a scout in the 1893 invasion of Matabeleland.

iii Later Lt. Colonel John Anthony Spreckley, CMG, (1865–1900). Spreckley's incredible life is worthy of a book all of its own. Born in England, he moved to South Africa where he worked as an ostrich farmer, Bechuanaland Border Policeman and gold prospector before entering Mashonaland as one of the 1890 pioneers. He fought in both Matabele Wars and went on to command the Rhodesia Horse in the Boer War, where he was killed in action. Baden-Powell's description of Spreckley was: 'Endowed with all the dash, pluck, and attractive force that make a man a born leader of men, he is also steeped in common sense, is careful in arrangement of details, and possesses a temperament that can sing 'wait till the clouds roll by' in crises where other men are tearing their hair out.'

himself escaped due to being out hunting at the time.[8] Man-yéze's knowledge of the country was considered to have been critical for the company's success and he had long warned that Lobengula's impis would strike when the Rhodesians attempted to cross the Shangani River.[9] Intelligence gathered by Forbes' scouts appeared to support this idea–they found the remains nearby, of five oxen, killed and eaten that day.[10]

Forbes' column reached the Shangani on the 24th. Just as Man-yéze had warned, the river crossing was indeed a perfect spot for an attack; the surrounding country was very broken, and strewn with rocky kopjes, and the dense bush was scarred with gullies and dongas– all of which would negate the firepower of the company men. With his men scattered about digging drifts and cutting bush, the best Forbes could do was to form a laager and deploy a couple of mounted troops with a pair of Maxims and a 7-pdr to high ground to provide cover. Another two mounted troops were sent out to patrol a little further from the crossing point.[11]

Nevertheless, there can be little doubt that a resolute Matabele attack on Forbes' scattered force would have been devastating, and the Rhodesians worked liked demons to prepare a route for the wagons. The crossing point was not ideal and the drifts were hastily dug, but when they were deemed ready, the Salisbury wagons only took 16 minutes to get across, while the Victoria ones took just 19. An hour-and-a-half after starting, all the wagons had negotiated the difficult terrain over the river and re-formed into laagers on the far bank of the Shangani.[12] Forbes has been criticized for selecting a position close to the river rather than pushing on into more open country,[13] though this seems a trifle pedantic, as the crossing was only completed at 16h30 and the Major no doubt felt he had risked enough for one afternoon.

Either way, the two laagers were formed about 150 yards apart and, for the first time in the campaign, connected by thick fences made of thorn bushes which created a secure place for the oxen, the horses and some of the Mashona allies. Due to animosity between the various Mashona contingents, Mr Quested's group of about 300 warriors—and a number of the women and children who had recently been liberated from slavery—made their own encampment about 600 yards to the north-east of the main position.

§

Mjaan's 5,000 Matabele warriors had missed their chance to ambush the Rhodesians in the Somabula Forest two days earlier and were too slow to catch them crossing the Shangani River, but on the evening of the 24th, the wily old general finally brought his forces within striking distance. Mjaan's major units were the Insukameni,[iv] Ihatli, Amaveni and Siseba impis, supported by contingents drawn from the Jingen, Enxna, Zinyangene and Induba kraals. All were in place and ready to attack at 22h30 that evening when the moon was at its highest. Understandably fearful of Rhodesian firepower, Mjaan's plan was to storm the laagers in an overwhelming night attack, using the darkness to negate the devastating effects of the company's machine guns and rifles, and rushing forward to have at them with cold steel.[14]

It was a solid enough plan and might well have worked, but Matabele superstition once again intervened. Moments before Mjaan's men were ready to attack, the Rhodesians sent up a couple of signal rockets to guide any stragglers or patrols, and the sight and sound of these streaking into the inky sky totally spooked the lurking Matabele.[15] If Dr Jameson's witchcraft was strong enough to knock the stars out of the sky, what was to stop him knocking the moon out too? Mjaan had no choice but to delay his attack until daybreak.

§

The company men were blissfully unaware of any of this, but as was usual, strong pickets[v] had been deployed and the standing orders for the rest of the force were to sleep fully clothed, with boots on and rifles at the ready. Sun-up had been recognized as a favourite time for a native attack, so the whole force always 'stood to' at 04h00[16]– perhaps an hour before dawn. A few minutes before 'stand to', however, thousands of Matabele warriors started creeping forward,[17] their stealthy approach completely undetected in the darkness.

In a remarkable twist of fate, it would appear that a couple of the Mashona pickets chose that precise moment to disappear into the bush to relieve themselves. When they failed to return, one of their comrades went looking for them and stumbled into the assembled attackers, lying in readiness for their assault. Unlike his luckless mates, this fellow managed to fire off a warning shot before being slashed and stabbed to death, his bravery alerting the whole position and triggering the attack.[18] Perhaps not expecting to find the kraal constructed by Mr Quested's natives so far from the main laagers, the attackers, who were surging forward from the north-east, blundered into it, and rushed into the encampment, stabbing indiscriminately in the old style. By then all hell had broken loose:

---

iv Generally regarded as Mjaan's best unit, 'Insukameni' translated as 'always ready'.

v Sentries placed some distance from the main body to give advance warning.

'A wild yell from the camp of the 'friendlies' roused the whole force. Then came several scattering shots followed by the terrific war cry of the Matabele as they rushed our laager and the battle of Shangani[vi] began.'[19]

In the main laagers, the company men got to their stations quickly, and began pouring a terrific fusillade into the darkness. One Matabele prisoner later said that the laagers 'became instantly a sheet of flame'.[20] The steady, relentless 'tut-tut-tut-tut' hammering of the Maxims was audible, even over the din of the rifle fire coming from both sides:

'... the roar of the Maxims, and the continuous crack of several thousand hostile rifles that rimmed our entire laager. Over and above the din of the firing rose the shrieks and yells of the friendly natives as they were stabbed and slaughtered by the onrushing Matabele.'[21]

As the witness suggests, the first few minutes of the battle were chaotic, with Mr Quested's Mashona contingent locked in ferocious hand-to-hand combat with the Matabele attackers in the blackness. The pickets and others of Quested's force tried to run for the safety of the main laagers, inter-mingling with the on-rushing Matabele as they sprinted through the gun fire. Major Forbes '...jumped up on the nearest waggon and tried to see into the darkness, but could distinguish nothing but the flashes, which were very close and frequent. The enemy were so close to us that I did not think it safe to stop firing, even had I been able to so in the noise that was going on, and I was very much afraid that some of the men on picket would be killed either by friends or enemies, and I was greatly relieved to hear shortly afterwards that they had all got safely in.'[22]

Mr Quested had been sleeping in the kraal alongside his Mashona warriors when the Matabele surged into them, slashing and stabbing in the blackness. Quested managed to rally some of his men and made a stand, but wounded in the arm and side, and with one thumb shot off, he was later forced to withdraw to the main laagers.

Perhaps more by good luck than good management, Quested's force had scuppered Mjaan's plans. Plenty of the Mashona allies—and the recently rescued women and children—were butchered in the frenzied melee, but they bought precious seconds for the Rhodesians, whose heavy fire broke up the attack. After half-an-hour, the Matabele rifles fell silent and the attacking warriors fell back into the blackness. Forbes recalled that it was 'still too dark to see any distance, but objects in the immediate vicinity were visible'.

---

vi   This action is known to the Matabele as the Battle of Bonko.

Battle of Shangani - Chronology of events

At about 15h50 on 24th October 1893 the Salisbury and Victoria columns cross the Shangani river and form a laager on the west bank.
A - Salisbury Column
B - Victoria Column
C - Enclosure for oxen
D - Enclosure for captured cattle

At 03h45 the laager is surrounded by 2 divisions of *amaNdebele* the first division consisting of the *Insukamini, Isiziba, Ihlati* and *Induba* Regiments, whilst the second contained the *amaKanda* and *amaVeni*.

First Attack

At 03h50 three Native Contingent members stumble upon the *amaNdebele* whilst getting water. Two are killed. The *amaNdebele* immediately attack Questeds camp, which contained NC troops and camp followers, killing approximately 50 more NC troops. They then attack the laager with rifle fire. They are driven off by rifle and Maxim gun fire.

At 04h30 Capt Spreckley and his troop circle the laager, keeping in open ground. They have a minor skirmish and return to the laager.

Second Attack

At 05h30 the *Insukameni* Regiment commence a vigourous and courageous series of frontal attacks on the laager from the small kopje to the south east. They are supported by rifle fire from other directions, and are beaten back by rifle, machine-gun and artillery fire from the laager with heavy losses.

At daylight, more patrols are sent out to harass the survivors. Capt Heaney's troop is sent north, Capt Spreckley west and Capt Bastard to the south. They encounter considerable *amaNdebele* presence within half a mile of the laager and all are forced to retire.

Third Attack

At about 08h10 probing patrols are sent out. The *amaVeni* and the *amaKanda*, from the second division, join the fight and attack the patrols. Capt Heany probes north west and is attacked by the *Exna* and falls back. Capt Spreckley goes east again without challenge whilst Capt's Fitzgerald and Bastard's troops, patrolling to the south west, are rushed and an attempt is made by the *amaVeni* to cut them off. They are forced to give ground briefly but, when supported by machine gun and artillery fire, the *amaNdebele* are driven off. Capt Borrow patrolled east, circling the small hill from which they had been attacked, without incident. By 08h00 the *amaNdebele* have had enough and had commenced retiring.

Casualties

Column

1 Killed (Tpr Walters)
6 Wounded

AmaNdebele

Killed & wounded ±500

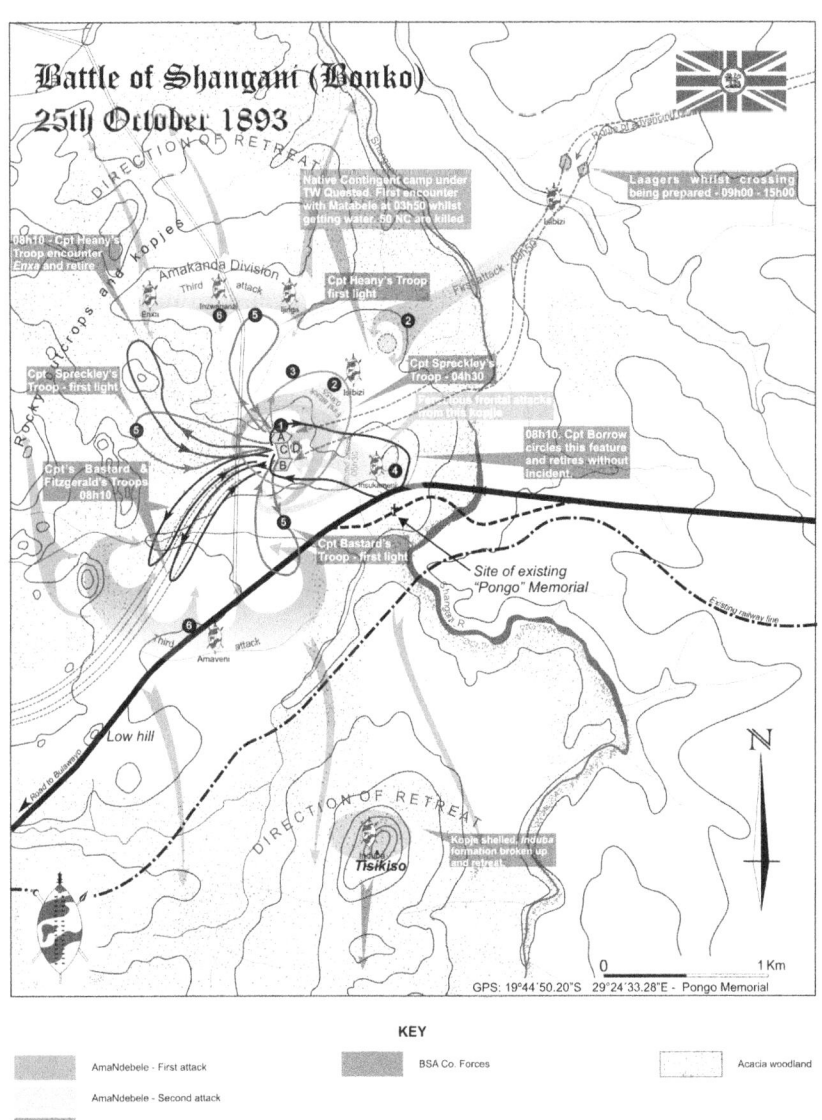

Battle of Shangani (Bonko)
25th October 1893

DIRECTION OF RETREAT

Native Contingent camp under TW Quested. First encounter with Matabele at 03h50 whilst getting water. 50 NC are killed

Laagers whilst crossing being prepared - 09h00 - 15h00

08h10 - Cpt Heany's Troop encounter Enxa and retire

Amakanda Division

Third attack

Cpt Heany's Troop first light

Cpt Spreckley's Troop - 04h30

Cpt. Spreckley's Troop - first light

Cpt's Bastard & Fitzgerald's Troops 08h10

08h10, Cpt Borrow circles this feature and retires without incident.

Cpt Bastard's Troop - first light

Site of existing "Pongo" Memorial

Third attack

Amaveni

Low hill

Road to Bulawayo

DIRECTION OF RETREAT

Tsikiso

Kopje shelled, induba formation broken up and retreat

N

0   1 Km

GPS: 19°44´50.20"S 29°24´33.28"E - Pongo Memorial

KEY

AmaNdebele - First attack

BSA Co. Forces

Acacia woodland

AmaNdebele - Second attack

AmaNdebele - Third attack

In the brief respite after the attack, Captain Spreckley led a mounted patrol out to look for any Mashona allies who might not have made it to the laagers and to bring in some loose horses. After about half-an-hour, and with the light by then much improved, a large group of natives was seen on a hill to the south-east. The company officers were unsure whether these were Matabele assembling for another assault, or a group of Mashona allies trying to make their way back to the laagers. In reality, they were a Matabele impi—the Insukameni—using a novel ruse de guerre: Forbes admitted to being one of those who initially mistook them for Mashona allies, and recalled that they had '...advanced down the slope in a most casual way, without hurrying or attempting to take cover and I allowed no firing on them.' When their true colours were revealed, however, 'a heavy fire was poured on them from two or three Maxims and about 200 rifles'.[23] Though many of the company men had never been under fire before, the relief of surviving the initial onslaught seemed to have settled any nerves and the fusillade was devastating: '...our men were now all very cool, and ammunition was not so recklessly expended.'[24] As soon as the Insukameni came under fire, the Matabele riflemen opened up again from positions all around the laagers, and other impis made a few half-hearted attempts to charge the company positions. These were soon beaten off and the firing stopped again.

One man who showed no nerves throughout the battle was old Man-yéze. This peculiar fellow had no interest in staying in the safety of the laagers. He strolled out into the open, placed his ancient musket in the fork of a tree, loosed off a shot, and then calmly returned to the laagers with a broad grin on his face.[25]

Again, mounted patrols were sent out to clear the bush in the wake of the second attack. These ran into Matabele lurking within half-a-mile of the laagers and the company horsemen withdrew under fire. Another force of Matabele was seen forming up on a kopje 2,000 yards to the west of the laagers, but this was quickly broken up by artillery fire. Once more, mounted patrols were sent out to clear the surrounding bush, and there were some skirmishes between these and small groups of Matabele warriors who were still lurking about. These marked the end of the action: by 08h30, it was all over.[vii]

Casualties among the company forces were relatively light: one white trooper was mortally wounded and would die that evening, and six others—including the plucky Mr Quested—were wounded, though not fatally. One 'Cape boy' was also killed along with 34 of the Mashona allies[26] and several of the recently rescued women and children:

---

vii   Company troops fired 3,645 rounds of Martini Henry ammunition in the action (this figure included the rounds fired by the Maxims and Nordenfelt gun).

'There was one child about two years old stabbed in three places; we found three women badly wounded and five dead.'[27]

Interestingly, and despite the determination of the company doctors to tend to them, the Mashona allies showed little inclination to assist their own wounded:

'"What's the good?" they said. "They no good, no hand for fight!" "Leave him; let him die!" and so forth. The wounded natives were also in some cases so afraid that their friends acting in the capacity of bearers would drop them that they positively refused to be moved. In one case a man who had been told off to carry a small boy was observed to put him down again, being much more anxious to carry his bundle of filthy rags and a few old goat skins than the poor little sufferer. He was, however, speedily compelled to bring along his human load. These incidents show in what light esteem they hold human life; the struggle for existence is so hard that every man looks first to himself, and thinks of nothing else.'[28]

Not surprisingly, Matabele casualties were much higher–probably in the region of 500 killed. This could only be guessed at, however, as many of the dead were dragged away from the battlefield by their comrades. Others were found to have hung themselves, or thrown themselves to their deaths in the river. The commander of the Insukameni impi was one of those who chose the soldier's way out; he was found hanging in a tree.[29] Whether he committed suicide due to the shame of defeat, or because he did not dare return to Bulawayo after failing, we shall never know.

One company officer commented:

'I attribute our success, and the few men killed and wounded on our side, to the arms of precision with which the enemy were equipped. Had they been simply dependent on their assegais and the old blunderbusses, the story might have been differently told.'[30]

It is certainly fair to say that the Matabele made poor use of the hundreds of Martini Henrys they had at Shangani River. Their marksmanship was truly atrocious, mainly due to their madcap belief that the higher one set the sights, the faster the bullet went.[31] Had Mjaan discarded the rifles altogether and managed to coordinate his attack so that all 5,000 of his warriors surged forward with their assegais before the company troops stood to, there can be little doubt this would have swamped the laagers. Indeed, one of the Matabele prisoners revealed that their orders had been to attack the Rhodesians on the march, not in laager–and that they were not to use their rifles, but instead, storm forward in the old style.

In contrast to the rather lacklustre performance of Mjaan's men, the company forces had fought well. Sir John Willoughby's report to the war office noted that the men, '... generally speaking, behaved with great coolness and steadiness... the fire control of the Victoria laager was excellent, while that of the Salisbury, although a little wild at first, became afterwards much improved.'[32] Willoughby was less complimentary about Brabant's native contingent who he claimed became 'panic stricken', whereas he noted, in contrast, that Quested's Mashona had '...stood their ground well, and inflicted considerable loss on the enemy, although he got right amongst them, and assegaied several, including many of the women and children... they eventually retired in good order on the laagers after daylight had dawned; but not till their leader was severely wounded.'[33]

The Maxim guns had also proved their worth, firing throughout the action without any jamming.[34] The sound of their relentless mechanical chatter caused the Matabele to name them 'J'kuto'kuto', and an eye-witness account of their success at Shangani was used in a sales brochure to promote the weapon:

> 'Immediately we stood to arms, and looking through the darkness we saw thousands of niggers rushing towards us. When the Maxim Guns started firing, there was a sudden check. They could not believe it, made another rush and were checked again, and so on till daylight broke...'[35]

Equally effective was the company's artillery: though the 7-pdrs only fired a total of seven rounds and the 2-pdr Hotchkiss gun only 28 in the action, they nevertheless did 'good execution, inflicting considerable losses on the retreating enemy'.[36] It was noticed that whenever a shell was flung into the midst of the Matabele, they would discharge their rifles into the explosion. When prisoners were later asked why, it was revealed that the Matabele believed each shell to contain several small, murderous fellows who sprung out when it exploded and they had been trying to shoot these diminutive killers.[37] Other perplexed prisoners asked, '...how we managed to wrap our bullets in a blanket[viii] and throw it at them.'[38]

§

---

viii Presumably in reference to the way artillery shells scattered shrapnel as they exploded.

All this talk of Matabele prisoners will be very confusing to those who watched the risible BBC 'epic' mini-series, Rhodes, and naïvely assumed that it might be any way historically accurate. Incredibly, and as touched on in Chapter 5, this multi-million pound piece of anti-British propaganda showed Dr Jameson and Major Frank Johnson shooting all the wounded Matabele in cold blood after the action. Leaving aside the salient fact that Johnson did not even serve in the war, there is simply no credible evidence to suggest that anything like this happened and it would seem the BBC based their version of events entirely on a couple of unsubstantiated claims made by Labouchère at the time–hardly an unbiased source.

Instead, accounts—be they from imperial officers, company troopers, journalists or anyone else who, unlike Labouchère, was actually there—are full of tales about prisoners and wounded Matabele being well treated: Forbes, for example, described, '...a very good-looking boy of about eighteen, being a pure Matabeli; he was shot through the lower part of the spine, which was all shattered, and was partially paralysed; he was very quiet and gentle, and very grateful for all that was done for him; he sent me messages on several occasions, warning me of certain localities where we were likely to be attacked.'[39]

As would be expected from a man of the cloth, Bishop Knight-Bruce took a cart out around the battlefield and collected wounded Mashona and Matabele alike so that they could be offered medical aid and water.[40] A couple of days later, our friend Captain Spreckley returned from a patrol of some abandoned Matabele kraals, bringing with him an 'enormously fat' Matabele boy, about two years old. This portly little fellow, who had been left behind all alone, charmed them all with his 'great composure' and was adopted by one of the Farrier-Sergeants–hardly the actions of men who would have slaughtered hordes of enemy wounded in cold blood.[41]

The reader will recall that a lengthy in-depth enquiry was held into Lendy's relatively innocuous action outside Fort Victoria. Similar enquires were held when a couple of escapees were shot at Tati... so it would be reasonable to assume that it might just have sparked a little bit of interest at the colonial office had there been even the tiniest shred of evidence that company troops had indulged in the mass murder of wounded Matabele.

When Labouchère started spreading these rumours via his Truth magazine, the Reuters News Agency appointed veteran reporter, Charles 'Noggs' Norris-Newman[ix] as their special correspondent for

---

ix   Charles Louis Marie William Norris-Newman (1852-1920), ex-British Army officer turned pioneering war correspondent, 'Noggs' (nicknamed after the character 'Newman Noggs' from Dickens' Nicholas Nickleby) reported on the Zulu War and the First Boer War as well as the 1893 Matabele Campaign. After his adventures in Africa, 'Noggs' moved to China and spent the remaining

Matabeleland, and briefed him to investigate the claims.[42] Noggs, who was not a man who minced words, arrived in Matabeleland before the end of the war and described Jameson as 'obstinate' and having an 'apparent frankness of manner which is so charming to observe and dangerous to believe in',[43] while Forbes was declared to have 'alienated all his best friends by his dictatorial conduct'.[44] Worse still, Noggs went on to describe Forbes as 'fidgety, bad-tempered, abusive in his language, and utterly lacking tact and courtesy'[45]–so no one can reasonably claim that 'Noggs' was some sort of company stooge, or sycophantic 'yes-man'. Noggs' investigation led him to confirm that a handful of Matabele prisoners had indeed been murdered after the Shangani battle–but that the killers had been Mashona allies, who had acted before company officers could prevent it. The only other vaguely similar incident was when Captain Francis of Raaff's Rangers shot two prisoners who tried to open fire on him while they were being disarmed–Captain Francis freely admitted to this and his action would seem to have been completely justified.

These relatively minor incidents aside, Noggs' investigation led him to utterly dismiss Labouchère's far-fetched claims of mass-murder committed by company troopers–indeed, he was even moved to declare, 'No campaign has ever been carried out, against natives, with more humanity or consideration for the natives generally, or with less cruelty to prisoners.'[46]

The Rev. Charles Helm, of Hopefontein Mission Station, Matabeleland, agreed, writing, 'The wounded that fell into the hands of the whites were well looked after... not a single person was killed outside the fighting, or that was not running away, refusing to give up his arms, and only two or three were killed in that latter way... the war was carried on as fairly and mercifully as a war can be. Dr Jameson was determined that no injustice should be done to the Matabele, especially the women.'[47]

It is telling that the self-loathing Marxists at the BBC fell over themselves to depict a fictitious atrocity—even to the extent of cheerfully showing a man who did not actually serve in the war committing the same—but showed no interest in portraying the battle's truly brutal incident: the chaotic and savage massacre of Mashona women and children by the Matabele who stumbled across Quested's kraal in the blackness.

Captain Donovan, who didn't much admire the company and had no axe to grind with the Matabele, was moved to give his own opinions of this butchery:

---

years of his life there, working as the highly respected editor of the China Critic newspaper.

'As I have said, I had no quarrel with the Matabeles, and at first was not altogether satisfied as to the justice of the war; but after the Shangani fight, the sights I witnessed stirred every feeling of humanity in my breast, and induced a wild desire to revenge the terrible brutalities which these savages wreaked on their helpless victims. Defenceless women lay killed, and mutilated in the most loathsome manner, simply because they had attempted to escape from the slavery into which they had been dragged years before. Here a young woman and her baby lay pinned to the ground by an assegai; there a poor little boy, who had tried to hide himself in an ant-bear hole, with half a dozen wounds in his miserable little black body. Again, another child with his intestines protruding through a cruel gash across his stomach, and still alive–left, by a refinement of cruelty, to linger in torment. Neither old nor young were spared, and the numbers of those so treated were appalling. The Matabele warrior does not appear to care how, or on whom, he 'bloods his assegai', so long as it is soaked in human gore... I left the laager that day, holding staunchly the opinions of Mr. Labouchère and his supporters, condemnatory of the slaughter of the black man; but a quarter of an hour among such sights as these sufficed to convert me.'[48]

§

Major Forbes was determined to prove to the Matabele that their attack had not interfered with his plans, and decided to move on as soon as it was confirmed that their attackers had finally retired. Company scouts reported a large open plain about three miles away–it was a perfect location from which to repel any follow-up attack, but could only be reached by pushing on through a narrow defile between two hills. Forbes decided to take the risk, but it was a very anxious move:

'If we had then been attacked and had had to laager, the natives could have fired right down into the laagers from the hills, and we would have had great trouble in dislodging them. The two columns moved close together, each in four parallel columns, and as many men as could be spared were kept on the flanks; we got out all right, but I felt inexpressibly relieved when we got round the ends of the hills into a large open valley. We headed for the widest part of it and laagered there, having done about three miles.'[49]

The laagers were built very sturdily that night, but no attack came. The next few days saw the company forces pushing steadily forward, throwing out fighting patrols to gather grain and cattle or burn down Matabele kraals along the line of march. This was dangerous work and even though the small mounted patrols often came under attack, the only fatality was Captain Owen Williams.[x] The patrol Captain Williams was part of, had come under attack and his horse had panicked and galloped off uncontrollably, carrying him with it. One of his brother officers told the tale:

'He had been out with several others, and they had been surrounded and very nearly entrapped by a large body of natives. They succeeded in getting through, however. Captain Williams' horse was fresh, but those of the others were completely knocked up, so that when the party came together later on he was missing. It was, however, confidently believed that he was ahead, and would turn up safely. As he did not return to laager that night, signal rockets were discharged, and two of our best native hunters were sent out to take up his spoor. This they did, but could only follow it a few miles, as natives pursued and fired on them continually. They reported that, as far as they could judge, his horse, though wounded, was going well and strong, and the track of his pursuers were growing fainter. I was sent out at once with a party and took up the track from where they had left it, following it for nearly ten miles, and not returning till late at night... nothing more could be done, for the enemy were about on all sides, and further delay was out of the question. We now learn that he was eventually overtaken, and after shooting some of his pursuers, sat down on a rock, revolver in hand, and faced the rest, who then retired about 200 yards and fired upon him, and he fell, shot through the temple.'[50]

Williams' body was stripped but not mutilated and his rifle, bandolier, and revolver were taken to Lobengula.[51]

While the king eyed these meagre returns, the rest of the company forces pushed on steadily. Their progress was shadowed by the Matabele but for the next few days, the only contacts were small skirmishes fought between patrols and raiding parties.

---

x   Captain Owen Gwynyth (spelled 'Gwynedd' by some sources) St. George Williams.

End Notes

1   Rhodesiana, No.15–December 1966, p.4
2   Wills and Collingridge, The Downfall of Lobengula, p.110
3   Gibbs, A Flag for the Matabele, p.133
4   Glass, The Matabele War, p.194
5   Wills and Collingridge, The Downfall of Lobengula, p.103
6   Wills and Collingridge, The Downfall of Lobengula, p.105
7   Donovan, With Wilson in Matabeleland, p.227
8   Donovan, With Wilson in Matabeleland, p.214
9   Donovan, With Wilson in Matabeleland, p.228
10 Jones, Rhodesian Genesis, p.85
11 Wills and Collingridge, The Downfall of Lobengula, p.104
12 Wills and Collingridge, The Downfall of Lobengula, p.105
13 Keppel-Jones, Rhodes and Rhodesia, p.268
14 Wills and Collingridge, The Downfall of Lobengula, p.110
15 Keppel-Jones, Rhodes and Rhodesia, p.269
16 Wills and Collingridge, The Downfall of Lobengula, p.106
17 Donovan, With Wilson in Matabeleland, p.229
18 Keppel-Jones, Rhodes and Rhodesia, p.270
19 Burnham, Scouting on Two Continents, p.136
20 Donovan, With Wilson in Matabeleland, p.229
21 Burnham, Scouting on Two Continents, p.136
22 Wills and Collingridge, The Downfall of Lobengula, p.107
23 Wills and Collingridge, The Downfall of Lobengula, p.108
24 Donovan, With Wilson in Matabeleland, p.230
25 Donovan, With Wilson in Matabeleland, p.216
26 Willoughby, Account of the Battle of Imbembizi, Fought at the Head Waters of the Bembizi River (Nov. 1893) found in Norris-Newman, Matabeleland and How We Got It, p.227-235
27 Wills and Collingridge, The Downfall of Lobengula, p.111
28 Donovan, With Wilson in Matabeleland, p.250
29 Glass, The Matabele War, p.194
30 Donovan, With Wilson in Matabeleland, p.238
31 Wills and Collingridge, The Downfall of Lobengula, p.110
32 Norris-Newman, Matabeleland and How We Got It, p.221
33 Norris-Newman, Matabeleland and How We Got It, p.222
34 Wills and Collingridge, The Downfall of Lobengula, p.111
35 Naval & Military Press,The Maxim Automatic Gun in Action, p.13
36 Norris-Newman, Matabeleland and How We Got It, p.224
37 Wills and Collingridge, The Downfall of Lobengula, p.112
38 Donovan, With Wilson in Matabeleland, p.233
39 Wills and Collingridge, The Downfall of Lobengula, p.113
40 Rhodesiana, No.18–July, 1968, p.99
41 Wills and Collingridge, The Downfall of Lobengula, p.116
42 Norris-Newman, Matabeleland and How We Got It, p.172
43 Norris-Newman, Matabeleland and How We Got It, p.184
44 Norris-Newman, Matabeleland and How We Got It, p.187
45 Norris-Newman, Matabeleland and How We Got It, p.188
46 Norris-Newman, Matabeleland and How We Got It, p.191
47 Norris-Newman, Matabeleland and How We Got It, p.192
48 Donovan, With Wilson in Matabeleland, p.240
49 Wills and Collingridge, The Downfall of Lobengula, p.112
50 Wills and Collingridge, The Downfall of Lobengula, p.254
51 Norris-Newman, Matabeleland and How We Got It, p.94

'On Friday last a Matabele impi opened a determined attack upon Major Forbes' column. The fight was vigorously sustained, but the Matabele could make no impression upon the white forces, who held a position in laager. The Matabele were mowed down on all sides, and finally retired with heavy loss.'
– Durban Mercury, 8 November 1893

'Sir Henry Loch telegraphed to Mr. Rhodes 'suggesting' that the Bechuana Police, imperial force, should garrison Bulawayo; and Mr. Rhodes politely told his high commissioner that the imperial force was not wanted at Lobengula's kraal, and that he preferred to retain the chartered company's police there... the radicals may rave; the colonial office may fuss; but the chartered company, rifle in hand, are on the spot, and their leader quietly intimates that there they propose to stay– till matters are settled to their satisfaction.'
– St James' Gazette[1]

Chapter 7
The Battle of Bembesi

When the battered survivors of the Shangani Battle staggered back into Bulawayo, the story they told provoked a remarkable response. The warriors of Lobengula's two royal regiments, the Imbezu[i] and Ingubu, jeered and mocked their counterparts in the Insukameni impi, laughing at their defeat. Totalling around 1,700 men,[2] these royal guards formed the king's best regiments and they declared it ridiculous that they should have to leave the capital and do the fighting. After years of unbroken victory against the Mashona, these doughty warriors were not short of confidence and did not seem to have any fear of facing the Rhodesians: indeed, they laughingly announced that—in stark contrast to the Insukameni—they would simply walk into the company laagers, kill all the older whites, and keep the younger ones as slaves.[3] In a final, desperate throw of the dice, Lobengula ordered the Imbezu and Ingubu out of Bulawayo to reinforce the main Matabele army which was still shadowing the company column. It would not be long before they got their chance to put their boastful words into action.

§

The Rhodesians started late on the morning of 1 November, waiting until about 08h00 for thick fog to clear before breaking up their laagers and moving off. By then they were within 20 miles of Bulawayo and there were skirmishes throughout the morning as patrols clashed with parties of Matabele, well away from the main force. The 7-pdrs were also used to good effect, flinging shells out to break up any groups of Matabele lurking a little too close to the main column.[4] Despite this, when the company forces stopped around lunchtime, they appear to have been surprisingly slack and were almost caught with their pants down.

The site selected for the halt was a poor one: the laagers were formed about 500 yards from some very thick bush, and on either side of a native kraal – a feature large enough to prevent them being mutually-supporting. The various Mashona contingents made themselves at home in this kraal which was also used to retain captured cattle. Worse still, only 150 yards from the Salisbury laager, there was an area of dead ground that offered cover from rifle fire

---

i Some accounts spell this unit's name, 'Umbezu'.

and into which any attacking force could move unseen. Incredibly, the Salisbury laager, which was to the north of the kraal and thus closest to the bush and the dead ground, had not been well-formed: there were wide gaps between some of the wagons and, showing little sense of urgency, some of the Mashona allies were still off gathering thorn bushes to fortify the position.[5] To further complicate the situation, the nearest water source was about a mile to the south, and almost all the company horses and oxen were down at this stream taking a drink while the troopers relaxed and enjoyed a late lunch. Pickets had been deployed, but it is remarkable that an officer as experienced as Major Forbes had allowed his command to be scattered to such a degree, and, with around 8,000 Matabele warriors[6] creeping forward through the thick bush to the north of the laagers, everything was in place for a massacre on the scale of Isandlwana.

§

Posted on the edge of the thick bush to the north of the Salisbury laager, two pickets—Troopers White and Thompson—seem to have been more interested in wondering what was for lunch and enjoying the sunshine than keeping watch. They were sitting chatting under a tree with their horses grazing some distance away when thousands of Matabele suddenly burst through the bush and were on them before they knew what was happening. Thompson tried to bolt up the tree but was dragged down and stabbed to death. White somehow made it to his horse, promptly fell off it, and had no choice but to make a desperate sprint for the Salisbury laager.[7] Bursting out of the bush, and hot on the heels of the panic-stricken trooper, surged thousands of Matabele warriors.

This was the famous 'chest of the buffalo'–the main thrust of the Matabele attack which included the royal Imbezu and Ingubu regiments. Other impis formed the 'horns' and charged out of the bush on either flank, rushing to encircle the company position and stampede their horses. Someone shouted, "Look, the bush is full of the bastards!"[8] and suddenly hundreds of hidden riflemen opened up on the laagers and the brush crackled with rifle fire. Buglers sounded the 'alarm' and 'pickets retire' as the Rhodesians threw aside their plates, snatched up rifles and bandoliers, and sprinted to their positions.[9]

Corporal Whittaker, who was in charge of the Salisbury laager's Gardner gun,[ii] was quickly at his post and opened up on the charging horde with 'great accuracy and coolness', calmly knocking down the Matabele warriors closest to poor Trooper White as he ran for his life.[10]

---

ii This gun stood as a monument in Bulawayo's main street for many years.

Incredibly, White made it to the laager, diving in and collapsing with exhaustion. As one trooper recalled:

'Then the fun started. The enemy came on splendidly, in short rushes, stopping to fire and so on. They were not in mass in or line, but advanced more in the shape of a lot of locusts than anything else.'[11]

In addition to Whittaker's Gardner, the Salisbury men quickly had one of their Maxims, a Nordenfelt, and a couple of hundred rifles, blasting away at the onrushing Matabele. The Matabele riflemen kept up a brisk return fire, but their aim was atrocious as ever.

The 'chest of the buffalo' was broken up and forced to take cover about 300 yards short of the Salisbury laager–a far cry from the Imbezu and Ingubu's boasts about 'walking in'. With astonishing courage, they rallied and surged forward once more, but were quickly checked by rifle fire and forced to take cover again. Small bands tried again, jumping up only to be blasted down in short order. Lobengula's executioner, '...a giant standing at least six feet six and weighing probably two hundred and fifty pounds, led one of the most heroic charges, running with his spear and rifle directly through the hail of lead until within a few yards of the laager. He dropped the closest to us of all who fell that day.'[12] Another group of attackers came under devastating machine gun fire as Lt. Tyndale-Biscoe[iii] found their range:

'He let them have a belt, and did great slaughter amidst the cheers of our crowd.'[13]

In their desperate attempts to charge the laagers, the bravery of the royal regiments bordered on fanaticism:

'The Umbezu and Ingubu regiments were practically annihilated. I cannot speak too highly of the pluck of these regiments. I believe that no civilized troops could have withstood the terrific fire they did for half as long.'[14]

With nothing to shoot at from the laager, the impressive Major Wilson acted on his initiative and ordered his Victoria Rangers out into

---

iii Lt. Edward Carey Tyndale-Biscoe, RN (1864–941). Despite being mentioned in despatches in the 1884 Sudan Campaign, Tyndale-Biscoe was invalided out of the Royal Navy for having a stammer. He was one of the 1890 pioneers, commanding the small 'Naval Brigade' and being given the honour of raising the Union Jack to establish the new colony. Tyndale-Biscoe would go on to serve in the 1896 Rebellions, the Boer War and the First World War.

Battle of Bembezi - Chronology of events

1 Salisbury and Victoria Columns laager on a tactically sound small hill. They deploy pickets and take the horses and oxen to water south of their position.

2 A large body of *amaNdebele* are seen to the west and shelled. These were identified as the the left horn of the attack.

3 A short while later another large group of *amaNdebele* are seen off to the east, being the right horn, and also shelled.

4 Unknown to the men in the laager, the elite *Imbizo* (Lobengula's bodyguard) and *Ingubo Regiments*, (1400 men) forming the "chest" of the attack, have moved unseen through dead ground and got to within 400 metres of the laager. At 13h00 they, accompanied by the 500 men of the *Ihlati* and *Isiziba* on the west horn and 1,100 men of the *Umcijo* and *Godhwayo* on the east horn, courageously rush the laager, getting to within 100 metres before being decimated by Maxim gun, rifle and artillery fire.

5 Horses, which were on their way back from being watered when the attack started, stampeded to the west but were eventually turned around by mounted men from the laager, but not before an attempt was made by the *Insuga* Regiment to capture them.

6 At 14h15, patrols of mounted men and infantry are sent out to clear the area. One patrol commander, with 100 men with fixed bayonets and a 7 pdr gun heads straight for the "chest", forcing the *amaNdebele* to retreat.   Capt's Borrow and Bastard head in the direction shown but split, Borrow going north west after *Inquobo*. Bastard goes after *Insukamini* which had advanced and after a skirmish with supporting artillery and machine gun fire, succeed in dispersing them. They clear the area and after sporadic encounters the *amaNdebele* retire at about 14h15, ending the battle.

Casualties
Columns   :   4 killed, 5 wounded
amaNdebele :   unknown but the Imbizo Regiment alone lost 500 men.

The words of Sir John Willoughby – "*I cannot speak too highly of the pluck of these two Regiments (Imbizo and Inguba). I believe that no civilised army could have withstood the terrific fire they did for half as long*"

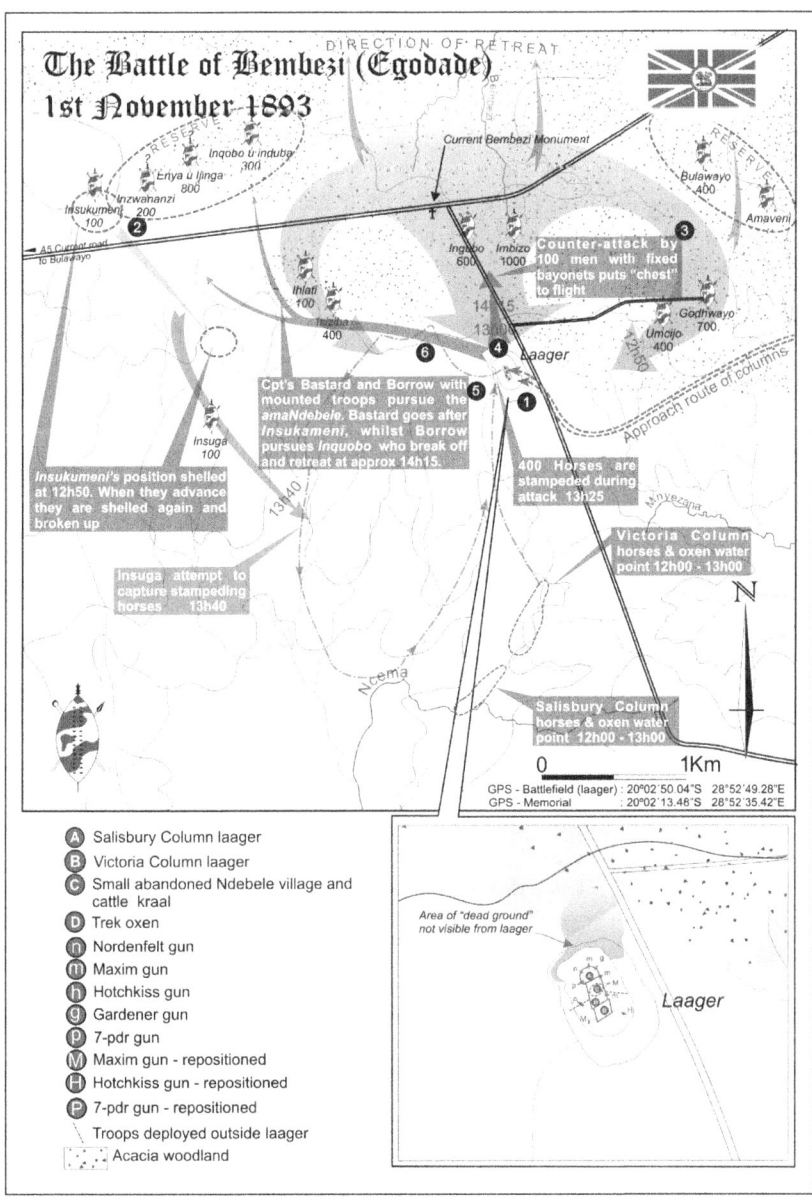

The Battle of Bembezi (Egodade) 1st November 1893

DIRECTION OF RETREAT

Current Bembezi Monument

Inqobo u induba 300
Eriya u Ijinga 800
Inzwahanzi
Insukumeni 200
100 ②

A5 Current road
To Bulawayo

Bulawayo 400
Amaveni

RESERVE

Ingobo 600   Imbizo 1000   Counter-attack by 100 men with fixed bayonets puts "chest" to flight ③

Ihlati 100

Godhwayo 700
Umicijo 400

Insiziba 400
14h15
13h35

⑥   ④ Laager   ⑤   ①

Cpt's Bastard and Borrow with mounted troops pursue the amaNdebele. Bastard goes after Insukameni, whilst Borrow pursues Inquobo who break off and retreat at approx 14h15.

Insuga 100

Insukumeni's position shelled at 12h50. When they advance they are shelled again and broken up

400 Horses are stampeded during attack 13h25

Insuga attempt to capture stampeding horses   13h40

Victoria Column horses & oxen water point 12h00 - 13h00

13h40

Ncema

Mnyezana

Approach route of columns

Salisbury Column horses & oxen water point 12h00 - 13h00

N

0   1Km

GPS - Battlefield (laager) : 20°02'50.04"S   28°52'49.28"E
GPS - Memorial   : 20°02'13.48"S   28°52'35.42"E

(A) Salisbury Column laager
(B) Victoria Column laager
(C) Small abandoned Ndebele village and cattle kraal
(D) Trek oxen
(n) Nordenfelt gun
(m) Maxim gun
(h) Hotchkiss gun
(g) Gardener gun
(P) 7-pdr gun
(M) Maxim gun - repositioned
(H) Hotchkiss gun - repositioned
(P) 7-pdr gun - repositioned
Troops deployed outside laager
Acacia woodland

Area of "dead ground" not visible from laager

Laager

the open so they could support their comrades. Soon the Victorians had three Maxims in position and were hammering the stalled attack. Their 2-pdr Hotchkiss was also quickly brought to bear, and dropped 'shell after shell into their midst as they lay in the thick bush'.[15] The raw courage of the Matabele was simply no match for the storm of lead.

The impis that formed the 'horns' fared no better; the luckless Insukameni emerged from the bush well to the north-east of the laagers, and—perhaps chastened by their mauling at Shangani—made a half-hearted push forward. They quickly came under fire from a well-handled 7-pdr and their day soon got much worse when a pair of machine guns opened up on them too. Ten minutes after emerging from the bush, the battered Insukameni were in full retreat.

Even with their main attacks smashed or stalled, the Matabele could still have won the day. The company horses, which were being watered down at the stream, stampeded in the middle of the fire fight, the witless beasts running directly towards the Matabele. Sir John Willoughby and Captain Henry Borrow reacted quickest. Leaping onto two of the few horses that had not been down at the stream, they bravely galloped out covered by Maxim and artillery fire from the laagers, and managed to head the horses off and turn them around.[16] It was a remarkably courageous act: the loss of the horses would have been absolutely devastating.

Forbes ordered Captain Delamore to take his infantry force out into the open, and to push forward in a skirmish line to clear the Matabele from the field. It cannot have been pleasant for these volunteers and gifted amateurs to leave the safety of the Victoria laager, but out they went, and pushed on in extended line, firing and loading as they trudged grimly forward.[17] Having cleared the bush of any lingering Matabele, they returned to cheers from the men in the Salisbury laager.[18] This effectively signalled the end of what became known as the Battle of Bembesi.[iv]

§

Compared to the important role they had played at Shangani, the Mashona contingents essentially sat out the fighting at Bembesi:

'The Mashonas were untouched, remaining huddled up in a heap together, inside the cattle kraal the whole time, and it was with difficulty they were persuaded, even after the field was clear of the enemy, to go out and collect fuel and water.'[19]

---

iv The battle became known to the Matabele as 'Egodade'.

Keen to find out who they had been up against, Forbes did manage to convince some to go out and fetch any wounded Matabele left on the field. Forbes recalled:

'...the first one brought in was a pure Matabeli–one of the Imbezu regiment; although he must have been in great agony—his left leg being shattered by a shell—he burst out laughing when he was brought into the laager, and said "Fancy the Imbezu being beaten by a lot of boys!"'[20]

It emerged that the Matabele force had comprised the survivors of the Shangani fight, with the addition of the two royal regiments, the N'Gobo impi, and other warriors from several other kraals.

Though the royal guardsmen of the Imbezu and Ingubu regiments were veterans, Captain Donovan of the Victoria Rangers commented on the ages of the other warriors:

'...it was noticeable that those who thus distinguished themselves were as a rule rather oldish men, being the same who had counselled their king not to fight the white man. The younger warriors were, on the contrary, eager for blood, but when it came to the pinch, failed to exhibit the same readiness to spill their own.'[21]

As at Shangani, there was a huge disparity in casualties between the two sides. While the Matabele losses could only be guessed at, they were reckoned to be in the region of between 800 and 1,000 killed and wounded.[22] The Imbezu regiment alone is thought to have sustained 500 casualties from a starting total of around 700 men. Company losses were negligible: as well as Trooper Thompson who was speared at the very start of the action, two other troopers were shot dead in the hail of rifle fire directed at the laagers by the Matabele riflemen.[23] Eight others were wounded and—thanks to Willoughby and Borrow—just four horses had been killed. The company troops had fired off 8,600 rounds of Martini Henry ammunition (which, in addition to the rifles, was also used by the Maxims and the Nordenfelt) 570 rounds from the Gardner, 25 shells from the 7-pdrs and 30 from the 2-pdr Hotchkiss.[24]

The usual excuse for any imperial victory is that it was 'like, you know, rifles against spears, man,' but this was certainly not the case at Bembesi. It was reckoned that the Matabele had at least three times as many firearms as the company forces[25] and a large, bewildering and varied haul of these were recovered from dead Matabele. Before the battle, Lobengula had issued the Imbezu 100 Martini Henrys, and a number of these were found along with various exotic weapons like muskets, express rifles and even four-bore elephant guns. More intriguingly, the Rhodesians also recovered a number of the latest .303 magazine rifles from their enemy. Quite how the Matabele had managed to get their hands on these was never explained, though it is not unlikely that agents from the Transvaal's ever-busy secret service were to blame. The Transvaal Boers had long considered Mashonaland and Matabeleland somehow 'theirs' and, in 1895, would be caught smuggling rifles into the territory to supply Matabele rebels.[26] Kruger's agents also supplied renegade chiefs in Bechuanaland[27] and continued supplying rifles and ammunition to the Matabele insurgents after they rebelled against company rule in 1896.

It is easy to criticize the Matabele for not attacking the Rhodesians while they were on the move, but actually achieving this would have been a lot harder than it sounds. In all but the very thickest bush and most difficult of terrain, Forbes' men could form laagers in a matter of minutes and bringing several impis close to a moving enemy would have been no easy feat. Some might claim that the Matabele should have rushed ahead of the column and lain in ambush, but they had no way of knowing where to wait as the Rhodesians were trail-blazing their route, rather than sticking to an established thoroughfare. Besides, the company scouts ranged far and wide while the column was on the move, and theoretically should have been able to give plenty of warning of any ambush. Indeed, the Matabele's best chance of victory would probably not have been to catch the Rhodesians moving at all, but rather to have steeled themselves to deliver an irresistible night attack, similar to the one Mjaan had planned at Shangani.

§

Though it could easily have ended differently but for Forbes' luck, Willoughby and Borrow's pluck and Whittaker's quick reactions, the Rhodesian victory at Bembesi was even more crushing than the one at Shangani had been a few days earlier. In just over an hour, the company men had smashed the very finest Lobengula could throw at them, and the war was as good as won. Major Forbes briefly considered taking advantage of his victory by immediately sending a flying column of 100 men on to seize Bulawayo, but was dissuaded by the state of the company's horses.[28] Indeed, it was the poor state of these which prevented a decisive follow up as the Matabele retreated from Bembesi–something which would undoubtedly have turned the retreat into a rout.

Instead, the whole column moved off the following morning—2 November—and continued their cautious march. Early on the 3rd, an enormous explosion shattered the stillness of the morning and a large column of smoke was seen rising from the direction of Bulawayo. Lobengula had ordered his capital destroyed, and his men had blown their magazine: a stock estimated to have consisted of 80,000 rounds of Martini Henry ammunition and around 2,000 pounds of black powder.[29] When company scouts entered the still smoking, shattered settlement shortly thereafter, they found it deserted with most of the huts and other structures flattened by the blast. Some days earlier, Lobengula, the gout ridden heavy weight, had gathered his court and fled to the hills–seemingly ready to start a career as a rather unlikely guerrilla. He had left orders for the capital to be destroyed if the attack at Bembesi failed but, much to his credit, taken care to ensure that two white traders who had stayed on in the town were left unharmed. Company scouts found these fellows—Messrs. Fairbairn and Usher—sitting on the roof of their store.[30]

The rest of the column marched into the remains of Bulawayo on the afternoon of the 4th, the '...wagons decorated with whatever handkerchiefs, or other articles capable of being stitched into some resemblance of a flag, might be obtained; Piper-Major McDonald, of Captain Delamore's 'Foot-sloggers', blowing the 'Bulawayo March' lustily on his beloved bag-pipes.'[31]

The laagers were formed around one of the few surviving huts, which was itself transformed into an impromptu hospital. Lobengula might have insisted they be left unmolested, but the stock in Fairbairn and Usher's store was instantly commandeered by the company and distributed for use at the hospital or for re-clothing the thread-bare troopers. Despite the explosion, a large amount of trophies and trinkets had survived, and the company men gathered up assegais, shields, ostrich feather head-dresses and the like. A large silver elephant that had been presented to Lobengula by the Tati Company some years before was found in the ruins of the king's house and raffled off.[32] Though this free-for-all sounds a bit unseemly, the fact was that—however rough and ready it might have been at first— British law and order had arrived in Matabeleland, and not before time:

'A Union Jack, surcharged with the yellow lion of the B.S.A. Company was placed on a pole fixed to the top of a tree alongside the headquarters, and proclaimed Britain's protection over a country where but a few weeks ago Lobengula had held absolute despotic sway.'[33]

Though they had run up the union's flag and seized Lobengula's silver elephant, the king himself remained at large–meaning that Jameson could not yet declare the war over. On 7 November, the

Doctor sent three 'colonial boys'[34] out with a letter to persuade the king to come in:

> 'Now to stop this useless slaughter you must at once come to see me at Bulawayo, when I guarantee that your life will be safe and that you will be kindly treated.'[35]

Jameson's messengers delivered the letter and returned with a reply from Lobengula, in which the king said he would come to Bulawayo. He also asked for some paper, pens, and ink, and wanted to know where he would stay, given that he had blown up all his houses.[36] Perhaps fearful after what had happened to his envoys at Tati—who Lobengula no doubt viewed as having been murdered—or perhaps just to buy more time to flee north, the king did not turn up as promised. Jameson was left with no choice but to hunt the renegade heavyweight down and bring him in, the plan being for him to be retained down in the Cape like other defeated chiefs.[37]

However, before we look at the company's attempts to chase the runaway king down, let us turn our attention to Goold-Adams' Southern Column as they pushed their way north from Tati.

End Notes
1 Reported in the Durban Mercury, 8 November 1893
2 Selous, Sunshine and Storm in Rhodesia, p.44
3 Colvin, The Life of Jameson, Vol.1, p.278
4 Wills and Collingridge, The Downfall of Lobengula, p.120
5 Willoughby, Account of the Battle of Imbembizi, Fought at the Head Waters of the Bembizi River (Nov. 1893) found in Norris-Newman, Matabeleland and How We Got It, p.227-235
6 Donovan, With Wilson in Matabeleland, p.267
7 Wills and Collingridge, The Downfall of Lobengula, p.121
8 Keppel-Jones, Rhodes and Rhodesia, p.273
9 Rhodesiana, December 1966 p.3
10 Wills and Collingridge, The Downfall of Lobengula, p.122
11 Rhodesiana, December 1966, p.4
12 Burnham, Scouting on Two Continents, p.150
13 Rhodesiana, December 1966, p.6
14 Gibbs, A Flag for the Matabele, p.135
15 Donovan, With Wilson in Matabeleland, p.260
16 Willoughby, Account of the Battle of Imbembizi, Fought at the Head Waters of the Bembizi River (Nov. 1893) found in Norris-Newman, Matabeleland and How We Got It, p.227-235
17 Donovan, With Wilson in Matabeleland, p.262
18 Wills and Collingridge, The Downfall of Lobengula, p.123
19 Donovan, With Wilson in Matabeleland, p.266
20 Wills and Collingridge, The Downfall of Lobengula, p.123
21 Donovan, With Wilson in Matabeleland, p.266
22 Willoughby, Account of the Battle of Imbembizi, Fought at the Head Waters of the Bembizi River (Nov. 1893) found in Norris-Newman, Matabeleland and How We Got It, p.227-235
23 Wills and Collingridge, The Downfall of Lobengula, p.124
24 Wills and Collingridge, The Downfall of Lobengula, p.125
25 Keppel-Jones, Rhodes and Rhodesia, p.274
26 A.E. Heyer, A Brief History of the Transvaal Secret Service System, p.15
27 A.E. Heyer, A Brief History of the Transvaal Secret Service System, p.20
28 Wills and Collingridge, The Downfall of Lobengula, p.125
29 Wills and Collingridge, The Downfall of Lobengula, p.129
30 Norris-Newman, Matabeleland and How We Got It, p.97
31 Donovan, With Wilson in Matabeleland, p.272
32 Donovan, With Wilson in Matabeleland, p.276
33 Donovan, With Wilson in Matabeleland, p.277
34 Keppel-Jones, Rhodes and Rhodesia, p.277
35 Glass, The Matabele War, p.227
36 Wills and Collingridge, The Downfall of Lobengula, p.132
37 Glass, The Matabele War, p.227

For better or worse — fair and foul — the world we know today is in large measure a product of Britain's age of empire. The question is not whether British imperialism was without blemish. It was not. The question is whether there could have been a less bloody path to modernity. Perhaps in theory there could have been. But in practice?
— Niall Ferguson, Empire

Ask any man what nationality he would prefer to be, and ninety nine out of a hundred will tell you that they would prefer to be Englishmen.
— Cecil John Rhodes

Chapter 8
The Southern Column

As we saw in Chapter 6, the Southern Column established themselves at Tati on 18 October, and Lobengula's envoys were killed shortly thereafter. Lt. Colonel Goold-Adams did not waste any time on these unfortunate incidents however, and continued the push forward from Tati on the 19th, at the head of '...about 440 Europeans and about 2,000 natives, 520 horses, and about 2,000 head of oxen. The proposed route was to the Monarch Mine, then to the Ramokabane River,[i] up and along the high veld to the eastward, striking the main road about the Fig Tree.'[1]

Unknown to Goold-Adams at the time, Lobengula had sent a large chunk of his army to block the Southern Column's advance. Matabeleland had been split up into four 'military divisions' and two of these[2]—which encompassed around 8,000 Matabele warriors from 23 kraals—had been assigned to the mission with the whole force under the command of Lobengula's splendidly named brother-in-law, Gambo. As was typical in Lobengula's court, the king did not entirely trust his brother-in-law and Dr Jameson confidently predicted that Gambo would defect to the company and bring his men with him. Though this did not happen, Lobengula was probably fearful of the possibility, and only assigned his southern force a measly 10 Martini Henrys and 1,000 rounds.[3]

§

Goold-Adams sent Raaff ahead with 100 of his mounted 'riff-raff' and another 100 of King Khama's mounted men. This force was to operate away on the flank of the slow-moving main column as it lumbered forward. The Southern Column had far more problems with their oxen than the company columns did. Whether this was due to the quality of the drivers, the beasts themselves or, most likely, the terrain they traversed is difficult to say, but it was a constant issue that hampered progress badly.

Compared to the relatively open terrain that Forbes had crossed, Goold-Adams had no obvious route and would have to pick his way through thick bush and broken, hilly country.[ii] At least he could be

---

i Sometimes written as 'Ramaquabane River'

ii Somewhat strangely, Stafford Glass claims that the Southern Column faced easier terrain than the Mashonaland column in his 'The Matabele War'. This is not a view shared by Selous or Goold-Adams.

grateful for the presence of the famous hunter and frontiersman, F.C. Selous, who had attached himself to the Southern Column as chief scout at Dr Jameson's request.[4] Selous led a small scouting party forward to try and determine if a route along the course of the Ramokabane River would be practical, but found it to be completely impossible due to the scarcity of water. Goold-Adams instead changed his plans, and 'decided to push forward on to the Mpakwe River, to try to get round the point of the hill by moving to the head waters of the Mpakwe or Nguisi Rivers'.[5] Adequate water was a constant issue for Goold-Adams, and—though splitting his force must have been the last thing he wanted to do—he had no choice other than to leave the bulk of his men behind for a time while he pressed on with just 190 mounted men from the Bechuanaland Border Police, 200 Raaff's Rangers (also mounted) 12 wagons, three Maxims and a pair of 7-pdrs. The balance of the column would wait in laager at Ramokabane until summoned.

Goold-Adams and his flying column arrived at the Singuesi River[iii] on 29 October, and learned from local Mashona that a large force of Matabele were occupying the hills directly to his front. To make matters worse, these locals also told the Colonel that the Matabele had cleared all the cattle from the area, and that there was no reliable water supply, even for the smaller force, should they try to push around the high ground. Goold-Adams decided that his only option was to call for the bulk of his men to come forward with all haste, and drive the Matabele from the hills. In the meantime, he selected a position close to water and his small force laagered as best they could. He later admitted:

'The position was not a good one, but was the best that could be found within reach of the water. There were high kopjes of from 150 to 300 feet about 1,000 yards to the south and south-east of the laager, and rising ground to the north from the bank of the river.'[6]

The flying column would pass a couple of anxious days waiting for the rest of the southern force to show up.

§

King Khama's contingent arrived at the Singuesi River position on 1 November, and laagered about 200 yards from the police position. Later that evening, Goold-Adams received word that some of the BBP wagons had outspanned about three miles short of his position, however, due to their oxen being knocked up, the unit commander,

---

iii This is spelt in various ways in different reports and accounts: 'Sangez', 'Singwesi',' Sinquesi', 'Sangesi' and 'Singesi' being some of the most common.

Founder of the Matabele nation, Chief Mzilikazi

'To be born an Englishman is to win the lottery of life' – a young Cecil Rhodes, eager to start painting the map pink

Lobengula, Matabele King in the early 1890s

The 'Colossus of Rhodes', linking Cape to Cairo

Lord Salisbury – Conservative Prime Minister after whom the Rhodesian capital was named

Empire builders: Rhodes and Beit ponder their next move

BSAC flag

Dr Leander Starr Jameson – right hand man to Rhodes who went in with the Pioneer Column and was Administrator of Mashonaland at the time of the 1893 war

Assembling the Pioneers at Tuli

F. C. Selous – the archetypal 'Great White Hunter' who acted as chief scout to the Pioneers and fought in both wars

Officers of the Pioneer Column, many of whom would serve in one or both of the Matabele Wars

Wider still and wider... the Pioneers cross into what would become Rhodesia

The Pioneer Column pushes onwards

Raising the flag at Fort Salisbury

'Send forth the best ye breed' Early Pioneers of Rhodesia

Fort Victoria –a massive raid on the settlement by Lobengula's warriors provoked the war of 1893

'Whatever happens, we have got, the Maxim gun – and they have not'

Battle of Shangani

Matabele prisoners – despite what the BBC would have their viewers believe, prisoners were taken and treated well

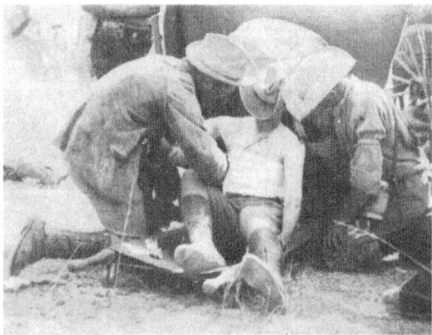

A wounded trooper is assisted by his mates

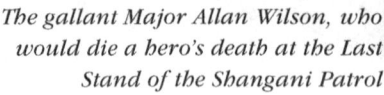

The gallant Major Allan Wilson, who would die a hero's death at the Last Stand of the Shangani Patrol

Captain Tancred, had decided to spend the night where he was. As Selous recalled:

'Owing to the miserable state of the oxen, a portion of the waggons did not get up to us on November 1st, but were left behind at a distance of about three miles from our main column and the oxen sent on to the water. After drinking, they were sent back at once, and early on the morning of November 2nd, the waggons came on.'[7]

About a mile-and-a-half away from the police laager, these 20 wagons blundered into an ambush and a force of about 700 Matabele surged forward in attack. Before anyone realized what was happening, one of the wagons in the middle of the convoy[iv] was rushed and Corporal Mundy, BBP, and the native driver were both assegaied. The oxen were cut free and dragged away by the attackers and the wagon quickly set ablaze. Captain Tancred, who had been at the rear of the convoy, immediately galloped forward with a troop of BBP and a Maxim. They opened fire on the ambushers, driving them away before they could wreak any more havoc.[8]

As soon as the shooting was heard, two more mounted BBP troops galloped out of the police laager to assist. Selous rode out ahead of them and described the action:

'I got hold of my horse long before the troop horses came in, and, saddling him up, galloped back alone to help the fellows with the waggons. They were not far off, and were being attacked on all sides by the Matabele, who were keeping up a hot fire and closing in on both flanks and from the rear. Our fellows were sticking to it well, though in small numbers. My appearance, I think, checked the Matabele a little, as, seeing one horseman gallop up, they naturally thought more were at hand.'[9]

Selous was almost immediately wounded in the fire fight, knocked off his horse by a Matabele bullet which struck him in the side but luckily glanced around his rib. Undaunted, he jumped back onto his horse and re-joined the fight.[10]

Selous and the two troops of the BBP, along with Tancred's troop coming up from the rear of the column, held the Matabele off for long enough to get the convoy safely to the laager, and then started falling back themselves, drawing the attackers on. The Matabele followed up closely, getting to within 150 yards of the laager–at which point

---

iv Other accounts say it was the rear-most wagon, but this does not tally with what happened thereafter.

Battle of Singuesi (Empandeni)
Chronology of Events

1 Lt-Col Goold-Adams, leading a section of the southern column consisting of BBP and BSA Company recruits coming up from Tati, goes on ahead of his wagons and arrives at a laager position close to the Singuesi River on the 29th October 1893. Khama, Chief of the Bamagwato arrived on the afternoon of the 1 st November with 130 men and wagons and set up camp next to the BBP. Goold-Adams wagon section, led by Capt Tancred with his troop, are forced to night stop three miles south of the laager on 1st November because of the poor condition of their oxen. After fresh oxen are sent out by Goold-Adams, they move out early the next day to join the camp.

2 At about 09h00 the wagons are ambushed one and a half miles from the laager by 700 Matabele from the *amabugudwana* and *inyamandhlovu* regiments who attack from the rear, left and right in the classic Matabele style. The rear wagon, containing quartermaster's stores, is burnt and its two attendants are killed.

3 Two troops of the BBP, with FC Selous at their head, ride out from the laager in support of the wagon train. Selous is wounded but continues the fight.

4 Tancred's troop in the rear, along with Selous and the two BBP troops, manage to hold off the Matabele whilst the wagon train moves on towards the laager. They gradually and intentionally fall back on the laager, pursued closely by the Matabele until at a point 150 yards from the laager the Maxim guns in the laager open fire. The Matabele themselves are now caught in an ambush. In disarray they break off their attack and retreat into the rough kopie country to the south.

5 Khama's men are ordered to flush the Matabele out of the hills from the north whilst the BBP forms a cordon at the base of the hills. Khama loses 3 men with 7 injured whilst the BBP suffers one killed and three wounded. Over 60 Matabele are killed and by 13h00 they are routed and retire.

6 On 3rd November Goold-Adams moves his laager further north to a better position near Mpandine village where Fort Adams is built.

the police Maxims suddenly opened up on them. The ambushers had become the ambushed, and fell back in disarray.[11] The Matabele, who were primarily from the Inyamandhlovu and Amabugudwana impis, took a hammering and began to flee for the kopjes. Trying to cut off their retreat,[12] Goold-Adams ordered a large force of BBP and Raaff's Rangers out after them, but these were too late to stop them from making it to the relative safety of the hills. Coming under heavy fire from the kopjes, the mounted troops fell back and Goold-Adams ordered two of King Khama's contingents out to clear the hills. This they did with great courage and élan, driving the Matabele from their positions in savage hand to hand fighting.[13] The bravery of the Bechuana was all the more remarkable given that—due to some bungling—they briefly came under fire from the column's seven-pounders.[14]

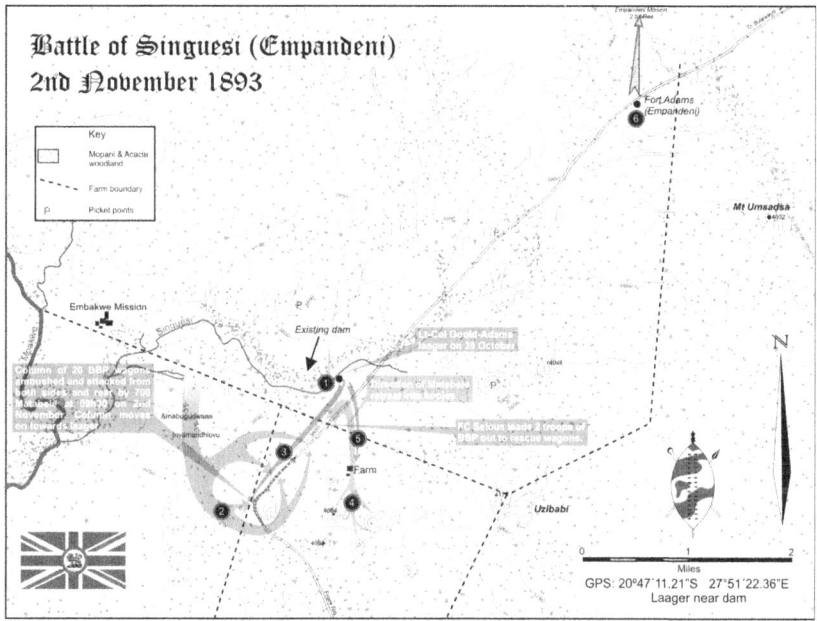

Battle of Singuesi (Empandeni)
2nd November 1893

The wagon convoy had been ambushed at 09h30. By 13h00, the Matabele had been well beaten and were streaming away in full retreat. The action would become known as Battle of Singuesi (sometimes the Battle of Empandeni).[15]

Imperial losses were fairly light: as well as the unfortunate Corporal Mundy and the native driver, three of Khama's Bechuana were killed as they cleared the kopjes, and Sgt Major Dahm, RSM of Raaff's Rangers, was shot dead in the attempt to cut off the Matabele retreat.[16] About another dozen men were wounded, and four horses were killed in the action. Over 60 Matabele bodies were found on the field, and it will never be known how many were dragged away after the battle.

Immediately the action was over, Goold-Adams moved his men about 4 miles to the north-east into more open country near Empandine (terrain that their machine guns and field guns could dominate more easily) and at least one member of the column declared himself 'thankful to be out of that rat trap'.

The cautious Goold-Adams remained in laager in this new spot until 6 November,[17] while he considered his next move. His men now held what he described as a capital position and he was not keen to press on from Empandine through waterless terrain with thousands of Matabele known to be lurking in the area. He thus cannot have been delighted to receive a message from the high commissioner, dated

23 October, ordering him to take up a commanding position near Bulawayo, and saying that he, rather than the company officers, was to negotiate the surrender of the Matabele.[18] Needless to say, it was somewhat easier for Sir Henry to make this demand than it was for Goold-Adams to comply with it.

§

Three days after the battle—on 5 November—and while the column was still laagered at the Empandine position, King Khama added to the Colonel's woes by dropping a bombshell and announcing that he would be leading his sizable contingent back to Bechuanaland. Goold-Adams was less than impressed by what he understandably took to be a form of desertion, but he could hardly accuse Khama's men of cowardice after the way they had fought at Singuesi. Either way, it was certainly a bolt from the blue, as Khama and the Colonel had always been on excellent terms. The reason Khama gave for turning back was that small-pox had broken out among his men, who would start dying in the veld unless he got them back to their own country. This all seemed a bit far-fetched and Khama did not help his case by refusing to leave any of his wagons or oxen with Goold-Adams, or even to hold his position near the Singuesi River until the police had moved on, thus hiding from the Matabele the fact that their enemies had divided their force.[19] Indeed, such was their haste to be on their way that the Bechuana were back in Tati just two days later. In fairness to Khama, the Southern Column had been advancing at a snail's pace, and he and his men had passed many days waiting at Tati and then twiddling their thumbs at the Ramokabane River. The column had not even made it halfway to Bulawayo by the time Khama decided to turn his men around. There were also worrying reports that a rival chief, Sebele, was planning to grab some of Khama's land in his absence, and a pressing concern about being back in Bechuanaland in time for ploughing before the rainy season.[20]

The king was baffled by the accusations of desertion and would later, with touching naivety, explain his reasoning to a missionary:

'I was with him [Adams] at the Sinquesi (sic) River, where we had to fight with the Matabele. After that fight, when we had moved out of the kopjes to the neighbourhood of Empandine and were in the open country, we saw that the Matabele had left us, and I took my men home because we saw that there was nothing but smallpox around us, and also because the time was passing for us to plough and there was no one left at home to do this work.'[21]

Though at the time the Colonel cannot have been pleased with Khama's 'desertion', his mood quickly improved when some local Mashona headmen came in to request protection for their people. They informed Goold-Adams that the company column had defeated the Matabele near Bulawayo[v] and that Lobengula had fled his capital. Better still was the news that this defeat had prompted the impis—which had been blocking the Southern Column—to pack in the fight and flee. The morning after they received this news, 6 November, and just as Goold-Adams was preparing to send Commandant Raaff forward with a flying column to confirm the reports, the two American scouts, Burnham and Ingram rode in from Bulawayo, bearing despatches and best wishes from Dr Jameson.[22] The scouts were no doubt delighted to see the Southern Column still intact, as Matabele prisoners taken at Bembesi claimed that Goold-Adams and his entire command had been annihilated.[23]

§

And so the Battle of Singuesi was the only significant action fought by the Southern Column. Goold-Adams left Lt. Munro at the Empandine position with 50 men and a pair of Maxims and, 'travelling by easy steps'[24] made it into Bulawayo with advance elements of the Southern Column on the 13th. Raaff arrived with another element the following day, and the exhausted oxen managed to drag the rest of the column into Bulawayo by 15 November. Given all the advantages their Matabele opponents had enjoyed in terms of terrain and the problems the invaders faced over water, they really should have given Goold-Adams a much tougher time of it. Indeed, Selous was to muse in a letter:

'The Matabele generalship has been abominably bad. They never did what they ought to have done, and we took advantage of their opportunities. The strong British column from the east [Forbes' Column], advancing through open country, with a large force of mounted men and a large number of machine guns, simply carried all before it, and on the two occasions when they attacked the 'laager' the machine guns simply mowed them down. No one, knowing their abominable history, can pity them or lament their downfall. They have been paid back in their own coin.
Our column advancing from the west had very great difficulties to contend with, as the whole country on that side is covered with thick bush and broken hills. Had the Matabele here made

---

v   This presumably refers to the Battle of Bembesi, which as we know, was fought on the 1st of November. The power of the 'Bush Telegraph' to spread news should not be underestimated.

a determined opposition we could never have got through, and should probably have met with a disaster.'[25]

Selous is right in that, by effectively splitting his army in half, Lobengula had forfeited the chance to overwhelm either of the invasion forces. Had Gambo's 8,000 men been deployed to stop the Mashona column, they might not have made too much of a difference against the company men's compact laagers and machine guns. However, if Lobengula had given some of Mjaan's men (or even more rifles) to Gambo for a determined attack against Goold-Adams' perennially scattered Southern Column, this would surely have been his best chance to inflict a morale shattering 'Isandlwana' on the invaders.

Goold-Adams' men may have arrived too late to beat the company forces to Bulawayo, but his column pulled in just in time to play a major role in the last act of the war–the pursuit of the king.

End Notes

[1] Wills and Collingridge, The Downfall of Lobengula, p.218
[2] Selous, Sunshine and Storm in Rhodesia, p.45
[3] Wills and Collingridge, The Downfall of Lobengula, p.129
[4] Millais, The Life of Frederick Courtney Selous, p.201
[5] Wills and Collingridge, The Downfall of Lobengula, p.218
[6] Wills and Collingridge, The Downfall of Lobengula, p.219
[7] Millais, The Life of Frederick Courtney Selous, p.201
[8] Norris-Newman, Matabeleland and How We Got It, p.109
[9] Millais, The Life of Frederick Courtney Selous, p.202
[10] Norris-Newman, Matabeleland and How We Got It, p.110
[11] Wills and Collingridge, The Downfall of Lobengula, p.219
[12] Keppel-Jones, Rhodes and Rhodesia, p.275
[13] Norris-Newman, Matabeleland and How We Got It, p.111
[14] Jones, Rhodesian Genesis, p.91
[15] Glass, The Matabele War, p.212
[16] Wills and Collingridge, The Downfall of Lobengula, p.220
[17] Glass, The Matabele War, p.213
[18] Glass, The Matabele War, p.214
[19] Wills and Collingridge, The Downfall of Lobengula, p.221
[20] Glass, The Matabele War, p.213
[21] Glass, The Matabele War, p.214
[22] Norris-Newman, Matabeleland and How We Got It, p.112
[23] Burnham, Scouting on Two Continents, p.153
[24] Keppel-Jones, Rhodes and Rhodesia, p.276
[25] Millais, The Life of Frederick Courtney Selous, p.204

'The story of how these thirty-four (nearly all of whom were great friends of my own) stood and fell, shoulder to shoulder, rather than desert two of their number who could not escape with them, will not only remain for ever in our history, but will be handed down through generations of the native tribes of Africa as an instance of how Englishmen can and will die, and the effect of their heroism on the natives, who above all else honour personal bravery, cannot be over-estimated.'[1]

– Major Forbes, on the courageous men of the Shangani Patrol

'The lands north of the Limpopo seem to be at least as productive of pocket-generals and dud politicians as our old home in the south. There are pudding-heads here who are determined to make heroes of us. For me, I had enough serving under these gentlemen in the Shangani Patrol.'[2]

– Johannes Colenbrander, on the same subject

Chapter 9
To Catch a King

As mentioned in Chapter 8, Jameson's attempts to coax Lobengula to return to Bulawayo had proven unsuccessful, perhaps due to the unfortunate killing of the Matabele envoys at Tati. When Goold-Adams' southern force arrived safely, it was quickly decided that a rather more proactive course of action would be needed and a flying column was assembled to go after the king and run him to ground. This force was drawn from various components of the invading columns: 90 from the Salisbury Horse, 60 from the Victoria Rangers, 60 from Raaff's 'riff-raff' and 90 from the Imperial Bechuanaland Border Police. They would be supported by 4 Maxims, a single seven-pounder and 200 native carriers under the command of Lieutenant Brabant.[3]

The command-structure was a complex one, and far from ideal: with political considerations at the forefront of their minds, both Dr Jameson and Lt. Colonel Goold-Adams would remain in Bulawayo. Major Forbes was therefore—perhaps surprisingly—chosen to be nominally in charge of the flying column, but the presence of Major Wilson cannot have been helpful: The dynamic and well-loved Wilson was three years older than Forbes. He had a good deal more experience and had commanded the Victoria Rangers, which was a much larger unit than Forbes' Salisbury Horse.[4] The simmering rivalry between the two had continued long after the invading columns united at Iron Mine Hill.

To make matters worse, Commandant Raaff[i]—who was junior to Major Wilson—was not only appointed as 2nd in command of the flying column[ii] but also placed in command of the BBP Imperial Troopers as well as retaining command over his own contingent of rangers.[5] Not only must this have put Wilson's nose out of joint, it cannot have gone down well with Captains Coventry and Tancred of the Bechuanaland Border Police–both of whom, as imperial officers, were technically his seniors. To their credit, both Tancred and Coventry seem to have accepted this strange turn of events with good grace, and both continued to go about their business.

As if all this was not chaotic enough, Jameson also instructed Forbes to consult Commandant Raaff over any steps he took whether

---

i The American scout, Major Frederick Burnham, said his first impression of Raaff was, 'Here's an insignificant Dutchman'. He was later to revise his opinion, and declared, 'A braver and kinder man there could not be; moreover, he was a strategist of the highest order.'

ii To add to the confusion, some accounts claim that Wilson was 2nd in command. It would be fair to say that it was a mess.

offensive or defensive[6]–an order which came within an ace of putting Raaff in effective overall command. Some writers have focused on the clash between Forbes and Wilson while neglecting the role that Raaff's presence played in the debacle that followed, but Colenbrander described the perverse three-headed beast that was the Forbes-Raaff-Wilson rivalry as three 'pocket generals [who on] principle could never agree with each other'.[7]

It is actually difficult to think of a way in which the command structure could have been organized more poorly. Had Jameson—always a man of action who liked to be in the very thick of things—ridden out with the flying column, his charm and leadership may well have papered over the cracks. As it was, Jameson fully expected Lobengula to return to Bulawayo, and wanted to be there to receive him. He no doubt feared that any company claim over Matabeleland might be undermined if he was absent and the king was instead greeted by Colonel Goold-Adams. In any case, Forbes did not seem to think the flying column would take long to bring the renegade king in. Raaff, who had a good deal more experience in native warfare but whose health was failing, was noticeably less blasé about the whole thing, and he pointed out that '…it was a very dangerous mission we were on with a handful of men'.

Though the flying column's leadership was riven with difficulties, it was still a good deal more formidable than Raaff's 'handful of men'. The rather complex order of battle was as follows:

Officer Commanding: Major Forbes
2IC: Commandant Raaff
Salisbury Horse contingent–90 strong
Captains Heany and Spreckley commanding
Lt. Tyndall-Biscoe, D.S.O., RN commanded a mule-Maxim gun
Victoria Rangers contingent–60 strong
Major Wilson commanding
Captain Lendy (RA) commanded a horse-Maxim gun
Raaff's Rangers–60 strong
Captain Coventry (BBP) commanding, but Commandant Raaff retained direct control
Bechuanaland Border Police–90 strong
Under the direct command of Commandant Raaff

Captain Tancred (BBP) commanded two horse-Maxims and one mule-seven pounder.

Each man drew 100 rounds of ammunition and carried food for just three days.[8]

In addition, there were 200 native carriers under Lt. Brabant.

§

The company men had been in Bulawayo for some time, but the reader will recall that Goold-Adams rode in with the leading units of the Southern Column on the 13th while Raaff's contingent only arrived a day later. Nevertheless, the flying column set off at 19h30 that evening–even before the last elements of Goold-Adams' force had arrived.

An uneventful 40 mile march over two days brought the flying column within striking distance of the mission station at Inyati, where intelligence reports suggested a Matabele impi was lurking. Jack Carruthers, one of the 1890 pioneers, rode forward with Selous to investigate:

'On approaching the mission, we chased two Matabele. Selous trailed one and I the other. When I caught my native up he turned for mercy and, to my surprise, I found it was my old boy, Charlie, of Angwa days. Shortly after Selous returned with his captive, he remarked, "I see you did not shoot him." "How could I?" I said, "This is a dear friend of mine." I told of my runaway. These two boys both served the column usefully afterwards.'[9]

The Mission was 'a litter of destruction' and, in addition to the two men Carruthers mentions, revealed the presence of nothing but a handful of other men and some women and children. From these prisoners, it was learned that the king and his retinue had headed north-east along the Bubye River,[iii] travelling towards the Shangani River[10] as fast as possible.

Forbes quickly revealed a somewhat alarming tendency to believe each and every native report he heard, and he remained optimistic that Lobengula could not be more than 20 miles up the Bubye River. Though their initial rations were all but exhausted, Forbes was confident that he would be able to run the king to ground within 48 hours.[11] He resolved to leave 80 men and one Maxim under Captain Fitzgerald at the mission station and press on with the rest. Our new friend, Jack Carruthers and some others were also sent back to Bulawayo with some of the cattle that had been taken. Jack Carruthers described his last sighting of his close friend, Major Wilson:

'As I wished him goodbye, Wilson rode away on his big cream horse in his shirtsleeves, riding trousers and top boots. In his belt was a tobacco bag with his clasp knife on the side hook. His

iii Sometimes spelt the 'Bubi River'

waterproof coat hung loosely over the pummel of his saddle and he carried no weapon. An easy going man, never perturbed, a leader of men, whom to know was to like.

When the column moved off, Brabant and his levies, Matabele Wilson[iv] and myself made south with the loot cattle, a bellowing confusion of oxen, cows and calves.'[12]

§

Even at this early stage, there were plenty who failed to share Forbes' optimism and grumbling had already started around the camp fires. Commandant Raaff's failing health seems, unsurprisingly, to have imbued him with a sense of fatalistic defeatism and Forbes simply dismissed the input of the two senior Salisbury Horse officers, Heany and Spreckley, despite the fact that they were both very loyal to him. Coventry and Tancred, the professional imperial officers from the BBP, appear to have remained aloof from the power struggle entirely, while— perhaps not surprisingly—Forbes seems to have grown increasingly reliant upon the opinions of the magnetic and dynamic Major Wilson. Though he was by no means a professional Sandhurst man, Forbes appears to have greatly approved of Wilson's keenness to close with the enemy, and the contempt he had for those who advocated a less aggressive approach.[13]

On the 18th, the now-much-reduced flying column arrived at a spot on the Bubye River where they had been led to believe Lobengula and his followers would be. Instead, they found nothing but a herd of cattle being tended by a few men. Once again, Forbes was told that the king was close, this time just 16 miles upriver. Rather than setting off in pursuit again, Forbes sent some of the herdsmen after the king with a message advising him to give up the pointless struggle. In the meantime, the flying column formed a thorn-bush zariba[v] and settled down to wait for the result.

The column had now been out of Bulawayo for four days, and their rations were finished. Never a happy force to begin with, the discontentment was getting worse. Lt. Tyndale-Biscoe RN, by all accounts a well-respected and thoroughly good and decent man, noted in his diary:

'We are now living on anything we can pick up, mostly meat and kaffir corn... there is a good deal of discontent among the men on account of the rations.'

---

iv   Not to be confused with Major Wilson

v   Common in many colonial conflicts, a zariba was a defensive barrier made of thorn-bushes. It served as a cheap and bio-degradable alternative to barbed wire.

But the rations were not the only problem: Commandant Raaff was behaving for all the world like Private Fraser from Dad's Army, and was now convinced that they were doomed, telling anyone who would listen, '...we were a small party with no adequate provision for the wounded... there must be large bodies of natives behind us.'[14]

Unbeknownst to Forbes, on the morning of the 19th, Raaff had even told his own men, the 'riff-raff' recruited from the seedier elements of Johannesburg, that they would be going back to Bulawayo that day. When these rumours found their way to members of the Salisbury Horse, two of the Salisbury men asked Captain Spreckley if they could also return. Spreckley was flabbergasted by this, and immediately approached Forbes.

What followed was not the finest episode in Britain's generally illustrious colonial military history. Forbes called a parade for 11h00 that morning, and directly asked the men under his fractured command whether or not they wanted to continue the mission. Democracy and military discipline do not make the best of bed fellows and this was a highly unusual response to the chattering in the ranks:

'Forbes barked, "Any of you men who are discontented with the rations or the way we are going on, step two paces to the front."'[15]

The result was astounding. Perhaps taken by surprise, all but 17 of the Salisbury men stepped forward, as did all but four of Raaff's Rangers. None of Wilson's Victoria Rangers chose to opt out, and, of course, the professional hard-men of the Bechuanaland Border Police were not given the option.[16] Understandably dismayed by this, Forbes, in the words of Captain Heany, addressed those who had paced forward:

"You will be sent back to Bulawayo." To those who had elected to stay, he said, "We are going forward to catch the king even if we can only get a dozen or twenty men to go with us."[17]

Perhaps seeing a chance to at least be rid of the doom-mongering Commandant Raaff, Forbes ordered him to return to Bulawayo with his rangers, but Raaff refused, claiming that he had to stay in order to command the BBP contingent.

The whole unhappy force withdrew to the small mission station at Shiloh to sort themselves out, arriving there on 23 November. Those who had elected not to continue were sent straight back to Bulawayo, the Salisbury men still grumbling about having been 'humbugged' into it, as they'd had no intention of refusing to fight. Captain Napier had come up to Shiloh with supplies and reinforcements sent by

Dr Jameson, and the flying column was reorganized accordingly. Jameson seems to have been frustrated by all this nonsense, and he sent a message instructing Forbes to 'get onto the king's spoor there and follow it right up'.[18] Surprisingly, however, the Doctor still remained in Bulawayo at a time during which he would have been much better served going up to Shiloh Mission Station instead of firing off messages.

§

The remains of Forbes' flying column, plus some reinforcements sent up by Jameson, set off again from Shiloh on 25 November, following in the tracks of Lobengula's wagons. The re-jigged force was made up as follows:

Salisbury Horse
22 mounted men under Captain Borrow
Raaff's Rangers
20 mounted men under Commandant Raaff (it would seem some changed their minds)
Bechuanaland Border Police
78 mounted men under Captain Coventry
Victoria Rangers
70 mounted men and 100 dismounted men under Major Wilson (it would appear that the reinforcements sent up by Jameson attached themselves to Wilson's command)

Support was now just four Maxim guns (two galloping, two on wagons) and a 2-pdr Hotchkiss.
Four wagons carried enough for ¾ rations for 12 days.
The large native contingent was dispersed.[19]
This force set out from Shiloh on the morning of 25 November and picked up Lobengula's spoor after just a mile. They pressed on for three days, but progress was slow: heavy rain hindered movement and the wagons quickly proved to be a serious encumbrance. On the evening of the 27th, Forbes realized that there was simply no way they would be able to run the king to ground at that pace—they were struggling to make eight miles a day—and the oxen were already completely exhausted. Faced with this situation, Forbes had no choice but to cut his force yet again, this time sending 130 men and all the wagons back to the mission station at Inyati. 158 men remained with the best horses, the vast majority of these drawn from the Victoria Rangers and the Bechuanaland Border Police's professional troopers. Just the two BBP Maxims—both mounted on galloping carriages—were retained.

Each man would carry 100 rounds, and each Maxim just 2,100. Ten days' worth of half-rations were carried on pack horses.[20]

It was a mobile, fast moving force with no artillery, very limited ammunition stocks and no wagons with which to form a laager–almost the exact opposite of the sort of forces which had proven successful at Shangani and Bembesi. However, it was probably the sort of column Forbes should have been commanding in the first place, rather than the half-arsed, half-way house he initially set off with.

Though the composition of the flying column made more sense in some respects, the thorny issue of the command structure had still not been resolved. Incredibly, Forbes did not seize this chance to rid himself of the top-heavy and fractious situation, and Wilson and Raaff both stayed with the drastically reduced force. With the company's Maxims having been sent back, Captain Lendy was also left without a role, but again, Forbes showed little desire to divest himself of any of his horde of officers. Seemingly loathe to lock horns with an experienced and well-respected officer like Lendy, and despite the fact that the two remaining Maxims were under Captain Tancred of the BBP's command, Forbes was not strong enough to make the call to send Lendy back with the others. Even by Forbes' standards, however, putting the police guns under Lendy's control would have been going a step too far. Instead, yet another ridiculous compromise was made: Lendy was unofficially appointed to work one of the guns, while the unit remained under Tancred's command. It was a pointless and unnecessary arrangement, and seems to have served only to alienate Lendy from Forbes, pushing him into Raaff's increasingly poisonous and defeatist orbit.

§

One of those who remained in the hunt, Walter Howard of the Bechuanaland Border Police,[vi] described the much-reduced flying column setting off:

'The journey to the banks of the Shangani was without much excitement except that caused by exceptionally heavy rains. We had no tents or any protection other than that afforded by our blankets or cloaks. The day we reached the Shangani we passed great numbers of armed Matabele who bluffed us that they were tired of war and were returning to make peace, in which laudable object we encouraged them. Little did we dream that their orders

---

vi Later, Major Walter Howard D.S.O. (1865-1949). Born in Surrey, England, Howard fought in the Matebele War of 1893, the Rebellion of 1896 and then in the Boer War, winning his D.S.O. at Spion Kop. He died in Bulawayo.

were that we were to be allowed to pass until we had crossed
the Shangani River and then none of us were to be allowed to
return.'[21]

Forbes seems to have been a little too keen to believe the best
of these bands and to avoid fighting them as this would only delay
his progress and give Lobengula more time to escape. In addition, he
explained:

'...our horses were in a poor state and our food supply very
limited, it was very important that we should catch up with him
as quickly as possible. I had not hesitated to leave these people
unmolested behind us as I always intended to come back up the
Shangani River.'[22]

It is somewhat surreal that Forbes was so trusting and seemingly
unconcerned about the large numbers of armed Matabele in the area.
This is even more remarkable given that the American scouts, Burnham
and Ingram, came across 'a party of about twenty armed Matabele—ugly
looking brutes—led by one of the most ferocious-looking characters
they had ever seen'. Worse, this band claimed to be from Gambo's
regiment. On hearing about this encounter, Colenbrander—formally
the company's man in Bulawayo—feared that the flying column was
blundering into a trap. Forbes and Wilson, however, both dismissed
the possibility.

Burnham, from his experience in the American Wild West, seems
to have found it strange that such discussions occurred between the
scouting groups of the opposing sides, and would later write:

'The South African niggers if they meet you scouting, and they are
alone or in small numbers, don't go for you but make tracks for
the nearest impi. This extraordinary conduct on their part saved
our lives over and over again. Indians kill you.'[23]

Nevertheless, Forbes noted that Burnham, who had previously
appeared fearless, seems to have been shaken by the encounter.

§

On 3 December, it seemed the patrol was finally getting
somewhere. Within a mile of the Shangani River, Forbes' men came
across a large herd of cattle and the boys looking after it confirmed
that the king and his retinue had only left the area that morning.
The trail was getting hot again and the column soon came across a

recently abandoned scherm.[vii] Fires had only recently been put out and the remains of hastily discarded meals could be seen. Another slave boy, who confirmed what the cow herds had said, was found. Better yet, the spoor of Lobengula's wagons was still clearly visible, running towards the river bank.

Believing that his luck had finally turned, and with two hours of daylight left, Forbes called for Wilson and ordered him to lead twelve men after the king on the best horses, find out where he had moved to and 'return by dark'.[24] There was no shortage of volunteers for what many realized could be the climax of the campaign, and men clamoured round, all eager to be picked. These were remarkable men:

> '...men like Sergeant-Major Sidney Charles Harding, son of the honorary colonel of one of the volunteer battalions of the Queen's Own Royal West Surrey Regiment; after being educated at Felsted and St. John's College, Cambridge, he had emigrated to South Africa where he served as a Lieutenant in the Natal Mounted Police and in the Bechuanaland Border Police; Sergeant Harold Brown, of Harrow and Exeter College, Oxford, a perpetual wanderer who had travelled in Europe, Asia and Africa and who had published a book on his adventures in Albania; Sergeant Clifford Bradburn, who had become dissatisfied with the life of a Birmingham bank clerk and had joined the Cape Mounted Rifles.'[25]

Ultimately, no less than eight officers, including Captains Kirton, Napier, Judd and Greenfield, quickly attached themselves to what was only ever meant to be a 12-strong fighting patrol, and off they went, leaving the main position at a gallop around 17h00,[26] and splashing their way through the Shangani to pick up Lobengula's spoor on the far side. Forbes later wrote:

> 'They all understood that they were to be back that night, and Kirton asked Dr Hogg, with whom he was messing, to keep some dinner hot for him as they would not be in till dark.'[27]

Seemingly on a whim, Forbes then ordered one of the two American scouts, Burnham, to join Wilson's patrol:

> '...as Burnham's horse was not very fit, I gave him my own, and sent him on after Major Wilson; Burnham, I thought, might be useful, and was very quick at following a spoor.'[viii]

---

vii   A temporary kraal or enclosure made from cut bushes

viii   The other American, Ingram, went out later with Captain Borrow's 'B' Troop.

Commandant Raaff thought splitting the patrol into two was 'lunacy'[28] while Walter Howard recalled that Major Wilson had:

> '...no intention of carrying out his orders to return at sundown to the main body. Let me here tell you that with us, as with all ill-disciplined troops, there is always ill-feeling and jealousy. The Victoria men had always felt that Major Wilson should have been in command of all the troops who came in from the north and this feeling was noticeable on many occasions. There is little doubt that they now thought they would, so to speak, do Forbes 'a shot in the eye' by capturing Lobengula on their own.'[29]

On the other hand, it would seem that Forbes himself harboured ambitions to be the one to bring in the king. He told in his trumpeter, Mr Chappé, that he would lead a 50-strong party with one Maxim gun to 'make one final rush for the king'[30] once Lobengula's position had been fixed (presumably by Wilson's reconnaissance that evening).

§

We will never know if Wilson somehow got wind of Forbes' plan, but as night fell, there was still no sign of his small party. Worse still, Forbes became aware of twinkling camp fires a few hundred yards away and called for silence:

> 'Sure enough, from all the way round in a large arc, he could hear, out of the bush, the low rumble of voices, the clatter of iron pots and weapons and occasionally the high-pitched laugh of some nervous and inexperienced youngster. The enemy was gathering for the attack.'[31]

It would later emerge that remnants of four Matabele regiments were in the area under the command of Mjaan and Gambo. No doubt chastened by their earlier defeats, neither induna was keen to take on the white men again, but their warriors—especially the younger ones—were furious at this reluctance, and demanded their chance to avenge their kinsmen.

There had been no sign of Wilson's patrol until around 23h00, when Captain Napier and two troopers rode into Forbes' main position with a message from the Major, requesting that Forbes bring the rest of the force forward so that they could attack the Matabele at first light.[32] This placed Forbes in an impossible position: Wilson had blatantly ignored his orders and was now essentially taking command of the whole force by asking Forbes to move forward and support his planned dawn attack. Forbes' correct course of action would have been to send Captain Napier back, ordering Wilson to return to the main position with his patrol. Perhaps knowing that Wilson would simply disregard such an order, Forbes did not waste any time issuing it. An alternative would have been to comply with Wilson's request and indeed move the whole force forward in the darkness, ready to pounce on the Matabele at day break, though this would by no means have been an easy under-taking, and with the enemy so close, attempting a river crossing in the darkness could have ended in absolute disaster.

Instead, Forbes has been accused of doing the very worst thing he could have done, though in truth, thanks to the hospital pass Wilson had thrown him, it might have been his only real option: Forbes sent Captain Henry Borrow forward with his 20-strong troop of the Salisbury Horse to join Wilson. As Walter Howard recalled:

'Forbes sent Capt. Borrow with his troops on as a reinforcement with a message that, as soon as it was light enough to move, he would come on in the morning. Napier did not return with Borrow and, as Mayne had a touch of fever, Robertson went as guide, taking food for Wilson's party with them. Of course, it was quite out of the question for the whole force to go on at midnight, and a night as black as ink at that. There were our slaughter cattle to drive—all our rations were now exhausted—native herd boys, galloping gun carriages and other impedimenta.'[33]

Remarkably, given what would happen a few hours later, it would seem that Captain Borrow even queried his men about taking their full ammunition supplies, as Forbes recalled:

'Just before Captain Borrow started, he asked me if it was necessary for his men to take their full 100 rounds of ammunition, as it was heavy for the horses, and I told him to; each man also had a revolver and twenty rounds ; they took out some food in their wallets for Major Wilson's men.'[34]

If true, this really would be a remarkable thing for Captain Borrow to have queried–it is a rare soldier who willingly takes less ammunition into a combat situation, and 100 rounds of rifle ammunition would only have weighed in the region of 5kg–hardly noticeable to a horse?

§

Dawn broke the following morning and events quickly started to spiral out of Forbes' control. Howard Walter continues:

'On the morning of the 4th December, as soon as it was light enough to see, we started to join up with Allan Wilson. We had scarcely gone half a mile when terrific firing began from the other side of the river. The column was closed up and hurried forward, our right flank being protected by the river down whose banks the column was marching. The heavy firing increased in intensity and Colenbrander called out to Major Forbes behind whom he was riding–"They cannot keep that up for long, sir, with their stock of ammunition." Almost at that moment a cloud of Matabele swept down through the bush and took up position across the vlei on the opposite edge of which the column was hurrying forward to join up with Wilson. At once they opened a heavy fire on us almost as they fired, our Maxims were returning their fire... Outnumbered by thirty to one and with less than 100 rounds of ammunition per man, our position was very precarious, but no ammunition was wasted for a man did not fire until he was certain of his mark.' [35]

For the first time in the campaign, Forbes had been caught on the move, but he reacted quickly and decisively. He bellowed orders, got his men into a rough defensive square against the river bank and quickly brought the two Maxims into action. Once again, Matabele marksmanship was appalling, but there was nowhere to hide the horses and these were slowly picked off. Unlike at the Battles of Shangani and Bembesi, however, the Matabele made no real attempt to charge Forbes' position, and the gun battle raged on for almost an hour. It was a much harder business than the earlier battles: the Matabele riflemen firing from the bush were almost invisible and the Rhodesians and police had to husband their limited ammunition carefully. Indeed, and despite their poor marksmanship, had the Matabele adopted similar tactics to the main set piece battles, the results might have been very different.

During a brief lull in the firing, the sounds of another battle raging on the other side of the river could clearly be heard.[36] Though many in the main force must have feared the worst, nobody could be sure what was happening to Wilson's party–besides, they had troubles enough of their own.

At about 07h30, having silenced most of the Matabele riflemen, Forbes began to extract his force, retreating back down along the river bank, back towards the position in which they had spent the previous night. Still being harried by the occasional shot, it was a thoroughly battered and demoralized patrol that got away from open ground and limped back to the relative safety of some thick bush beside the river–a river that had risen considerably since Borrow's troop had crossed it just a few hours earlier.

With their slaughter cattle having been driven off in the attack and unable to find a place to cross the swollen river even had he been inclined so to do, Forbes was not in a good position. The Matabele riflemen seem to have targeted the horses deliberately: 16 were killed in the action, along with five mules. No men were killed, though five—all Bechuanaland Border Policemen—were wounded.[37] Just as Forbes was considering his next move, at perhaps 08h00 on the 5th, the soaking wet figures of the American scouts, Burnham and Ingram, together with young Trooper Gooding, cantered into the position having swum their horses through the flooded river.

Desperate for news about Wilson's party, Forbes demanded to know what was happening. Burnham replied, "I think I may say we are the sole survivors of that party."[38]

End Notes
[1] Wills and Collingridge, The Downfall of Lobengula, p.188
[2] O'Reilly, Pursuit of the King, p.156
[3] Glass, The Matabele War, p.227
[4] O'Reilly, Pursuit of the King, p.32
[5] Cary, A Time to Die, p.39
[6] Cary, A Time to Die, p.40
[7] O'Reilly, Pursuit of the King, p.33
[8] O'Reilly, Pursuit of the King, p.31
[9] Jones, Rhodesian Genesis, p.92
[10] O'Reilly, Pursuit of the King, p.41
[11] Cary, A Time to Die, p.41
[12] Jones, Rhodesian Genesis, p.94
[13] Cary, A Time to Die, p.42
[14] O'Reilly, Pursuit of the King, p.42
[15] Cary, A Time to Die, p.43
[16] O'Reilly, Pursuit of the King, p.43
[17] Cary, A Time to Die, p.43
[18] O'Reilly, Pursuit of the King, p.44
[19] O'Reilly, Pursuit of the King, p.46
[20] Cary, A Time to Die, p.49
[21] Jones, Rhodesian Genesis, p.95
[22] O'Reilly, Pursuit of the King, p.49
[23] O'Reilly, Pursuit of the King, p.50
[24] Cary, A Time to Die, p.52
[25] Cary, A Time to Die, p.57
[26] Glass, The Matabele War, p.228
[27] Wills and Collingridge, The Downfall of Lobengula, p.157
[28] O'Reilly, Pursuit of the King, p.66
[29] Jones, Rhodesian Genesis, p.96
[30] Cary, A Time to Die, p.54
[31] Cary, A Time to Die, p.68
[32] Glass, The Matabele War, p.229
[33] Jones, Rhodesian Genesis, p.96
[34] Wills and Collingridge, The Downfall of Lobengula, p.162
[35] Jones, Rhodesian Genesis, p.97
[36] Cary, A Time to Die, p.99
[37] O'Reilly, Pursuit of the King, p.68
[38] O'Reilly, Pursuit of the King, p.69

'I have entered Major Wilson's party as killed. I think it is impossible that any can have escaped death, more especially as natives have reported that they have seen the bodies lying stripped and mutilated.'[1]

'...they do not die like Mashonas. They never cry or groan. They are men. No! I will never fight whites again. They are not afraid to die: They are men.'[2]
– A Matabele assessment of the men of the Shangani Patrol

'We marched fifteen miles that night, did not halt until day light, horses being led, guns and tripods and ammunition being carried. A hard task for half-starved men. Our march continued for ten days.'
– A trooper of the Bechuanaland Border Police
describes Forbes' retreat from the Shangani[3]

Chapter 10
Men of Men

To find out what happened to the rest of Wilson's party, let us now return to the previous evening, hours before Captain Borrow's troop rode out, and re-join the patrol on the far side of the Shangani River. In the fading light, but sensing their quarry nearby, Wilson's patrol followed the scouts, Burnham and Bain, as they tracked Lobengula's spoor. Before long, they came across a hastily-constructed scherm and were able to see Matabele men, women and children inside it. These people pointed out the route the king had taken, and one even ran alongside Burnham's horse, keen to show him the way. They passed large numbers of Matabele as they rode, but none showed any sign of hostility.

Just as night was falling, the patrol came across another scherm where camp fires were being lit. Seeing his chance to end the war at a stroke, Wilson ordered his men forward at a canter. Captain Napier recalled:

> "As we dashed through the scherms occupied by the king's guard and their families, with boys milking, women and girls grinding the evening meal, the howling scurrying and shouting must be left in the imagination."[4]

The horsemen pressed on, riding through various enclosures as the Matabele merely looked on with a mixture of bewilderment and confusion on their faces. Wilson and his small band pushed on through the enclosures regardless, finally stumbling into two wagons which they not unreasonably presumed to be Lobengula's.

Burnham recalled the event:

> 'As we lined up, Captain Napier, who spoke the Zulu language excellently, shouted to the king. He addressed Lobengula in the grandiloquent native style, giving him all his titles and assuring him that we were distinguished messengers sent by Dr Jameson's fighting induna to escort him to Bulawayo and there conclude a treaty of peace; that his life would be spared and all honour shown to him, etc.'[5]

Even as Wilson ordered Captain Napier to call for the king's surrender, the baffled Matabele finally started reacting to events. In the growing darkness, hundreds of warriors snatched up rifles and assegais and closed in on Wilson's party from behind, threatening to cut them off. With no reply coming from the wagons, and the previously stupefied Matabele now galvanized into action, Wilson shouted for his men to retreat. A heavy storm broke as the Rhodesians withdrew, and thunder and lightning shattered the night.[6] The event ended as bizarrely as it had begun, with the Matabele warriors, who just moments earlier had snapped out of their collective reverie and been ready to massacre the patrol, now just as suddenly more interested in finding shelter from the torrential rain storm. Wilson's rather surreal attempt at a coup de main had failed, but he could still have made it back over the river and re-joined the main body of the flying column.

It would seem that Wilson's thinking was clouded by the fact that three of his men were separated during the retreat from the king's wagons. So strong was the bond between Wilson and his Victoria Rangers (from whom his patrol had been picked) that the Major, perhaps understandably, felt he could not simply withdraw and leave them to a decidedly grizzly fate. Instead of pulling back over the river to re-join Forbes, Wilson had his men bed down for the night while he and Burnham searched for those who were missing. At the same time, about 21h00, Wilson—as we know—sent Captain Napier and two troopers back to the main force, bearing a message urging Forbes to join his patrol.

§

With the departure of Captain Napier and his party, we are beginning to run out of witnesses to the final act. As we know, Burnham, Ingram and Gooding would survive to tell a bit more of the tale, but Burnham was really the only one who wrote about the events at length, and many question the accuracy of his version. This seems a little unfair, but should still be borne in mind. The Matabele also gave verbal accounts after the war, but these were often contradictory and rather hazy–so all anyone can really do is use them to make a best guess at piecing together the most likely course of events.

Guided by Trooper Robertson and accompanied by Ingram (the American scout) Captain Borrow's troop arrived at Wilson's position in the early hours. Burnham claims that they initially assumed the whole column to have arrived when they heard men and horses approaching in the darkness, and it was a 'stunning moment'[7] when they realized that only Borrow's B-Troop of the Salisbury Horse had come. It is difficult to know why it should have been so stunning though: Borrow had brought his troop safely to them, so it is clear that the Matabele net had not yet closed on Wilson's patrol, and, despite the continuing heavy rain, the river had not yet risen to such a level as to be impassable. Wilson could even then have withdrawn back across the still-fordable Shangani–and most certainly should have, when he realized that Forbes had not come on with the whole flying column.

Instead, it would seem he and Borrow consulted on their next move and agreed that their best option was to mount another attempt to snatch Lobengula at first light. Burnham later told the court of inquiry:

> "Major Wilson asked what I thought of attacking the king's wagons and scherms. I was opposed to this plan without the Maxim but [Wilson] said if we did not attack we would be attacked in retreat, so we may as well have a go at them at once."[8]

Burnham claims that several other officers—including Captains Judd and Kirton—shared his concerns and also thought that taking the offensive was bound to end in tears.

If Burnham's claim about what Wilson said is accurate, this seems a very odd stance for the Major to have taken. As just mentioned, Borrow had managed to get his troop through, so it stands to reason that retreating back along the same path was still an option. Why Wilson would have assumed they would be attacked if they withdrew is not clear. Ingram, who had accompanied Borrow and survived the action, recalled not having seen or heard a single native on their march.[9] There can be little doubt that Wilson could have extracted his patrol had he withdrawn as soon as Borrow's troop arrived and while it was still dark. Even if Wilson did not wish to consider retreating, the next best option would have been to go firm where he was, and await the anticipated arrival of Forbes and the rest of the column.

Either way, by the time dawn was breaking, Wilson had indeed lost any chance of pulling back without a fight. The Matabele were thought to be encircling them and placing men between Wilson's reinforced, but increasingly beleaguered patrol and the now swollen river by that stage.

None of this seemed to bother the indomitable Major Wilson, though. We will never know why he made the decision he did, though it seems likely he feared Lobengula would once more escape if he did not act immediately. With the addition of Borrow's troop to the initial patrol, Wilson's command totalled 37 men[i] and, rather than hold their

---

i This number varies very slightly depending on which account one reads, but is based on those who came and went over the previous 12 hours–two of the initial party were sent back as their horses were lame; Captain Napier and two others returned with the message at 23h00, though one of these returned to Wilson to guide Borrow's group. Two of Borrow's troop became separated on their night march and returned to the main body without having made it to Wilson's position.

ground, they mounted up at first light on the 4th, determined to bring the war to a close. It was a very wet and grey morning, and many of Wilson's initial patrol were tired, hungry and soaked through after what must have been a very miserable night. They moved forward at a slow walk, partly to conserve the energy of the horses and partly so that they would not startle the Matabele they soon came into contact with. In a repeat of the previous evening, Wilson's patrol picked their way through the various Matabele scherms and encampments, this time just as the women-folk were lighting fires and starting to go about their business.

Just as they had the evening before, they approached the king's wagons without incident. The Matabele watched them with interest, but there was no hostility on either side. About 100 yards from the wagons, Wilson told his patrol to halt, and then urged his horse on a few more yards before calling out that 'the white men had not come to fight; all they wanted was to speak to the king'.[10]

It is worth noting that Wilson's patrol approached Lobengula's position—or, at least, where he is presumed to have been—without firing, and called upon him to surrender twice within a 12 hour period. We will return to the significance of this later. Wilson had been able to withdraw without serious incident the previous evening, but he pushed his luck too far on the morning of the 4th. While Wilson and his troopers waited anxiously for some sort of response from the wagons, the still of the morning was suddenly shattered by a hail of rifle fire. In an instant, the edge of the bush was alive with Matabele riflemen, moving and firing.

Wilson shouted for his men to dismount and return fire, killing or driving back those brave souls who ventured into the open. The previously calm and passive Matabele villagers that Wilson's men had ridden past just moments before, excitedly joined the ambush, charging forward to join the mayhem. Within seconds, two horses had been hit, and one trooper, young William Britton,[ii] had been shot in the face and horribly injured.

Wilson called a retreat, and the patrol remounted as best they could. It was more of a helter-skelter flight than a withdrawal, as more and more Matabele broke cover from all sides, surging forward to block the fleeing horsemen. After half a mile or so, Wilson reined in his breathless horse and called a halt next to an enormous ant hill; Burnham recalled it being '20ft high–enough to screen our horses'.[11] Here, Wilson ordered his men to dismount and shelter the precious horses. Clambering onto the ant hill, he bellowed orders for his men to shake out and get ready. Perhaps thinking that the white men were

ii Trooper William Henry Britton (1870–1893), B-Troop, Salisbury Horse. Originally from Halstead in Essex, England.

already as good as dead, their pursuers enthusiastically followed up, sprinting into the open without a care. When the Matabele were 200 yards away, Wilson gave the order to fire. The effect was dramatic. The troopers opened up on their would-be killers, bowling them over, knocking them down and forcing the rest to run for cover.

It was a temporary reprieve though. More warriors moved quickly through the bush, unseen by the troopers until they were level with the ant hill, and able to pour fire into the position at point blank range. Within a moment, five more horses had been shot down and three men were wounded. Wilson had no choice but to pull back again. Trooper Gooding, who was one of the survivors, described how they mounted up and pulled back once more, 'this time, two horses carrying double'.[12] It was at this point, it would appear, that Wilson decided to try and send a galloper back to Forbes to report his predicament and summon assistance.

Based, presumably, on what the three survivors told him, Forbes reported:

'Major Wilson asked Burnham if he thought he could get through to me and he expressed himself ready to try if Major Wilson gave him a man to accompany him. Captain Borrow told Gooding, who was about the best mounted of his party to go with him, and Ingram, Burnham's mate, also asked to go, and the three started off. The three gallopers burst through some Matabele, turning away to avoid an attack and hit upon the by-then impassable river.

Burnham recalled, '…the river was a swift yellow torrent 200 yards wide with floating grass in its swirling eddies…it had been a stream the night before.'[13]

Galloping another one-and-a-half miles along the river bank, they eventually found a spot where they could swim their horses across.[14]

§

With the departure of Burnham's group—who as we know, made it back to Forbes just as he was extracting the rest of the patrol from the attack that morning—we have lost our last western witnesses to the final act.

Judging from Matabele verbal accounts (many of which were taken some time later, and several of which are a little contradictory) it would seem that the rest of Wilson's patrol was soon cut off. Realizing that his retreat had been blocked, Wilson found a small clearing in the bush and elected to make his last stand. There was no cover but at least the grass was short and the troopers would have clear fields of fire. The horses were doomed in any case, so they were formed into a rough circle and made to lie down, creating an impromptu laager. Wilson's men crouched behind their doomed steeds and prepared to sell their lives dearly.[15]

They soon came under fire from Matabele riflemen hiding in the bush and the fight raged on for some time. Unwilling to wait, many of the braver or more reckless warriors charged into the open, only to be blasted down in detail.[16] One induna recalled:

> 'We surrounded them and started to fight. They got off their horses and fired at us over them. All the horses were killed, and then the white men, those of them that were left, lay down behind the dead horses, and fired at us. After many of the white men were killed, the few that were left, all of whom were wounded, lay on their backs, and held their rifles between their feet and fired. After a little, the firing stopped, and we knew the cartridges were finished. We then rushed up and assegaied the remainder, who covered their eyes with their hands. We lost many more than the number of white men, for they were men indeed, and fought us for many hours.'[17]

Wilson's now 34-strong patrol was set upon by the remains of five impis, the Imbezu, Ingubu, Insukameni, Inyamandhlovu and Ihatli– perhaps as many as two thousand warriors in all. Their position utterly hopeless, Wilson's men still fought like tigers, pulling out their revolvers when they ran out of Martini Henry ammunition. These were no ordinary men: they were brave, hardy and skilful. Many had been 1890 pioneers and there were a disproportionate number of officers and NCOs. They were also fiercely loyal to Wilson; everyone knew how to shoot and all were determined to make every bullet count and to die hard.

Other Matabele accounts record:

> 'And so died every one; not one escaped to tell how all had met their end–without a cry for mercy or thought of surrender, they fought, not like men, but spirits.'[18]

No two such accounts agree on how long the fighting lasted, but it would seem that by mid-morning, Wilson's men—out of ammunition and with all their horses killed—were finally swamped by the sheer weight of numbers. The Matabele — themselves no strangers to courage—were impressed by the bravery of the patrol, later stating:

> '...they could not understand why all should have stayed, as some of them could have escaped, had they tried. But they had not tried

because some of their horses had been killed, and those who had horses resolved not to desert their comrades in distress. So they stood there and fought the thing out.'[19]

By all accounts, the imposing Major Wilson was one of the last to die. Near the end, with just a few men left, Matabele witnesses claimed the troopers gave three cheers and then belted out a plucky and defiant rendition of 'God Save the Queen':

'Six only left. Men or gods. Fell asinging as though their breasts were bursting with a wondrous joy. I knew not meaning of song, but some amongst us knew it for the song of the last things of all–song of triumph which tells of the glories of the great white mother who rules the impis of the English.'[20]

It was a fitting final show of defiance by the beleaguered troopers. Shortly thereafter, however, they were swamped and the last few were killed. The 34 men of, what became immortalized as 'The Shangani Patrol', had killed between 300 and 400 of their enemy.[21] A full list of the officers and men who died can be found in Appendix 4.

§

Over on the southern bank of the Shangani River, Forbes was obviously unaware of the details, but having heard the sounds of battle and listened to what Burnham's party had to say, he must have feared the worst. Forbes had his men dig in on the afternoon of the 4th and they also remained in place throughout 5 December, desperately hoping to hear something from Wilson's party. Two gallopers, Ingram and Lynch, were sent off to Bulawayo on the evening of the 4th, riding out under the cover of a 'terrific thunder storm' to try and get word to Dr Jameson. Forbes' message to the Doctor explained what had happened, and stated that he was going to retreat down the Shangani River with the remains of the flying column. He also asked Jameson to send ammunition, food and medical support.[22]

The fact that Ingram was prepared to undertake such a hazardous mission is noteworthy. Some later claimed—without much evidence—that he, Burnham and young Gooding were not sent back by Wilson at all, but actually deserted their comrades and fled. This rather unpleasant rumour appears to have come from a third-hand account of a death-bed confession allegedly made by Gooding.[23]

Though we can never be 100% sure either way, Robert Cary, who wrote, probably the most authoritative account of the Shangani

Chronology of events - The Allan Wilson Patrol

On 12th November 1893 Dr Leander Starr Jameson despatched Major Patrick Forbes with a column to pursue and capture Lobengula, the last Matabele King. Lobengula had torched his kraal at Gubulawayo and fled north, away from advancing troops of the BSA Company and Raaf's British Bechuanaland Police. The king, travelling in a wagon, was escorted by several thousand warriors of the Ingubo, Inshlati and Isiziba regiments under the chief induna, Miaan.

1 On 3rd December Forbes column reaches the Shangani River. It is learned that Lobengula has already crossed to the north bank and is not far away.

2 Forbes sends Major Allan Wilson and 20 men, including scouts Burnham and Ingram, across the river to find the exact position. They make camp near a place called *pupu*.

3 At last light Wilsons scouts locate Lobengulas wagons and report back. Captain Napier is sent back to Forbes with a request for reinforcements and a Maxim gun. Because the river is now in flood, only Capt Barrow and 20 men arrive just before dawn.

4 At dawn Wilson advances on the camp and is ambushed by a vastly superior force. Wilson withdraws 600 metres and faces determined frontal attacks from Lobengula's camp.

5 A large group of Ndebele circle the patrols right flank, cutting them off from the river and their likely direction of retreat.

6 At dawn Wilson is attacked again and again as they retreat, and, after having four members of the BBP wounded and 17 horses killed, he is forced to withdraw towards their original night camp at *pupu*. They form a hollow square. Wilson sends Burnham, Ingram and trooper Gooding back to Forbes to demand immediate reinforcements.

7 Finally, Wilson can retreat no more, and forms a laager using the remaining horses as cover. After facing impossible odds, Wilsons patrol are overrun and all are killed.

Patrol's Last Stand, dismissed the possibility, pointing out the consistencies between the accounts given by Burnham, Ingram and Gooding;

> 'It is almost inconceivable that the three men together concocted, and resolutely maintained, an identical 'cover story'; one may therefore conclude that Burnham, although guilty as usual of exaggerating his own share of glory, was not lying when he reported that it was on Wilson's orders that he rode away from the rest of the patrol.'[24]

As well as the consistency of their accounts, one should also bear in mind the valour displayed by Burnham and Ingram, in particular,

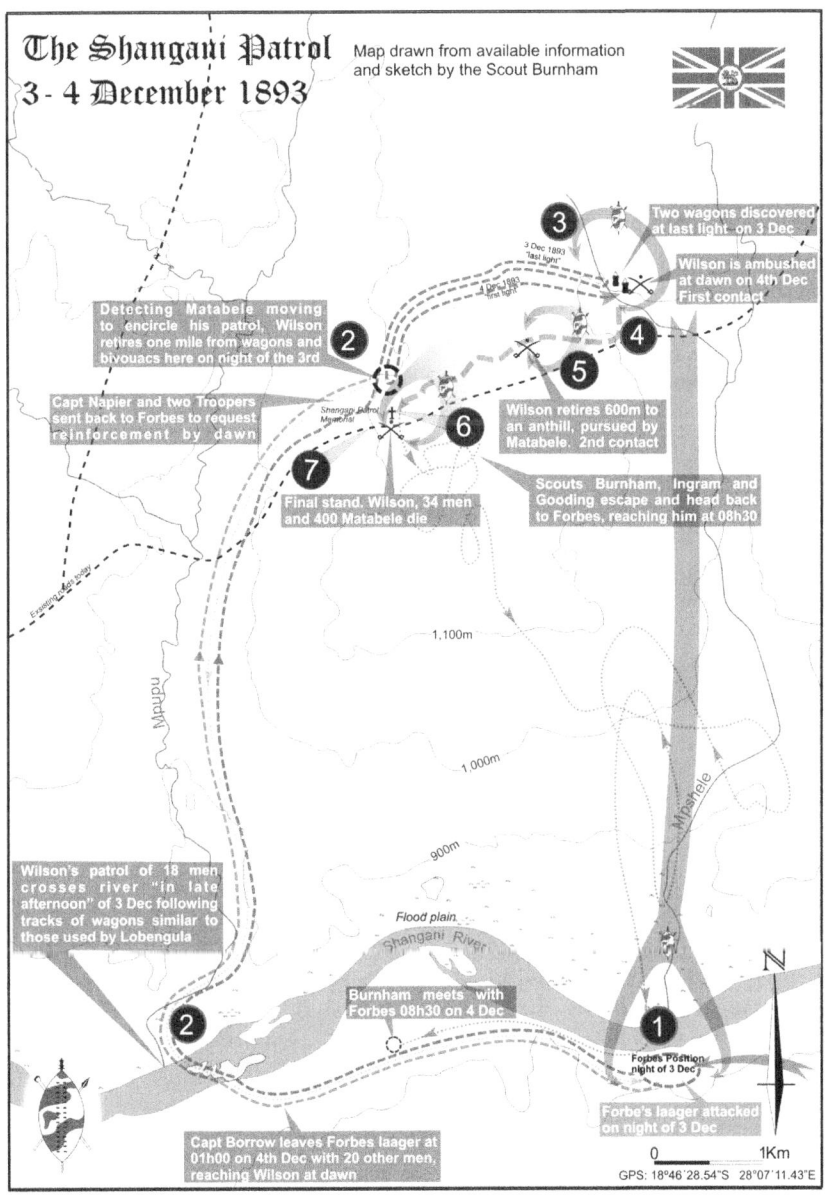

The Shangani Patrol 3 - 4 December 1893

Map drawn from available information and sketch by the Scout Burnham

3 Two wagons discovered at last light on 3 Dec

Wilson is ambushed at dawn on 4th Dec First contact

2 Detecting Matabele moving to encircle his patrol, Wilson retires one mile from wagons and bivouacs here on night of the 3rd

Capt Napier and two Troopers sent back to Forbes to request reinforcement by dawn

4

5 Wilson retires 600m to an anthill, pursued by Matabele. 2nd contact

6

7 Final stand. Wilson, 34 men and 400 Matabele die

Scouts Burnham, Ingram and Gooding escape and head back to Forbes, reaching him at 08h30

1,100m

1,000m

900m

Wilson's patrol of 18 men crosses river "in late afternoon" of 3 Dec following tracks of wagons similar to those used by Lobengula

Flood plain

Shangani River

Burnham meets with Forbes 08h30 on 4 Dec

2

1 Forbes Position night of 3 Dec

Forbe's laager attacked on night of 3 Dec

Capt Borrow leaves Forbes laager at 01h00 on 4th Dec with 20 other men, reaching Wilson at dawn

0   1Km

GPS: 18°46'28.54"S 28°07'11.43"E

thereafter. Ingram's ride to Bulawayo to deliver the message was an extraordinarily courageous thing to have done,[iii] while Burnham fought with distinction, both in the Matabele Rebellion of 1896 (as we shall discuss later) and the Boer War. Indeed, such was Burnham's reputation that, early in the Boer War, Lord Roberts summoned him from Canada to serve as his chief of scouts in South Africa. Burnham spent much of 1900 gathering information and blowing up railway lines deep inside Boer territory. He was wounded twice, escaped twice, won a DSO, was promoted to Major, received letters of commendation from Baden-Powell, Rhodes, and Field Marshal Roberts[iv] and, on his return to London, was invited to dine with Queen Victoria in recognition of his service in South Africa. None of this gives anyone cause or justification to even start questioning the man's honour and valour.

On the 6th, Forbes decided that he had no choice but to give up on Wilson's party and begin the long trudge back to Bulawayo. The men who took part can be forgiven for thinking that the retreat would end up like that from Kabul in 1847:

> 'The column was in a parlous state. The horses could do little more than walk and the men were in not much better condition. Very wet weather, only horseflesh for food, and the constant strain were beginning to tell on everyone except Major Forbes.'[25]

Worse still was the shortage of ammunition: the flying column had not had much to begin with, and had fired off much of that on the morning of the 4th. The constant Matabele sniping and attempts to drive off the horses had to be answered sparingly as the troopers desperately tried to husband their rounds.

Though lucky to be helped by friendly villagers along the way, the column was again attacked on the 8th but the Matabele were driven off. On the 9th, the Matabele had another go:

> 'The column was resting for a short spell in some kopjes divided by a deep spruit in which the horses were grazing. Suddenly one of the horses made a most unusual sound, and a man who had been brought up amongst horses knew there was something

---

iii Ingram and Lynch had been given the best two horses available—the splendidly named 'Brandy' and 'Soda'—but even these indomitable steeds were so emaciated that they could only proceed at a walk. When tracks indicated that around 15 Matabele had been sent after them, everyone feared the very worst.

iv Writing in 1900, Lord Roberts declared, 'I take this opportunity of thanking you for the valuable services you have rendered since you joined my headquarters at Paardeberg last February. I doubt if any other man in the force could have successfully carried out the thrilling enterprises in demanding as they did the training of a lifetime, combined with exceptional courage, caution, and powers of endurance.'

wrong. He went over to the edge of the deep spruit and found the Matabele swarming up on top of the column. It seemed that one of the enemy had assegaied a horse and the noise it made caused this man to go and see what was wrong, and he gave the alarm. This firing of his revolver caused everyone to jump up and Forbes at once gave the order to man the kopjes. It was a stiff fight while it lasted but the Matabele were soon driven off.'[26]

Torrential rain made the retreat all the more unpleasant and that evening, the men huddled in what shelter they could find. The wounded suffered the worst, lying in water which was up to the horses' knees, but 'both then and right through they were marvellously plucky'.[27] Their pursuers were close enough taunt them, claiming that they had already '…finished off one white impi and tomorrow would finish us off' too. Forbes was alive to this, however, and word was quietly passed around that they would secretly withdraw at 21h00 that evening. The weak or sick horses were left standing, the two Maxim gun carriages were abandoned, and the guns themselves were carried off in blankets in the darkness. The men each took a blanket or cloak, and the rest of the clothes were left behind, bundled up to give the impression that the position was still manned. The hardest act must have been killing the dogs, lest their barking betray the withdrawal:

> 'We were now obliged to destroy seven of our faithful dogs, who had followed us so loyally through storm and flood and war into this wilderness of trouble. They were knocked on the head with choppers and dispatched without sound. To kill such friends is one of the most trying ordeals a soldier can experience. But there was only one way to escape from the trap in which we were caught, and that would have been closed for ever had a single yelp or bark reached the ears of the alert enemy enclosing us.'[28]

It was an audacious and cunning ploy, but it could have been devastating had the Matabele realized what was happening and caught the column strung out on the move:

> 'What a night's march that was. Not a sound was made. The few prisoners we had who carried the boxes of reserve ammunition for the Maxims were told that if they uttered a sound they would be promptly assegaied and a man was told off for this job if necessary, but no sound was uttered by anyone and even the horses seemed to scent the danger and trod through the kopjes as it they understood… by dawn, we were out of the difficult country, but what a haggard and worn-out crew the column now looked.

Ragged and bootless they had been for some time and their only
rations were about two pounds of horse flesh per day per man,
but that dawn, all looked particularly woebegone.
The Matabele were a long time in discovering that our laager was
empty. It seems that they attacked it at dawn. That the fire was
not returned they thought was a trick. At last some of the more
venturesome crawled close enough to see how they had been
deceived.'[29]

The ruse was successful, but the Matabele didn't take long to catch
up to the retreating column, and soon attacked them again. Forbes'
men were in better country by then, however, and broke up the attack
without loss.

Whatever command structure issues there may have been,
Commandant Raaff proved his worth on that sorry retreat, and his
skill and experience was recognized and appreciated by all. Indeed,
Burnham even claimed that the safety of the column was increasingly
due to Raaff's judgement and reckoned the diminutive Afrikaner to be,
'…the most experienced Kaffir fighter in Rhodesia at that time. Most
Boers are large men, but Raaff did not weigh more than 120 pounds. It
was jokingly said of him that he had engaged in a Kaffir fight for every
pound of his weight.'[30]

Marching 18 hours out of every 24, the bedraggled, exhausted and
hungry men limped along the Shangani, the enemy shadowing and
harrying them every step of the way. Another attack was driven off
on the 12th, but in so doing, the column used up even more of their
precious ammunition supply. On the 14th, however:

'…two white men suddenly appeared across the vlei at the edge
of which we had halted. How the column cheered and yelled, for
this meant that at length we were in touch with the long-looked-
for relief. The two men were Selous and Acutt who had ridden out
from their column to see if they could get any news of us, for we
had been lost so long that the gravest fears were entertained for
our safety. The relief column was barely three miles away, with
them being, among others, Mr Rhodes and Dr Jameson. How light-
heartedly all the old cripples covered those three miles, arriving
not very long after dark guided by rockets that were sent up at
Selous' request. There we found ready for us tons of bully beef,
cookies, coffee with sugar in it, and all that we could want for.'[31]

As soon as Ingram and Lynch had arrived in Bulawayo, Dr Jameson
had formed all the available men into a relief column and personally
led it up the Shangani to meet the retreating patrol. One of those in

the relief force, our friend Jack Carruthers, recalled meeting Forbes' column on the evening of the 14th:

'I hardly knew my few surviving friends they were so worn and unkept. Most of us gave up our mounts, everybody finding their way back to Inyati, various kit lying discarded all along the road... It was a sorry disorderly column that found its way back to Bulawayo.'[32]

Another who served in the relief force was moved by the condition of the various stretcher cases and walking wounded who had been brought safely out:

'Several men of Forbes's party had been killed or wounded during the retreat, and Pike had been carried with a shattered arm over 100 miles. Dr Jameson took the arm off at the shoulder as soon as we got back to Inyati. It was an operation under very difficult conditions and it was a wonder that Pike survived. It also showed the great surgical skill of 'Dr Jim'.'[33]

Yet another remembered the distinctly cool reception with which Major Forbes was greeted:

'Selous brought Major Forbes–he was the first to arrive. Dr Jameson and Rhodes shook hands with him, but Rhodes walked away from Forbes and the Doctor spoke to Forbes for some time. I think no one knows what he said. Was he accused of, or was he blamed that Wilson's party lost their lives? But when Commandant Raaff and his men came, three hearty cheers went up for Raaff. This must have been very humiliating for Forbes–there were no cheers for him. Did he [Forbes] not also go through all the dangers, hardships, hunger etc.? He was also in rags. I for my part felt very sorry for him.'[34]

§

Indeed, and though Forbes had brought the rest of the patrol safely back to Bulawayo, the politics were only just beginning. Jameson seemed determined to hang Forbes out to dry and went so far as to tell Lt. Col. Goold-Adams that he wanted an inquiry into the loss of Wilson's patrol in order 'to show the friends and relatives of the poor fellows killed that some steps were being taken at once to ascertain where anyone was to blame for their deaths'.[35]

With Goold-Adams presiding, the court of inquiry assembled in Bulawayo on 20 December 1893 and began hearing evidence from everyone involved. This process was not helped, however, by the ailing Commandant Raaff's condition, which worsened on the 24th. With remarkable determination to tell his side of the story, he had been dictating his version of events from his death bed but had only got as far as 3 December when he croaked on the 26th. Another key witness, Captain Lendy, died on around 15 January 1894,[v] but not before testifying that Forbes had put too much faith in things he was told by natives and, '...there is no doubt that most of the men looked to Raaff as the leader of the retreat'.[36]

Though no official report was ever issued by the court, the basic thrust of the procedure was to criticize Forbes' leadership, and to find that he had underestimated his enemy. He was found to have proceeded with insufficient ammunition and his decision to split his force on the night of the 3rd was roundly condemned. Sir Henry Loch, perhaps a little unfairly, condemned the fighting retreat down the Shangani as having 'degenerated into a complete rout'.[37]

The high commissioner did, however, quash Jameson's plan to make the court's judgement public while keeping the evidence by which it came to this conclusion secret. Sir Henry was having none of this and said it was an impossible stance to adopt. He informed Jameson that the British South Africa Company could deal with its officers (including Forbes) while he would deal with the imperial officers of the BBP if needed. Due mainly to this ruling, many of the details of the loss of the Shangani Patrol remain cloaked in a shroud of mystery.[38]

§

Either way, Lobengula would never be caught, and is thought to have died, either on the 22nd or 23rd of January 1894, apparently from fever. He was only about 30 miles south of the Zambezi and (he must have hoped) safety.[39] With the king's death, the First Matabele War fizzled out, rather than ending conclusively, though one last piece of intrigue would still emerge from it.

In the month during which Lobengula died, rumours began to spread in Bulawayo, about the king having sent some messengers back towards Forbes' column with a bag of gold sovereigns and a message stating that he realized he was beaten and wanted to talk peace. Furthermore, the messengers returned, claiming they had indeed passed on the dispatch and delivered the gold–so why had Forbes not mentioned this? No one was terribly convinced by these tales at first: surely the most logical explanation was that Lobengula's own

v Tragically for their family, Lendy's brother, Captain Edward Lendy, DSO had been killed in action in West Africa just three weeks earlier. He is buried in Sierra Leone.

messengers must have stashed the gold somewhere and then returned to the king, informing him that they had passed on his message.[40]

A few weeks later, however, Dr Jameson, received a letter from James Dawson, the trader we last met at the killing of the two Matabele envoys at Tati. Dawson had set off from Bulawayo some weeks previously, intending to bury the remains of Wilson's patrol and track Lobengula down. After a time, and satisfied that the king had died, Dawson sent his long letter south in the hand of a runner.

Along with confirmation of Lobengula's death, the letter contained the following passage:

'With regard to the suspicion that some of the men had received money, I am told that Petcham (who has gone in) with Sehuluhulu and another man, were sent by Lobengula with £1,000 to give to the man in command of the white men and to ask him to stop that they might talk… they met two men who appeared to hear what they had to say: took the money and told them to go back, it was alright, they would tell the white induna.'[41]

Jameson quickly showed this to Goold-Adams and, with remarkable alacrity, focus quickly turned to a pair of Bechuanaland Border Police men, William Charles Daniel and James Wilson. The evidence against these two was basically that they had bought up farm rights for £70, had a propensity to lag behind the column on the march, and 'were known to have gold in their possession'.[42] Amazingly, this was deemed sufficient to have them arrested. Perhaps still smarting from his own part in having sent off the unsuccessful patrol rather than leading it, Jameson seems to have become obsessed with these two, saying that morally, they had murdered Wilson's party and Lobengula.[43] It was suggested that they should face a general court-martial for 'imperilling a portion of HM Forces'–a charge which carried the death penalty.

Instead, they were charged with theft of £1,000 sterling by embezzlement 'by which act the lives of the men on Major Forbes' Column were endangered whilst on the Shangani River in December 1893, and 33 men of Major Wilson's patrol ultimately lost their lives on December 4th, 1893, on or near the Shangani River'.[44]

Both men pleaded 'not guilty' and several of their comrades in the BBP spoke in their defence, but they had really had no chance from the outset. It was a rather long and confused case which smacked of kangaroo court rather than crown court–especially when one of the presiding officers, Captain Heyman openly declared he would 'hang the men if he could'. Sure enough, both were found guilty and sent down for 14 years imprisonment with hard labour. In addition, all their property in Matabeleland was confiscated.[45] When word of the sentence reached Cape Town, the severity of it caused alarm, as the court had no right to impose such a lengthy jail term and the whole affair came under greater scrutiny. Eventually, in 1896, after the men had served two years and two months, their convictions were quashed on five counts:

1.   there was no evidence, or not sufficient evidence, against the prisoner James Wilson[vi] to justify his conviction
2.   the magistrate awarded a greater punishment than the constitution of his court permitted
3.   the magistrate failed to forward the records of the case to the registrar of the court of the Chief Magistrate of Mashonaland or of the High Court of Matabeleland, as required by Section 47 of Act No.20 of 1856
4.   illegal or incompetent evidence was admitted at the trial
5.   the proceedings before the resident magistrate at Bulawayo were otherwise wholly irregular and contrary to law

The two men were thus released and disappeared from history. Many contemporary accounts take the view that they were crooks who 'got away with it,' but this seems a little unfair and contrary to the 'innocent until proven guilty' principal–however 'unlovely' they might appear to have been, their convictions were over-turned for a range of reasons, and so we must accept this.

Of more interest, is whether or not, if they did indeed steal the money, this had any impact on Major Wilson's patrol being massacred: was there any reason to think that they were in any way 'moral murderers' rather than just common thieves?

It is difficult to believe that things would have been any different, even if the money and the message had found their way to Major Forbes. As we know, Lobengula had previously told Jameson he was coming in, but took advantage of this ploy to get his wagons moving north. It is also worth recalling, as we noted earlier, that when Wilson's small patrol approached the king's wagons, on the evening of the 3rd and again on the morning of the 4th, they did so without firing, and called for Lobengula to surrender on both occasions. Had the money and the message reached Forbes, he could surely have been expected to send out a small patrol like Wilson's to bring the king in. And if Lobengula was indeed keen to give himself up, why did he not turn himself in when Wilson arrived saying that he wanted to talk? Instead, the Matabele response, when Wilson tried this again the following morning, was to ambush the small party of horsemen.

---

vi   No mention was made of William Daniel, but he would also be released for the same reasons.

With this in mind, it is difficult to believe that Lobengula ever had any intention of turning himself in. If the gold and the message were indeed sent, this seems likely just to have been another time-wasting ploy to allow the king to cross the Zambezi to, supposedly, safety. Whatever else Wilson and Daniel were, and whether or not they pocketed the cash, they cannot reasonably be considered the 'moral murderers' of Wilson's Shangani Patrol.

End Notes
[1] The Graphic, London, 10 March 1894
[2] Baxter, Rhodesia: Last Outpost of the British Empire, 1890-1980, p.96
[3] The Graphic, London, 10 March 1894
[4] Cary, A Time to Die, p.63
[5] Burnham, Scouting on Two Continents, p.95
[6] Cary, A Time to Die, p.66
[7] Westminster Gazette, 7th January 1895
[8] Cary, A Time to Die, p.85
[9] Cary, A Time to Die, p.87
[10] Cary, A Time to Die, p.89
[11] Burnham, Scouting on Two Continents, p.98
[12] O'Reilly, Pursuit of the King, p.71
[13] Burnham, Scouting on Two Continents, p.187
[14] O'Reilly, Pursuit of the King, p.72
[15] Cary, A Time to Die, p.104
[16] Cary, A Time to Die, p.105
[17] Keppel-Jones, Rhodes and Rhodesia, p.282
[18] O'Reilly, Pursuit of the King, p.108
[19] O'Reilly, Pursuit of the King, p.91
[20] O'Reilly, Pursuit of the King, p.94
[21] O'Reilly, Pursuit of the King, p.100
[22] Jones, Rhodesian Genesis, p.98
[23] O'Reilly, Pursuit of the King, p.77
[24] Cary, A Time to Die, p.103
[25] Jones, Rhodesian Genesis, p.99
[26] Jones, Rhodesian Genesis, p.100
[27] O'Reilly, Pursuit of the King, p.119
[28] Burnham, Scouting on Two Continents, p.103
[29] Jones, Rhodesian Genesis, p.101
[30] Burnham, Scouting on Two Continents, p.103
[31] Jones, Rhodesian Genesis, p.102
[32] O'Reilly, Pursuit of the King, p.124
[33] Jones, Rhodesian Genesis, p.104
[34] Jones, Rhodesian Genesis, p.103
[35] Glass, The Matabele War, p.230
[36] O'Reilly, Pursuit of the King, p.147
[37] Glass, The Matabele War, p.232
[38] Glass, The Matabele War, p.233
[39] Glass, The Matabele War, p.238
[40] Cary, A Time to Die, p.150
[41] Cary, A Time to Die, p.151
[42] Keppel-Jones, Rhodes and Rhodesia, p.279
[43] Cary, A Time to Die, p.152
[44] Cary, A Time to Die, p.154
[45] Glass, The Matabele War, p.255

'Although treated with great consideration by the government;
although no taxes were levied, and although every precaution was
taken to prevent harassing and unnecessary interference by the white
settlers; the fact remained that a warlike and hitherto unconquered
people were daily reminded, that they, the former lords of the earth,
were now expected to wear the livery of inferiority, and to perform
industrial duties which formerly they had exacted from their slaves.'[1]

'We travelled, unarmed and unconcerned, by night as well as by
day, through villages where five months later the Kaffirs rose and
murdered every European within reach.'[2]

– James Bryce, a 'scholar-statesman', describes the trip he
and his wife made through Matabeleland in late 1895

Chapter 11
Drawing Breath

Despite the way it rather fizzled out, the 1893 campaign ended in victory for the company. Lobengula's power had been broken and the spectre of murderous Matabele raids into Mashonaland was no more. Just as the Second World War is considered to have been the direct result of the First, however, so the 1893 Matabele War planted the seeds for the rebellion that flared up just three years later. Many identify the failure of the Jameson Raid as the direct reason for the rebellion, but in reality, there was no one single cause and the significance of the raid is perhaps overblown by many. No nation—and especially not a warlike people like the Matabele—can be expected to submit to conquest with a smile, and between 1893 and 1896, a variety of poor decisions, misunderstandings, cock-ups and acts of God combined to turn Matabeleland into a powder keg.

§

As early as 12 November 1893, Sir Henry Loch confirmed in a telegram, that he had decided against the idea of taking Lobengula's dominions under the imperial wing temporarily. Due to the chartered company's 'great success', Sir Henry concluded that there was no reason to impose imperial control over the newly conquered territory, and instead, proposed that Matabeleland and Mashonaland be governed as one country under the administration of the company with safeguards in place for the protection of native and imperial interests.[3] So it was that Matabeleland was added to Mashonaland, the two thus forming the company territory of Rhodesia under the 'common sense' rule of Dr Jameson. This is not to say that the dreaded 'imperial factor' would not see fit to meddle in Rhodes' personal fiefdom though, or that this interference would not play a significant part in sparking the 1896 rebellion as we shall soon see.

Development in the newly acquired region was rapid: the Doctor personally planned a new Bulawayo, famously decreeing that the streets should be wide enough to turn 16-span of oxen around. Jameson remained in Bulawayo until May 1894, supervising the building of three forts, the establishment of a postal service and the building of roads. A hospital and other buildings were quickly thrown up, legal practices were established, and a pair of rival newspapers were soon at loggerheads. By the time the Doctor returned to Salisbury, over

800 farms and almost 6,000 mining claims[4] had been pegged out and registered by enthusiastic settlers.

The company also dealt with the thorny issue of the vast number of captured cattle swiftly. Jameson had always said that only the king's cattle were to be considered 'loot' and that privately owned herds should not be impacted. The problem lay in defining which was which.

In the (admittedly, not unbiased, though not entirely unreasonable) view of the company, virtually every cow in Matabeleland had belonged to Lobengula, many of them having been looted from his neighbours in various raids and wars. Assuming that no one else held significant numbers of cattle, it made sense for the company to award itself, say, two-thirds of the total herd, and hand out one third to be owned outright by individuals, believing that this would be viewed very positively by all concerned.

Many Matabele actually did rather well out of the company's confiscation of Lobengula's personal herd. Even an important induna might only have owned a dozen cattle before the 1893 war, while the rest of 'his herd' would actually have belonged to the king. Not surprisingly, many indunas claimed large numbers of Lobengula's cattle, thereby vastly increasing their herds. What was more, the company's portion of Lobengula's herd was also assigned according to the needs of various kraals, meaning that the Matabele now simply tended these cows for the company rather than for Lobengula, and they were able to use the milk as they wished.[5] On the face of it, this all seemed rather equitable, so it is unsurprising that the land commission broadly accepted the company's position on the subject. Sir Henry Loch, the high commissioner also saw things in a similar way. The colonial office however, sounded a note of caution, with the Marquess of Ripon commenting, '...experience in former wars, especially in Zululand, shows that distinction between King's cattle and people's cattle is fallacious, in all cattle being in some sense King's...' before going on to insist that 'ample cattle for their requirements should be secured to the Matabele'.

In the event, some 90,000 cattle[i] were branded with the BSAC mark and registered as belonging to the company but left in native hands. From time to time some of these would be called in for slaughter, sale, or re-distribution. Later, when it was believed that some 70,000 were still being held by natives, the company decided to take ownership of about another 28,000 and to confirm the absolute possession of the rest to Lobengula's former subjects.

F.C. Selous, who was no admirer of the Matabele, took a slightly different view, claiming that 'almost every man of standing

---

i It is worth noting that Sir Henry Loch estimated Lobengula's herd at somewhere over 200,000.

in Matabeleland had been a cattle-owner, some of the chief indunas possessing large herds of private cattle'. It was suggested, however, that he too had misunderstood the reality of the situation and blurred the distinction between 'royal' and 'private' cattle.[6]

Aside from the fact that privately owned cattle were not included in the 'loot, it should also be remembered that the king had pillaged his vast herds in the first place—so the reader should be wary of wasting too much sympathy on the confiscation of these cattle by the company.

There was definitely plenty of skulduggery and even something of a feeding frenzy as everyone tried to grab a piece of the pie. Groups of Mashona crossed into Matabeleland and seized cattle they claimed to have been stolen while some white settlers seem to have considered any cattle they came across theirs for the grabbing. All in all, it got a great deal of attention and no doubt ruffled some feathers, but the confiscation of the 'loot' cannot reasonably be thought of as the primary reason for widespread dissatisfaction and simmering resentment among the Matabele.

§

A more serious issue was the sheer number of whites who had settled in Matabeleland, (especially in the area around Bulawayo) so soon after the war. Many of these had taken opportunities to peg out large farms and by 1895, there were well over 1,000 such ranches, covering an area of over 10,000 square miles. This area, which had the best soil and the best climate, had been prized by the Matabele, and was their nation's 'heartland'—which obviously led to serious complications. That is not to say, however, that the Matabele were driven from this area en masse–indeed, many farmers viewed the 'resident natives' as a valuable source of labour. There were other ranchers, however, who took a dim view of the Matabele's reluctance to work 'year in and year out' and thus moved them on.[7]

This was very different to the situation in Mashonaland where there had been virtually no competition for land. The lives of huge numbers of Shona carried on without any real interruption after the arrival of company rule, since relatively few of the Mashonaland settlers decided to make a go of farming.[ii] Indeed, even by 1896, many Shona had still had no contact with white men at all:

'...with no access to markets, and with the dream of golden riches not yet faded, the settlers [of Mashonaland] were too busy on their mining claims to bother about farming.'[8]

---

ii   One exception was the District of Melsetter which had more white settlers than the whole of northern Mashonaland.

The arrival of white settlers and the termination of Lobengula's tyrannical power were overwhelmingly positive for the vast majority of Mashona. Edward Knight, writing for The Times in 1894 explained:

'Up to this year, the progress in Mashonaland has been kept back by the perpetual menace of the Matabele raids. Capitalists hesitated to invest in so dangerous a land; it appeared a reckless venture to send valuable mining plants to the rich reefs on the ever-disturbed border. In cases where men attempted to develop their properties and put up batteries, repeated Matabele scares would interrupt all work for weeks or months at a time, the native labourers deserting en masse to take refuge in their mountain strongholds.

But these harassing conditions exist no longer, and there are already many signs to show that the Matabele war has produced an excellent effect in Mashonaland. While I was at Fort Salisbury several deputations of headmen came in from all parts of the country to thank Captain Duncan, as acting administrator, for all the blessings which the chartered company's victories had brought to their people... They fully realize that for the future they will be able to accumulate property and enjoy a prosperity quite unknown to them before. While riding from Bulawayo to Salisbury I crossed the belt of neutral country which lies between the Matabele and the Mashonas. The former do not occupy it, and the Mashonas, before the war, were afraid to venture so near their formidable neighbours. The region was therefore left desolate, despite its rich pastures; but now I met several families of Mashonas, who, no longer fearful of Matabele raids, were migrating to this favoured portion of the High Veldt. Dr Jameson, who was with me, conversed with some of these people, approved of their enterprise, and urged them to advise their friends to follow their example.'[9]

Despite the modern politically correct take on matters, many Matabele were actually far better off with Lobengula out of the picture too. As the likes of Man-yéze and the villagers who assisted Forbes' retreating column illustrate, Lobengula had been a despot who reigned over a divided and fractured land, and many of his subjects had been kept in check by sheer terror, not bonds of loyalty. Many 'Matabele' were not Matabele at all, but captured slaves and their descendants, or members of other tribes who had been 'assimilated' and dragged into the Matabele nation whether they liked it or not.

Not surprisingly, many of Lobengula's indunas quickly appreciated the law and order the company brought, and embraced it enthusiastically. In fact, a delegation of eight senior Matabele chiefs met with Jameson shortly after the war and asked him to station a white policeman in each of their districts so as to strengthen their authority and arbitrate their disputes.[10]

For his part, Jameson was utterly determined to replace Lobengula's savage chaos with the rule of law. Writing in 1899, he remembered:

'...an important part of my work... was to teach the native indunas the change in the law, which was considered necessary in substituting the chartered company's rule for that of Lobengula. This change consisted mainly in the much more serious view we took of the prevalent crimes of rape, murder, and witchcraft leading to murder... As far as possible, the natives were to remain under their own tribal law; but the white man's laws for the protection of life and property, and also for the protection of the women from rape, were to be strictly enforced.'[11]

Jameson was as good as his word: the company's police were employed in a tireless effort to suppress the previously wide-spread practice of witchcraft; a huge benefit to the average Matabele–though whether or not they realized this is another issue. Either way, and thanks entirely to the company, they no longer lived in fear of being 'smelled-out', a fear which had made them deeply reluctant to work harder or acquire more cattle than their fellows lest this draw the attentions of jealous relatives or neighbours who might tip the witch doctors off. Tall Poppy Syndrome, or the philosophy of 'the nail that sticks out gets hammered down' had been taken to an extreme and existing under such terror utterly stagnated development and progress. The stamping out of such medieval barbarism was a great boon to everyone except perhaps the witch doctors themselves.[12]

§

The reader will be forgiven for wondering why, if company rule was seemingly so beneficial, the Matabele rose up in rebellion as they did. One problem was that the very law and order brought by the company also spelled the end of the glorious free-for-all that many Matabele men had enjoyed for so long. Selous—who knew the Matabele better than most and who was in Rhodesia throughout the rebellion—did not think for a moment that the Matabele had risen against some sort of intolerable injustice or cruelty by the company. Rather, they were motivated by a simple desire to return to the 'good old days'. Selous went on to relate what he perceived to be the causes of the uprising:

'...the Matabele broke out in rebellion because they disliked their position as a conquered people and imagined they were strong enough to throw off the yoke of their conquerors... We Europeans make the mistake of thinking that, when we free a tribe of savages from what we consider a most oppressive and tyrannical form of government, we ought to earn their gratitude–we invariably fail to do so.'[13]

Selous continued by saying that the 'savage' instead, took the view:

'...hang your Pax Britannica; give me the good old times of superstition and bloodshed; then, even if I did not know the hour when I might be smelt out as a witch and forthwith be knocked on the head, I could have basked in the sun till my time came; and then, too, when the impi went forth, what glorious times I had and how I revelled in blood and loot!'[14]

Though his plain speaking will no doubt upset a few modern-day bleeding hearts, and is certainly not how such issues are viewed through western eyes, Selous makes some interesting points. He is quite correct in saying that no nation happily accedes to being invaded, and pretty much whatever the Rhodesians had done after 1893, however well they had governed the Matabele, an uprising was always going to be likely. Similarly, and as hard as this is for a modern, suburban, Euro-centric mind to grasp, Selous is no doubt correct in saying that many Matabele men must have rather enjoyed their previous lives of pillage and murder. To plenty of hot-headed young Matabele bucks, an existence where they could regularly rampage into neighbouring territory to snatch women, slaves and loot from a weaker tribe must have seemed rather jolly–certainly a good deal jollier than one restricted by the pesky new 'white man's laws'.

In a striking parallel to what happened in Germany in the wake of the First World War, many such young Matabele firebrands convinced themselves that they hadn't really lost in 1893. Whole impis had not seen action,[15] and there can be little doubt that the defeat of the Shangani Patrol—and the way that Forbes' battered column was sent limping back to Bulawayo with their collective tails firmly between their legs—caused many warriors to feel they could indeed beat the white invaders. Again, and just as whole divisions of the German Army were allowed to march home with their rifles in 1918/19, the failure to disarm the Matabele impis after they had been defeated was a huge factor in convincing them that they hadn't really been beaten.

This remarkable oversight was by no means the company's fault, however. Rather, it was due to meddling from the 'imperial factor' in the wake of sanctimonious bleating from Labouchère and his sheep-like ilk. Under pressure from a rogue's gallery of naïve hand-wringers,

Lord Ripon—the secretary of state for the colonies—compelled the company to accept peace with the Matabele without insisting that they surrender their weapons.[16] An astounded Jameson argued strongly against this, explaining that the natives would never understand that they had been conquered without some disarmament,[17] but he was over-ruled.[18] Sitting safely in their London Clubs, these meddling liberals no doubt congratulated themselves on their success and convinced one another that this lunatic leniency would be well received by the Matabele. Instead, as everyone with half a brain predicted, the warrior nation interpreted this as a weakness and when the call to arms was received, these weapons were simply snatched up again.

As well as a failure to collect the physical weaponry of the Matabele, there was also little or no attempt to dismantle the military apparatus of Lobengula's state, essentially leaving this 'command structure' intact to plot and scheme rebellion. The great dance was permitted to continue and the regimental system of the Matabele army, based as it was on indunas and their villages and kraals, had not been interfered with since the defeat of Lobengula.[19]

§

The short-sighted failure to collect weapons and break up command structures left the rebels with a ready-made army in waiting, but more importantly, the Matabele took this as yet more evidence that the white-man was indecisive and feeble. It was never likely that a nation hardened and desensitized by years of Lobengula's casual executions and bouts of mass murder would suddenly respect the company's infinitely less brutal and dictatorial rules:

'The native idea of government is based so entirely upon submission to the supreme head, that as Sikombo said at the last indaba, they felt, after the white man had taken over the country, "like a flock without a leader". Thus, then, an ever-present grievance that the Matabele as a nation had against the Government was the constant changing of the head white man in the country to whom they could look up, and from whom they could obtain redress. That they had some cause to complain on this point is beyond dispute. "No sooner do we get to know him that he goes away." This is true enough, and had always been their trouble. The influence of the strong personality of such men as Mr Rhodes and Dr Jameson is not only beneficial, but an absolute necessity to maintain evenly balanced relations between white and black. Whether the rebellion would have been averted had either of those two leaders remained in the country permanently is a matter of conjecture.'[20]

Another important factor was company's decision to establish a 'native police force' in Matabeleland after the war–indeed, this is arguably the most critical of the many factors which led to the uprising. Of all the grievances aired during the indabas at the end of the rebellion, the behaviour of the native police was always brought up as one of the worst.[21] Often recruited from the pick of Lobengula's pre-war army,[22] the young policemen quickly became drunk on their new-found authority, destroying the traditional power structure of the Matabele people as they swaggered about, brazenly offending and insulting their elders.

One Matabele induna described the native police as men who:

'...ravished their daughters, and insulted their young men, who tweaked the beards of their chieftains and made lewd jokes with the elder women of the Great House, who abused the law they were expected to uphold, who respected none but the Native Commissioners and officer of the police, who collected taxes[iii] at the point of their assegais, and ground the people in tyranny and oppression.'[23]

Even before the uprising, a senior Matabele induna had visited Selous to complain about these native policemen, and told the hunter:

'I have no problems with the white policemen, but the black police, wa duba, wa duba sebele: they give me trouble, they really give me trouble.'[24]

'Curio' Brown, an American zoologist who had served in the 1890 pioneer column, also voiced his worries over this:

'As is known the world over, power cannot be placed in the hands of the negro without turning his head so far that he feels it incumbent upon him to be domineering. Thus with the authority which their official position gave them, the Matabele police practiced all manner of abuses upon their brethren.'[25]

It had, in fact, been thought that the Matabele would appreciate being policed by their own officers, but this was to backfire spectacularly.[26] As one veteran of the war was to write, the establishment of this constabulary was:

---

iii They would actually have been gathering loot cattle or else extracting bribes as no taxes were being levied in Matabeleland at that stage.

'...an experiment which, contrary to all expectation, turned out badly. As events proved, the natives should not have been trusted. Sent out under no supervision but that of their own native non-commissioned officers, to enforce the authority of the new government, they, under cover of this authority, took the opportunity to pay off old scores against, and generally tyrannize over, any of their own people who against whom they had a grudge.'[27]

Needless to say, however, it does not suit today's politically correct outlook to concede that the arrogant behaviour of power-crazed Matabele police officers played a large role—indeed, was possibly the biggest single factor—in prompting the Matabele to rise up against 'white oppression'.

There can be no denying that the poor quality of some of the company-appointed officials was also a significant factor in stoking Matabele discontent. Sir Alfred Milner,[iv] the newly appointed high commissioner in Cape Town, visited Rhodesia shortly after the rebellions and reported that 'a lot of unfit people' had been 'allowed to exercise power, or at any rate did exercise it, especially with regard to the natives' in a manner which could not have been defended. While acknowledging the difficulties faced by company, Milner's report continued:

'The number of competent men available is small and the amount of riff-raff having some sort of claim on the company, or its principal members, is considerable. This would not matter so much, if the worthless people were only appointed to small clerkships and sinecures... the danger comes in, when they are sent to important administrative posts, especially native commissionerships... it is extremely difficult to get a sufficient number of men at all fitted to exercise such wide powers, liable as they are to abuse.'[28]

§

On top of the failure to disarm the Matabele, the confiscation of Lobengula's cattle, the establishment of modern law and order, and the introduction of native police, came other factors rather more out of the company's control. A particularly severe drought blighted Matabeleland at the same time that company rule was imposed in 1893, and this unhappy state of affairs dragged on for several years,

---

iv Alfred Milner, later 1st Viscount Milner KG, GCB, GCMG, PC (1854–1925). A brilliant colonial statesman, most famous for demanding a fair franchise for the English-speaking residents of Kruger's Transvaal; demands which led to Kruger's invasion of Natal and sparked the Boer War.

with rainfall dropping to about half the normal amount.[29] On top of this came a devastating plague of locusts that:

> '...appeared in swarms which literally darkened the sky, devastating both the veld and the gardens of the country, and eating up the crops on which the natives depended for their food. It is stated, on the authority of Umjaan and Sekombo, that until the occupation of Mashonaland, no locusts had been seen in any numbers for twenty-five years in Matabeleland. The simultaneous advent in Rhodesia of the white man and of swarms of locusts, of a kind unknown in the country for forty years, and much more destructive than the ordinary species, caused the locusts to be called by the Matabele 'Tsintete za makiwa' (locusts of the white man).'[30] Another witness described them as 'great black clouds sweeping up from the horizon, blotting out the sun.'[31]

In the wake of the locusts came an even more devastating act of God–an outbreak of rinderpest, a highly infectious, viral cattle plague. The outbreak appears to have originated in Somalia in 1889, and spread down through the continent, reaching Matabeleland in March of 1896. It absolutely decimated the Matabele cattle herds, and was especially hard to bear as it arrived shortly after the company had confiscated Lobengula's 'loot'. To makes matters worse, the unschooled Matabele saw the company's rational attempts at stemming the outbreak by culling herds as yet more evidence of the white man's determination to rob them of their precious livestock. The impact was certainly enormous and the rinderpest outbreak was reckoned to have accounted for around 2,500,000 cattle south of the Zambezi by the time it reached the Cape at the end of 1897.[32]

Not even the maddest self-loathing liberal can reasonably blame the company for the drought, the locusts or the rinderpest, but demented Matabele witch doctors quickly used them to whip their people up into rebellion. The most deranged of these followed a shadowy figure, 'the M'Limo', who was either one of various self-styled high priests, or perhaps even a God–all depending on one's point of view. Whatever he was (if he ever existed at all) the M'Limo's prophesy, 'Until the blood of the white man be spilt, there will be no rain,'[33] soon spread throughout Matabeleland like wildfire.

For reasons of political correctness, it is fashionable today for writers to downplay the superstitious nature of the Matabele of the period; this is to ignore the reality that the Matabele were, in terms of development, essentially still in the Iron Age, many hundreds of years behind the western world. As upsetting as it might be for some to admit, there can be little doubt that widespread belief in utter nonsense like 'the M'Limo', and the equally insane babblings of the host of lunatic charlatans and witch doctors who spread these prophesies, played a major role in working the Matabele up into a frenzy of blood-lust.[v]

§

There are various views, but little agreement as to which of the multitude of factors was the most important. Neville Jones, in his Rhodesian Genesis, for example, listed the causes as follows:

1. the incomplete subjugation of the Matabele in 1893
2. the disinclination of the Matabele to settle down peacefully
3. the overbearing attitude of the native police which was deeply resented
4. the conviction, on the part of the natives, that all the evils that had visited them (droughts, locusts, and the rinderpest) were directly attributable to the white man
5. it must also be remembered that many of the armed men in Matabeleland were captured with Jameson after the abortive raid into the Transvaal[34]

It is interesting that Jones only lists the Jameson Raid as number five, since many modern writers put a great deal more emphasis on this event. If anything, the raid provided a catalyst for the rebellion, rather than being a cause; indeed, as Earl Grey,[vi] who was appointed as the administrator of Rhodesia after Dr Jameson was incarcerated wrote:

'It would thus appear that the withdrawal of the white police from the country did not supply the cause for the rebellion, but merely pointed the opportunity.'[35]

But what was the real impact of the raid and how much responsibility does Dr Jameson really bear for the rebellion that followed in its wake? This is not the place for an exhaustive account of the Jameson Raid, so the reader will forgive me for giving a brief overview of the event.

---

v　Frederick Burnham would later claim to have tracked the M'Limo to a cave and shot him dead while he was performing a bizarre ritual. Burnham's account of having slayed this 'God' was reported all over the globe. His version would later be challenged, however, and while it was accepted that Burnham had indeed shot a Matabele in a cave, it was asserted that his victim was simply a random unfortunate fellow, rather than a God or even a witch doctor. It is likely that there was never a single 'M'Limo' at all. Rather, various witch doctors and priests pretended to be able to converse with him. Nevertheless, Burnham's 'killing of him' was probably still significant in terms of a propaganda coup, and word of his demise quickly spread among the rebels.

vi　Albert Henry George Grey, 4th Earl Grey PC GCB GCMG GCVO (1851–1917). Educated at Harrow and Cambridge, Grey entered politics as the Liberal MP for South Northumberland. After serving as the administrator of Rhodesia, Grey went on to be Governor General of Canada.

All but surrounded by the British territories of Rhodesia, Natal, Bechuanaland, Basutoland and the Cape Colony, were two Boer republics–the Transvaal and the Orange Free State. The early 1890s had seen increasing tensions between British South Africa and the Boers; indeed, as early as 1887,[36] Paul Kruger (then president) had tried to create an offensive alliance with the Orange Free State with a view to replacing the British as the pre-eminent power in southern Africa.

The British, for their part, were unhappy about the way in which large numbers of Britons who had been drawn in by the Johannesburg Gold Rush and made their homes in Kruger's Transvaal, were being treated. Known as 'Uitlanders', these subjects only wanted the same voting rights that Afrikaners enjoyed in the British territories of southern Africa. It is difficult to deny that they had a case (though, for reasons known only to themselves, many modern writers still do). The British government had involved itself in the matter and was putting increasing pressure on Kruger with the objective of getting a fair franchise for the Transvaal's English-speaking residents. By 1895, however, the Uitlanders were widely accepted to have become the political majority in the republic and, though a religious fanatic who firmly believed the world was flat, Kruger was cunning enough to realize that introducing normal franchise qualifications in the Transvaal would see him booted out of power in short order. The corrupt old misery had absolutely no intention of letting that happen.

Infuriated by what they perceived to be a lack of action from the British Government, and with Kruger's clique laughing at their peaceful attempts to address the problem, an influential group of Uitlanders decided to take matters into their own hands and began to plot what was essentially a coup d'état. Rhodes became heavily involved in this scheme, and in so doing, drew in Jameson and Rhodesia in general. The Uitlanders' basic plan was to seize control of Johannesburg (which was overwhelmingly populated by Uitlanders) after which, Dr Jameson would ride into the Transvaal with a 'relief force' to stabilize the situation. This force would become infamous as the Jameson Raiders, which some claim denuded Rhodesia of her police.

As the planned date of the coup approached, things began to unravel in Johannesburg, and the various plotters started getting cold feet. Jameson was having none of this, however, and decided to ride in anyway, no doubt hoping to galvanize the wavering Johannesburg plotters into action by grabbing the bull by the horns. On 29 December 1895, Jameson's 478-strong column crossed into the Transvaal and struck out towards Gold Reef City.

It was a decisive and audacious move, but it was all over by 2 January 1896. With shameless cowardice, the Johannesburg Uitlanders sat tight, leaving Jameson's men to fight an unequal running battle with the Transvaal's commandos. The raiders fought hard but were cornered just outside Johannesburg, and blasted into submission by the Boer's newly acquired artillery. Jameson and his men were marched into captivity.

At first glance, the reader would be forgiven for assuming that Jameson's impetuosity cost Rhodesia 478 of her policemen at a stroke, thus the theory that he was largely responsible for the rebellion seems reasonable.

On closer inspection, however, there is much more to this than meets the eye. The initial plan called for Jameson to ride in with 800 men, but recruiting such numbers proved impossible. Of the 478 he eventually led into the Transvaal, around 100 were recent transferees from the Bechuanaland Border Police, who would not have been patrolling in Matabeleland in any case. A further 100 of the Raiders were recruited from the ranks of the Cape Town based Duke of Edinburgh's Own Volunteer Rifles–so again, no one could claim their involvement weakened the normal police presence in Matabeleland. Around 40 of the raiders were never caught and these made their way back into company territory. This leaves about 250 men who can reasonably be assumed to have acted as a deterrent to any rebellion, and many of these do not seem to have been experienced, seasoned police officers in any case. Mark Twain, who was in South Africa on one of his Tramps Abroad at the time, described the raiders as 'green youths, raw young fellows, not trained or war-worn British soldiers'.[37]

Even if Jameson's impetuosity can be blamed for removing 250 men from Rhodesia (not all of whom would have been in Matabeleland in any case) there is no way the Doctor can be blamed for them not being back there well before the uprising. Though many of the Transvaal's ruling clique wanted the raiders strung up, Kruger was far too shrewd an operator to make martyrs out of them and threw this hot potato straight back into the hands of the British Colonial Authorities. The first batch of raiders were loaded onto trains and sent to the Natal border as early as 11 January. Jameson and his officers were the last to leave the Transvaal and even they were on their way out of Pretoria by 19 January.

Despite the way Jameson's group are portrayed today, the ill-conceived, though undoubtedly gallant, attempt at toppling Kruger's corrupt oligarchy had actually been supported by many who lived in the republic. One of the Rhodesian medical officers recalled:

'We were cheered as we left the station (Pretoria) and at every station we passed.'[38]

The colonial authorities in Natal wasted no time in putting Jameson and his officers onto the SS Victoria and sending them off to England to face trial. The rank and file left Durban on the Harlech Castle a few days later. These men had not been charged with anything and, while the few without homes in the colonies were taken home to Great Britain, all those who resided in southern Africa were allowed to disembark in Cape Town.[39] This would surely have included any and all of the officers who had been serving in the Rhodesian Mounted Police before the raid. So apart from Jameson and a few of his senior officers, all the survivors were free men before the end of January and most would never even have left southern Africa.

As the rebellion only erupted in late March of that year (a full two months later) there is no reason whatsoever why the bulk of these policemen would not have been back up in Rhodesia long before it started. So though the Jameson Raid certainly removed a couple of hundred mounted policemen from Rhodesia for a few weeks, they were not—as some claim—locked up at the time of the rebellion, and there was simply no reason why these men could not have been back on duty weeks before the Matabele rose up. That most were not, cannot be considered Jameson's fault. Indeed, had the raid been successful, it is likely that these forces would have been out of Rhodesia for even longer, as they would surely have been needed for duty in the Transvaal. Writing just after the conflict—which he served in—Selous called the allegations against Jameson 'the height of meanness and injustice'.[40] To illustrate his point, it is worth noting that one of the raiders, Captain Maurice Heany, even made it all the way to New York by the first week in March–the New York Times covered his arrival on the 8th of that month.

It is also often forgotten that the largest single unit in Rhodesia, the 1,000-strong Rhodesia Horse (under the command of Lt. Colonel Spreckley) remained in reserve up in Bulawayo, and never crossed the Limpopo throughout the fiasco. Though a part-time militia unit, rather than a standing police force, the Rhodesia Horse was still a powerful regiment. In addition, there were also 300 native police officers[41]– though it would soon turn out that the loyalty of many was suspect to say the least.

Interestingly, there are reports of rebels plotting as early as November 1895–long before the Matabele could have known about plans for the raid. One witness recalled:

'After talking a long time, Lekuni [the late Lobengula's brother] told us there was a big meeting of the chiefs in the hills, and that they wanted to kill all the white men in the country... Next day I went into town, saw the acting administrator and told him exactly what I had seen and heard. He said "For God's sake Wilson do not tell anyone in town what you are telling me, or you will create a panic"... of course, I did not'[42]

Once the result of the raid became known, however, other reports from loyal natives unsurprisingly confirmed that it had given a fillip to already rebellious elements:

'These boys say that the Matabili know that there are only a few men here and no guns [Maxims?]... also that the Matabili have been waiting for an opportunity to pounce down on Salisbury and Bulawayo for months. These boys say further that there are immense numbers of Matabili ready to come down on the town at once. These boys are absolutely reliable.'[43]

So whether the raid was the cause of, or just one of the catalysts for, the uprising, what it most certainly did do was remove Dr Jameson from the scene for the duration of the rebellion. It is not unreasonable to suggest that his decisive, 'blood and iron' leadership style might have helped nip the rebellion in the bud before it even got going. When rumours that the natives were polishing guns and sharpening assegais began to circulate, Jameson's temporary replacement as administrator did not take them seriously and failed to act.[44] Whether or not the Doctor would have acted more decisively can never be known–but most agree he would have been of more use in the thick of things in Bulawayo than lingering in a London gaol.[vii]

Perhaps the most important part played by the Jameson Raiders, however, was that their defeat boosted the morale of Matabele malcontents–coming on top of the victory over Wilson's patrol, this latest company defeat must have been greeted with delight and helped to convince any doubters that the white man was eminently conquerable.

§

In the rush to pile all the blame for the rebellion on Jameson, however, another potential spark has been largely over-looked: the role played by the ever-active Transvaal Secret Service. Even before the Jameson Raid, in December 1895, a certain Henning Pretorius,[viii]

---

vii Not all shared this view though: when the rebellion broke out, Johannes Colenbrander, who had bitter memories of the loss of the Shangani Patrol, seemed to take a dim view of Jameson's impetuosity and daring. He wrote, 'Thank God Jameson isn't here: he'd have us all immortalized by now as the late heroes of some glorious piece of bunkum.'

viii Henning Petrus Nicolaas Pretorius, 1844–1897. His father, Marthinus Pretorius, was killed in the

Lt. Colonel of the Transvaal Staats Artillerie, entered Rhodesia on an ostensible hunting trip. In reality, the Colonel was an active agent in the Transvaal's secret service, and after much more dangerous game.[45] According to the Daily Telegraph's correspondent, Pretorius and his confederates smuggled 175 rifles and 30 cases of ammunition into Rhodesia. These all bore the Transvaal government mark, and, worse still, were stamped 'made in Germany'. They had been drawn from the Transvaal's magazine in Middleburg and covertly distributed to potential rebels and trouble-makers in Rhodesia.[46] The reader will recall that modern magazine rifles had also been recovered after the Battle of Bembesi back in the 1893 war–a mystery that has never been resolved.

Kruger's Transvaal Boers had long considered the territory which became Rhodesia their own, and believed that Rhodes had cheated them out of it. Despite attempts to reinvent Kruger as some sort of poor, misunderstood innocent, he and his mob considered pretty much all of Africa south of the Zambezi, rightfully theirs. We shall never know how important a part this smuggling of weaponry, or the nefarious encouragement of the Transvaal's secret agents, played. It was confirmed, however, that when the Matabele duly rebelled in 1896, the Transvaal delivered another 200 rifles and 16 cases of ammunition to the insurgents.

Rhodesian settlers at the time certainly believed that the long arm of the Transvaal's secret service was at least partly responsible: one, writing in the Pall Mall Gazette on the 17 April, noted the presence of:

'...a number of Boers in Matabeleland: all of whom are agents—in some cases, paid agents—of the South African Republic. These Boers who are as a body more in touch with the natives than the British settlers, have undoubtedly spread abroad exaggerated reports of the defeat of Dr Jameson's expedition and the collapse of the Jo'burg insurrection and have led the natives to believe that their conquerors are not as formidable as they imagined. There can be no doubt also that the Boers have bought cattle largely from the natives... and that the cattle so purchased... have been paid for by the surreptitious sale of guns... Had it not been for the action of the Boers the native rising against the authority of the chartered co. would never have assumed serious proportions even supposing it had taken place.'

Another report, this time in the Morning Post on 28 March, stated: '[It is]...an open secret that the Boers have long had their agents in Matabeleland, and it is not at all impossible that the witch doctor

First Boer War, and his maternal grandfather was the famous Voortrekker, Piet Retief.

considered that the moment was a convenient one to remind the natives of the increasing power of President Kruger.'

In October 1897, Rhodes himself wrote to the administrator of Rhodesia in confidence, saying, 'let the world know that from the evidence in your possession you believe the Transvaal did assist the Matabele with arms'.[47]

Strangely, and without troubling himself to provide any reason whatsoever, Professor Ranger simply dismisses this as 'improbable' in his 1967 history of the revolt. In fact, given the Transvaal's long-standing enthusiasm to expand her borders north of the Limpopo, and the propensity of her large and well-funded secret service to get involved in such things, there is no reason simply to dismiss this as a significant factor. It is not as though it was in any way unusual for the Transvaal to indulge in such skullduggery–the republic had a long and unpleasant history of using Africans to fight shadow wars for them; in one of their attempts to conquer the Orange Free State, Transvaal secret agents had been sent into Basutoland[ix] to persuade King Moshesh to attack the Free Staters.[48] They would also later be caught provoking and supporting the rebels in the 1896/97 Langberg Revolt against British rule in Bechuanaland.[49] It is also interesting that the rebellion flared up a few weeks after the Jameson Raid–did the raid perhaps prompt the Transvaal's secret service to re-double their efforts to destabilize company rule north of the Limpopo?

§

The reality is that the rebellion didn't have one true cause, or even one over-riding cause. It was probably bound to happen sooner or later, no matter whether company rule had been harsher or more lenient. One should also bear in mind that different groups of rebels had different reasons for rising up—Rather than being a precisely coordinated, homogenous uprising, it spread with a momentum of its own as natives decided whether to join the rebellion or sit it out— which plenty did. Many may have been inspired to throw their lot in with the rebels for very personal reasons–perhaps a cruel white boss, or else one who just made them work a little harder than they would have preferred. Indeed, one commentator considered the way that Matabele labourers were treated to be 'one of the greatest causes of the rebellion'.[50] Another suggests an even less pleasant cause, coyly mentioning 'the conduct of many of the whites towards their black sisters, married or virgin'.[51]

---

ix Modern day Lesotho

The fact is that by late March 1896, whichever combination of causes and catalysts can be blamed, Matabeleland was ready to explode in rebellion.

End Notes
[1] British South Africa Company, The '96 Rebellions, p.5
[2] Hanna, The Story of the Rhodesias and Nyasaland, p.140
[3] Mason, The Birth of a Dilemma, p.184
[4] Cary, A Time to Die, p.145
[5] Knight, Rhodesia of Today, p.13
[6] Mason, The Birth of a Dilemma, p.189
[7] Keppel-Jones, Rhodes and Rhodesia, p.392
[8] Keppel-Jones, Rhodes and Rhodesia, p.389
[9] Knight, Rhodesia of Today, p.6
[10] Knight, Rhodesia of Today, p.11
[11] Imperialist, Cecil Rhodes: A Biography and an Appreciation, p.408
[12] Knight, Rhodesia of Today, p.12
[13] Mason, The Birth of a Dilemma, p.192
[14] Mason, The Birth of a Dilemma, p.192
[15] British South Africa Company, The '96 Rebellions, p.5
[16] Hanna, The Story of the Rhodesias and Nyasaland, p.140
[17] Mason, The Birth of a Dilemma, p.190
[18] Mason, The Birth of a Dilemma, p.192
[19] Keppel-Jones, Rhodes and Rhodesia, p.439
[20] Sykes, With Plumer in Matabeleland, p.5
[21] Keppel-Jones, Rhodes and Rhodesia, p.408
[22] Sykes, With Plumer in Matabeleland, p.9
[23] Keppel-Jones, Rhodes and Rhodesia, p.409
[24] Selous, Sunshine and Storm in Rhodesia, p.11
[25] Brown, On the South African Frontier, p.323
[26] Baxter, Rhodesia: Last Outpost of the British Empire, 1890-1980, p.99
[27] Sykes, With Plumer in Matabeleland, p.9
[28] Hanna, The Story of the Rhodesias and Nyasaland, p.139
[29] Keppel-Jones, Rhodes and Rhodesia, p.432
[30] British South Africa Company, The '96 Rebellions, p.6
[31] Keppel-Jones, Rhodes and Rhodesia, p.432
[32] Keppel-Jones, Rhodes and Rhodesia, p.433
[33] British South Africa Company, The '96 Rebellions, p.6
[34] Jones, Rhodesian Genesis, p.120
[35] British South Africa Company, The '96 Rebellions, p.6
[36] Cook, Rights and Wrongs of the Transvaal War, p.92
[37] Twain, More Tramps Abroad, p.458
[38] Gibbs, The History of the BSAP, Vol.1, p.151
[39] Gibbs, The History of the BSAP, Vol.1, p.152
[40] Selous, Sunshine and Storm in Rhodesia, p.9
[41] Hensman, A History of Rhodesia, p.167
[42] Keppel-Jones, Rhodes and Rhodesia, p.435
[43] Ranger, Revolt in Southern Rhodesia, 1896-7, p.124
[44] Sykes, With Plumer in Matabeleland, p.14
[45] A.E.Heyer, A Brief History of the Transvaal Secret Service System, p.16
[46] A.E.Heyer, A Brief History of the Transvaal Secret Service System, p.15
[47] Ranger, Revolt in Southern Rhodesia, 1896-7, p.166
[48] Botha, From Boer to Boer and Englishman, p.15
[49] A.E.Heyer, A Brief History of the Transvaal Secret Service System, p.20
[50] Keppel-Jones, Rhodes and Rhodesia, p.406
[51] Sykes, With Plumer in Matabeleland, p.10

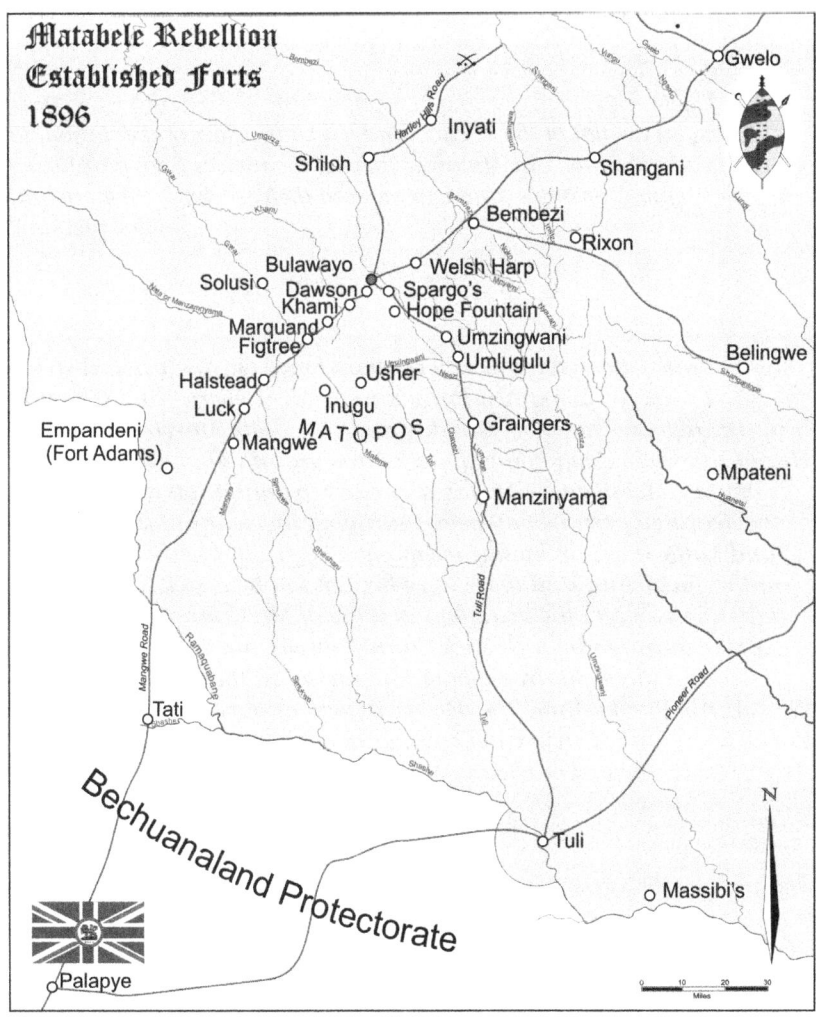

Matabele Rebellion
Established Forts
1896

'We had the news from the Matopos that M'Limo was going to help us, so we just decided among ourselves that there were white people over there and we had better go there... We were going to kill all the white people because we had the news that the M'Limo was going to help us.'
    – One rebel explains why he and his friends butchered a white family[1]

'Acting on the fiat of the M'Limo and the counsellors of the nation, to 'slay and spare not', the Matabele formed themselves into marauding gangs, or impis, and commenced their work of massacre and destruction.'[2]

'I am an assistant native commissioner for the Insiza district. I accompanied last witness—Mr. Liebert—and Orpen to Cunningham's farm on Tuesday morning, 24th March. On arrival there I saw eight dead bodies lying on the ground about twenty yards from the homestead. We made a cursory examination and saw that the deceased persons had been murdered by means of knob-kerries and battle-axes, or similar weapons. The ground was covered with native footprints, and there were broken knob-kerries lying about. I identified among the dead bodies those of Mr. Cunningham senior, Mrs. Cunningham, two Miss Cunninghams, Master Cunningham, and three children whom I identified as the grandchildren of Mr. Cunningham senior. The deceased persons appeared to have been killed inside the house and afterwards dragged out and thrown outside in the position in which we found them.'
    – Sworn statement by Herbert Pomeroy Fynn[3]

'A lot of friendly natives have come in and the authorities have set them on to burying the dead rinderpest cattle. What a horrible disease it is. We have lost every beast we possessed, and I am sad to say that the Matabele have taken my colonial cow–but I am putting in a claim of £30 for it. The scouts picked up a Mrs O'Maker who had been walking for four days without food with her husband. Now she lives with them and cooks and bosses up generally; she calls herself a scout and wears their colours.'[4]
    – Annie Fletcher describes the situation in Bulawayo in a letter dated 15 April, 1896

Chapter 12
The Storm Breaks

The Matabele people had no obvious or widely accepted leader after Lobengula died in early 1894. As we know, Mhlaba, who should be have been able to step into the breach, the 'regent in waiting' as it were, had been murdered on Lobengula's orders back in 1892–the futile, desperate act of a brutal man. Two of his sons were also out of the running, having been sent to school in Cape Town by Rhodes[5]– an act, either of munificence or shrewdness, depending on one's point of view. With these two out of the picture, another of Lobengula's sons, Nyamanda, was thought by many to be his rightful heir, though other senior indunas preferred the late king's brother, Mfezela.[6] With the Matabele on the verge of splintering into factions, the closest thing the rebels had to a leader was Mlugulu, who was the old 'head dance doctor' and thus, holder of the highest ritual position in the land.

It would seem that plans were hatched in various secret meetings during which the rebel leaders grasped at the unifying force of 'the M'Limo' to form an unholy alliance with the associated Mwari Priesthood[i]. Selous revealed the generally accepted version of the time when he wrote, 'I believe, however, that the Umlimo, was made use of for the purposes of the present rebellion by Mlugulu, and other members of the king's family.'

More recently, Julian Cobbing has claimed that the Mwari Priests played no significant role in the rebellion at all, while others have suggested that they were actually the driving force behind the uprising, and that the alliance with Mlugulu was a 'marriage of convenience.'[7]

We shall probably never know for sure, but given the number of times that the name, M'Limo appears in contemporary accounts about the uprising, it seems short-sighted to dismiss the impact of this cult-like priesthood. The likes of Professor Ranger have suggested that the uprisings were the result of a well-organized and coordinated plan, but in fact, it was a rebellion that spluttered into action over a couple of weeks as various rebel groups rose up for a variety of reasons.

It should also not be forgotten that a great many of the Africans in Matabeleland remained loyal to the company or stayed neutral. A couple of weeks into the uprising, a Jesuit missionary, Father Prestage, left his mission station near Mangwe with a single attendant, 'bravely to go into the Matopos Hills, and endeavour to alienate many chiefs

---

i Mwari was the Shona name for the deity of rain and agriculture worshipped as M'Limo by the Matabele.

known to him from taking the rebel side'. When he got back, he brought with him, '...18 representatives of the leading 10 indunas, representing some 600 people, who were desirous of being protected by us, and granted special protection passes'.

Shortly thereafter, passes were given to 125 Matabele headmen in the Bulawayo area, representing about 600 men, and a further 1,200 were issued to servants.[8]

When Selous, who lived outside Bulawayo on his farm in Essexvale[ii] heard of the rebellion, he sent messengers to summon the headmen of all the kraals in the immediate vicinity of the homestead. In his own words:

> 'These men, I may say, were all in possession of cattle belonging to my company, and as none of them were pure-blooded Matabele, I imagined they would have no sympathy with the insurgents. They all answered my summons, accompanied by many of their people, and before leaving I spoke to them, and did my best to impress upon them the folly of rebelling against the white man. They professed themselves in perfect accord with all I said; averred that they were quite content to live with me as their 'inkosi'[iii] and protested that they had nothing to hope for from the overthrow of the white man by the Matabele.'[9]

For all the attention given to the impact of the Jameson Raid, the rebellion was not unleashed until many weeks after it. In an unconventional piece of military planning, Mlugulu took the partial eclipse of the moon on 28 February as some sort of divine signal to move, and he, along with a group of senior indunas, decided to hold the great dance on 29 March. The plan was to inaugurate the late-Lobengula's son, Nyamanda, as the new king at the dance, and then to unleash hell on the white settlers in a coordinated attack on Bulawayo. Unfortunately for Mlugulu, some of his more enthusiastic elements, decided to unleash hell a little earlier than planned.

As Frederick Burnham put it:

> 'So well were the plans of the native laid, and so weak the colonists that, had the orders of the M'Limo been carried out, it is probable that all the whites in Rhodesia would have been killed within twenty-four hours from the hour set, and every town left a smoking ruin. Fortunately the black brain cannot be trusted to carry through so comprehensive a measure, although

---

ii Now renamed 'Esigodini'

iii Selous defined this word: 'Literally, king; but the word is commonly used in addressing Europeans, as a complimentary title, conveying the idea of dependence on the part of the speaker.'

its secretiveness is ample... What upset the M'Limo's plans was the zeal of certain young warriors on the Insesi River, forty-five miles from Bulawayo. Instead of waiting for the full of the moon, as ordered, they began killing the settlers three days in advance.'[10]

These elements seem to have been sparked into premature action by an attack on a patrol of the hated native police which occurred on the evening of 20 March. According to Selous, eight native policemen and their accompanying bearers were approached by a body of armed Matabele warriors while sitting around their campfire near the Umgorshwini Kraal to the south of Bulawayo. The policemen were not attacked immediately, but taunted and insulted before a scuffle broke out. Shots were fired, killing one of the attackers and then one of the bearers. A second bearer was clubbed to death with a knobkerrie. Later that night, the attackers struck again, killing a lone native policeman in a neighbouring kraal.

§

The attack on the police prompted an uncoordinated outbreak of murders, with gangs of Matabele descending on outlying white farmsteads and stores, savagely smiting anyone unlucky enough to be there at the time. In truth, and despite Burnham's claims of well laid plans, it was a poorly organized revolt. The rebels had no supreme leader or coherent strategy[11] but the sheer brutality of the initial murders was truly shocking, with women and children hacked and slashed to death.

In one of the first attacks, a gang of rebels led by Mfezela himself (one of the pretenders to the throne) burst in to the Edkins Store and quickly butchered the storekeeper, three other whites, two black servants and a 'coolie' cook. Native Commissioner, Arthur Bentley, had an office nearby and was stabbed in the back while seated at his desk, the last words he had written dated 23 March 1896. The attackers followed by killing a miner by the name of Maddox, and another two men, one at the Celtic mining camp, and the other between the camp and the store.

Details of the attacks were supplied by a 'colonial boy'–a euphemism for a black servant of Cape origin. The attackers had split this poor devil's mouth from ear to ear and left him for dead, but he survived to report that the attacks had been mounted by rebel detachments of the native police aided by local natives under the command of Lobengula's two brothers.[12]

An equally brutal attack was made against the Cunningham family farm near the Insiza River. Grandfather Cunningham had been lying

on the couch reading a newspaper while the rest of the family enjoyed
their lunch. A gang of Matabele rebels had burst in without warning
and hacked and clubbed the family to death: grandfather, two parents
and five of their six children. The sixth of the Cunningham children,
a little girl of about seven, managed to escape the bloodbath, running
away in terror to hide near the river. There she sheltered for a few
days until found by a group of Matabele women. In an act of almost
unbelievable barbarity, one of these women held the poor little girl
down while another smashed her head in with a rock.[13]

The savagery spread like wildfire, as any remote farm, mine
or outpost was targeted. One rebel later testified that he and some
friends had murdered a trio of whites: 'We had no grievance against
these people. We killed them merely because they were white.'[14] After
detailing how the three unsuspecting settlers had been murdered, this
fellow also confirmed that their Zulu servant had also been killed
'because he was as good as a European', before stating, 'These white
people were our friends, and so did not expect that we were coming
to kill them.'[15]

Selous recalled similar tragedies all over Matabeleland:

'From the Umzingwani, the flame of rebellion spread through the
Filibusi [Filabusi] and Insiza districts, to the Tchangani [Shangani]
and Inyati, and thence to the mining camps in the neighbourhood
of the Gwelo and Ingwenia rivers, and indeed throughout
the country wherever white men, women, and children could
be taken by surprise and murdered either singly or in small
parties; and so quickly was this cruel work accomplished, that
although it was only on 23rd March that the first Europeans were
murdered, there is reason to believe that by the evening of the
30th not a white man was left alive in the outlying districts of
Matabeleland.'[16]

This was no exaggeration. Scores of white settlers were brutally
murdered together with many of their black and Indian servants and
workers in the first few confused days of the rebellion. Many of the
killings were truly gruesome, with bodies literally hacked apart. As
Selous wrote:

'I went down to the scene of the massacre of the Fourie family
early in the morning and found the remains of four people–a
woman and three children, the body of Mr. Fourie and those of
three of the children being missing. The murders had evidently
been committed with knob-kerries and axes, as the skulls of all
these poor people had been very much shattered. The remains

had been much pulled about by dogs or jackals, but the long fair hair of the young Dutch girls was still intact, and it is needless to say that these blood-stained tresses awoke the most bitter wrath in the hearts of all those who looked upon them.'[17]

A letter written by a female resident of Bulawayo in April gives more details about the opening phase of the uprising:

'...we are expecting nightly to see our homes in flames; the Matabele are only a quarter of a mile out—as near as that— and have driven off cattle. They are so daring. A Matabele servant went into his Mistress's bedroom with an open knife, evidently with the intention of murder. He was caught, tried and shot... There have been some wonderful escapes. One man, Joe O'Conner, was warned that the Kaffirs were just behind the house. He ran out and was attacked by 20 Matabele. He fought his way down to a mine about half a mile off. He arrived there half dead, and slipped down the rope on to some of his own boys coming up in a box. They then attacked him. He fought and fought and got into a drive. They left him and threw two charges of dynamite (they knew how to use it) into the shaft. Luckily it exploded and left him unharmed in the drive. He fainted and came round in the night and crept out. He dragged himself up to the house which was burned and there lay his two chums murdered. Then he struck out for Bulawayo. He had on only a shirt and a pair of trousers. He took off his shirt and tied it round his head which had eight wounds. In this half-dead condition he travelled on. Some miles on he met two men he knew well, but he was so swollen and bruised and full of blood that he was not recognized. The next day they were picked up by Spreckley's column. O'Conner is now in the hospital recovering.' [18]

§

The opening attacks saw 128 white men, eight women and eight children murdered.[19] The losses among 'loyal natives' are unfortunately not recorded but the numbers are probably similar if not higher. By springing the rebellion early, however, the Matabele rebels had lost their best chance of inflicting a devastating defeat on the Rhodesians. The horrific murders of outlying farmers and traders was tragic and appalling, but it was never going to drive the white settlers out–indeed, it served both to galvanize their resolve and to give them time to organize their defences.

The first reports of the massacres were received in Bulawayo on the 24th and Mr Duncan,[iv] the acting administrator in Jameson's absence, gathered a 60-strong mounted force to investigate.[20] Led by Captain William Napier,[v] these men rode out at 20h00 that evening, taking a Maxim gun with them. As news of further murders continued rolling in on the 25th, Duncan quickly expanded his volunteer force, summoned everyone in from the outlying districts, and prepared Bulawayo for attack:

> '...no time was lost in constructing a strong laager round the market hall in the centre of the town. The Sanitary Board (or Town Council) with Mr Sidney Redrup J.P. as chairman, insisted upon a strong laager being formed of wagons, sandbags and barbed wire fencing, with broken glass bottles covering the ground on the outer defences for about ten yards in breadth.'[21]

Despite claims that the Jameson Raid had left Rhodesia short of weaponry, the Bulawayo magazine contained 12 guns–an assorted mix of machine guns, 7-pdrs and a 12-pdr, though this latter piece had no carriage and there was only limited ammunition for the others.[22] There were also 600 rifles and carbines (primarily the latest .303 magazine Lee Metfords together with 1,500,000 rounds) which were handed out to volunteers.[23] A council of defence was established, comprising Duncan, 'General' Digby Willoughby[vi] as his chief of staff and Captains Nicholson and Carden.[24] Captain Napier–whisked in from relative obscurity and hastily appointed full colonel–was placed in command of all company forces in Matabeleland.

The Boer residents of the town formed their own 'Afrikander Corps' under Commandant A.H. van Rensburg, a force which was to give valuable service throughout the rebellion.[vii] Given that there was essentially a 'cold war' between the two white races in southern Africa at the time, this was more remarkable than the modern reader might realize. One observer noted:

---

iv Andrew Henry Farrell Duncan (1855-1931). An ex-Royal Navy Officer, Duncan had been Jameson's under-study and would shortly be replaced in the primary position by Earl Grey.

v Colonel William Napier CMG (1861-1920), who narrowly survived the Shangani Patrol, was born in Natal and served in the Natal Carbineers before moving to Mashonaland in 1891. After serving in the Matabele War of 1893, Napier was appointed as an officer in the Rhodesia Horse, serving in the rebellions and then in the Boer War. In 1903, he was elected to serve on the Rhodesian Legislative Council.

vi 'General' Digby Willoughby (1845-1901) was a highly colourful soldier of fortune. Though 'General' was only a nickname, Willoughby had served in the Zulu War and had also had a go at being variously an auctioneer, war-correspondent, guerrilla leader, financier, pioneer and even—it was said—a King; the latter due to the close relations he enjoyed with a Malagasy Queen during her war with the French.

vii The Afrikander Corps consisted of three companies and a small staff group. As well as Commandant van Rensburg, the other officers were Commandant Barnard and Captains van Niekerk, Pittendrigh and Brand.

'...we have the strange spectacle of Dutch and English—who, even yet, in the Transvaal, were straining at the leash as it were, to engage in a tussle for supremacy—here in far-off Matabeleland, ranging shoulder to shoulder for common defence against a common foe.'[25]

§

It was not all hands to the pump, however, and there was a good deal of antagonism within Bulawayo. Some thought that the company was doing everything it could to downplay the severity of the uprising, and were even intercepting mail to do so. So furious was this section of the populace, that there was even intemperate talk of lynching the acting administrator. When his replacement, Lord Grey, made it to Bulawayo, he was just as poorly received by some and wrote to his son saying:

'Shortly after my arrival here, they held a public meeting in the square and passed a resolution unanimously to the effect that the gaol should be cleared of all its occupants and the administrator and other members of the government take their place.'[26]

There was similar conflict in respect to the native police, and due to fears over their dubious loyalty, the decision was taken to disarm the entire force–even the thirty officers stationed in the Bulalima region who, on hearing rumours that their native commissioner was going to be murdered, escorted him to safety in Bulawayo and reported for duty.[27] While the treatment of these loyal officers seems more than a little shoddy, it is perhaps not surprising, given that 200 of their comrades had already deserted to the rebels,[28] a mass defection made even more remarkable by the fact that the arrogant behaviour of these braggarts had been one of the major causes of discontent in Matabeleland. Professor Keppel-Jones wrote: 'such collaborators with the regime have usually been prime targets in a revolution'[29] and could expect some pretty brutal retribution. Strangely, this does not seem to have been the case in the Matabele rebellion, and deserters from the native police were welcomed by the rebels.

Equally remarkable was the decision to disband the units of the Rhodesia Horse based in Matabeleland, so that their troopers could be reformed into a new regiment called the Bulawayo Field Force.[30] Virtually every able bodied man in the town would soon be a member of this or one of the smaller regiments–quite why this was done in the middle of the panic is baffling, though it seems to have had little negative impact. Colonel Spreckley was to command the new unit, with

Lt. Colonel the Rt. Hon Maurice Gifford as his second-in-command. The Bulawayo Field Force comprised 14 troops, an engineer troop, and an artillery troop. Other units in the town were Grey's Scouts,[viii] Dawson's Scouts, and the 200-strong Afrikander Corps–for a total of about 800 men, plus a 150-strong native corps under Colenbrander.[31] Horses were less abundant–there were about 200 company-owned horses in Matabeleland on the 25th, but no time was wasted in buying up hundreds of privately owned steeds.[32] This meant that there were soon in the region of 680 horses available for work.[33]

Given that this force had been formed within a couple of days of the rebellion starting, it was hardly an insignificant one–and shows that it is somewhat far-fetched to claim that the Jameson Raid left Matabeleland defenceless. On the other hand, it would seem the Doctor himself was missed: Annie Fletcher, who was trapped in Bulawayo during the rebellion, wrote to friends to reassure them:

'...we are very well protected in Bulawayo in a strong laager. There are about seven hundred armed men. Then you see, many cannot be spared to go out and fight as it weakens the laager, so until reinforcements come there will be little skirmishing round about the town. There are supposed to be fully two hundred people murdered. That is not counting ten men killed in action and twenty or twenty-five women in action... If only you knew how Dr Jameson is missed.'[34]

The three small settlements of Mangwe (60 miles to the south of Bulawayo), Belingwe[ix] (60 miles to the east) and Gwelo[x] (120 miles to the north)[35] also prepared for a siege, the defences initially manned by mere handfuls of volunteers until the outlying farmers all came in. Gwelo had been on the telegraph line, but the rebels quickly cut this.[36]

Belingwe had not been connected, so was essentially isolated throughout and it would be some time before any word was received from the settlement. It later emerged, however, that the resident native commissioner had been forewarned of the uprising[37] and sent a native constable to inform the military commander of the area, Captain Laing. The policeman had dutifully delivered the message and Laing, '...recognizing the gravity of the situation, at once acted with the promptitude and decision which always distinguish him, and

---

viii Grey's Scouts was one of the more famous regiments formed during the war. Raised on 26 March by a mine owner, Mr George Grey, the unit was formed around a nucleus of 23 picked men. The unit would be reformed in 1975 and would serve with distinction in the Rhodesian Bush War.

ix The area was pointlessly renamed Mberengwa after Mugabe took power.

x The town was pointlessly renamed 'Gweru' in 1982.

ordered all the whites in his district to immediately come in to laager at Belingwe'.[38] A large force of rebels arrived shortly thereafter, and, not keen to brave an attack on the hastily-formed laager, contented themselves by driving off a large herd of cattle. Captain Laing, with just nine others, immediately saddled up and rode out after them, attacking the insurgents and recapturing some of the herd.[39]

Somewhat remarkably, the native policeman who had obediently carried the message to Captain Laing (thus probably saving the lives of most of the settlers in the Belingwe district) never returned to duty, defecting to the rebels with his rifle and bandoleer full of cartridges. It would be reasonable to assume that he, and many other such rebels, had no idea when the insurrection was going to begin, and did not understand the significance of the early murders.

Most would-be rebels were in a state of expectancy due to the widely circulated ravings and prophetic utterances of the M'Limo; but this policeman, at least, seems to have been taken rather by surprise, and remained loyal to the government until he was informed that the first murders had been part of a greater plot.[40]

As the third settlement, Mangwe, lay on the route south from Bulawayo, holding it was deemed vital in maintaining communications down to Mafeking. Indeed, a series of small forts would soon be built to protect the road between Bulawayo and Mangwe.[41] The Matabele, however, made little effort to cut this route, which was considered somewhat bizarre by all concerned given how easy it would have been. The rumour was that the M'Limo had insisted on an escape route to the south being left open to tempt the whites to retreat.[42] Equally plausible is that the Matabele commanders simply made a schoolboy error, as Selous suggests in rather blunt terms:

'Here the road descends for a distance of three miles into the Shashani valley, winding continually in and out amongst thickly-wooded granite hills. Had the Kaffirs, at the commencement of the insurrection, put a force of 1,000 men armed with rifles, backed by another 1,000 with assegais, into this pass, it is my opinion that they would have completely cut off all communication between Bulawayo and the south until a body of troops at least 1,000 strong had been sent up from Mafeking to open the road. However, luckily they missed this opportunity, as they have missed every other chance they have had of striking a really effective blow at the white men. In fact, they have shown a general want of intelligence that stamps them as an altogether inferior people, in brain capacity at least, to the European.'[43]

§

In addition to Napier's patrol, various others were sent out from Bulawayo over the first few days of the rebellion as Acting-Administrator Duncan desperately tried to respond to the various reports of murders which were by then flooding in, and to have his men escort any survivors in. Several of these patrols came under attack, and we shall turn our attention to these small, but hard-fought, battles.

On the evening of the 24th, Lt. Colonel Gifford led a patrol out of Bulawayo, heading south-east towards the Insiza River. Gifford's force comprised 30 mounted volunteers and 14 Matabeleland Mounted Police under Inspector Southey.[44] They were in a hurry; word had been received that about 30 settlers, gathered at a store owned by a man named Cumming, were in urgent need of relief.

25 miles out of Bulawayo, Gifford's men came across a wagon which had obviously been ambushed. The sixteen mules, still in their traces, had been cruelly slashed and hacked to death with assegais. The wagoners were later found to have been murdered and abandoned in the bush.[45] The fighting patrol made it to Cumming's store on the night of the 27th, and found that only half-a-dozen of the settlers sheltering there were armed.[46] Deciding to stay the night and extract his force first thing in the morning, Gifford ordered his men to take up their positions.

It was by no means an ideal spot to make a stand: the main store was a brick-built, single-storied structure with a thatched roof, though the flammable thatch had already been removed, loop holes cut in the walls and sacks of earth placed in the windows before Gifford's men arrived. A few yards away was a small corrugated-iron shed and a few native huts stood at the back of the store. Gifford ordered the building of a zariba to link the store and the iron shed so as to form a bit of a scherm to keep the horses in for the night.

The main weakness of the position was the high ground a couple of hundred yards to the south which completely dominated the store. The loyal natives were put in the iron shed, pickets were placed on this high ground—and on all other approaches—and the Rhodesians settled down for a nervous night.

At 04h15 on the 28th, a Matabele attack force bumped into the pickets posted on the high ground, and shots were exchanged. Suddenly, rebel riflemen opened fire on the position from three sides, while others charged forward through the night in large numbers. Gifford ordered all his men into the main store building and returned fire. Sgt-Major O'Leary of the Matabeleland Mounted Police had been outside and was shot dead before he could get in. Another man was stabbed in the arm by an assegai.

Fighting in the blackness, the battle was intense with groups of rebels charging right up to the veranda on the front of the store before being shot down by the defenders. One was even shot as he tried to tear the sandbags away from the windows. The battle raged for almost an hour, with the firing described as 'very hot' in the official report. As the sun rose, the Matabele gave up the attack, and pulled back to the high ground.[47]

Rhodesian casualties were one killed (Sgt-Major O'Leary) and six others lightly wounded. Matabele casualties were unknown, but it was reckoned they suffered at least 25 dead.[48] Some of the rebels were spotted still up on the high ground when Gifford extracted his force as planned that morning, but did not intervene. The patrol brought the 33 refugees safely into Bulawayo the following day. It is remarkable that the Matabele waited until the arrival of Gifford's force before launching their attack–an oversight which is as astonishing as it is indicative of the poor quality of their commanders. Had the rebels stormed the beleaguered refugees at any time during the previous few days, they would surely have been able to slaughter them all. Attacking the store after the arrival of Gifford's patrol was a different proposition altogether and they suffered accordingly. Captain Dawson and Colonel Spreckley led similar patrols out from Bulawayo in the final week of March, though both returned without incident.

§

Selous, having brought his wife into Bulawayo,[xi] set off back towards Essexvale late on the 25th, leading a patrol of about 35 men.[49] Such was his status in Rhodesia, that Selous appears to have decided upon this mission himself, with his self-appointed object being:

'...to endeavour by prompt action to strike terror into the hearts of some of the rebels before they had time to concentrate, and at the same time to reassure those who were content with the white man's rule, but who, in the absence of any display of power on the part of the government, might be led to believe that their only chance of safety from the vengeance of the Matabele lay in taking part with them in the rebellion. In conclusion, I told them [the members of his patrol] that any Kaffirs we might find with arms in their hands, who had left their kraals and gone off into the hills with stolen cattle, ought to be shot without question and without mercy, as they were every one of them more or less responsible for the cruel murders of white men that had already been committed.'[50]

---

xi Selous' wife would stay with their close friends, Colonel and Mrs Spreckley. Mrs Spreckley was a sister of Captain Henry Borrow who had been killed at Wilson's Last Stand.

Early the following morning, the 26th, Selous' men came across a native herdsman who had been in charge of over thirty head of company-owned cattle. This fellow claimed that the headman of a nearby Matabele kraal had turned up with several armed followers and driven the herd off the previous evening. Selous immediately set off in the direction of the kraal in question, but there was no sign of the rebels though they found the cattle. Selous' men torched the kraal and sent the re-captured cattle off with the herdsman while he led the patrol in search of any other company cattle that the rebels might have snatched.[51] Selous' patrol spent the following couple of days recapturing cattle, engaging in running skirmishes with small groups of rebels and torching their kraals. It was not practical to drive the re-captured company cattle into Bulawayo so they were left in the care of loyal Matabele.

On the morning of the 29th, Selous decided to take his patrol into the Matopos Hills. Many in Bulawayo claimed this was the hotbed of rebel activity and that large numbers of insurgents were holed up in the caves and ravines. Selous, however, explained why he made what seems a very brazen decision:

'As, however, I had very good reasons for believing that as yet no large number of Matabele had assembled in this part of the country, I was anxious to make a reconnaissance through them in order to see what the difficulties of the country really were.'[52]

The Matopos Hills are perfect bandit country and no place for a small, mounted patrol to venture into. As soon as Selous' men entered the foothills and began riding up a gorge, they started to hear rebels calling to one another but pressed on in any case. The neck of this ravine was cut by a stream that could only be crossed on flat, slippery stones and they suddenly came under fire as they struggled to cross.[53] The rebels were perfectly positioned behind rocks and the troopers could not see them well, but nevertheless pushed forward and drove them off. Once more, the Rhodesians benefited from the poor shooting of the Matabele and suffered no losses in the skirmish.

With the rebels put to flight, Selous' men rounded up a hundred captured company cattle, and tried to drive them out of the hills and on to Bulawayo. It proved impossible to get them over the stream and back down the ravine, however, and the time wasted in attempting this allowed the rebels to return with reinforcements.

These Matabele took up positions in the wooded cliffs above the patrol and opened fire, as Selous recalled:

'I at once sent Mr. Blöcker and a few men who were good shots to take up a position beyond the stream, from which they could check the enemy's fire, whilst the rest of the men were crossing. I myself with Mr. Claude Grenfell and a few more men protected the rear. However, before we got down into the open ground, we had four horses killed and two men wounded, Mr. Stracey and Mr. Munzberg. How it was that more men were not hit, I don't know, as the bullets were pinging about pretty freely. Everyone, I think, although I spread the men out as much as possible, had some narrow shaves, and my Sergeant-Major got two bullets through his gaiter, and one through his trousers between his legs, yet he was not touched. Not knowing how many Kaffirs we had to deal with, nor whether some of them would not try to get round in front of us, I now sent Mr. Blöcker on with half the troop and the wounded men to take up a position on ahead, on our line of retreat; whilst Mr. Grenfell and I with the rest of the men remained behind to keep the Kaffirs from coming out of the broken ground behind us. However, having lost a few of their number, they showed no disposition to leave the shelter of the rocks, so we retired slowly and off-saddled on an open spot just beyond the hills.'

It would seem that most of their opponents had been erstwhile members of the native police force, and these turncoats were given away by their tell-tale white knickerbocker trousers. They were all reported to have been fairly young men, shooting with Winchester repeating rifles–and, as Selous recalled, 'did not shoot badly either—that is for natives.'[54]

The two wounded Rhodesians were not mortally hit, and after an hour's rest, the patrol saddled up again and made their way cross country to Dawson's store, at the Umzingwani Ford on the Tuli road, about twenty-five miles from Bulawayo. A stretcher was obtained on which to carry one of the wounded, while the other was able to ride his own horse. Rather amazingly, the store keeper, a Mr Boyce, was still at his post but was quickly persuaded to lock everything up and accompany the patrol into Bulawayo. Selous' men made it back to the town on the 30th.

§

Captain Pittendrigh rode north-east out of Bulawayo on the evening of the 28th, leading yet another patrol. Pittendrigh commanded 12 men of the Afrikander Corps, the mission being to bring in a native commissioner, Mr Graham, who was thought to be besieged with some others at his post at Inyati. The patrol stopped in at Jenkins' store on the way, rescuing 10 men who had been sheltering there. These ten rather sportingly volunteered to join Pittendrigh on his mission, bringing the total up to 22 men.[55]

The horsemen came under fire from rebels while crossing the Elibani Hills on the 29th, and pluckily spurred their horses forward to engage these riflemen. In so doing, they almost rode straight into a 300-strong rebel force, which were also surging forward in the famous crescent formation of the Zulus. Pittendrigh wisely pulled his patrol back, and they went firm in a patch of brushwood and poured fire into the onrushing horde. The rebel riflemen returned this fire and, with two of his men badly wounded, Pittendrigh had no choice but to withdraw his patrol again, mounting up and galloping for the Bembesi River as fast as they could. They managed to outpace their pursuers.[56]

Pittendrigh's patrol pushed on to Campbell's store and discovered an Irishman called Madden sheltering there. Madden claimed to be the only survivor of a party that had been holed-up with Mr Graham, the native commissioner at Inyati, the others already having been murdered by the rebels in a 5-hour battle.[57] When it was also claimed that there were about 1,500 Matabele in the area–in addition to the 300 or so they had already bumped into–Pittendrigh decided his best option was to fortify Campbell's store and call for reinforcements.

The thatch roof was quickly dismantled and loop holes cut into the walls. Somewhat fortuitously, a case of dynamite was found, and used to make mines which were laid all around the store. Other sticks of dynamite were fashioned into make-shift hand grenades. Two gallopers were sent back to Bulawayo and the rest of the small patrol settled down to wait.[58] It could be argued that Pittendrigh, rather than sending gallopers back on a decidedly risky errand, and then expecting a relief force to fight their way through to him, would actually have been much better served by simply withdrawing his whole command that evening.

The gallopers made it through safely and Captain Macfarlane was sent out with 35 men to bring Pittendrigh's beleaguered patrol in.[59] Unsurprisingly, the relief force quickly ran into trouble itself, coming under fire in the early hours of 30 March. The running battle went on for half an hour, but Macfarlane's men got through alright. It was found, however, that two men who had been riding in advance of his patrol were missing and we shall return to these fellows in a moment.

The remainder arrived at Campbell's store safely, and, together with Pittendrigh's patrol, started back to Bulawayo as soon as the horses had had a chance to rest. The combined force came under fire as it passed through the Shiloh Hills, but the marksmanship of the rebels was decidedly poor and they suffered badly when the Rhodesians returned fire. To the cheers of the defenders, they arrived safely back in Bulawayo late on the 30th.

Thoughts turned to the two missing men, Troopers Henderson[xii] and Celliers, who had become separated when Macfarlane's relief column came under fire that morning. It had been hoped that they might have made their own way back to Bulawayo but there was no sign of either man. Instead, it would later transpire that some rebel riflemen had got between Henderson and Celliers and the main body of the patrol, and the two had come under heavy fire. Celliers was shot through the knee and his horse killed under him. Trooper Henderson rode back for him, dismounted and put Celliers up onto his own horse. Ignoring Celliers' calls to save himself, Henderson instead resolved to walk, leading the horse (and his comrade) to safety. After travelling for 35 miles through enemy territory, the two men staggered into Bulawayo on 1 April, having somehow dodged the thousands of rebels who were roaming the hills.[60] Henderson was awarded the VC for his courage. There is little doubt that he would have been able to gallop away to safety, but instead risked everything to go back and rescue his comrade–something that the modern commentator should bear in mind when spitting out criticism about the character of these admittedly rough-and-ready frontiersmen.

§

While these, and other, fighting patrols were being despatched to desperately try and bring in any survivors, Bulawayo remained in a state-of-siege:

> 'All women and children were ordered into laager at night, the large market hall being served for this purpose. Strong defence outposts were established on the outskirts of the town, each guarded by a troop of about 50 men of the BFF[xiii] who, in the event of attack, were to endeavour by cross-fire to keep the enemy in check, this acting as a first line of defence for the main laager, where a reserve of ammunition and general stores were kept in case of a close and long siege. At night, all men capable of bearing arms had to sleep on the first line of wagons, standing to arms by bugle call in the evening and in the early morning. In addition strong guards were furnished by the BFF who performed all military duties and sent out mounted patrols round the town at all hours of the day and night.'[61]

---

xii Herbert Stephen Henderson VC (1870-1942). Born in Glasgow, and educated at Kelvinside Academy, Henderson moved to the Johannesburg goldfields in 1892, then on to Rhodesia in 1894 to work as an engineer on the Queen's Gold Mine to the north of Bulawayo. He volunteered for service in the 1896 rebellion and remained in Matabeleland until his death in 1942.

xiii Bulawayo Field Force

As could perhaps be expected, given the savagery of the murders being reported, tensions were running high early in the siege. When a sentry suffered a negligent discharge on the night of the 25th, the shot prompted panic in the town and it took a while for order to be restored.[62] Some men even ran to the market hall, seeking sanctuary with the 200 or so women and children gathered there. These cowards were quickly thrown back out by the officer stationed at the door, who threatened to shoot anyone who tried again.[63] Captain MacFarlane later wrote of how 'the gallant inhabitants lost their heads and scrambled and fought for what rifles were left in the Government Store. It was a disgraceful scene and the less said about it the better'.[64]

Another witness, a lady who endured the siege with her two infant children, recalled the event with similar disgust:

'Some of the men were more frightened than the women. About twenty of them one night broke open the doors on the building and rushed in, but were soon sent to the right about. Another time a miserable little Jew managed to creep in unobserved and concealed himself under a blanket until morning. When he was discovered he had a bad time of it. My husband at this time was out on patrol, and I had to manage as best I could. My baby died simply for the want of proper nourishment–preserved milk and maizena, the only things it could take, being unprocurable; and a friend of mine lost hers from the same cause.'[65]

These rather unseemly—and distinctly un-British—scenes of panic prompted a reorganisation of the defences. 'William's Buildings'–a half built double-storey affair which had a splendid view all around, was adopted as a lookout point and connected to the command post in the main laager by field telephone.[66] A gun was also positioned on the top of William's Buildings, the commanding position giving it a range of about 4,000 yards. Better still, a 'crow's nest' was established by building an 80 foot tower which gave a perfect view of enemy movements; there were even attempts to fashion an observation balloon, but these came to naught.

One witness recalled other defence systems that were put in place:

'...a large bell was also placed in a position in the market buildings which was to be rung as a signal that the enemy were going to attack, or as a warning to the women and children that they had to take shelter in the laager. Signal rockets were also in readiness in case of a night attack and, as an additional means of defence, mines were laid along all the principal streets and in positions where a possible attack would come from.'[67]

§

By the first few days of April, Bulawayo had essentially been made safe from attack, and all the surviving settlers brought in. The rebels had murdered around 150 whites in brutal attacks on isolated settlements, but had blown their chance to deal a truly decisive blow against the Rhodesians.

As thoughts turned to taking the fight to the rebels, the Bishop of Mashonaland tried to preach understanding, reminding his flock:

'...we must be patient and strong and just, remembering on the one hand that we have the responsibility of 19 centuries of Christianity, while the native has inherited the tendencies of at least 50 centuries of heathenism and its accompanying triple tyranny of cannibalism, polygamy and slavery.'[68]

After the savage murders of the previous couple of weeks, few were interested in restraint.

End Notes

[1] Keppel-Jones, Rhodes and Rhodesia, p.442
[2] Sykes, With Plumer in Matabeleland, p.39
[3] Selous, Sunshine and Storm in Rhodesia, p.35
[4] Kane, The World's View: The Story of Southern Rhodesia, p.106
[5] Baxter, Rhodesia: Last Outpost of the British Empire, 1890-1980, p.100
[6] Keppel-Jones, Rhodes and Rhodesia, p.434
[7] Keppel-Jones, Rhodes and Rhodesia, p.435
[8] Keppel-Jones, Rhodes and Rhodesia, p.439
[9] Selous, Sunshine and Storm in Rhodesia, p.28

[10] Burnham, Scouting on Two Continents, p.122
[11] Hanna, The Story of the Rhodesias and Nyasaland, p.141
[12] Selous, Sunshine and Storm in Rhodesia, p.33
[13] Keppel-Jones, Rhodes and Rhodesia, p.442
[14] Ranger, Revolt in Southern Rhodesia, 1896-7, p.129
[15] Ranger, Revolt in Southern Rhodesia, 1896-7, p.130
[16] Selous, Sunshine and Storm in Rhodesia, p.32
[17] Keppel-Jones, Rhodes and Rhodesia, p.443
[18] Kane, The World's View: The Story of Southern Rhodesia, p.106
[19] Hanna, The Story of the Rhodesias and Nyasaland, p.141
[20] British South Africa Company, The '96 Rebellions, p.23
[21] Jones, Rhodesian Genesis, p.121
[22] Plumer, An Irregular Corps in Matabeleland, p.3
[23] Hensman, A History of Rhodesia, p.175
[24] Sykes, With Plumer in Matabeleland, p.14
[25] Sykes, With Plumer in Matabeleland, p.16
[26] Ranger, Revolt in Southern Rhodesia, 1896-7, p.164
[27] Gibbs, The History of the BSAP, Vol.1, p.164
[28] Baxter, Rhodesia: Last Outpost of the British Empire, 1890-1980, p.105
[29] Keppel-Jones, Rhodes and Rhodesia, p.448
[30] Jones, Rhodesian Genesis, p.121
[31] Hensman, A History of Rhodesia, p.174
[32] Selous, Sunshine and Storm in Rhodesia, p.55
[33] Sykes, With Plumer in Matabeleland, p.22
[34] Kane, The World's View: The Story of Southern Rhodesia, p.105
[35] Hensman, A History of Rhodesia, p.178
[36] Keppel-Jones, Rhodes and Rhodesia, p.444
[37] Selous, Sunshine and Storm in Rhodesia, p.135
[38] Selous, Sunshine and Storm in Rhodesia, p.136
[39] Hensman, A History of Rhodesia, p.199
[40] Selous, Sunshine and Storm in Rhodesia, p.136
[41] Selous, Sunshine and Storm in Rhodesia, p.139
[42] Hensman, A History of Rhodesia, p.179
[43] Selous, Sunshine and Storm in Rhodesia, p.141
[44] British South Africa Company, The '96 Rebellions, p.26
[45] Hensman, A History of Rhodesia, p.180
[46] Hensman, A History of Rhodesia, p.182
[47] British South Africa Company, The '96 Rebellions, p.26
[48] Hensman, A History of Rhodesia, p.182
[49] British South Africa Company, The '96 Rebellions, p.23
[50] Selous, Sunshine and Storm in Rhodesia, p.62
[51] Selous, Sunshine and Storm in Rhodesia, p.63
[52] Selous, Sunshine and Storm in Rhodesia, p.73
[53] Selous, Sunshine and Storm in Rhodesia, p.75
[54] Selous, Sunshine and Storm in Rhodesia, p.78
[55] Hensman, A History of Rhodesia, p.183
[56] Hensman, A History of Rhodesia, p.184
[57] Keppel-Jones, Rhodes and Rhodesia, p.444
[58] Hensman, A History of Rhodesia, p.185
[59] British South Africa Company, The '96 Rebellions, p.23
[60] Hensman, A History of Rhodesia, p.186
[61] Jones, Rhodesian Genesis, p.122
[62] Sykes, With Plumer in Matabeleland, p.16
[63] Sykes, With Plumer in Matabeleland, p.18
[64] Ranger, Revolt in Southern Rhodesia, 1896-7, p.129
[65] Sykes, With Plumer in Matabeleland, p.25
[66] Sykes, With Plumer in Matabeleland, p.20
[67] Jones, Rhodesian Genesis, p.123
[68] Ranger, Revolt in Southern Rhodesia, 1896-7, p.132

'The events of the last three months have taught me at least this, that it
is impossible for a European to understand the workings of a native's
mind; and, speaking personally, after having spent over twenty
years of my life amongst the Kaffirs, I now see that I know nothing
about them, and recognize that I am quite incompetent to express an
opinion as to the line of conduct they would be likely to adopt under
any given circumstances.'[1]

F.C. Selous confesses his bewilderment a few months after the start of the rebellion

'These men formed the nucleus of a force which has done splendid
service in the suppression of the present rebellion, under the name
of Grey's Scouts. They were a picked body of men, and neither their
name nor their brave deeds will ever be forgotten in Rhodesia, whilst I
think we all regard Captain Grey as one of the finest specimens of an
Englishman in the country–quiet, self-contained and unassuming,
but at the same time, brave, capable, and energetic.'[2]

Selous' description of the stalwart men of Grey's Scouts

'Sure enough on a ridge about 1,000 yards away we made out a body
of men hiding under cover. We at once put the Maxim on them, and
as they retreated in haste up the side of the hill, we found that several
hundreds of them had been waiting in ambush.'[3]

Lieutenant Webb describes how Captain Brand's patrol was attacked on the Tuli Road

'...in a running fight, when they are flurried and hustled, Kaffirs
cannot get the time they require to take good aim, and if you are near
them they always shoot over you. The golden rule is to scatter out,
each man firing independently in the Boer fashion.'

One veteran's advice on how best to fight the rebels

Chapter 13
The Empire Strikes Back

As soon as the severity of the rebellion had been understood, urgent appeals for relief were sent to the high commissioner[i] down in Cape Town.[4] Rhodes' chartered company immediately started recruiting a relief force, offering would be troopers the princely sum of 7/6 to march up to Bulawayo.[5] There was no shortage of volunteers. Men were mustered in the 'company towns' of Kimberley and Mafeking, and another 150 were raised in Johannesburg. Initially, the force was to be 500-strong, but under instructions from the high commissioner, this was increased to 750 so as incorporate the BSACP officers who had still not made it back to Rhodesia after the Jameson Raid.[6] Many of the other recruits were ex-Bechuanaland Border Police, or ex-Cape Mounted Riflemen and the like, and were tough, experienced men.[7]

An additional unit of 'Cape Boys' was also authorized. This 200–strong mixture of Africans and Cape Coloureds was recruited from among non-white mine workers in Johannesburg to be commanded by a Major Robertson. Strangely, these men were issued rifles and bayonets, but no frogs–meaning they had to leave their bayonets affixed to their rifles at all times. This no doubt added to the frightening reputation this corps would gain.[8] The Cape Boys would be attached to the main force then mustering in Mafeking.

Command of the relief column was given to Lt. Colonel Plumer[ii] who happened to be in South Africa at the time, having earlier been sent to Bulawayo to forestall a rumoured attempt to march on Pretoria and rescue Dr Jameson. It had fallen to the redoubtable Plumer to tell these elements that such a scheme would not be tolerated, and to take control of the company's ammunition stocks.[9] Plumer had handed this task over to a replacement but was still in Cape Town when the rebellion started, and he hurried back up the line to Mafeking to take command of the relief column.[10] He quickly organized the purchase of two Maxims from the Royal Navy base at Simon's Town, and another

---

i Sir Henry Loch had by this time been replaced by Hercules George Robert Robinson, 1st Baron Rosmead, GCMG, PC (1824–1897). Robinson had previously served as governor in Hong Kong, and was returning to the Cape for his second stint as high commissioner, having previously held the post between 1881and 1889.

ii Later Field Marshal Herbert Charles Onslow Plumer, 1st Viscount Plumer, GCB, GCMG, GCVO, GBE (1857–1932). One of the finest officers of his era, Plumer was a product of Eton and Sandhurst and served in Egypt, the Matabele Rebellion, the Boer War and the Great War, ultimately commanding the British 2nd Army in the war-winning 'Hundred Days Offensive' in 1918.

Matabele Rebellion - Key to incidents

(1) On 27th March 1896 Lt Col Gifford rides out from Bulawayo to rescue 33 refugees trapped at Cummins Store, near Fort Rixon. At 04h15 on 28th he is attacked at the store by a large force of Matabele but drives them off and effects the rescue

(2) On 30th March 1896 a Bulawayo Field Force (BFF) patrol, sent out to rescue another beleaguered patrol at Campbell's Store, was itself ambushed. Trpr HS Henderson was awarded the VC after being cut off and rescuing a wounded comrade.

(3) On 4th April Lt Col Gifford fights an action at Fonsesca's farm on the Umguza river, 22 miles north of Bulawayo

(4) On 10th April 1896 Capt Brand fights a rearguard action on the Tuli Road, at the Umzingwani crossing, 23 miles south of Bulawayo.

(5) On 17th April, 45 men under Captains Van Niekirk and George Grey skirmish with a Matabele *ibutho* (regiment) on the Umguza River barely three miles from Bulawayo.

(6) At about the same time, a Ndebele *ibutho* attacks Colonel Napier's fortified farmstead at Matsheumhlope, The 16-man white garrison, supported by friendly natives, drive off the attackers.

(7) Napiers relief force, finding no Ndebele, swept northward to the Umguza, and after crossing the road that led to Salisbury, the troopers clashed with natives near Colenbrander's Farm. As the Matabele attempted to outflank the colonials, Frederick Selous crossed a nearby stream and prevented a large war party from advancing on the main column's rear

(8) On 25th April, troopers and friendly natives under the command of Capt R Macfarlane left Bulawayo to scout the Unguza. Supported by a 1-Pdr Hotchkiss gun and a Maxim, they clash fiercely with the *amaNdebele*.

(9) On May 11, a relief column of 600 Rhodesians from Salisbury led by Cecil Rhodes fought its way through an opposing force of Ndebele between Movene Kraal and Gwelo, linking up with a mounted troop from Bulawayo. The combined columns combed the district northeast of the city, skirmishing with Ndebele regiments and burning native kraals.

(10) After information identified the place of the mlimo's secret cave in the Matopo Hills, scouts, Burnham and Armstrong, riding by night, located the medicine man, and allegedly assassinated him.

(11) At 5:30 am on 5th June 1896, Plumer's column, supported by two 2.5-inch mountain guns, attack Tabas-I-Mhamba, 65 miles north east of Bulawayo and after stiff fighting, capture the area.

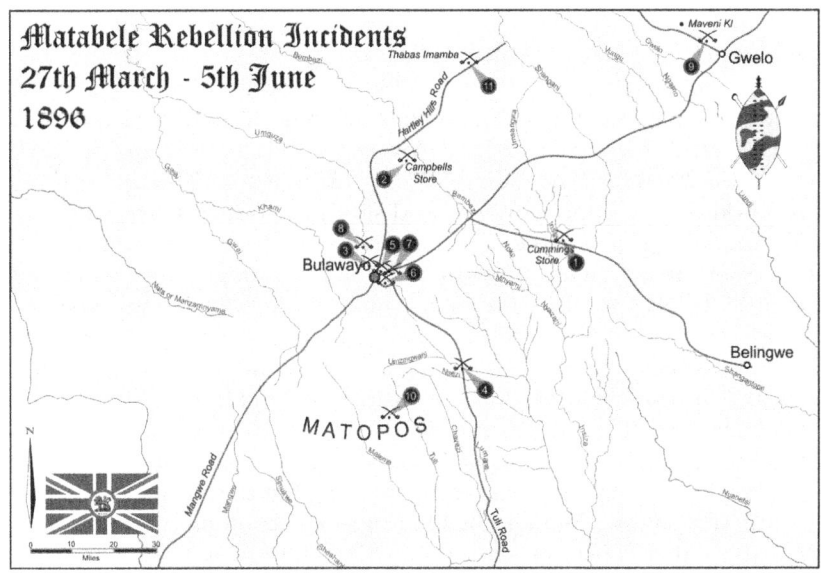

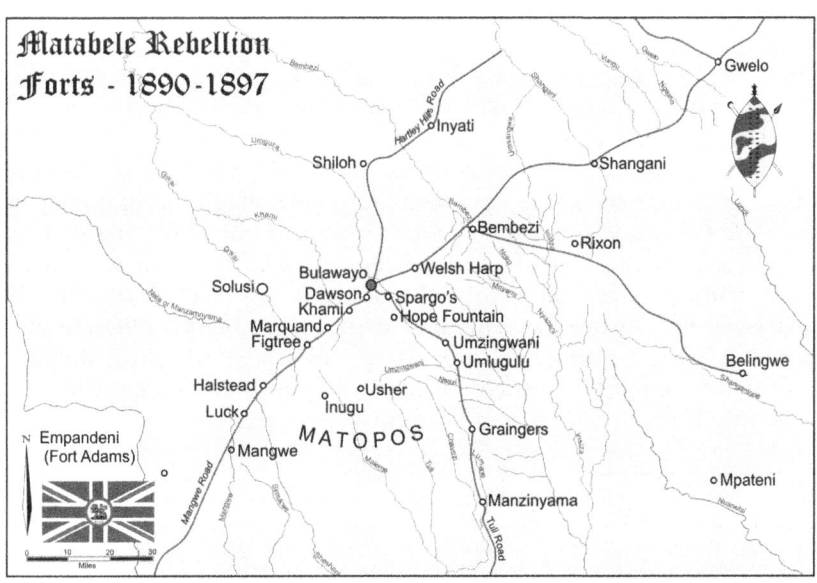

ten from 'a Mr Warren from Durban'. It is not explained quite how or why Mr Warren had ten tripod-mounted Maxims to hand, but he got the handsome price of £4,500 for them–a fee Plumer thought to be 'considerably in excess of their value'.[11]

The understanding was that Plumer would relinquish control to the newly appointed 'commandant general' of all armed forces in Mashonaland, Matabeleland and Bechuanaland, Sir Richard Martin,[iii] when he arrived from London to take up his new role. This change was forced onto the company by a very disgruntled British Government in the wake of the Jameson Raid, as a way of exerting more control over Rhodes' company, determined that it would no longer have an armed force of its own to do with as it would, while still being expected stump up the costs for troops in company territory.[12] Sir Richard would also act as the deputy commissioner for Rhodesia–basically, the British Government's man on the inside.[13] A stickler for routine and regulations, Sir Richard was not overly popular with the settlers. One wrote of him as being '...a nice man but a great deal too much the stereotypical official. We don't want anything but rough and ready men for this sort of job'.[14] Others were even more damning, describing Mr Richard as 'that consummate ass,' and 'that silly old woman'.

§

While Plumer's 'Matabeleland Relief Force' was still mustering, Administrator Grey pressed the high commissioner for even more white troops[iv], though Robinson, understandably wary about HM forces being under company control, pushed for regular imperial units, rather than additional company-raised volunteer units, and seemed to feel that, as the war was by no means a small uprising, it should be handled by the imperial authorities. There was also the continuing desire (whether conscious or unconscious) to stamp a bit of authority over Rhodesia and exert a bit more formal control of the place. This debate was the subject of various telegrams sent between 12 and 14 April, with Grey reluctant to let the dreaded 'imperial factor' play an important role in the war. This was already a bit messy: Plumer, who was still busily raising and organising the relief force in Mafeking, was a serving imperial officer, but described himself as one who was 'appointed by the high commissioner in connection with the forces of

---

iii   Colonel Sir Richard E.R. Martin, K.C.M.G., K.C.B. (1847–1907). A retired colonel of the 6th Dragoons, Sir Richard was described as 'a handsome, courteous officer of the old school' but events moved too quickly for him to play a major role in the war, and he quickly earned the nickname, 'Whistling Dick'–'an allusion to his principal occupation while in Rhodesia'.

iv   Not because of race preference but rather because he wanted well trained men who could ride and shoot.

the British South Africa Company'[15]–and besides, Sir Richard was to take command when he arrived.

The decision was taken to deploy a handful of imperial units and this prompted the colonial secretary to cable on 17 April, saying, 'As imperial troops are being employed, war office insist on command being entrusted to military officers on full pay and approved by them.' Sir Richard Martin did not fit the bill, therefore, and so Major General Sir Frederick Carrington[v] was quickly drafted in as commander in chief of all forces involved.[vi] Carrington seems to have been regarded as a decent sort by the Rhodesians, with one police officer declaring:

> 'When fighting or sport of any kind is going on, he is in his element, and the more the danger, the greater the element. To see him ride and shoot is to understand how, in his younger days, he raised a colonial corps and commanded them by sheer force of strength and skill of fisticuffs; and to see him stand on his own strong legs, or bestriding a horse, he is a splendid specimen of a man and a soldier–tall, active and daring.'[16]

Despite all this courage and dynamism, even his admirers wondered about his intelligence and imagination; a concern which would become more widespread as the fighting in the Matopos dragged on. As it turned out, and though the company-financed volunteers of Plumer's Matabele Relief Force would see plenty of action, there would only be very small numbers of imperial troops employed, and few of these would arrive in time to see action in Matabeleland.

Commanded by Lt. Col E.A.H. Alderson[vii], a mounted infantry (MI) battalion was formed in Aldershot from mounted companies from a variety of regiments of the British home garrison. To give the reader an idea of what a mishmash of units this formation was, the Highland Company, commanded by Captain G R Tod of the Seaforths, consisted of 4 detachments of about 30 men each from the 2nd Gordon Highlanders, 2nd Black Watch, 2nd Argyll, Sutherland Highlanders and 1st Seaforth Highlanders (please see Appendix 6 for full details on this remarkable battalion).

---

v   Major General Sir Frederick Carrington KCB, KCMG (1844–1913). Born and educated in Cheltenham, Carrington served in many southern African wars in the period, ultimately commanding the Rhodesian Field Force in the Boer War.

vi   Captain J. S. Nicholson of the 7th Hussars also arrived to take command of the Matabele Mounted Police

vii   Later, Lieutenant General Sir Edwin Alfred Hervey Alderson, KCB (1859–1927). A keen fox hunter and yachtsman, Alderson saw active service in many colonial wars, and went on to command the 1st Canadian Division, and then the Canadian Corps in the First World War.

The first elements of the composite mounted infantry battalion left Southampton on the Warwick Castle on 25 April and arrived in Cape Town on 19 May. Together with a detachment from the Duke of Wellington's (West Riding) Regiment–which had been part of the Natal garrison, the scratch mounted infantry battalion would later be shipped round to Beira and serve in Mashonaland so we shall return to these units later.

Other imperial units from the Natal Garrison—including three squadrons of 7th Hussars, and a Royal Artillery detachment manning a pair of mountain guns[17]—were moved inland and deployed up to Mafeking. In addition, two mounted infantry companies from the York and Lancaster Regiment were also sent up from the Cape Garrison.[18] The presence of these troops so close to the Transvaal's border was not terribly well received by Kruger, who, ever the drama queen, claimed, 'British troops are massing there.'[19] While 'B' Squadron of the 7th Hussars remained at Mafeking, the other two squadrons, 'A' and 'D'[viii]—along with the guns and the mounted infantry—marched north into Matabeleland on 22 June.[20]

It had been slow going, but matters were not helped by Kruger's refusal to let imperial units traverse the Transvaal–perhaps understandable, given the recent Jameson Raid, but one should also bear in mind that his agents were supplying the rebels behind the scenes. Kruger's offer to send commandos into Matabeleland to 'help' was also politely refused–military interventions by the Transvaal invariably ended with them annexing additional land for their republic.[21]

§

While the Matabele Relief Force was still being recruited and equipped, and the might of the British Empire was busy hacking its way through all the red tape and tiptoeing around Kruger's sensitivities, settlers from Mashonaland were a little quicker to come to the aid of their fellow Rhodesians over in Matabeleland. Word of the murders had reached Fort Salisbury almost immediately, and on 25 March, Captain Gibbs rode out with 10 Rhodesia Horse troopers, a pair of Maxims, 50 spare rifles and a large stock of ammunition. This small contingent arrived in Gwelo on the 29th and Gibbs assumed command of that town. He quickly raised his force to '284 volunteers, 52 burghers and 180 natives' which he used to patrol the area aggressively and to man various small forts.[22]

Delayed by the effect of the rinderpest epidemic on their transport, a rather more substantial relief column trotted out of Salisbury on 6

---

viii 'C' Squadron remained in Natal throughout the rebellions

April.[23] Commanded by Lt. Col Robert Beal, this force comprised 150 men from the Rhodesia Horse–and Cecil John Rhodes himself.[24] At the time, Rhodes was supposed to have been in Cape Town facing a parliamentary committee that was investigating his role in the Jameson Raid. Instead of wasting time on such things while men's lives were at stake, Rhodes simply absented himself from the whole affair and took a steamer to Beira. Despite suffering an attack of fever, he made his way to Salisbury in time to attach himself to Beal's column. The relief force advanced to the Gwelo laager without significant incident, and—with the telegram line repaired—Rhodes took the chance to send a typically dismissive message to explain his absence: 'Let resignation wait'.[25]

§

By early April, Bulawayo's defenders were also looking to take the fight back to the Matabele. Lt. Colonel Gifford led a sizable force out of the laager on the 4th with a 'roving commission' to seek out and engage the enemy. The column would be known as the Shiloh Patrol, and was made up of his own 'Gifford's Horse', 'F' Troop of the Bulawayo Field Force under Captain Dawson, a small number of Grey's Scouts, and a wagon-mounted Maxim gun team–a total of 118 all ranks, plus 49 Colonial Boys under Captain Bisset.[26]

The Shiloh Patrol had not gone far when word was received of an impi encamped about 14 miles away, near Fonseca's Farm on the Umguza River,[27] and Gifford gamely decided to attack. As the column changed direction, their scouts soon came under fire and then the rear guard was attacked by about 300 rebels. These were beaten off, and the Shiloh Patrol pushed on the following morning, only for the advance guard to come under attack from about 500 Matabele. The Maxim was brought forward and quickly broke up the rebels while the Colonial Boys worked their way round the flank and fell upon the Matabele, killing about thirty of them.[28] The force laagered again, but the evening and night passed without further incident.

The following morning, Monday 6 April, patrols were sent out and the laager was broken up. After receiving reports that there were cattle down at the Umguza, Gifford ordered the Colonial Boys out to bring them in, but they came under fire just a few hundred yards out. In the face of this very brisk fusillade, the Colonial Boys retreated, back to where Gifford was deploying the main force into a natural defensive position in a dry donga.

The Colonial Boys were safely brought down to the main position, though Trooper Mackenzie of Gifford's Horse[29] was killed while covering their retreat. The attackers then turned their attention to

Gifford's main force and a fierce fire fight raged. The Maxim gun, which was mounted on a tripod atop a wagon, attracted much of the enemy fire, and Corporal Reynolds (Gifford's Horse) was hit while near it and died later. Gifford himself clambered onto the wagon to get a better view of the action, and was soon shot through the shoulder. Two of the Colonial Boys were also shot dead in the action. By 09h30, the company forces seemed to have won the fire fight and the rebels sulkily withdrew, though some continued to fire long-range dropping shots into the position long afterwards.[30] The Matabele had not made any real effort to storm Gifford's position in the old style, but their riflemen had managed to kill three of his force and wound another five (including Gifford himself). The rebels' generally good shooting led to speculation about many of them being deserters from the native police–trained in marksmanship by the very men they were trying to kill.

Gallopers were sent back to Bulawayo—about 22 miles away—to request reinforcements. In response, Captain Macfarlane rode out of the laager with 60 mounted troopers, a Maxim, a doctor and a heliograph team, that evening.

The following morning, 7 April, and before Macfarlane's reinforcements arrived, the rebels attacked Gifford's position again. They came on much more aggressively this time, attacking from two directions 'with great violence' as they charged forward 'with a desperate rush of the old Zulu type'.[31] These courageous charges were quickly broken up and repulsed by rapid fire, though Captain Lumsden, who had taken over command from the wounded Gifford, was himself shot through the ankle. Two other company troopers were wounded, one very severely.[32] The rebels shook themselves out into more open order and charged again, attacking from all sides of the position at once.[33] By midday, however, they'd had enough and pulled back. Macfarlane's relief column arrived at 16h00. There were no further attacks and the whole force withdrew back to Bulawayo on the 8th, arriving there at 10h30.

Though rebel losses are unknown, the action at Fonseca's Farm had certainly been a fierce engagement. The company forces had fired off 3,850 rounds of Martini Henry ammunition and another 2,600 of Lee Metford.[34] Captain Lumsden would die from his wounds two days later, while Gifford's injury was so bad that his arm had to be amputated at the shoulder. One of the men killed in the action was a retired officer from the Scottish Rifles who had been big game hunting in Matabeleland when the rebellion broke out.[35]

§

A similarly sized unit had set out from Bulawayo two days before the Shiloh Patrol, with the object of bringing in any remaining white settlers from the Gwanda district[36] which lies around 80 miles to the south. This force was made up of the 50 men of 'C' Troop, Bulawayo Field Force,[37] 50 of the Afrikander Corps and a Maxim gun team. Dr Levy accompanied the patrol with an ambulance and Captain Brand was in overall command. The patrol had not come into contact with the enemy and finding that the white settlers of the region had retired down to Tuli, decided to start the return march back up to Bulawayo on the 9th.[38]

On the afternoon of the following day with the column about 25 miles from Bulawayo, the advance party came under fire at about 1,000 yards from some kopjes which commanded the road. The Maxim was quickly brought forward and silenced the rebel riflemen after just a few bursts. Flanking parties were thrown out to clear the kopjes and the main body pushed on. Disaster struck when the disselboom[ix] of the mule wagon snapped just as the patrol was passing between the two kopjes, and the delay prompted the Matabele to surge forward for an attack.

Captain Brand managed to get some of his men onto high ground while the Maxim was deployed to cover the road to the east. One witness described what must have been a terrifying experience in the quaint, stiff-upper-lipped style of the time: 'Mr. Jobson, who was in command of the Maxim, brought his gun into action with the greatest coolness and promptitude.'[39] The rebels charged forward with great dash from three sides before being shot down just 30 yards from the firing lines. The Maxim was very well handled and was reported as having done 'great execution'. Indeed, it probably saved Brand's patrol from being over-run.[40]

Displaying phenomenal élan, the rebels regrouped and charged three more times but were broken up or driven off at each instance. Captain van Niekerk then ordered half of his Afrikanders to mount up, and led them out in a charge to clear the Matabele from some thick bush. The rebels panicked and fled out into the open and many were shot down as a result.

Brand seized this moment of respite to get his patrol moving again, and they pushed on as best they could. Though seemingly loathe to risk another charge, about 1,000 rebels closely followed the retreating column, shooting at them from cover. Lieutenant Webb later recalled:

'...when I tell you that [the Matabele] were over 1,000 strong and followed us for over five miles at a distance of little more than

---

ix   The main shaft or pole of a wagon, to which horses, oxen or mules were harnessed. From the Afrikaans 'dissel shaft + boom beam'.

200 yards, you will be better able to judge of the task we had in hand. Our route lay over successive ranges of ridges and valleys, and afforded plenty of cover for the enemy, as the grass was about three feet high, and the country thickly studded with bush and trees. They formed a half-moon round us and skirmished excellently, taking advantage of every bit of cover. They also fought with ferocious determination, and often showed pluck verging on lunacy. They were kept well in hand by their leaders, who constantly urged them to fire low. Our horses and men were now falling with deadly monotony, and we all saw the importance of getting into more open country. Our men were firing steadily and rapidly all this time, and the Maxim did good service; but being on the move and owing to the tactics of the enemy, did not do the execution we were accustomed to see in the first Matabele war.'[41]

Not surprisingly, the new tactics were certainly a lot more successful than the old style Zulu charge and, sniping from the rocks, the rebels harried Brand's retreating column every step of the way. We shall let Webb continue describing that unpleasant afternoon:

'At last, after about three hours' fighting, we saw about a mile ahead of us a round stone kopje, for which we made in order to take a short halt. The enemy at once saw through our movement, and a number of them endeavoured to defeat our object by out-flanking our advance. Our horsemen, however, were too sharp for them, and by hard riding reached the kopje first, and held them in check until the main body arrived. The kopje we thus reached was nothing but a huge flat rock, showing out about twelve or fifteen feet above the surrounding country. It was almost surrounded by broken rocks and trees, and under this cover—in some instances only some thirty to forty yards from where we were standing—the Matabele concealed themselves, and continued their fire upon us. This alone will give you some idea of their astounding audacity and bravery. We had to charge them four times to make them at last give in and retire. It was now about sundown (5.30 p.m.) and we had actually been about six hours fighting over five miles of country.'[42]

By then, the Matabele seemed to have had had enough and backed off a little. Brand took a few minutes to reorganize and load the most seriously wounded onto the mule cart or the Maxim wagon. The wounded who could not fit had no choice but to ride. Brand led his battered, blooded but—thus far—somehow still unbowed, patrol off again at dusk, determined to risk pushing on through the darkness,

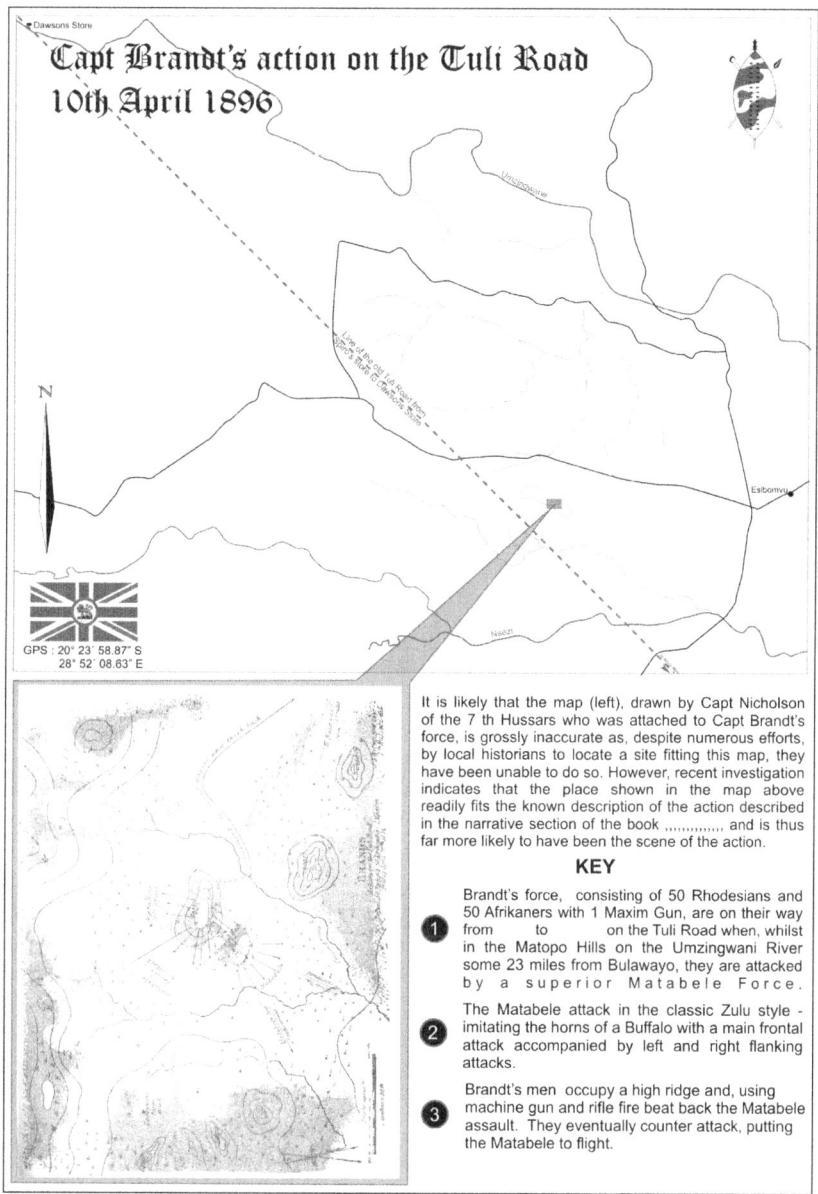

Capt Brandt's action on the Tuli Road 10th April 1896

Dawsons Store

N

GPS : 20° 23' 58.87" S
28° 52' 08.63" E

It is likely that the map (left), drawn by Capt Nicholson of the 7 th Hussars who was attached to Capt Brandt's force, is grossly inaccurate as, despite numerous efforts, by local historians to locate a site fitting this map, they have been unable to do so. However, recent investigation indicates that the place shown in the map above readily fits the known description of the action described in the narrative section of the book ,,,,,,,,,,,,, and is thus far more likely to have been the scene of the action.

KEY

1 Brandt's force, consisting of 50 Rhodesians and 50 Afrikaners with 1 Maxim Gun, are on their way from   to   on the Tuli Road when, whilst in the Matopo Hills on the Umzingwani River some 23 miles from Bulawayo, they are attacked by a superior Matabele Force.

2 The Matabele attack in the classic Zulu style - imitating the horns of a Buffalo with a main frontal attack accompanied by left and right flanking attacks.

3 Brandt's men occupy a high ridge and, using machine gun and rifle fire beat back the Matabele assault. They eventually counter attack, putting the Matabele to flight.

rather than giving the rebels time to sort themselves out for another onslaught. Lt. Webb finished his account:

> 'We left the kopje at dusk, and for the next sixteen miles had a most unpleasant section of the road to traverse, on any portion of which the Matabele had us at their mercy had they chosen to attack. Whether they had had enough fighting, or whether they did not suspect our departure, is not known, but we were all heartily glad to get through that section of the country unmolested. At half-past four on the morning of the 11th of April, we met the relief force sent to meet us, and two hours later we halted in front of the government offices in Bulawayo. That afternoon we buried one of my most intimate friends, poor Baker, who had been shot in the fight, and died on the homeward march.'[43]

The engagement would become known by the less-than-catchy name, 'The Rearguard Action On The Tuli Road' and Captain Brand was very fortunate to have escaped the fate suffered by Major Wilson three years earlier: indeed, one history stated, 'How the little force of 100 men escaped complete annihilation was a mystery.'[44] One could argue that fortune shone on them, but Brand kept his head, his men were steady and fought bravely, and the Maxim gun was very well handled. Captain van Niekerk's Afrikanders, described as 'old and experienced campaigners', came in for special praise. Another observer put it a little more bluntly:

> 'Amongst the Afrikanders there were many old Kaffir fighters, such as old Mr. Steyn and Messrs. Loots and Ferreira, and these old campaigners were naturally more useful than inexperienced men.'

As was only to be expected and, indeed, as proved to be the norm at the height of empire, the young officers of British stock also proved to be unflappable and resolute under pressure:

> 'Lieutenants Webb and Holland, Purssell and Jobson—the latter in charge of the Maxim gun—did their duty throughout the engagement as coolly as if they were on parade.'[45]

Nevertheless, Brand's patrol still lost five men killed and another 25 wounded, two of which would subsequently die–a total of perhaps 30% of his force. 33 horses were also killed in the action. Brand had no choice other than to leave his dead on the field. Rebel losses were estimated to be around 250.[46]

§

While Captain Brand's men were fighting for their lives on the Tuli Road, there was also drama at Bulawayo. On 10 April, three rebel prisoners were brought into the town by loyal natives. These three, who had been caught in the act of burning and looting a white-owned property about 20 miles to the west of Bulawayo, were summarily sentenced to death and hanged in a tree on the outskirts of the town.[47] This was rough and ready, frontier-style justice, for sure, but there was also little doubt of the men's guilt and the storm of protest this prompted in the left-leaning London press was the normal manufactured, self-loathing rubbish. It is difficult to think of a more suitable punishment for the rebels and, though perhaps shocking to the soft-hearted modern reader, one can hardly blame the settlers for not feeling too 'touchy-feely' in the wake of so many horrific murders.

By mid-April, the situation had stabilized to a degree. Around 1,500 white men, women and children were sheltered in Bulawayo, able to visit their houses in different parts of the town by day, but spending their nights within the laager. The rest of Matabeleland, with the exceptions of the laagers at Gwelo and Belingwe, and the string of small forts protecting the road to Mangwe, was in the hands of the rebels, although the main road south to Mafeking remained open.

We shall let Selous describe the deployment and intentions of the rebel forces at that time:

'A large impi lay at Mr. Crewe's farm, Redbank, on the Khami river, about twelve miles to the west of the town, besides which some thousands of rebels, amongst whom it was said was Lobengula's eldest son, Nyamanda, were camped all along the Umguza, considerable numbers of them being actually within three miles of Bulawayo, whilst other two large impis had taken up their quarters amongst the Elibani Hills, and in the neighbourhood of Intaba Induna, there being altogether not less than 10,000 hostile natives spread out in a semicircle from the west to the north-east of the town. Had these different impis only combined and acted in concert under one leader they might have accomplished something; but each impi appears to have been acting independently of the others, and my own belief is that they kept hanging round the town without any general plan of action, in the expectation of some supernatural interference by the deity on their behalf. At least this is what we hear from themselves, and I think it is the truth. Besides the impis to the north and west, there were others encamped within the edge of the Matopos Hills.'[48]

It is unclear quite who—if anyone—was in charge of these sizable forces. Lobengula's son, Nyamanda, would appear to have been involved, but not in the role of a fighting general.[49] Some suggest that the induna of the Ingubu Impi was calling the shots. One historian points to the powerful influence of various witch-doctors and the like. Either way, this lack of coherent command structure was hardly conducive to a successful uprising.

On 12 April, a large force of rebels approached Bulawayo, coming within about a mile and a half of the beleaguered settlement. They made no attempt to storm the fortified town, but rather seem to have hoped to draw the settlers out into the open, where the odds would be much more favourable to the Matabele. Unable to simply ignore this mass of warriors, the Rhodesians duly obliged and a series of actions were fought between 16 and 25 April.[50]

The first clash occurred near the Umguza River, when a 45-strong mounted patrol under Captain Grey came under fire.[51] The rebels opened up at 800 yards, which was optimistic to say the least. Grey's response was to shake his men out into skirmishing order and make straight for the rebels at a canter. The Matabele riflemen were on the far side of the river, but the Rhodesians forded this and then charged the nearest band of rebels. This group was put to flight, but Captain Grey soon realized he had led his men into a fairly large impi and was in danger of being out-flanked. Wisely, he called a halt and pulled his men back over the river. Their retreat was closely followed-up by the rebels, but the patrol made it back to the safety of Bulawayo with just one man wounded.[52]

On the 19th, a three-man patrol from the Afrikander Corps was isolated and killed by the rebels and, at the same time, an impi raided Colonel Napier's farm which lay about three miles south of Bulawayo. Remarkably, there were still cattle and a group of sixteen white men[53] at Napier's farm, and the rebels drove off the former and attempted to storm the latter. A relief column consisting of a troop of the Afrikander Corps, 'K' troop of the Bulawayo Field Force and a detachment of Grey's Scouts rode out from Bulawayo to the rescue, with Captain Macfarlane in command.[54]

On approaching the farm, Macfarlane learned that the settlers had quickly repulsed their attackers, and their loyal natives had chased after them, clubbing and stabbing six to death as they fled.[55] Determined to give them an even bloodier nose, Captain Macfarlane led his column to try and catch up with the fleeing rebels before they got clean away. Sure enough, they caught the raiders at the Umguza River, but—as on the 16th—the Matabele were on the far side. With his scouts reporting that other impis were closing in on him, Macfarlane decided against crossing the river. Instead, he took up a defensive position near a farm house belonging to Johannes Colenbrander, and waited for the seemingly inevitable attack.

The rebels did indeed attempt to take Macfarlane's men on, and there was a short, sharp skirmish, an action most notable because the single Maxim gun jammed at an inconvenient time. Depending on which account one believes, this either spared the rebels greater loss than the twenty or so casualties they took, or else brought the company troops to the edge of 'near disaster'.[56] Given that Macfarlane's column lost only one man killed and another wounded, it would seem far-fetched in the extreme to claim that the jamming of their single machine gun almost saw them over-run and it ignores the fearsome firepower of the hundred rifles of his patrol.[x] It is also noteworthy that, according to the ubiquitous Selous, he had been asked to draw the attackers onto the machine gun, and it jammed, not just as an unstoppable rebel horde was about to charge home, but while they were skirmishing at about 400 yards:

'There was a really good chance for the Maxim to do some execution, for although the Kaffirs were nowhere in masses, there was a straggling line of a couple of hundred of them right out in the open, and not more than 400 yards from the gun. But when the word was given to fire it most unfortunately jammed at the sixth shot, and the Kaffirs had to be driven back by rifle fire. The cause of the mishap was that a cartridge-case had broken off at the rim in the barrel of the Maxim, rendering it for the time being useless.'[57]

Either way, Macfarlane realized that the Matabele were steadily working their way around his position, and were close to completely surrounding his column. It was at this point that he decided to order his men to re-mount and retreat back to Bulawayo.[58] Some accounts claim that the rebels called their pursuit off when a spring hare ran in front of them–an unpropitious omen, apparently.[59] It is easy to claim, as many modern writers do, that such things were said to discredit and belittle the Matabele as simple and overly-superstitious people–but this is to ignore the fact that many such accounts came from Matabele witnesses, and also to disregard the reality that, political correctness aside, they were indeed a primitive people, highly influenced by omens and superstition.

§

---

x The reader should bear in mind that, in a defensive action, a well sited Maxim was reckoned to be equivalent to 30 magazine rifles. It was a formidable weapon, but the effect of it having jammed temporarily should be kept in perspective.

The inconclusive actions fought on the 16th and 19th were enough to convince Colonel Napier that he needed to break up and drive off the impis which were by then closely investing Bulawayo. Napier assembled a sizable force—230 whites and 100 Colonial Boys (some armed only with assegais) a Hotchkiss, a 7-pdr, and a Maxim gun[60]—and, on the 20th, led them out towards the Umguza River. Napier's force sighted a rebel impi of about 3,000, but once more these were on the far side of the river, and seemed keen to draw Napier's men across and then cut them off. Outnumbered about 10 to 1, Napier had no intention of falling into such a trap, and withdrew to Bulawayo.[61]

Two days later, on the 22nd, another force was sent to the area, this time under the command of Captain Bisset. It was a smaller column than what Napier had led out on the 20th, and comprised 120 whites drawn from various units, the Hotchkiss, a Maxim and a unit of about 100 Colonial Boys to which our old friend, Selous, was attached. Things did not start well, however, and an accident on the road broke the Hotchkiss' limber, rendering it unusable in the action which quickly followed.

This time, the rebels had occupied a small ridgeline on the near side of the river and they opened fire on the approaching column before it got to the Umguza:

'On proceeding we changed our direction and made straight for the Umguza, and it was soon evident that the Kaffirs intended to dispute our advance, as they commenced to fire on us from the low ridges covered with scrubby bush which here border the river on both sides. Captain Van Niekerk and his Afrikanders were soon hotly engaged on the left flank, and as the Kaffirs were in possession of some ridges just in front of us as well, I was asked to advance with the Colonial Boys from the centre, and endeavour to chase them across the river. My instructions were to attack and, if possible, drive them before me, but to retire on the guns if I found them too strong.

The boys came on capitally, led by their officers, who were all mounted, and we soon drove all the Matabele in this part of the field through the Umguza, and following them up at once, pursued them for about a mile over some stony ridges covered with scrubby bush.

Up to this time I had not fired a shot, as I had been principally engaged in encouraging the Colonial Boys to come on quickly and give our enemies no breathing time. But by this time we had got right up amongst them, and I began to use my rifle.

A number of the Matabele had built little fortifications of loose stones near the bank of the river, from behind the shelter of which they fired on us; but the warlike Amakhosa and Zulus [many of whom made up the Colonial Boys] charged them most gallantly, and engaging them hand to hand drove them out of their shelters into the river, and killed many of them in the water. Several of the Colonial Boys were here wounded with assegais and axes, but none were killed.

It was at this time that I saw John Grootboom, a Xhosa Kaffir—who has distinguished himself for bravery on many occasions both during the first war and the present campaign—galloping after a Matabele just in front of me, who was armed only with assegais and shield. As the horse came upon him he ducked down, and only just escaped a blow on the head from John's rifle, which was dealt with such vigour that the rider lost his balance and fell off, and his foot catching in the stirrup, he was dragged along the road for some yards. If the Matabele had but kept his presence of mind and been quick, he might have assegaied his antagonist easily, and possibly would have done so had not Captain Fynn and myself been close to him.'[62]

The courageous assault by the Colonial Boys, and a dashing charge by a small unit of Grey's Scouts, had essentially shattered the rebel position, and many were fleeing for their lives. Had the rest of Bisset's force been unleashed at that point, there is little doubt that a pursuit would have been little short of a massacre, and a serious blow would have been dealt to the rebels. Instead, only a few mounted Colonial Boys and some of the Grey's Scouts followed up, with Bisset not keen to commit the rest of his units. It is easy to criticize this decision in hindsight, but Bisset probably felt that he had landed a sizeable blow on the rebels and did not wish to risk his men galloping off into an ambush. The swirling, uncontrollable running battle of a mounted pursuit through close terrain was a good deal more dangerous than the 'typical' colonial battle where the imperial forces could fight in tight, well ordered, dismounted formations, and make best use of their fire-power.

Those few who had taken it upon themselves to pursue the routing rebels were quickly recalled and the whole force then withdrew back to Bulawayo. The rebels, who must have suffered very severely, made no attempt to interfere with the withdrawal. Company losses were just one man killed and half a dozen wounded–none seriously.

Selous, who (true to form) took an active part in the pursuit, emerged unscathed but without his horse. It had run off when Selous dismounted to engage the enemy and he had to be brought out on the back of a friend's mount. Selous regretfully recorded that his horse,

'...must have been captured by the Matabele, as he did not return to Bulawayo, and has not since been heard of. The lucky savage into whose hands he fell became possessed at the same time of a very good saddle and bridle, and a brand new Government coat.'[63]

§

On the 25th, another attempt was made to land a knock-out blow on the rebels. Captain Macfarlane led another column out of Bulawayo, and down towards the Umguza River; this time the patrol was made up of 35 Grey's Scouts under Captain Grey, the 25-strong 'B' Troop of the BFF under Captain Fynn, 15 of Captain Dawson's troop, 35 of the Afrikander Corps under Commandant Van Rensburg, 100 Colonial Boys under Captain Cardigan, and 60 to 70 friendly natives under Chief Native Commissioner Taylor. In support, there was the Hotchkiss gun, a Maxim under Captain Rixon, and an ambulance with stretchers under Dr Vigne–all in all, some 120 whites and about 170 Colonial Boys and friendlies.[64]

Macfarlane's plan was to push his scouts out to provoke a rebel response and then to pull back, drawing the Matabele onto the main body 'where the guns were, so as to give the quick-firing weapons an opportunity of inflicting a much-needed lesson on the rebels'.[65] While his scouts set about this work, the rest of Macfarlane's force took up a position near a burned out farmhouse some three miles from Bulawayo and close to the Umguza River. Though the position allowed the Hotchkiss and the Maxim to be well sited, there was little in the way of cover for the men.

Sure enough, Macfarlane's scouts encountered a large force of rebels, and slowly began to withdraw, leading them on to the main position. The Matabele were not going to blunder into the trap, however, and drew up about 200 yards short, going to ground in the bush and sparking a fierce fire-fight.

As the company forces' rifles and machine guns opened up, flaying the bush, the rebels gamely returned fire:

'...bullets of all sorts came whistling along, from elephant guns, Martinis, Winchesters, and Lee-Metfords, and for about an hour things were decidedly unpleasant, though up to this time we had only one man killed and one wounded. Our firing was incessant, and the shooting, though mostly at long range, very steady, and as effective probably as our exposed position and the cover afforded our assailants by the bush would allow. After the rebels had made two determined efforts to approach the Maxim, in both of which they were foiled, their fire slackened, and they apparently sent their best marksmen to the front to see what they could do.'[66]

Macfarlane seized his chance, and ordered the Afrikanders out to charge the rebels on the left. The Dutchmen rode straight at them, shouting and whooping 'they use rather more "noise" fighting than the Britishers do'—and sent the Matabele running for the river in a panic-stricken stampede. The Afrikanders got in about the fleeing rebels at the river crossing, killing at least seventy,[67] and completely smashing that wing of their attack. To add to the carnage, the Hotchkiss gun flung several shells out into the midst of the rout.

On the other side of the line, the Matabele were quickly cleared from the bush in front of Captain Dawson's men and soon the rebels were in full flight all across the field. Another impi attempted to intervene, but they too, were swiftly driven off by fire from the Maxim and the Hotchkiss gun.[68]

It had not, perhaps, been the mass slaughter which veterans of the First Matabele War might have hoped for, but Macfarlane's men had landed a telling blow nonetheless. The rebels had had enough and pulled their impis back from the area at the Umguza River, shifting them back to a more remote spot. It was reckoned Macfarlane's men had killed around 150 of the 2,000-strong rebel force that day. As usual, company losses were much lower, but by no means insignificant: 4 white men killed and another 4 wounded. Three friendly natives were also wounded.

The action on the 25th bought Colonel Napier some breathing space and a few days later, he received word of a relief column pushing west from Mashonaland. We shall therefore leave Napier and the plucky defenders of Bulawayo for a moment, and turn our attention to the force coming to his rescue.

§

As we know, Lt. Colonel Beal's column—complete with heavy artillery in the form of Cecil John Rhodes himself—had arrived safely at the Gwelo laager despite the havoc the rinderpest outbreak had played with his transport. This was not the only problem though: the Rhodesian settlers were nothing if not an individualistic bunch, and anyone who was anyone in the Gwelo laager seems to have felt he should be in charge. With two squabbling Lt. Colonels (neither of whom would serve under the other) to deal with, Cecil Rhodes took the logical, though still rather audacious, step of simply conferring himself the rank of full colonel. As the two prima donnas were both willing to serve under him, this solved the problem at a stroke, but raised more than a few eyebrows at the colonial office in London. Rhodes waved away the concerns of Joe Chamberlain[xi] in his usual style, telegramming from Gwelo on 14 May:

'For Secretary of State for Colonies. Tell him there is no colonel more unhappy than I am; obliged to take position to smooth over individual jealousies as to rank between the various officers. The result is I have to go out into the field and be fired at by the horrid Matabeles with their beastly elephant guns, which make a fearful row. It is a new and most unpleasant sensation.'[69]

Despite all this fuss, Beal's 'relief force' was not entirely worthy of the name; as it pushed on from Gwelo, it still comprised only 150 men from the Rhodesia Horse. On 19 May, Beal's relief column met the force Colonel Napier had led out from Bulawayo to meet them—a force which was, rather perversely, four times larger than the one coming to its rescue.70 Various fighting patrols were sent out to dominate the area, but these did little more than skirmish with small bands of rebels, and indulge in some tit-for-tat burning of kraals.

By 27 May, the combined columns were back in Bulawayo and discovered that events had been moving quickly in their absence.

---

xi Joseph Chamberlain (1836-1914). Self-made businessman and one-time Mayor of Birmingham, 'Pushful Joe' Chamberlain initially joined the Liberal party but sided with the Liberal Unionists when the party split in 1886, and became a passionate exponent of the British Imperial cause. He served as Secretary of State for the colonies from 1895 to 1903 and was deeply implicated in the Jameson Raid—an event which left a lasting schism between him and Rhodes and caused Jameson to describe him as 'the callous devil from Birmingham'. He was the father of Neville Chamberlain, Conservative PM most famous for his appeasement of Hitler.

End Notes
1   Selous, Sunshine and Storm in Rhodesia, p.25
2   Selous, Sunshine and Storm in Rhodesia, p.97
3   Selous, Sunshine and Storm in Rhodesia, p.121
4   Jones, Rhodesian Genesis, p.121
5   Sykes, With Plumer in Matabeleland, p.56
6   Sykes, With Plumer in Matabeleland, p.57
7   Plumer, An Irregular Corps in Matabeleland, p.16
8   Keppel-Jones, Rhodes and Rhodesia, p.455
9   Plumer, An Irregular Corps in Matabeleland, p.2
10 Plumer, An Irregular Corps in Matabeleland, p.14
11 Plumer, An Irregular Corps in Matabeleland, p.28

[12] Keppel-Jones, Rhodes and Rhodesia, p.431
[13] Keppel-Jones, Rhodes and Rhodesia, p.432
[14] Ranger, Revolt in Southern Rhodesia, 1896-7, p.173
[15] Keppel-Jones, Rhodes and Rhodesia, p.454
[16] Ranger, Revolt in Southern Rhodesia, 1896-7, p.172
[17] Barrett, The 7th (Queen's Own) Hussars, Volume 3: 1818-1914, p.171
[18] Barrett, The 7th (Queen's Own) Hussars, Volume 3: 1818-1914, p.172
[19] Barrett, The 7th (Queen's Own) Hussars, Volume 3: 1818-1914, p.140
[20] Barrett, The 7th (Queen's Own) Hussars, Volume 3: 1818-1914, p.172
[21] Theal, History of South Africa from 1873-1884, p.146
[22] Keppel-Jones, Rhodes and Rhodesia, p.455
[23] Gibbs, The History of the BSAP, Vol.1, p.169
[24] Keppel-Jones, Rhodes and Rhodesia, p.456
[25] Robert I. Rotberg, The Founder: Cecil Rhodes and the Pursuit of Power, p.556
[26] Hensman, A History of Rhodesia, p.193
[27] British South Africa Company, The '96 Rebellions, p.30
[28] Hensman, A History of Rhodesia, p.194
[29] British South Africa Company, The '96 Rebellions, p.40
[30] British South Africa Company, The '96 Rebellions, p.30
[31] Hensman, A History of Rhodesia, p.196
[32] British South Africa Company, The '96 Rebellions, p.32
[33] Hensman, A History of Rhodesia, p.196
[34] British South Africa Company, The '96 Rebellions, p.32
[35] Hensman, A History of Rhodesia, p.197
[36] British South Africa Company, The '96 Rebellions, p.28
[37] Hensman, A History of Rhodesia, p.188
[38] Hensman, A History of Rhodesia, p.190
[39] Selous, Sunshine and Storm in Rhodesia, p.122
[40] British South Africa Company, The '96 Rebellions, p.28
[41] Selous, Sunshine and Storm in Rhodesia, p.122
[42] Selous, Sunshine and Storm in Rhodesia, p.123
[43] Selous, Sunshine and Storm in Rhodesia, p.124
[44] Hensman, A History of Rhodesia, p.193
[45] Selous, Sunshine and Storm in Rhodesia, p.125
[46] Hensman, A History of Rhodesia, p.192
[47] Selous, Sunshine and Storm in Rhodesia, p.137
[48] Selous, Sunshine and Storm in Rhodesia, p.143
[49] Keppel-Jones, Rhodes and Rhodesia, p.449
[50] Keppel-Jones, Rhodes and Rhodesia, p.450
[51] Selous, Sunshine and Storm in Rhodesia, p.144
[52] Hensman, A History of Rhodesia, p.200
[53] Selous, Sunshine and Storm in Rhodesia, p.148
[54] Hensman, A History of Rhodesia, p.200
[55] Selous, Sunshine and Storm in Rhodesia, p.148
[56] Keppel-Jones, Rhodes and Rhodesia, p.450
[57] Selous, Sunshine and Storm in Rhodesia, p.152
[58] Hensman, A History of Rhodesia, p.201
[59] Keppel-Jones, Rhodes and Rhodesia, p.451
[60] Hensman, A History of Rhodesia, p.201
[61] Keppel-Jones, Rhodes and Rhodesia, p.451
[62] Selous, Sunshine and Storm in Rhodesia, p.158
[63] Selous, Sunshine and Storm in Rhodesia, p.166
[64] Selous, Sunshine and Storm in Rhodesia, p.171
[65] Hensman, A History of Rhodesia, p.205
[66] Selous, Sunshine and Storm in Rhodesia, p.173
[67] Hensman, A History of Rhodesia, p.206
[68] Selous, Sunshine and Storm in Rhodesia, p.174
[69] Keppel-Jones, Rhodes and Rhodesia, p.456
[70] Hensman, A History of Rhodesia, p.209

'...the M'Limo had instructed them to approach Bulawayo and to draw out the garrison, and get us to cross the Umguza, because he (the M'Limo) would then cause the stream to open and swallow up every man of us... something must have gone wrong with the M'Limo 's machinery, and we crossed the stream without any contretemps.'[1]

'One of our men got somewhat detached from the rest, and came on a bunch of eight of the enemy. These fired on him and killed his horse, but he himself was up in a trice, and, using his magazine fore, he let them have it with such effect that before they could close on him with their clubs and assegais, he had floored half their number, and the rest just turned and fled.'[2]

'The 'friendlies' Mr. Thomas had brought were very useful... they knew the country thoroughly, although their idea of distance was peculiar.'[3]

Lt. Colonel Plumer recalls the limitations of the loyal natives

'We came to the approach of the cave which was curtained with grass... I told the M'Limo the message I had been given by the indunas and told him the whites had gone on towards the Shangani. The M'Limo who, invisible to me, spoke from the cave told me to return to the impi and tell them to follow the white man.'[4]

A Matabele captive, Malima, who served as a messenger in the rebellion, gives his account of communicating with the 'god' M'Limo

Chapter 14
The Imperial Factor

While Napier's column was out rendezvousing with the relief force from Mashonaland, events were marching on in Bulawayo. Sir Richard Martin—the government appointed 'commandant general' of all the troops in the area—arrived in the town on 14 May. As we know, poor 'Whistling Dick' had already been side-lined before he even arrived in Rhodesia, and was not to play a significant role in the remainder of the war; indeed, his military functions were soon taken over entirely by Major General Carrington when he and his chief of staff——a certain Lt. Colonel Robert Baden-Powell[i]—arrived a couple of weeks later.

Lt. Colonel Herbert Plumer arrived in Bulawayo on the same coach as Sir Richard,[5] ahead of the Matabeleland Relief Force. As he stepped off his coach in Bulawayo, the rest of his hastily-raised 850-strong light horse regiment were still strung out on their 587 mile march north from Mafeking.[6] The first elements had moved out on 14 April (the last units only departed on 1 May). When they reached the old Bechuanaland Border Police Headquarters at Macloutsie, about 30 miles south of Francistown in modern-day Botswana, they reorganized themselves into five squadrons, each made up of fourteen troops (please see appendix 5 for details). The leading squadrons of the well drilled and efficient force —'A', 'B' and 'C'—rode into Bulawayo on 24 May and were, not surprisingly, 'vociferously welcomed' by the townspeople. They were accompanied by a rather less well-turned out force of about 250 Bechuana allies:

> 'Radicladi's Bamangwato, a motley crew of natives, in every conceivable style of dress and undress, but for the most part armed with rifles.'[7]

For their part, the newly arrived Matabele Relief Force troopers seemed impressed with the rather eclectic collection of miners, farmers, ex-pioneers and gifted-amateurs who had rolled up their sleeves to form a rough-and-ready volunteer force that would take the fight to the rebels. One observer stated that each of these colourful 'swashbucklers' was 'more picturesque than his neighbour':

---

i Lt. General Robert Stephenson Smyth Baden-Powell, 1st Baron Baden-Powell, OM, GCMG, GCVO, KCB (1857–1941). 'B-P' was commissioned into the 13th Hussars in 1876 and saw active service in various African colonial conflicts. His finest hour was his successful defence of Mafeking in the Boer War and he would go on to establish the Boy Scout Movement.

'Cowboy hat, with puggree of the colour of his corps, short-sleeved canvas shirt, cord breeches, and puttees, with bandolier across his chest, and pistol on his hip, is approximately the kit of every man you meet. The strong brown arms and sunburned faces, the bold and springy gait, all show them soldiers, ready-made and ripe for any kind of work. Good shots and riders, and very much at home upon the veldt, no wonder that they form a "useful" crew–especially when led, as they were, by men of their own kidney.

Among the leaders are Mickey MacFarlane, erstwhile the dandy lancer, now a bearded buccaneer and good soldier all the time; Selous, the famous hunter-pioneer of Matabeleland; Napier and Spreckley, the light-hearted blade, who is nevertheless possessed of profound and business-like capacity; Beal, Laing and Robertson, cool, level-headed Scotsmen with a military training; George Grey, "Charlie" White and Maurice Gifford, for whom rough miners and impetuous cowboys work like well-broken hounds.'[8]

§

Plumer was not a man to hang about, and the moment his first troops arrived, he gave orders for them to expect to be in the field for three days as he would be leading them out that evening. Probably not what everyone wanted to hear, but the troopers all seemed keen to get into action and there was a state of barely supressed excitement in the town that afternoon. One can only admire their enthusiasm.

The leading elements of the Matabele Relief Force—and their native allies—were formed into two columns, one under Major Watts and the other under the command of Plumer himself. As night fell, they headed out of Bulawayo towards the north-west where the rebels were thought to have gathered. About eight miles from the town, Major Watts' column came upon a great number of rebels occupying a strong position behind scherms of bush. The Matabele opened fire on Watts' men, but this was quickly answered and crushed and Watts swiftly brought his Maxim guns up into action. After an hour, Watts' men had driven the rebels from the position. Plumer marched his men towards the sound of the firing, and arrived just after the action had been won. Watts had sustained casualties of one man killed, one wounded and three horses lost. It was decided that the combined columns would spend the rest of the night in this location, and push on at sun up.[9]

Plumer threw scouts out at first light and then advanced forward with his three squadrons in line, the Maxims at the rear and his native contingent out on the right flank.[10] The terrain was dense and broken with limited visibility and after only half a mile, they suddenly came under fire all along their front. Plumer quickly ordered his men to dismount and, pressing on in skirmishing order, they quickly won the fire-fight. The rebels broke in the face of the rifles and Maxims of the MRF and took to their heels, fleeing from the bush and routing across open ground. Plumer had his men re-mount quickly and the whole force galloped forward, chasing the fleeing Matabele and shooting them down as they ran. The pursuit went on for three miles and left the rebels completely shattered.[11] Plumer reckoned the enemy to have been around 1,000 strong and reported about 60 killed.[12] The Matabele Relief Force engaged another 1,500-strong impi that evening; again, the enemy was broken but this time no follow-up was possible due to the failing light.[13] Plumer lost three men against 70–80 of the enemy killed in this later action.[14] The Matabele Relief Force had hit the ground running.

§

In the first few days of June, Napier and Beal arrived in Bulawayo with their respective columns and 'Colonel' Cecil Rhodes:

'...on Mr Rhodes's arrival in Bulawayo he was entertained at a banquet given by the leading men of the town and, in a vigorous speech displayed the policy which would govern his actions in Matabeleland during the crisis through which the country was passing and, to the satisfaction of all, he prophesied a speedy termination to the war.'[15]

The newly-arrived Carrington had no intention of taking undue risks to achieve a speedy victory, however, and even with the arrival of the 'D' and 'E' squadrons of the Matabele Relief Force at Bulawayo, he was still hesitant to clear the rebels from the Matopos Hills. It was reckoned that three strong impis were established there, and clearing hundreds of square miles of broken, rocky terrain would not be easy. Instead, it was decided first to clear the rebel impis from the area around Bulawayo, and then combine columns to advance on the Matopos.[16]

To this end, Colonel Plumer led a 450-strong column out on 5 June, riding north-west along the Khami River to its confluence with the Gwai River, where it was believed a rebel impi was encamped. Plumer took three of the precious Maxims and sixteen supply wagons with him, expecting the 'Gwai patrol' to be out for 20 days.[17] At the same time, Captain Macfarlane led another 400 men out, also heading north in a coordinated sweep.[18] Showing no fear of risking his neck in the field with the rest, Cecil Rhodes rode out with Macfarlane's column.[19]

No plan survives contact with the enemy however, and the day after these two columns had ridden out, Carrington received word that a large impi had taken up a position on the Salisbury Road, near the Umguza River–perhaps six miles from Bulawayo. Beal's Column—the 150 men from the Rhodesia Horse who had ridden in from Fort Salisbury—were camped out of town, only two-and-a-half miles away from the 1,200-strong impi.

Carrington reacted quickly and ordered Colonel Spreckley—who was just about to head north with a third column[20]—to instead ride out against this impi, taking with him pretty much every mounted man in Bulawayo. This hastily organized scratch-force consisted of about 200 men, made up of the Grey's Scouts, the Afrikander Corps and about 45 troopers from the Bulawayo Field Force under Captain Brand.[21] As usual, Selous, Baden-Powell and some other officers attached themselves to the force and there were also 'one hundred men from the native contingent, under Captain Colenbrander', who gamely followed the horsemen at a quick march.

As they approached the Umguza, Spreckley's column met with Beal's Salisbury men who had been observing the impi for some time. Beal reported that the rebels had broken camp a little earlier and were evidently expecting the attack. What Spreckley did not know, however, was that the rebel leaders had assembled an elite force, drawn from the best men of eight regiments and somehow convinced these naïve fellows that the whites would either be struck blind or swallowed by the waters if they even attempted to cross the river.[22]

Needless to say, this lunatic prophecy did not come to pass, and Spreckley's troopers splashed their horses through the Umguza at various points, deploying on the far bank unspotted by the rebels:

'...we were hidden from the Kaffirs by the slope of rising ground behind which they had retreated, but when this was crested they were seen in the bush little more than a hundred yards in front of the foremost horseman. The order was at once given to charge, on which a whirlwind of horsemen bore down on them, Grey's Scouts and Brand's men being in the centre, the Africanders on the left, and the Salisbury men on the right.' [23]

Baden-Powell recalled that this order momentarily confused a few of the volunteers who were used to dismounting to fight:

'...some of our men, accustomed to mounted infantry work, were now jumping off to return the fire, but the order was given: "No; make a cavalry fight of it. Forward! Gallop!" Then, as we came up close, the niggers let us have an irregular, rackety volley, and in another moment we were among them.'[24]

Selous described the battle:

'[The rebels were] spread out in skirmishing order through the open bush in face of the long line of advancing horsemen, yet they never stood for a moment, but were seized with a panic … they fired a hurried ill-aimed volley and then turned and ran. In the chase which followed, a large number of them were shot down, and the pursuit was only abandoned when the fleetest-footed amongst them had gained the shelter of the belt of thick bush which runs down from the western side of Thaba Induna towards the Umguza. I am of opinion myself that the Matabele lost more heavily on this occasion than at any other fight during the campaign, for the very reason that it was not a fight but only a pursuit in which the natives were killed as fast as they were overtaken.'[25]

Baden-Powell takes up the story:

'…we were close upon their heels, zigzagging through the thorns, jumping off now and then, or pulling up to fire a shot (we had not a sword among us, worst luck!) and on again. The men that I was with—Grey's Scouts—never seemed to miss a shot'.[26]

Despite the lack of swords or lances, it was still essentially a cavalry charge and quite simply too much for the rebels who were quickly gripped by sheer terror. The action soon descended into more of a rout than a battle and the broken, panic-stricken rebels were pursued and charged down for about five miles. Some attempted to loose off shots, but it was a very one-sided affair–Spreckley only lost four men wounded against rebel losses of well over 200. Worse still for the rebels, the nonsensical ravings of the witch-doctors had—once again— been shown up for the rubbish they were and the influence of these leaders was shattered. The disheartened elements retreated to the Matopos Hills.[27]

His departure had been delayed, but on the 7th, Colonel Spreckley headed out on his sweep north, leading 'a fine body of 400 of the roughest, most workman-like fighters one could wish to see' comprising 'infantry and mounted infantry, artillery, and a levy of wild-looking friendly Matabele'.[28] That Carrington was willing to send so many men off the day after a battle just a few miles from Bulawayo demonstrates just how total Spreckley's victory on the 6th must have been, as did a letter written by Lady Victoria Grey[ii] who visited the battlefield in August–two months later:

---

ii Lord Grey's daughter

'...all the ant-bear holes are filled with the corpses of niggers, they are only skeletons now. In several places we came across skeletons lying in the bush with the shield and assegai and sandals lying beside them.'[29]

§

The three columns that were sent to sweep to the north and north-west, failed to bring significant numbers of rebels to battle, though they encountered the usual small skirmishes. Towards the end of June, these columns had returned to Bulawayo, and the remaining Matabele rebels had essentially been confined to two areas: the large, rugged expanse of the Matopos Hills to the south of Bulawayo, and a smaller, though just as rugged, area of hills called Thabas Amamba (also Tabas-i-Mhamba[30] or Intaba zikaMambo[31]) about 65 miles north of the town.

Despite latter-day attempts to present the insurgency as some sort of mass uprising, the Matabele in the south-west of the country did not rebel at all, and the route down to Mafeking remained open throughout the conflict. In mid-June, however there were rumours that these people were being stirred into action by one of the M'Limo's priests (or, according to some, rather remarkably, the M'Limo himself) who lived in a cave in the western extremity of the Matopos Hills.[32] Responding to intelligence, Carrington despatched Burnham to kill this rabble-rouser, and a degree of controversy still remains over who (or what) exactly the American shot. Burnham—never one to hide his light under a bushel—claimed he had killed the M'Limo himself, while others were not surprisingly, rather more sceptical. More plausibly, especially given that his version was later supported by locals from the area,[33] Baden-Powell reckoned that the American had shot some sort of a high priest, rather than a god; either way, and more importantly, the news of this slaying spread like wild fire.[34]

Other, even more worrying, reports were received at about the same time. On 16 June, Baden-Powell wrote:

'To-day, a thunderclap has come. Telegrams from Salisbury (sent round by Victoria and Macloutsie, owing to the direct wire being cut) tell us of murders of whites in three widely separate parts of Mashonaland. It almost looks as though the Matabele Rebellion were repeating itself there. If so, the outlook is very bad indeed. Salisbury is 270 miles from here by road. We have here a number of troops who were sent from Salisbury to help us, and now their want will be acutely felt over there.'[35]

The news was every bit as bad as he feared. Large numbers of Mashona—a people almost universally considered to be meek and peaceful—had indeed risen up in brutal, murderous rebellion. We shall deal with the Mashona uprising later, however, and finish with the war in Matabeleland first.

Satisfied that the M'Limo (or at least someone the Matabele would believe to be him) was out of the way and that his lines of communication remained secure, General Carrington decided to strike the rebel stronghold at Thabas Amamba. Colonel Plumer would lead the attack, and rode out of Bulawayo at the head of a formidable column: mainly the newly arrived forces, about 750 men in total (perhaps 450 of whom were white, including 400 men from the Matabele Relief Force[36]) with the usual Maxim and 7-pdrs, and a very keen, Cecil John Rhodes himself:

'...one man drew out ahead in spite of warnings and expostulations. I spurred to see. It was Rhodes himself, riding unarmed, switch in hand, leading the hunt.'[37]

After a few days, Plumer halted his force at Inyati and gave orders for a night march towards Thabas Amamba—about 16 miles away—followed by a dawn attack.[38] Famously—and brilliantly—used by Lord Wolseley at Tel el-Kebir in 1882, it was a fairly standard tactic at the time and would be widely employed in the Boer War a few years later, though not always with great success.

Major Robertson, commanding the Cape Boys, described the natural fortress that Plumer's men were about to storm:

'Thabas Amamba consists of a range of hills running north and south, and rising abruptly from a plain which is seen gradually ascending in an easterly direction. The range is about five miles in length. Along the western slope the face of the hills is almost precipitous, with numerous clefts and gorges opening to the country beyond, that is to say, to the east. The top of the range may be described as a series of peaks, somewhat elongated in a northerly and southerly direction, having for their summits gigantic granite boulders piled on the top of each other, frequently to a height of 400 or 500 feet... shooting out from the eastern slope of the range are numerous spurs, now descending, now ascending, and finally culminating in other hills... between the spurs above described there are numerous valleys, some not more than 100 yards, others nearly a mile in width, all of them intersected with watercourses and overgrown with dense bush, with but few clearings. Towards the eastern extremity of the hills may be seen what is now known as the rebel stronghold. This consists of a conical-shaped hill rising abruptly to a height of about 400 feet, and divided from the main stronghold, still further east, by a broad, sandy-bedded watercourse. The stronghold itself rises out of this watercourse, with an almost precipitous face, to a height of from 500 to 600 feet, formed of gigantic boulders, with innumerable caves of great dimensions, and a perfect maze of thorns and shrubbery. Along the eastern base of this fastness, the Insungu River is seen, enclosed by another range of lofty hills, almost as precipitous and equally as high as the stronghold itself. The whole group covers an area of some 25 miles square.'[39]

Robertson's rather lengthy description will leave the reader in no doubt that Plumer and his men were facing a difficult task. The dismounted troops left the Inyati camp on the afternoon of 4 July, and the others followed on just after sundown. The ambulance and transport wagons were the last to set off, leaving at 02h00 on the 5th.[40] Mr Stent, a recently arrived correspondent for The London Times, described the approach march vividly:

'All through the night we rode–a stealthy band of khaki grey intruders... on towards the mountain looming indistinct before us. Then the picket fires of the rebels lifted through the cumber of the night. Men gripped their rifles, loosened a round or two in the bandoliers, and peered grimly out into the murk. Now the column broke–some to outflank the position, others to move into the heart of the enemy's fastness... grey dawn found us standing to our horses. In front of us a crop of isolated granite kopjes which formed the object of Plumer's attack. Clear upon the cool wind of the morning, the wind that wakes, came the crack! crack! of the Martinis, answering the dull heavy explosions of the old elephant guns which the Matabili carried.'[41]

The attack came at first light and the 7-pdrs started flinging shells into the rocks and outcrops. The only way to clear the rebels was with bayonets, however, and the Cape Boys were to bear the brunt of the fighting on the 5th, supported by about 40 men from the Bulawayo Field Force.[42] Stent of the Times carried on describing how some of the enemy immediately routed and:

'...came streaming across our front. The machine-guns spat viciously at them as they ran. Among the hills the musketry began to babble incessantly. The dawn glowed red. The Matabili were making a stand in a central kopje–a nasty one to tackle.'[43]

Major Robertson describes the action to clear this hill:

'Foot by foot we ascended the dangerous heights, taking advantage of every cover, nook, and crevice, now creeping along, now rushing across some opening between the rocks. The ascent was slowly but surely progressing. ... we made a rush into it, and took the enemy by surprise. Here hand-to-hand struggles took place both in the open and in the caves where my men had pursued the rebels. ... During this four and a half hours' fighting, there were several instances of bayonet versus assegai, the former in each case proving the superior weapon. Captain Nash assisted me most gallantly. I personally saw him shoot four rebels (one of them a chief) in quick succession with his revolver.'[44]

Some of the rebels had been driven into the caves. Robertson's men started fires to smoke these unfortunates out and shot them down as they fled into the open. Captain Boggie led the dismounted white troopers that day, and vividly recounted their attack on a conical hill:

'Ordered to lead the storming party, I placed myself in the centre at front of the line, giving the 'right wing' to Lieutenant Hunt, and the 'left' to Sergeant-Major Brooker. At a distance of about fifty yards from the kopje, I gave a signal for the usual cheer, which was at once responded to by all the line. Whether it could be called a British cheer, I did not know; but the loud rolling and hearty cheer heard on the football and cricket fields appeared to have given place to a sort of war whoop, and for a second or so a deep, revengeful yell echoed from the granite rocks on our front.
A moment later, we were in hand-to-hand conflict with our dusky foes. The engagement was brief and decisive. A succession of rapid reports, a pattering and singing of bullets, a cracking of revolvers, a brief impression of blood-bespattered rocks, wounded, dying and dead warriors, and the position was carried. We were on the top, with the enemy speeding down the far side.'[45]

Though his men had cleared the rebels from a series of positions, Plumer called the attack off at about 14h30, by which time the fighting had disintegrated into a number of more or less independent actions.[46] The exhausted men could not root every single rebel out of the mountains, and (such was the chaos of the hand-to-hand fighting among the rocks) had sustained much heavier causalities than was the norm for the war: around 30 killed and wounded.[47] Rhodes had been intimately involved in urging the assault onward, riding around unarmed, and showing no signs of fear. One observer said this was because of his deep conviction that, as a great man with so much work still to do, 'he was not intended to be killed by a damned nigger'.[48] For all this bravado and self-assurance, Rhodes was, however, deeply moved by the losses sustained by his young settlers and volunteers, and it would seem that this made him determined to end the war as soon as possible.[49] Mr Stent recalled a dejected and visibly moved Rhodes brooding over the camp fire that evening, 'cut to the heart' by the casualties of the day:

> 'Soldiers of fortune, if you will; having their faults, not too overburdened with humane considerations; they asked no quarter; they probably would have given none. But they were the men that Rhodesia wanted to smooth her rugged ways; to break her in. They were the price of victory and the price was heavy... this rough and hurried burial of the men who had given their lives for Rhodesia brought home to him, as nothing else could have done, the meaning of war–the cruel bloodiness of war... there came to him the idea of meeting the Matabili themselves, learning what they fought for, and trying to bring about peace.'[50]

Despite Rhodes' sadness, Plumer had landed a devastating blow against the rebels. They had been defeated, not by white man's machine guns in the open field, but by hand-to-hand fighting in broken, rocky terrain. An estimated 1,500 to 2,000 rebels had been sheltering in the hills of Thabas Amamba, and perhaps up to 200 of these had been killed in the attack, with the same again wounded. Some six hundred of their women and children were captured by Plumer's men[51] and an enormous haul of loot (including 1,000 cattle and 2,000 sheep and goats) was taken

The northern rebel impi had thus been shattered in one morning of savage close-quarter battle, and the surviving chiefs and their followers went bomb-bursting off in different directions. Some fled south to join the rebels still holding out in the Matopos, and others headed east to join the Mashonaland rebellion, or gave up the fight altogether and headed north, looking for new lands away from company rule.[52]

§

The victory won by the Matabele Relief Force's quasi-imperial (though company financed) troops led Carrington to disband the Bulawayo Field Force volunteers–something that was done with surprising alacrity given the news coming from Mashonaland, and the fact that even the Matabele Rebellion was still far from over. The volunteers were inspected by General Carrington and then addressed

Wilson (3rd from left) with his officers

The Last Stand of the Shangani Patrol

'Men of Men'

Monument to the men of the Shangani   *Memorial at the battlefield*
Patrol. Designed by the tireless Sir
Herbert Baker, the main inscription is
simply: 'To Brave Men'

Detail on the Monument – 'Erected to the enduring memory of Allan Wilson
and his Men who fell in fight against the Matabele on the Shangani River
December 4th, 1893. There was no survivor'

President Paul Kruger of the Transvaal – his refusal to grant a fair franchise to the Uitlanders prompted the Jameson Raid

'Clive would have done it!' – Jameson throw caution to the wind and goes in, thoroughly upsetting Rhodes' apple cart

Boer commandos assemble to repel the raiders

BSAP garrison of Fort Belingwe, 1896

*A well-turned out lady,
making the most of life
in the laager*

*'Linger Laager Longer...' such laagers were hastily established all over
Matabeleland when the rebellion broke out*

Selous' 'H' troop which operated out of Bulawayo

Both sides showed great courage in the fighting around Bulawayo: Lt. Fred Crewe gives his horse to a wounded comrade and fights his way out on foot

BSAP troopers on parade at Mt Darwin

Matabele Field Force officers

Major General Sir Frederick Carrington was placed in command of all forces (Imperial and Company) in the theatre

Mazoe Patrol officers looking very dapper

Mazoe Patrol survivors, posing on the armoured wagon

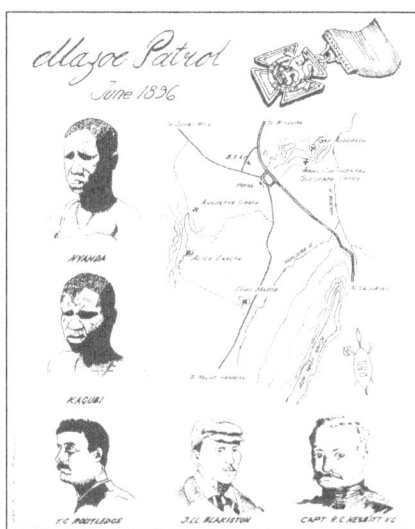

Sketch of the route of the Mazoe Patrol

SOUTH AFRICAN AFFAIRS.

RECRUITING RHODESIAN POLICE.

London, October 19.

It is reported that twelve thousand men have applied in London alone for admission to the Rhodesian police force.

RENEWED FIGHTING.

THE REBELS DEFEATED.

London, October 19.

Advices from Buluwayo state that Captain Thorold has succeeded in capturing Chena's Kraal after six hours' hard fighting.

Recruits rushed to join the BSAP

The Shona witch doctors, Kagubi and Nehanda looking a little crestfallen – both were hung for stirring rebellion, with the harridan Nehanda remaining 'defiant, loquacious and savage to the last'. Their executions signaled the end of the war in Mashonaland

Company forces on parade

*Two officers who would go onto greater fame
in later conflicts: Baden-Powell and Plumer*

*Rhodes holds his Indaba with the rebels in Matapos Hills, bringing the war to
a close in Matabeleland*

by Lord Grey after mustering one last time. The administrator concluded his address saying:

"All of you have acquitted yourselves as brave men, and I would particularly commend the conduct of Colonel Napier, who throughout the campaign has performed his very arduous duties so satisfactorily. But mingled with our enjoyment there must be some pain in looking back upon many of the episodes of this rebellion. The company has done its best to look after your comfort, but you have undergone notwithstanding some severe hardships, which, however, you have borne like men; and the only complaint I have heard is that you were not always able to go out against the enemy, but had to perform as well the hard and monotonous work of laager and fort duty.

Many of you have a Matabele memento in the shape of a wound, the mark of which you will carry to your graves. Many too have lost friends; and possibly none of us realize the loss of life which has taken place both before and during hostilities; for our losses have been heavy, and form a large percentage of the total number of people who were engaged in the exploitation of the country. I cannot refer to individual cases of bravery where all have done so well, but I would again especially mention Colonel Napier's services to the country. He has exhibited remarkable tact and judgment, and has freely given great assistance to the government. I regret that he is to-day retiring from the service, but I hope that he will continue to give us the benefit of his experience.

I do not like to mention any particular troop, as each has acted so creditably, but I would note the excellent services rendered by the Africander Corps in this war, as showing the whole world the complete brotherhood which exists between the two races of Dutchmen and Britons in Rhodesia. I trust that an Africander troop will again form part of the new force which is now being raised by the government. Information reached this country by last mail that Her Majesty has been pleased to allow a medal to be worn for the last Matabele war, and I shall represent strongly to Her Majesty that the same honour ought to be conferred on the members of the Bulawayo Field Force. You have as much right and title to the distinction as those who fought in the first war, and I hope there will be a sufficient number struck for both those who fought in the first war and those who have fought during the present rebellion. I thank you for your assistance in the past, and I hope you will remain in the country to witness the prosperity which is certain to come."[53]

With the storming of Thabas Amamba, the only rebel stronghold
still remaining in Matabeleland was the Matopos Hills–but if clearing
the former had been costly, driving the rebels out of the Matopos
would be even more so. The northern extremity of the Matopos is
just 15 or so miles south of Bulawayo, but the hills cover an area
roughly 50 miles by 30, and this broken jumble of kopjes, valleys,
caves, tangled bushes and precipitous rock faces was described by one
observer as 'just about the most difficult country in the world–worse
than Afghanistan or Chitral'.

None of this was enough to put a man like General Carrington off,
however–though, in truth, he had little option but to try and clear the
hills if he wanted to end the rebellion. Accordingly, Plumer's column
was ordered to march there, and camped at a farm 12 miles south of
Bulawayo for a few days to reorganize. On 17 July, Carrington himself
rode into the camp to take personal command of operations, and the
whole force was moved to forward base camp at the very foot of the
Matopos Hills, five miles further south.[54]

Carrington's first target was the stronghold of a rebel leader
called Babayana, which lay inside the Matopos about 10 miles from
the base camp. True to form, Baden-Powell had scouted this position
meticulously and confirmed the presence of a large force of rebels.
On the evening of the 19th, Baden-Powell led the assaulting troops in
on their night approach march, with the plan being to launch a dawn
attack on the 20th. The troops pushed forwards through the darkness:

'First of all the Scouts, supported by native "friendlies" on either
flank ; then the Matabeleland Mounted Police, on this occasion
dismounted ; A and B Squadrons, M.R.F., supported by the Cape
Boys Corps on the left and Colenbrander's Native Contingent on
the right ; Maxim guns and Hotchkiss of the M.M.P. ; Mountain
Battery, R.A. ; Maxim, M.R.F. ; Lieutenant Mathias' troop ; and E
Squadron, M.R.F.'[55]

Though the Bulawayo Field Force had been disbanded a few days
earlier, some of the more enthusiastic 'swashbucklers' were still keen
to join the fight–as was a certain Cecil John Rhodes.[56] There was no
way the Maxims' carriages could be dragged into the broken terrain of
the Matopos. Instead, two of them were broken down and loaded onto
eight mules, along with tripods and ammunition. Another especially
unfortunate beast would carry the Maxim ammunition stocks–eight
boxes containing 1,200 rounds.[57]

After a two mile march, a halt was called to allow the men to snatch
some sleep–though a combination of the excitement and extreme cold
ensured that few did. It was still dark when the men were roused. They

discarded their greatcoats, left the ambulance wagon and a Maxim gun at the entrance to a valley and pressed on. First light revealed the rebel stronghold which 'consisted of an intricate labyrinth of caves and boulders, strengthened with scherms'[58] on the far side of a valley. The Royal Artillery mountain guns quickly deployed and opened fire while Colenbrander's friendlies swarmed forward for an assault.

The Cape Boys—who had fought so well at Thabas Amamba—also pushed forward under cover of artillery fire, supporting the assault of the native friendlies. This latter corps proved utterly worthless that day, however, and '...completely lost their heads and fired their rifles off wildly as fast as they could load without any definite object. They were a useless rabble, as well as a considerable source of danger to those near them.'[59]

In contrast, Robertson's Cape Boys again fought well, their assaults succeeding at all points. They quickly drove the rebels from their initial positions, sending them running to find cover elsewhere. The Cape Boys pushed forward again, driving the rebels from three successive positions. By this time, they were being supported by the Maxims and the Hotchkiss gun which opened up with devastating effect, and the rebels gave up and fled away to the south. It is noteworthy that virtually all the close-in fighting was left to the non-white troops. All but the scouts were kept in reserve all day and simply watched the action. A cynic might suggest reasons why this was done.

Imperial losses were three Cape Boys and one white scout killed, and a small number of others wounded. Rebel losses were uncertain, and guesses varied from a few dozen to over a hundred. The reality is probably somewhere in between.

§

As Plumer's men stormed Babayana's stronghold, Captain Laing— who we last met when he took charge of the Belingwe laager—led another force into the Matopos from the north-west, intending to link up with the main body on the 20th. Laing commanded 170 white troops and around 300 'friendlies' together with a Nordenfelt, a Maxim and a 7-pdr.[60] This force laagered up at the entrance to a valley named Inungu Gorge—a spot soon to become known as 'Laing's Graveyard'— on the night of the 19th.

Inungu Gorge was almost purpose built for defence: about 50 yards wide, the walls of the valley rose steeply on either side and cover of the 'best kind' was afforded by the 'thick stunted bush and huge boulders'. Situated in the defile, the laager site—'Laing's Graveyard'— was overlooked by this high ground. Pickets reported plenty of rebel movement up in the rocks throughout the night and it soon became obvious that the Matabele were moving men into position. Indeed, as soon as day broke, rebel riflemen poured fire onto Laing's laager from the commanding heights. Laing's men grabbed their rifles, ran to their positions and quickly returned this fire. Amazingly, given all their advantages, the rebels showed little interest in a fire-fight with the troopers and instead, suddenly returned to the old, Zulu-style charge, running down the hillside and getting to within 20 yards of the laager.[61] It was courageous and dashing, but utterly unsuccessful. Laing's men blasted the onrushing rebels to pieces, with the case shot from the 7-pdr ripping through them and sending them running back for cover.[62]

The simultaneous attack on Laing's friendlies was more successful, however. Camped about 50 yards from the white laager, the friendlies panicked and fled, dashing for the safety of the main position and running helter-skelter into the rifle fire of their white comrades. While all this was going on, other rebels took up better positions in the rocks above the laager and opened fire on Laing's men at less than 30 yards. Several troopers were shot through the head by these snipers and they were only finally rooted out with great difficulty.

Though it is easy to criticize Laing's decision to place his laager where he did, no one can question his courage or steadiness:

> 'Capt. Laing was here, there and everywhere encouraging the men with quiet remarks such as "Steady boys", "Give it to them", "Don't waste your ammunition"... Whilst I was sitting up against a wagon I couldn't help admiring old Laing. He was bringing up the 7-pounder into action and to bring the gun round smartly he manned the wheel himself, sighted the gun and then remarked "Now then boys give them Hell". Bang went the seven pounder and he remarked "Good shot".'[63]

Laing's men were in a tight corner for a while, but he was magnificent throughout, pushing men back into the firing line and threatening to shoot anyone who hung back under the wagons.

Realizing they had blown their chance, however, the rebels began slipping away and the fighting ended after about an hour. Laing's bravery and leadership had saved his force from annihilation, but his poor placement of the laager had cost the lives of 4 whites and 28 'friendlies', and about 30 or so were wounded. Rebel losses were reckoned at around 100. After the attack on the 20th, Laing's mission rather fizzled out, and he decided to retire back out of the Matopos the following day.[64]

On the night of the 24th, another attempt was made to push up the Inungu Gorge to clear the rebels.[65] Captain Nicholson (7th Hussars) led a strong fighting patrol back into the valley but fared little better than Laing had four days earlier. Nicholson's men fought their way forward, pushing the rebel marksmen from the sides of the gorge, only for them to fall back to the next natural vantage point. With several of his men killed, Nicholson called the attack off, and withdrew his force back to the base camp.[66]

Though the imperial forces always claimed to have inflicted much greater losses than they had taken, this action suggested that clearing the Matopos Hills was simply going to be too costly to undertake. As one war veteran put it, 'If to every ten rebels killed or disabled one white man is killed or disabled, how many of Plumer's Column, 500 strong, will remain by the time the 5,000 rebels in the hills are killed or disabled?'

A Press report of the time agreed:

'Carrington has to choose between two alternatives–either he must storm the hills and drive the rebels out at a heavy sacrifice of valuable lives, or he must build a chain of forts at enormous expenditure, and so, in course of time, starve them into submission.'[67]

No doubt aware of these mutterings, Plumer assembled his men for another push into the Matopos, this time planning to strike further to the east.[68] He marched his column around the hills, mainly moving at night and doing what he could to disguise his intentions, and led his men into the Mtshabezi Valley before day break on 1 August.

Daylight saw the column coming under fire from rebel riflemen up in the rocks above, and 'C' Squadron was told to clear these. Dismounting, the troopers started clambering up the steep slopes and performed the task with alacrity. As the troopers of 'C' Squadron cleared the high ground, Plumer's guns busily shelled other suspected rebel positions. The rest of the column could do nothing but wait.[69]

They pushed into the Matopos for two more days and reached their objective—the strongholds of two rebel chiefs—on the 3rd, but found these abandoned. Plumer's men destroyed the large stores of grain that had been left behind, but this was a poor return for their efforts. Having achieved virtually nothing, Plumer pulled his column back out of the hills and met with his supply wagons to re-stock for another go.

Leaving 'B' Squadron, a 7-pdr, and a pair of Maxims to defend their new camp,[70] Plumer led the rest of his column[iii] back into the Matopos on the 5th, pressing on to attack the stronghold of chief Sikombo. Captain the Honourable J. Beresford, 7th Hussars,[71] had been sent forward with the artillery and a strong escort (138 men of the Matabele

---

iii 89 officers and men from the Matabeleland Mounted Police, 359 of the Matabeleland Relief Force, 57 Royal Artillery, 158 of Colenbrander's native friendlies and 101 of Robertson's Cape Boys. The force had three Maxims, one Hotchkiss and a pair of 7-pdrs.

Relief Force and MMP) so as to bombard the objective–but they were soon in trouble.[72]

Beresford's pair of native guides took fright and refused to lead the detachment as a result of which, Beresford lost his way. Groping their way forward, his strung-out command stumbled into some Matabele at just 150 yards and were instantly charged.[73] While the escorting infantry opened up on the onrushing rebels, the friendlies, who were carrying the Hotchkiss, 'behaved in a most cowardly manner, dropping the pole and running off behind some rocks as soon as the firing began; part of the gun could not be found, and it was consequently never brought into action'.[74]

Luckily, the Maxim was better handled and the quickly assembled 7-pdrs were soon blasting case shot at the rebels.[75]

The men from the main column could hear the rattle of the Maxims and rapid rifle fire, and they soon espied a signal flag which indicated that Beresford's force had been surrounded. Plumer sent 'A' Squadron to their assistance, and continued the main assault on Sikombo's stronghold with 'C' and 'E' Squadrons. These latter formations galloped across the mealie fields to the foot of the slope, dismounted and, covered by the Maxims, rushed up the rock faces in great style.[76] Rebels quickly opened fire on these assaulting troops but this did not seem to concern them unduly:

> 'Major Kershaw, eager and active as ever, led his men up the almost vertical walls of bare granite, where scarce a foothold could be obtained, under a heavy fire from above.'[77]

Unfortunately, Kershaw's enthusiasm saw him mortally wounded just a few feet short of the summit.[78] The troopers nevertheless drove the rebels from the hilltop and then from another to which they had retired. The rebel retreat then descended into a rout, and many were shot down as they fled.

Plumer had his hands full coordinating such a confused, swirling action spread across a swathe of broken and difficult terrain; even as the main attack was going in, 'A' Squadron arrived at Beresford's position and the situation there stabilized. Elsewhere, Major Robertson and the hard-fighting Cape Boys were storming another side of the stronghold, fighting their way up a steep ravine and driving the rebels back before them.[79]

By 15h00, the rebels had been driven off completely, and the 'assembly' was sounded. The wounded were placed on stretchers and Plumer's men retired back down and out of the Matopos once more. It was 20h00 before they got back to their camp, victorious, but with very little to show for it.

Imperial losses were seven killed: the gallant Major Kershaw, Lieutenant Hervey, two Sergeant-Majors, two Sergeants and just one trooper. About another dozen were wounded.[80] Lieutenant Hervey's magnificent last words were, 'Well, I suppose before long I shall be extending the British Empire in Jupiter or somewhere else.'[81]

It was becoming increasingly obvious to all, that—though dashing and courageous—such attacks were also essentially fruitless. Both the British and the local Rhodesian press had already started airing such views by late July, and the Bulawayo Sketch opined that, if things did not look up in the campaign to clear the Matopos Hills, '...it will be our backbone that will be broken, not that of the rebels.'[82] Further afield, the Westminster Gazette asked whether all the engagements so optimistically described as 'draws' were not really defeats, as it was always the company and the imperial troops that ended up pulling back.[83] The London Times reported '...the extreme confidence and arrogant bearing of the rebels who jeer at the whites and call them cowards... there is a growing fear that the troops are insufficient to put down the rebellion effectively.'[84]

By then, General Carrington had no doubt that he had too few troops for the job, and seemed content to settle in for the long haul. He declared that nothing else could be achieved before the rains came and brought an end to the fighting for a few months. In the meantime, he requested another 2,500 imperial troops, a couple of thousand bearers, some engineers and more mountain guns so as to blast the remaining rebels out of the Matopos in the dry season of 1897.[85] Others even thought that this commitment was optimistic, and one experienced officer claimed, '...it would take an army of ten thousand men to thoroughly sweep the place and even then there would be a great loss of life and you would have to calculate how many men you could afford to lose in order to gain each position.'[86]

Not a man blessed with much in the way of patience, and ever-concerned about the financial viability of his personal fiefdom, Rhodes was infuriated by all of this and constantly demanded to know how long it would take. But Rhodes was also not one to leave the fate of a project in the hands of others. Even before the battle on 5 August, he had shown a good deal more imagination than the military men and approached Lukini (a brother of Lobengula's who had remained loyal to the company and was living in a fortified kraal just outside Bulawayo) in an attempt to start a dialogue with the rebel leaders. This had come to nothing because of the hatred that existed between the rebel Matabele and those who had remained loyal to the company, and Lukini claimed that he would be killed on sight if he tried to act as a go-between.[87]

Rhodes was not a man who gave up easily, however. While accompanying a patrol that had gone into the hills to destroy stocks of grain, he came across an old Matabele woman[88] who turned out to be the mother of one of the rebel leaders and one of the widows of the late Mzilikazi himself.[89] From this rather fortuitous chance meeting, a message was passed to the rebels and an indaba was arranged to discuss peace. Whatever one thinks of Cecil Rhodes, and there are many today who prefer to think the very worst of this truly remarkable man, one has to admire his pluck as he set off into the hills for this indaba on 21 August, completely unarmed[90] and accompanied only by three other white men (one of whom was a correspondent for the Cape Times) and a couple of 'Colonial Boys' who had helped set up the event. The small band found the bluff full of rebels when they arrived at the designated meeting point. If any of the others were feeling nervous, Rhodes remained calm throughout, even commenting to one of his comrades, 'This is one of the occasions which make life worth living.'[91]

The indaba began with a predictably long, rambling, and rather pointless soliloquy from an old rebel commander, Somabulana. On and on he went, talking about the earliest days of the Matabele people and how Mzilikazi had brought them up over the Limpopo, before going on to talk about the war of 1893 and the theft of Lobengula's peace offering (the bag of gold sovereigns that Lobengula was supposed to have sent to Forbe's column). This long-winded diatribe contained an interesting passage which will give the reader an idea of the Matabele's world view and their thoughts on the Mashona:

> "...the Mashona... what are they? Dogs! Sneaking cattle thieves! Slaves! But we are the Amandabili, the sons of Kumalo, the Izulu, children of the stars; we are no dogs! You came, you conquered. The strongest takes the land. We accepted your rule. We lived under you. But not as dogs! If we are to be dogs it is better to be dead."[92]

Somabulana finally got to the point, and declared that the tyranny of the native commissioners and the arrogant abuse of power by the native police had made them feel like dogs. Rhodes, speaking through his interpreter, Colenbrander, announced that there would be no more native police–a declaration that was greeted by thunderous applause from the rebels.[93] In truth, all but the most hot-headed rebels must have realized that, they would not win the war even though they might have been able to hang on as renegades in the fastness of the Matopos. The imperial troops were also targeting their food stocks–so Rhodes was arguing from a position of considerable strength. The indaba dragged on for five hours, but at the end, the rebel leaders threw their sticks on the ground, to show that they would submit to the new 'King of Rhodesia', swear allegiance to Rhodes, and regard him as their chief and father.[94] It was progress, but the war was not over yet.

While Rhodes was talking peace, the fighting continued. Plumer's men kept probing and forcing their way into the Matopos Hills, skirmishing with the rebels, and capturing grain and livestock.[95] Elsewhere, the two squadrons of the 7th Hussars and supporting troops finally rode into Bulawayo on about 10 August[96]–some six weeks after they had moved out from Mafeking. They were soon in action, patrolling aggressively up the Gwai River, in concert with 800 loyal natives.[97]

Lt. Colonel Baden-Powell assumed command of the Hussars on 12 September, and led them in operations to clear rebels from around the Somabula forest and Umvungu and Shangani Rivers. Baden-Powell's first act on assuming command was to convene a general court martial on the rebel chief Uwini, who had just been captured. Uwini was found guilty of murder and executed that afternoon.[98] This execution dealt a devastating blow to the morale of his people, and before long the Hussars had accepted the surrender of over 1,000 rebels.[99]

Even as the Hussars skirmished their way through the forests that September, Rhodes conducted more meetings with the rebel leaders and made it clear to the more bellicose indunas that he was offering them a very stark choice: to continue a war they could not win, or surrender.[100] By 12 October, and on the eve of the fourth such indaba, rebel surrenders in Matabeleland amounted to 2,354 men, 2,892 women, 4,144 children, 329 rifles, 3,275 assegais and a really rather dismal 150 rounds of ammunition.[101] It was not a haul which overly-impressed the military men, but it was decent progress nonetheless– and a lot more than continued attacks into the Matopos Hills would have netted. The fourth, and final indaba on 13 October tied up the various lose ends and essentially ended the Matabele Rebellion.

The rebels who had argued to carry on the fight were, unsurprisingly, the same sort of young hot-heads who had pestered Lobengula to defy the whites back in 1893. Indeed, one of the demands made by the older, wiser chiefs at the indabas was that they be given more power and authority over these uncontrollable young-bloods. Rhodes agreed whole-heartedly, and announced that these wise old heads would receive government appointments and monthly salaries, and that their authority would be upheld. Used to a highly structured society, the chiefs also demanded someone to whom they could go 'before we go to Mr Rhodes' to report their troubles. Rhodes explained that this 'go to guy' was the administrator, Lord Grey. The chiefs were delighted by this news, and one even declared, rather remarkably, that they would 'lick the ground he [Grey] was standing on'.[102] As one observer put it:

'What force of arms failed to do, Mr Rhodes by diplomatic means succeeded in accomplishing. Thus a happy conclusion was brought to a long and costly war, which was likely to have dragged on for an indefinite time with the loss of many more valuable lives.'[103]

In truth, the hard-fighting and resolve of the settlers and imperial troops had broken the back of the rebellion, but it was indeed the courage and conciliation shown by Rhodes that ended it and brought peace to Matabeleland. Over in Mashonaland, however, the copy-cat rebellion was still very much under way, and it is to that which we shall now turn our attention.

End Notes

[1] Baden-Powell, The Matabele Campaign 1896, p.54
[2] Baden-Powell, The Matabele Campaign 1896, p.57
[3] Plumer, An Irregular Corps in Matabeleland, p.104
[4] Ranger, Revolt in Southern Rhodesia, 1896-7, p.180
[5] Keppel-Jones, Rhodes and Rhodesia, p.456
[6] Sykes, With Plumer in Matabeleland, p.87
[7] Sykes, With Plumer in Matabeleland, p.89
[8] Baden-Powell, The Matabele Campaign 1896, p.45
[9] Hensman, A History of Rhodesia, p.212
[10] Sykes, With Plumer in Matabeleland, p.91
[11] Hensman, A History of Rhodesia, p.213
[12] Plumer, An Irregular Corps in Matabeleland, p.95
[13] Sykes, With Plumer in Matabeleland, p.92
[14] Plumer, An Irregular Corps in Matabeleland, p.96
[15] Jones, Rhodesian Genesis, p.124
[16] Hensman, A History of Rhodesia, p.216
[17] Sykes, With Plumer in Matabeleland, p.92
[18] Keppel-Jones, Rhodes and Rhodesia, p.456
[19] Selous, Sunshine and Storm in Rhodesia, p.222
[20] Baden-Powell, The Matabele Campaign 1896, p.51
[21] Hensman, A History of Rhodesia, p.217
[22] Keppel-Jones, Rhodes and Rhodesia, p.456
[23] Selous, Sunshine and Storm in Rhodesia, p.224
[24] Baden-Powell, The Matabele Campaign 1896, p.54
[25] Selous, Sunshine and Storm in Rhodesia, p.224
[26] Baden-Powell, The Matabele Campaign 1896
[27] Keppel-Jones, Rhodes and Rhodesia, p.457
[28] Baden-Powell, The Matabele Campaign 1896, p.65
[29] Ranger, Revolt in Southern Rhodesia, 1896-7, p.176
[30] Plumer, An Irregular Corps in Matabeleland, p.121
[31] Keppel-Jones, Rhodes and Rhodesia, p.459
[32] Baden-Powell, The Matabele Campaign 1896, p.81
[33] Ranger, Revolt in Southern Rhodesia, 1896-7, p.187
[34] Baden-Powell, The Matabele Campaign 1896, p.82
[35] Baden-Powell, The Matabele Campaign 1896, p.72
[36] Plumer, An Irregular Corps in Matabeleland, p.121
[37] Keppel-Jones, Rhodes and Rhodesia, p.459
[38] Sykes, With Plumer in Matabeleland, p.136
[39] Sykes, With Plumer in Matabeleland, p.138
[40] Plumer, An Irregular Corps in Matabeleland, p.135
[41] Ranger, Revolt in Southern Rhodesia, 1896-7, p.230
[42] Plumer, An Irregular Corps in Matabeleland, p.136
[43] Ranger, Revolt in Southern Rhodesia, 1896-7, p.231
[44] Sykes, With Plumer in Matabeleland, p.147

[45] Sykes, With Plumer in Matabeleland, p.154
[46] Plumer, An Irregular Corps in Matabeleland, p.137
[47] Keppel-Jones, Rhodes and Rhodesia, p.459
[48] Ranger, Revolt in Southern Rhodesia, 1896-7, p.234
[49] Blake, A History of Rhodesia, p.135
[50] Ranger, Revolt in Southern Rhodesia, 1896-7, p.234
[51] Baden-Powell, The Matabele Campaign 1896, p.125
[52] Keppel-Jones, Rhodes and Rhodesia, p.460
[53] Selous, Sunshine and Storm in Rhodesia, p.240
[54] Plumer, An Irregular Corps in Matabeleland, p.151
[55] Sykes, With Plumer in Matabeleland, p.170
[56] Baden-Powell, The Matabele Campaign 1896, p.147
[57] Plumer, An Irregular Corps in Matabeleland, p.149
[58] Plumer, An Irregular Corps in Matabeleland, p.156
[59] Sykes, With Plumer in Matabeleland, p.172
[60] Sykes, With Plumer in Matabeleland, p.176
[61] Baden-Powell, The Matabele Campaign 1896 p.165
[62] Plumer, An Irregular Corps in Matabeleland, p.158
[63] Keppel-Jones, Rhodes and Rhodesia, p.461
[64] Sykes, With Plumer in Matabeleland, p.180
[65] Baden-Powell, The Matabele Campaign 1896, p.168
[66] Sykes, With Plumer in Matabeleland, p.184
[67] Sykes, With Plumer in Matabeleland, p.185
[68] Keppel-Jones, Rhodes and Rhodesia, p.461
[69] Sykes, With Plumer in Matabeleland, p.190
[70] Plumer, An Irregular Corps in Matabeleland, p.172
[71] Baden-Powell, The Matabele Campaign 1896, p.207
[72] Keppel-Jones, Rhodes and Rhodesia, p.462
[73] Plumer, An Irregular Corps in Matabeleland, p.173
[74] Plumer, An Irregular Corps in Matabeleland, p.175
[75] Plumer, An Irregular Corps in Matabeleland, p.174
[76] Sykes, With Plumer in Matabeleland, p.194
[77] Sykes, With Plumer in Matabeleland, p.195
[78] Plumer, An Irregular Corps in Matabeleland, p.177
[79] Sykes, With Plumer in Matabeleland, p.198
[80] Baden-Powell, The Matabele Campaign 1896, p.227
[81] Sykes, With Plumer in Matabeleland, p.200
[82] Bulawayo Sketch, 25 July 1896
[83] Westminster Gazette, 27 July 1896
[84] Ranger, Revolt in Southern Rhodesia, 1896-7, p.236
[85] Keppel-Jones, Rhodes and Rhodesia, p.462
[86] Ranger, Revolt in Southern Rhodesia, 1896-7, p.237
[87] Sauer, Ex Africa, p.309
[88] Blake, A History of Rhodesia, p.137
[89] Keppel-Jones, Rhodes and Rhodesia, p.496
[90] Sauer, Ex Africa, p.317
[91] Sauer, Ex Africa, p.322
[92] Blake, A History of Rhodesia, p.138
[93] Keppel-Jones, Rhodes and Rhodesia, p.499
[94] Jones, Rhodesian Genesis, p.126
[95] Plumer, An Irregular Corps in Matabeleland, p.181
[96] Barrett, The 7th (Queen's Own) Hussars, Volume 3: 1818-1914, p.180
[97] Barrett, The 7th (Queen's Own) Hussars, Volume 3: 1818-1914, p.173
[98] Barrett, The 7th (Queen's Own) Hussars, Volume 3: 1818-1914, p.174
[99] Barrett, The 7th (Queen's Own) Hussars, Volume 3: 1818-1914, p.180
[100] Blake, A History of Rhodesia, p.139
[101] Keppel-Jones, Rhodes and Rhodesia, p.506
[102] Keppel-Jones, Rhodes and Rhodesia, p.508
[103] Jones, Rhodesian Genesis, p.127

'The Mashona race has always been regarded as composed of disintegrated groups of natives, having no common organization and owning allegiance to no single authority, cowed by a long series of raids from Matabeleland into a condition of abject pusillanimity, and incapable of planning any combined or premeditated action.'[1]

Hugh Marshall Hole gives the view commonly-held at the time

'Those who know Mashonaland well are not uneasy–they are unanimous in the belief that the rising will not prove formidable.'

– Lord Grey

'If you let the men smoke on a night march, you might as well let the band play too.'

– Colonel Baden-Powell

'You only want a sjambok and a box of matches to take any Mashona kraal.'

No one seemed to consider the Mashona a formidable foe

'The first essential for a mounted infantry man is that he be a thoroughly good infantry soldier. In this he differs from a mounted rifleman, who need only be a good shot, and does not require the cohesion and solidity necessary to produce the discipline which enables the former to stand steady in square, or face a severe fire when attacking a position.'[2]

Lt. Colonel Alderson talks about the calibre of men in his regiment

'We had under-rated the Mashona native. They were certainly not a warrior race like the Zulu, but they were steeped in superstition, and were cunning and clever, far more so than their late over-lords, the Matabele... we were sitting on a smouldering fire and didn't know it.'[3]

Native Commissioner, 'Wiri' Edwards looks back ruefully on
Rhodesian complacency in Mashonaland

Chapter 15
Sunshine and Storm in Mashonaland

When the Matabele rose in rebellion in March of 1896, few even considered the possibility that the Mashona might do likewise. Unlike the warlike and aggressive Matabele, the Mashona were regarded as a very docile and placid bunch, and, what is more, surely indebted to the white man for putting an end to Lobengula's reign of terror and pillage. As the missionary, Carnegie, put it shortly after Lobengula's defeat: '...they will be no longer in fear and dread of that heathen monarch's tyrannical power to crush their ambition, enterprise and desire for knowledge.'[4] We saw earlier that there had been little hesitation in sending Colonel Beal off to Matabeleland with 150 men of the Rhodesia Horse, since few seemed concerned that this would leave the Mashonaland settlers exposed. Even those who did anticipate trouble in Mashonaland thought that it would come from Matabele rebels and there was even a discussion about the need to defend the Mashona from possible attacks.[5] Indeed, the acting administrator in Salisbury, Mr Justice Joseph Vintcent, went so far as to announce, in the Gazette, that there was 'no reason to believe' that there was 'any probability of a similar rising of natives in Mashonaland'.[6]

As predictions go, it was a shockingly inaccurate one.

§

Various theories abound as to why the Mashona rebelled. As with the theories surrounding the Matabele Rebellion, there is probably a degree of truth in most of them. Mugabe's modern-day propaganda machine endeavours to present the insurgency as some sort of 'first Chimurenga'—the initial blows of a popular struggle for independence and a black-ruled Zimbabwe—but it was far from that.

Just as with the Matabele Rebellion, during which large numbers of Matabele 'friendlies' stayed loyal and served the company, only certain groups of Mashona rebelled while others fought to help the Rhodesians. In addition, large areas of Mashonaland saw no rebellion whatsoever; examples include the Melsetter area where there had been no rinderpest outbreak, and Fort Victoria, where the local Mashona showed no desire to see the end of white rule and protection, having suffered terribly until 1893.[7] Selous recalled:

'Captain Laing received very valuable assistance from Matibi, a Mashona chief living near the Bubyi River, who sent several hundred of his men to accompany him on his march to Bulawayo. These men did good service and fought well when supported by white men. They accompanied the column as far as the Umzingwani River, twenty-five miles from Bulawayo, returning home from this point loaded up with loot of all kinds which they had taken from their rebel countrymen. Besides Matibi, it is worthy of remark that Chibi and Chilimanzi, the two most important chiefs in the district between Belingwe and Victoria, have both not only held aloof from the present rebellion, but have given active assistance to the whites since the outbreak of hostilities, whilst Gutu's people—the Zinjanja—have also remained loyal to the government.'[8]

This support continued throughout the Mashonaland rebellion. Many at the time claimed that the Mashona had rebelled at the bidding of Matabele who had made their way into the territory to stir up trouble.[9] Though this might not be convenient for those who prefer to argue that the Mashona rose up to throw off the dreadful yoke of colonialism, there seems to be more than a grain of truth in these claims, given the reports of Matabele leaders 'haranguing' their Mashona comrades and 'scolding them for not fighting better' in several of the opening actions. The strong impact that these Matabele rabble rousers had on chiefs who had always lived in fear of them is not surprising–especially considering that they claimed to have killed every white man in Matabeleland, and threatened to make Mashona who did not rebel in support, suffer terribly, just as they had in Lobengula's day.[10] In fact others have since shown that the most important factor in determining whether or not various Mashona chiefs would rebel, was their relationship with the Matabele. There were some exceptions, but generally speaking, those who had accepted Matabele subjection before the 1893 war rebelled while those who had always resisted the Matabele stayed loyal and, indeed, mostly fought on the side of the white government.[11]

As in the Matabele Rebellion, the part played by spirit medium cults cannot be overlooked, however uncomfortable this may be for the politically-correct historian. The most influential of these rejoiced in the catchy name of Gumsporehumba, but adopted the title 'Kagubi' as he claimed to be a medium for the Shona spirit of the same name.[12] A mysterious and blood-thirsty 'witch' called Nehanda played a similar role in the Mazoe area.[13] While Kagubi and Nehanda indulged in whipping the Mashona into a murderous frenzy, it would seem that the spirits didn't always sing from the same song sheet; when one of Chief Chibi's indunas argued passionately in favour of joining in the revolt, Chibi consulted the spirits through his own witch-doctor, and found them strongly opposed to the rebellion.[14] A cynic (or anyone with a brain) might suggest that Chibi had other reasons for declining to revolt, but being able to claim that the spirits agreed with him was not a bad thing.

After the rebellions had been quelled, a Wesleyan Minister in Salisbury, the Rev. John White, wrote a lengthy letter to the Methodist Times, laying out what he considered to have been the causes of the uprising in Mashonaland. He came up with five main reasons, but qualified these by saying that the problems had been caused by a few bad-eggs: the poor quality of some native administrators, the 'native constable nuisance', the poor behaviour of some settlers, the rinderpest and locusts, and the 'pernicious influence of the witch-doctors'–all of which had caused some of the Mashona to rebel at the 'opportune moment' while the Rhodesians were embroiled in Matabeleland.[15]

All the chiefs in a swathe of central Mashonaland (an area encompassing Chilimanzi, Fort Victoria, Chibi and Ndanga) either stayed neutral or actively supported the company's operations against the rebels. This large chunk of loyalist land formed a sort of 'cordon sanitaire' and, whatever their feelings might have been, chiefs who were cut off by this area were separated from fellow insurgents and dared not rebel.[16] Other than three murders at the very beginning of the rebellion, the area around Umtali on the border of Portuguese East Africa, remained quiet throughout. A laager was formed in the town, and settlers summoned in from the scattered settlements, but despite premature reports in the British press of Umtali having been wiped out, it seems actually to have been a rather jolly spot throughout the war. One nurse recalled a musical evening in the town:

'The Umtalians are most kind-hearted, hospitable people, they vie with each other in acts of kindness. This musical evening was a complete success. Mr Sawerthall, the chartered company's agent, is a very accomplished pianist, and is a host in himself. After the music, tables were cleared out and an impromptu dance took place. A waggon-sail spread tightly over the mud floor forms an excellent substitute for a wood floor and is not unpleasant to dance upon. This was the first of many pleasant evenings.'[17]

With dances and even weddings taking place,[i] it was soon realized that keeping the laager formed—and martial law in effect—was a little pointless, since the local Mashona clearly had no interest in joining the

---

i Miss Emily Hewett married Mr Herbert Blatch and apparently, '...it was a very pretty wedding. The whole of Umtali seemed gathered together in the little church, including the dogs of the town, which were numerous and enterprising.'

rebellion.[18] Likewise, the chiefs to the north of the colony all remained neutral–neither the Matabele nor company rule had really impacted their lives at all, and they seemed happy enough with the status-quo.

The Mashona system of rotating chieftainships among a number of leading families was also a major factor. Some Mashona chiefs stayed loyal (and actively fought the insurgents) simply because neighbouring rival chiefs, happened to have rebelled. Claimants to chieftainships popped up and led loyalist factions against would-be rebel chiefs, and other would-be paramounts used the uprising as an excuse to seize control by being more radically committed to the rebellion.[19] Though it was no doubt simply the straw that broke the camel's back, one of the most prominent rebels, Mashongombi, seems to have joined the uprising because a native commissioner had flogged his nephew for having flogged the wife of one of the commissioner's messengers.[20] Chiefs who fought on the company's side in the 1893 war against Lobengula knew that a successful rebellion would probably be fatal to them, and thus remained staunchly loyal.[21] Such family feuds, petty power games and endless squabbles give a lie to the latter day claims that the uprising was some sort of universally popular resistance movement.

§

Whatever the individual motivations and grievances might have been, the uprising spluttered into life over a period of weeks, rather than erupting in a devastating thunderclap. Troublesome rumours started circulating long before any killing took place, and native commissioners started receiving reports that some of the chiefs were assembling warriors.[22] A lone prospector was murdered as early as 24 April, and while many did not consider this the beginning of a general uprising, the inhabitants of nearby Hartley[ii] formed a laager on a commanding piece of high ground just in case.[23] Hartley was very close to the border of Matabeleland, so it was not unreasonable to assume that the prospector had been killed by renegades who had crossed into Mashonaland.

More alarm bells went off when a when a native policeman was murdered on 7 June, but this killing was thought be related to the fact that he had been collecting hut-tax at the time.[24]

When in mid-June, a rash of brutal murders was suddenly committed in various places across Mashonaland, many still maintained that these were not the start of a popular uprising. On 17 June, the Rhodesia Herald declared, 'We do not see sufficient evidence in the

---

ii Now called Chegutu, Hartley (sometimes known as 'Hartley Hills') was named in honour of Henry Hartley, a pioneer and hunter.

murders and the attitude of the natives to conclude that anything like a general, or even a partial, rising is contemplated.' One must bear in mind that these were the days before the internet and 24-hour rolling news channels, so it is perhaps not surprising that the full extent of the insurgency was not grasped immediately.

Nevertheless, it is still remarkable that, as late as the 20th, the editor of the Bulawayo Chronicle still seemed to think the murders would not amount to much:

'The rebellion, if such it be, has been started in a similar manner to the one in Matabeleland by the massacring of isolated parties, and unless checked at the beginning will assume large dimensions. However, we do not anticipate an insurrection of anything like the magnitude it is here, as the Mashonas are notorious cowards, and have not got the quantity of arms and ammunition which the Matabele had secreted.'[25]

He was absolutely correct in saying that the two rebellions had started in the same way. As had been the case in Matabeleland, the thinly-stretched company forces and volunteers desperately tried to bring scattered groups of settlers to safety. One resident of Salisbury recalled the horrific attacks that marked the start of the uprising:

'Mr Norton, accompanied by a coloured man, had gone off to a kraal on the farm to make enquiries about some of the natives who had left their work without permission the previous evening. It was not known how he met his end and his body was never found. The police patrol sent out from Salisbury to warn the Nortons of the rising found the rest of the family all murdered–Mrs Norton, their baby, their white nurse and their farm assistant... At Headlands, all possible arrangements for bringing the people together for self-protection were made. Those living in the vicinity of Marandellas were brought there also. Three men out trading were murdered while making their way in. At Bromley three men refused to go in to Salisbury when they had the chance and left it too late. They were murdered while trying to make their way into town.'[26]

When the native commissioner, 'Wiri' Edwards, received a letter from his boss informing him that Chief Makoni was playing-up, he rode out with a few men to nip the trouble in the bud.[27] As the small party travelled, they saw 'fires on the tops of mountains in different parts of the district' and realized that something serious was going on. Edwards' camp was attacked and looted by rebels on the 20th and the local whites barricaded themselves in a nearby store. When Edwards returned to draw ammunition, he had to crawl through the bush to evade the besiegers:

> 'We were surrounded by a horde of savages out for our blood. They kept shouting out what they would do with us when daylight came.'[28]

Others rode to their deaths in blissful ignorance of what was happening. When three Indian traders vanished (later found to have been murdered) the local native commissioner visited the kraal where they had last been seen, only to be hacked apart himself.[29] His 'faithful native', a fellow by the splendid name of 'January', fled and hid in a cave, a vantage point from which he witnessed two more white men– Messrs Stunt and Shell[30]–riding into the kraal that afternoon. These visitors were well received at first, but then grabbed, bound hand-and-foot, and thrown into a river to drown.[31]

Several native commissioners were killed, mainly because they were isolated, easy targets in the middle of native areas, rather than because of any desire for specific revenge. Traders, policemen, miners and prospectors were surprised and hacked or stabbed to death just as readily. Even a Mashona Anglican clergyman—Bernard Mizeki—was brutally murdered by rebels in front of his terrified wife.[32]

As rumours continued to fly, a Basuto known as Jan rode into Salisbury, bringing word of an attack on the small settlement at Beatrice Mine. He gave his report to the secretary of the BSACP, explaining that he had seen 'twenty boys' on the road:

> 'Some of them were Matabeles and some were Mashonas. They killed two white men and four natives with kerries. This happened yesterday afternoon about sundown. I knew the natives who killed the two white men; they live six miles from the mine. I saw them killing the white men and the boys, and when I ran away I saw them looting the house.'

One of the murdered settlers was mutilated and his remains thrown down a well.[33]

Like the Matabele settlers a few weeks earlier, the whites of Mashonaland were shocked and enraged by the sheer savagery of the murders and the way that the rebels had killed and maimed women and children as readily as men. Whatever the rights and wrongs of the insurgency, it is difficult to forgive the rebels for having indulged in such utter brutality, and these outrages spurred the Rhodesians—and the wider empire—into action.

Martial law was declared. A laager was quickly formed at Fort Salisbury and the kopje that overlooked the town occupied, just as had been done at Bulawayo. There were around 250 women and children to protect, but company forces in the town were meagre; about 60 Rhodesia Horse troopers who (much to their disgust) had been left behind when their colleagues had ridden to Matabeleland a few weeks earlier, and a handful of officers from the Mashonaland Mounted Police. These were supplemented by 250 settlers who had been called up for service by 'burger law', but this was far from an effective fighting force: when these men had initially mustered in response to the Matabele uprising, turnout had been very poor and some of those who did parade only did so in the hope of being issued rifles.[34]

When the burgers were again called up to face the Mashona, they were allowed to elect their own officers in the Boer style–though with the insane stipulation that no man who had previously held a commissioned rank could be elected so that 'others might have experience of being in control'.[35] This farce instantly turned the burgers into a very ineffective unit, and one which was ludicrously top-heavy with all manner of officers and NCOs–so much so that various wags in Salisbury commented that if the Mashona attacked, there would be few casualties among the men but slaughter among the officers. To make matters worse, many of these fellows un-sportingly declared that they would only serve within the confines of the town, and refused to take part in any patrols.[36]

A 'defence committee' was set up, and a 'genial and loquacious Scotsman', William 'Mazoe' Smith[iii] was elected chairman[37]–this despite his only military experience being a few years with the Royal Navy Volunteer Reserve. Smith was a fierce critic of the government and his defence committee was not to play a particularly impressive part in the rebellion, being determined only to defend the laager and opposing any operation that would weaken the town's garrison.

Fortunately for all concerned, the Mashonaland Mounted Police and Rhodesia Horse were under independent command[38] and, just as in the Matabele Rebellion, the first phase of the insurgency involved skirmishes fought by these scratch forces of police and volunteers as they bravely sallied into the countryside on their mercy missions.

The most famous such operation went down in Rhodesian folklore as the 'Mazoe Patrol' and it is a tale of endeavour and valour worthy of a Hollywood epic. When the rebellion broke out, a small group of settlers got stuck out in the Mazoe Valley,[iv] perhaps 30 miles to the north of Salisbury. They had gathered in a little cluster of dwellings:

---

iii He earned his nickname as the manager of the Mazoe Development Company, which no doubt helped to distinguish him from all the other Smiths.

iv Since renamed 'Mazowe'

the houses of the native commissioner and mining commissioner, a few huts, a store, the nearby Alice Mine, and the telegraph office.[39]

Thanks to the telegraph office, the manager of the Alice Mine, Mr J.W. Salthouse, had been informed of the murders at Beatrice Mine and advised to gather all the nearby settlers together. Unfortunately Pollard, the native commissioner, was away from the settlement when word of the rebellion was received, and was murdered before he could make it back, but Salthouse quickly gathered some 15 settlers—including 3 ladies—and a dozen loyal Mashona at the position (please see Appendix 7 for a list of those involved).

On the morning of 18 June, some of these settlers made an attempt to get to Fort Salisbury but didn't get far before being attacked. Three men were quickly killed, and the survivors fled back to the small laager which had been built at Alice Mine. This was quickly besieged by pursuing rebels.[40] Interestingly, and like Jan the Basuto, the defenders of the Alice Mine laager reported having heard Matabele voices among their attackers–indeed, one such Matabele was even heard chastising the Mashona for leaving him in his position without tobacco.[41]

The only way to raise the alarm was to make a dash to the telegraph office—which lay about a mile from the laager—and send a plea for help to Salisbury. Not surprisingly, the telegraph operator, a man called Routledge, was not keen to embark on what was essentially a suicide mission,[42] but a rather unlikely hero stepped up to the mark: a telegraph operator from Salisbury by the name of Blakiston, who had only just arrived at the mine with two other men from the capital and a wagon to bring in the ladies.[43] Blakiston was distinctly un-Rhodesian: a quiet, intellectual, studious fellow whose brother would later become the president of Trinity College, Oxford– but cometh the hour, cometh the man. He had been unhappy in Rhodesia, and found he had little in common with his fellow settlers, but 'some ironic twist of fortune destined the shy young man to become a martyr for the country's hard-riding, hard-drinking white frontier community'.[44] By offering to go with him, Blakiston managed to convince Routledge to make the run.

Dodging fire from the rebels, the plucky pair somehow made it to the office and tapped out most of their message–it was short and poignant, but enough to raise the alarm in Fort Salisbury: 'Three men killed. Alice Mine surrounded. Send help at once. Goodbye'.[45] Neither man made it back to the laager.

Down in Salisbury, the man who received the message, Lieutenant Judson[v] of the Rhodesia Horse, was ordered to ride out to the Mazoe

---

v   Like all the other volunteers, Lt. Dan Judson only served in the Rhodesia Horse on a part time basis. He held a day job as the Inspector of Telegraphs in Salisbury, so one can assume he knew both Routledge and Blakiston quite well.

Valley and bring the settlers in immediately. Judson, with just four troopers, rode out of the laager on the evening of the 18th, and soon bumped into paymaster Captain Brown, who sportingly attached himself to the patrol.[46] Judson was reinforced by another five troopers the following morning, but some of the horses had knocked up, and he had no choice but to send several of his men back. The patrol—by then just seven strong—continued its mission.

Judson's men came under fire as they entered the Mazoe Valley and the last seven miles to the Alice Mine were done at a gallop as they fought a running battle. Two horses were killed and one trooper badly wounded, but Judson's tiny force made it to the Alice Mine laager just as the rebels were attempting to storm it.

Though Mr Salthouse reckoned that Judson's men had saved the laager from being over-run, the rebels still surrounded the settlement, and loosed off pot-shots into the laager from a few hundred yards. Judson quickly realized that they had no chance of fighting their way out and instead waited until nightfall to send a 'Cape Boy' called Hendrik out with another plea for assistance.[47] The decision to send Judson out with such a small force was a bizarre one and, for all their bravery and dash, their arrival had not really improved the situation in the Mazoe Valley.

Luckily, this had been recognized fairly swiftly, and before Judson's runner made it anywhere near Salisbury, Inspector Nesbitt[vi]—sometimes referred to as 'Captain Nesbitt' which was the equivalent military rank—of the Mashonaland Mounted Police had been sent out with a second patrol to assist. Nesbitt and his 12-man party rode out of the Salisbury laager on the 19th, and soon encountered the messenger Judson had sent. Hendrik, the galloper, bravely opted to return to Alice Mine with Nesbitt's men.

Nesbitt's patrol came under fire as it pushed down into the Mazoe Valley, but reached the Alice Mine laager in the early hours of the 20th, with the loss of just one horse wounded. It was quickly decided to evacuate the laager as soon as possible, so as to give the rebels no further chance to consolidate their stranglehold on the valley. Mr Salthouse, who seems to have been a very practical and steady fellow, fixed sheets of iron to the sides of a wagon, to make a kind of impromptu 'armoured car' to protect the ladies on the withdrawal. The three ladies were placed into this wagon, and the rest of the force formed up: twelve mounted men ranged in front, on the flanks and to the rear of the wagon, while the rest of the men—eighteen of them—would have to walk beside it, for lack of horses. At midday on the 20th,

---

vi Inspector Randolph Cosby Nesbitt VC (1867–1956). Born in Queenstown in the Cape Colony, Nesbitt became a native commissioner after the war and retired after 40 years' service with the Rhodesian police and civil service, returning to South Africa due to his wife's poor health.

the small band pushed out of the Mazoe Valley. Nesbitt later reported the events of that afternoon:

'On starting I sent on an advance guard of four mounted men, the same number being left as rear guard, the dismounted and four remaining mounted men being with the coach. After proceeding about a mile the advance guard were fired on, when almost immediately my whole party were engaged, and silenced the enemy's fire, thus enabling the coach to pass through a very dangerous 'donga'; from this spot a heavy fire was kept up from my right flank, until, when passing the Vesuvius camp, the enemy were reinforced. The fire becoming hotter, they succeeded in killing McGeer, Jacobs and two horses; from here we were constantly harassed, so pushed the advance guard further forward to hold all rising ground on the line of march, they being thus enabled to cover our advance.

I proceeded in this order till I reached a spot some two and a half miles from the Salvation Army Farm, where, from the nature of the country and the fact of having so few horses left, it was impossible to hold any rising ground, so rushed an ugly gorge, where a heavy and sustained fire was opened on my party from either side of the road, where dense reed beds, long grass, rocks and creepers effectually hid the enemy, who were only about ten yards off and sometimes nearer. At this spot Tpr. Van Staaden and four horses were shot dead, Mr. Burton and Tpr. Hendricks wounded dangerously, Ogilvie, Berry and two horses wounded slightly. Mr. Arnott and Tpr. Hendricks, part of my advance guard, who had pushed through this trap, thinking all was over, rode for Salisbury. The enemy followed us for another four miles, keeping up a harassing fire and wounding another horse, this making a total of about 14 miles' constant fighting, occupying about three and half hours. When arriving near Mount Hampden and getting into the open, the enemy retired, and I proceeded without further delay, arriving in Salisbury about 9.30 p.m.

I estimated the enemy's strength to be at least 1,500, many of them being armed with Lee-Metford, Martini and Winchester rifles, and appearing to be well supplied with ammunition. I have every reason to believe that Cape Boys and Matabeles were the leaders of this attacking party. I compute that the enemy's loss must be about 100.

The men of the patrol behaved splendidly all through; many of them had never been under fire before. I would especially mention the good services rendered by Messrs. Ogilvie, Pascoe and Harbord.'[48]

Mr Salthouse gave a rather more personal account of the chaotic and terrifying retreat:

'It was almost impossible to see the enemy, owing to the long grass and reeds which grew right up the roadside, and all we could do was to continually fire in all directions from the wagonette to clear the way as we struggled forward. Our horses and men gradually became weaker and weaker, and at times many of us had not the strength to lift our rifles. We supported and rallied ourselves from time to time by holding to a companion's stirrup or to some portion of the wagon until we had regained sufficient strength to fire a few more shots. When our bandoliers were emptied the ladies, who never uttered a sound, though the bullets—slug and shot—rattled incessantly on the armour of the wagon, gave out handful after handful of ammunition to their gasping and exhausted protectors. About a mile from the Tatagora River drift, or crossing, the road winds round between the foot of a large kopje and the river. It was at this point that it appeared to us more than ever that our advance must come to an end. The grass to within three yards of the road was swarming with blacks, and from every quarter the bullets seemed to shower. Here one of our leaders was shot through the head, and immediately after the off-side wheeler fell mortally wounded. Mr. Brown and I struggled to cut him loose. Our task was hardly completed when our hearts sank to see the other wheeler also fall.

I was just able to save myself as he fell towards me. We cut him loose also. At about the same time Van Staaden and Jacobs were shot dead and Ogilvie and Burton wounded; the latter received a wound—a terrible one—right through the face. He nevertheless, without assistance, struggled into the wagon and fell bleeding amongst the horrified women. Arnott and Hendricks also, two of our advance guard, were cut off.

We afterwards learned that they reached Salisbury–one of them, Hendricks, with a bullet wound right through his jaws and mouth. Our four remaining horses dragged on the wagonette, blood pouring from the nose and mouth of the wounded leader. We passed the body of Van Staaden lying on the road, one side of his head having been blown away. We picked up his rifle and bandolier. Our advance guard then left the road and, continually taking up positions on any little hills or knolls that they could see, kept pouring lead on the black demons waylaying us in the grass ahead and across the Tatagora River, which was now in sight. Here we had hoped to quench our raging thirst, which had been growing momentarily more and more unbearable. But it was

The Mazoe Patrols - Chronology

1 17th June - Mine manager of the Alice Mine, Mr Salthouse, on receiving news of the murder of the Norton family and the Mashona uprising, calls all Mazoe residents to the Alice Mine and builds a fortification "on a small rocky hill close behind the west side" It is overlooked on 3 sides by hills.

2 17th June - At 11h00 a cart with 6 men (Cass, Dickenson, Faull, Pascoe, Fairburn and Stoddart) leaves Alice mine for Salisbury. The women, left at the Mine under the care of manager Salthouse, follow on in the wagonette shortly after. (3 women and 3 men as escort.) After 3 miles the 6 men in the cart are attacked by rebels, 3 are killed. They turn back and are able to stop and warn the wagonette with the three women who had left just after them. They are harassed by fifty rebels all the way back to the mine.

3 18th June - At 17h30 Lt. Judson of the Rhodesia Horse leaves Salisbury to go and assist at Mazoe. At 03h30 on 19th June he is joined at Mt Hampden by 5 more men. They enter the "valley of death" at 12h00 on the 19th June. Just after Mt Hampden they start to see evidence of rebels, but arrive safely at Mazoe.

4 19th June - Alice Mine laager comes under attack from rebel leader Mhasvi (later found to be an ex BSAC policeman)

5 19th June – Inspector RC Nesbitt plus 12 men of the Mashonaland Mounted Police leave at 22h30 for Mazoe to rescue the survivors. They meet Cnst. Hendrik coming on his own from Mazoe to request help. They proceed straight through the bush, and at dawn on the 20th they reach the area where Mazoe Dam is today . They gallop through "the poort" and are fired on from both sides of a carefully planned ambush. They survive and arrive at Alice Mine.

6 20th June - At 12h00 Inspector RC Nesbitt sets off for Salisbury, having armour plated the sides of the wagonette. Their party consists of 30 men and three women. They put out an advanced guard on foot and a mounted rearguard behind. They are fired on within the first half mile and from there on they are attacked continuously from both sides of the road. At the first donga near the Vesuvious Mine there is a furious attack and two men are killed. They continue the advance – harassed from both sides and the rear by some mounted rebels. They are heavily attacked again at the Tetagura drift. At the head of the valley the rebels give up the chase.

7 At 10h30 pm on the 20th June Inspector Nesbitt's patrol reaches Salisbury. Three of his 13 man patrol are dead and five are wounded. The women and rest of the party are safe. 15 horses had either been killed or injured. On 12th August 1897 Inspector Nesbitt is awarded the Victoria Cross in Salisbury for his bravery and leadership.

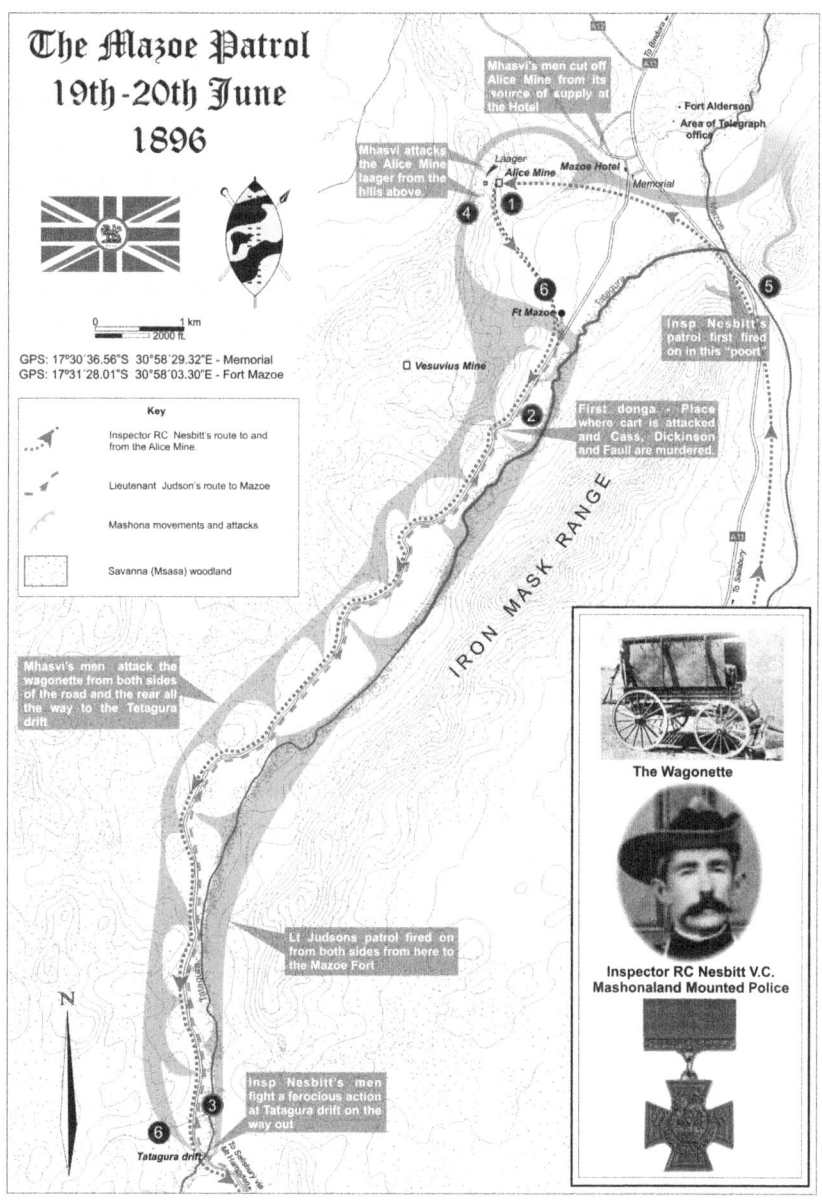

The Mazoe Patrol
19th-20th June
1896

Mhasvi's men cut off Alice Mine from its source of supply at the Hotel

· Fort Alderson
· Area of Telegraph office

Mhasvi attacks the Alice Mine laager from the hills above.

Laager
Alice Mine   Mazoe Hotel
Memorial

GPS: 17°30'36.56"S 30°58'29.32"E - Memorial
GPS: 17°31'28.01"S 30°58'03.30"E - Fort Mazoe

Ft Mazoe

Insp Nesbitt's patrol first fired on in this "poort"

☐ Vesuvius Mine

First donga - Place where cart is attacked and Cass, Dickinson and Faull are murdered.

Key

Inspector RC Nesbitt's route to and from the Alice Mine.

Lieutenant Judson's route to Mazoe

Mashona movements and attacks

Savanna (Msasa) woodland

IRON MASK RANGE

To Salisbury

Mhasvi's men attack the wagonette from both sides of the road and the rear all the way to the Tetagura drift

The Wagonette

Lt Judsons patrol fired on from both sides from here to the Mazoe Fort

Inspector RC Nesbitt V.C.
Mashonaland Mounted Police

N

Insp Nesbitt's men fight a ferocious action at Tatagura drift on the way out

Tatagura drift

0   1 km
2000 ft.

not to be. The firing was too terrific, and only one or two as they rushed past the water behind the wagon were able to catch up in their hats a mouthful of mud and water.

Beyond the river the ground became more open, and we were able to put out small flanking parties to aid our advance guard in clearing the way for the wagon. Hope revived, and with it our struggle seemed to rise again.

We were now able at times to see our enemy and to use our rifles with more effect. We reached the end of the valley, and, faint and exhausted, almost at our last gasp, sighted the open country. We were still 17 miles from home. Had our treacherous and cowardly pursuers faced our rifles and followed us further, we could never have reached it; but here they gave up the chase.'[49]

Nesbitt would be awarded the Victoria Cross for his gallant leadership in the action and there is no doubt that it was well deserved. Everyone involved showed similar courage though, including the 'Cape Boys', Hendrik and George. Hendrik (though admittedly encouraged by a £100 reward) had left the laager to take Judson's message to Fort Salisbury and returned with Nesbitt's men to drive the armoured wagon out. George was singled out for special praise by Mr Salthouse for the bravery and selflessness he showed while defending the laager.[50]

The Rhodesia Times perhaps put it best:

'And well they deserved the cheers that were showered upon them. They had done a deed that will be remembered as long as Mashonaland lasts, and have proved that a body of Mashonalanders chosen practically at random is just as plucky a set of men as the world can show.'[51]

Telegrams arrived from London and Cape Town to congratulate the garrison on the gallantry of the Mazoe Patrol, but for sheer stiff-upper lipness, it is hard to beat the cable from London which ignored the rebellion and the patrol altogether, instead simply declaring: 'England has beaten the Australians by six wickets.'[52]

§

Away to the south-east of Fort Salisbury, another remarkable rescue mission was underway. A few days earlier, reinforcements from Natal (originally destined for the fight in Matabeleland) had landed at Beira in Portuguese East Africa and travelled up the road between Salisbury and the border town of Umtali.[vii] A large wagon train containing 38,000 rounds of Martini Henry ammunition had followed in their wake. To the alarm of the defenders of Salisbury, their oxen had been struck down by the rinderpest and the wagons were now stuck near Marandellas.[viii] There was no question of letting this haul fall into the hands of the rebels.

The Native Commissioner for Marandellas, Mr Edwards, and a small group of volunteers shifted the ammunition crates onto mule carts on the night of 20 June. The wife of one settler, Mrs van der Spuy, and her baby, were loaded onto one of the wagons, protected by sacks of flour and the ammunition boxes themselves–which must have been a little disconcerting for her. Early on the 21st, the party set off, but luckily struck south back towards Headlands and Umtali, rather than pushing on to Fort Salisbury as the rebels had assumed they would. The time this bought the party was crucial and, though there was a short exchange of gun fire, the wagons were safely brought down to Umtali.[53] Not where the ammunition was most urgently needed, perhaps, but better than in the hands of the rebels.

§

Another beleaguered group—a small party of miners from the Ayrshire Mine—felt they had no choice but to fight their own way to safety. These men had been alerted to the trouble by a Zambezi 'boy' who had run in on the afternoon of the 21st. This fellow explained that he had witnessed the murder of a native policeman and managed to slip away after being captured.[54] Another 'boy' ran in shortly thereafter—he had also escaped from the rebels, but brought news that seven white settlers at a nearby camp had been attacked and no doubt, murdered.[55] The miners—10 in number, plus 20 unarmed 'friendlies'—passed a nervous night in laager and then decided to make their own way to Fort Salisbury the following morning.

The small party came under fire after just a mile and a half, but pressed on. A little further on, they were set upon by about 80 rebels, who rushed and overwhelmed the advance guard before those further back could get forward to assist.

The survivors took to the bush, and made their way to a nearby river, hoping to use it as cover. The rebels tracked them mercilessly and hunted them through the bush for days. On the evening of the 27th, the survivors—just 5 whites and a 'boy', the rest having either been murdered or scattered—were found by a patrol about 12 miles from Salisbury, and brought in to the laager.[56]

---

vii   Pointlessly renamed Mutare by Mugabe's regime

viii Renamed Marondera in 1982

§

It was believed that a small band of settlers were still holed-up in a laager in Hartley, about 65 miles south-west of Salisbury. An early attempt to get through to them had failed[57] and it was not until 19 July that the company forces were strong enough to risk a second rescue mission. The patrol was led by Captain the Honourable Charles White (his brother, Bobby, was languishing in a London prison for his part in the Jameson Raid) and comprised 65 of the Grey's and Gifford's Scouts which White had led up from Bulawayo, 42 men of the Natal Troop, 60 dismounted volunteers from Salisbury, 2 Maxims, a 7-pdr and 40 'friendlies'.[58]

This sizable force came under fire on their second day out of Salisbury, and fought an action to clear rebels from the kopjes near Norton's farm–the scene of some of the earliest murders. One trooper was killed and another three men, including one of the 'friendlies', were wounded. Satisfied that they had cleared their route, White's men made their way through the Hunyani River, turned their 7-pdr on some rebels who tried to interfere, and then laagered for the night some 23 miles from Salisbury.

White's men pressed on early on the 21st and soon came across the skeletons of three men who had been murdered in the opening phase of the war. Letters were found next to these grisly remains, one of which—dated 17 June—was a request for help from the men at Hartley. There was more fighting on the afternoon of the 21st, but the rebels were driven from their positions without any loss to the column.[59]

White's men arrived at the Hartley laager on the morning of the 22nd, and were no doubt delighted to find ten settlers there, still alive and well.[60] For their part, these fellows had no idea that they were involved in a wider rebellion, and had thought it had merely been a local uprising.[61] Taking these ten fellows with them, White's men withdrew the following day, intending to burn several rebel kraals on the way back to Salisbury–which, after five weeks of siege, might not have been exactly what the recently rescued men wanted to hear.

After a couple of fruitless days, White's scouts surprised an enemy kraal before first light on the 26th and rushed it immediately, killing up to 40 rebels. They also captured 500 head of cattle, 50 sheep and goats, a small number of horses and mules and a few firearms. With the rebels put to flight, the kraal was set ablaze and the scouts returned to the main encampment, driving their spoils along. It was probably the biggest company victory of the Mashonaland rebellion to that point.[62] The column—and the rescued men—made it into Salisbury on the 28th and the Rhodesia Herald noted approvingly:

'No small praise is due to Captain White and his staff officers for the success of the patrol, and the same can be said of the men themselves, especially White's scouts. A finer body of men than those scouts it would be hard to find. They did their work with smartness and pluck. There was a healthy dash about them which was assuring to all behind them. The Natal men and artillery also are a plucky lot, and will prove so when their turn comes.'

Towards the end of July 1896, the situation had stabilized to a degree, and the 'nightmare' month was over.[63] 118 whites were murdered between 17 and 24 June (the first week or so of the Mashonaland uprising) but not too many after that. It is not known how many loyal natives were slain by the rebels in these opening atrocities, but this number could easily have been the same again if not more.

It would not be until the end of July that there were enough imperial troops in theatre to carry the offensive to the rebels, but after the first deadly week of the uprising, the rebels had run out of easy targets to pick off. Though we have only covered a handful, no less than 28 patrols were sent out from Salisbury[ix] before imperial reinforcements arrived,[64] but these were primarily tasked with rescuing isolated parties, or bringing in supplies and cattle, rather than actively striking at the rebels. Indeed, and though these gallant patrols no doubt provided a much-needed fillip at the time, the rebellion quickly came to something of a stalemate, with neither side able to score a knockout blow to the other.

By this time, the vast majority of settlers were safely gathered into five main laagers: Salisbury, Charter, Enkeldoorn,[x] Victoria, and Umtali–only the first three being in rebel territory.[65] There were to be no more isolated, unready homesteads or trading posts for the murderers to fall upon, no more lone native commissioners or trusting missionaries who could be hacked apart. It is difficult to know what the rebels had really hoped to achieve by slaughtering handfuls of settlers in penny packets–what was meant to happen next?

The brutal murders that started the Matabele Rebellion had achieved virtually nothing, and the killing of settlers had essentially fizzled out as soon as the company forces got organized. The Mashona rebellion was even more fractured and poorly coordinated than that of the Matabele and it quickly followed exactly the same pattern. Other than perhaps a vague intention of starving the Salisbury laager into

---

ix Another nine were sent out from other settlements

x Renamed Chivhu in 1982, Enkeldoorn is considered the oldest white settlement in Zimbabwe, having been established by Boer trekkers long before the arrival of the 1890 pioneers. It retained a very Afrikaans identity in the midst of a Rhodesia which, for decades, was proud to be 'more British than the British'.

submission, there seemed to be no real plan as to what would happen after the initial murders–no scheme for a 'second phase' of operations. With the settlers now safely inside their hastily-formed laagers, it was time for the company forces and the newly arrived imperial regiments to take the fight to the insurgents.

End Notes

1   British South Africa Company, The '96 Rebellions, p.69
2   Alderson, With the Mounted Infantry and the Mashonaland Field Force 1896, p.5
3   Ranger, Revolt in Southern Rhodesia, 1896-7, p.191
4   Hanna, The Story of the Rhodesias and Nyasaland, p.73
5   Tanser, A Scantling of Time: The Story of Salisbury, Rhodesia, 1890-1900, p.151
6   Gibbs, The History of the BSAP, Vol.1, p.169

[7] Blake, A History of Rhodesia, p.135
[8] Selous, Sunshine and Storm in Rhodesia, p.238
[9] Baden-Powell, The Matabele Campaign 1896, p.261
[10] Baden-Powell, The Matabele Campaign 1896, p.262
[11] Keppel-Jones, Rhodes and Rhodesia, p.474
[12] Baxter, Rhodesia: Last Outpost of the British Empire, 1890-1980, p.134
[13] Blake, A History of Rhodesia, p.134
[14] Keppel-Jones, Rhodes and Rhodesia, p.474
[15] Thomson, Rhodesia and its Government, p.239
[16] Keppel-Jones, Rhodes and Rhodesia, p.475
[17] Goodwin-Green, Raiders and Rebels in South Africa, p.84
[18] Jones, Rhodesian Genesis, p.141
[19] Ranger, Revolt in Southern Rhodesia, 1896-7, p.197
[20] Keppel-Jones, Rhodes and Rhodesia, p.475
[21] Keppel-Jones, Rhodes and Rhodesia, p.474
[22] British South Africa Company, The '96 Rebellions, p.53
[23] British South Africa Company, The '96 Rebellions, p.52
[24] British South Africa Company, The '96 Rebellions, p.53
[25] Keppel-Jones, Rhodes and Rhodesia, p.477
[26] Jones, Rhodesian Genesis, p.128
[27] Ranger, Revolt in Southern Rhodesia, 1896-7, p.192
[28] Ranger, Revolt in Southern Rhodesia, 1896-7, p.193
[29] British South Africa Company, The '96 Rebellions, p.55
[30] Bond, Remember Mazoe, p.31
[31] British South Africa Company, The '96 Rebellions, p.56
[32] Keppel-Jones, Rhodes and Rhodesia, p.482
[33] Bond, Remember Mazoe, p.36
[34] Tanser, A Scantling of Time, The Story of Salisbury, Rhodesia, 1890-1900, p.151
[35] Tanser, A Scantling of Time, The Story of Salisbury, Rhodesia, 1890-1900, p.157
[36] Tanser, A Scantling of Time, The Story of Salisbury, Rhodesia, 1890-1900, p.158
[37] Tanser, A Scantling of Time, The Story of Salisbury, Rhodesia, 1890-1900, p.157
[38] Tanser, A Scantling of Time, The Story of Salisbury, Rhodesia, 1890-1900, p.158
[39] Keppel-Jones, Rhodes and Rhodesia, p.479
[40] Keppel-Jones, Rhodes and Rhodesia, p.480
[41] Keppel-Jones, Rhodes and Rhodesia, p.481
[42] Jones, Rhodesian Genesis, p.131
[43] Bond, Remember Mazoe, p.65
[44] Blake, A History of Rhodesia, p.134
[45] Bond, Remember Mazoe, p.93
[46] British South Africa Company, The '96 Rebellions, p.83
[47] British South Africa Company, The '96 Rebellions, p.84
[48] British South Africa Company, The '96 Rebellions, p.86
[49] British South Africa Company, The '96 Rebellions, p.90
[50] Keppel-Jones, Rhodes and Rhodesia, p.482
[51] Bond, Remember Mazoe, p.153
[52] Bond, Remember Mazoe, p.154
[53] Keppel-Jones, Rhodes and Rhodesia, p.483
[54] Keppel-Jones, Rhodes and Rhodesia, p.485
[55] British South Africa Company, The '96 Rebellions, p.101
[56] Keppel-Jones, Rhodes and Rhodesia, p.485
[57] British South Africa Company, The '96 Rebellions, p.67
[58] British South Africa Company, The '96 Rebellions, p.125
[59] British South Africa Company, The '96 Rebellions, p.102
[60] British South Africa Company, The '96 Rebellions, p.103
[61] Keppel-Jones, Rhodes and Rhodesia, p.484
[62] British South Africa Company, The '96 Rebellions, p.103
[63] Keppel-Jones, Rhodes and Rhodesia, p.486
[64] British South Africa Company, The '96 Rebellions, p.123
[65] Keppel-Jones, Rhodes and Rhodesia, p.487

Some incidents of the Mashona Rebellion
Key

1 24 th April 1896 - Prospector murdered. At the time it was not thought to be part of the rebellion but later appeared to be so.

2 June 1896 - 3 murders in Umtali area

3 7th June 1896 - A Policeman is murdered whilst collecting hut tax in the Hartley area

4 16th June 1896 - 2 Traders murdered on the Hunyani.

5 14th June 1896 - Native Commissioner DE Mooney and later 2 prospectors are murdered at Beatrice, not far from Hartley, on the Umfuli River.

6 16th June 1896 - Porta Farm, Norton. Mr & Mrs Norton, her baby, nurse and assistant are murdered

7 18th June 1896 - Hwata clan attack Mr Salthouse, manager of the Alice Mine, killing 3 men in his party. They then attack the mine, killing Blakiston and Routledge, two employees of the Telegraphic Office. Native Commissioner Pollard was also murdered.

19th June. Survivors are rescued by a patrol of the Mashonaland Mounted Police led by (Insp. Nesbitt (VC). 9 persons, including civilians and Police, are killed.

8 21st June 1896 - 10 miners and 20 friendlies are attacked near Ayrshire Mine after hearing of the rebellion and setting off for Ft Salisbury. Only 6 arrive - the rest are either missing or murdered.

9 20 th June 1896 - Uprising in the Fort Charter and Enkeldoorn area. 16 Europeans are killed after Capt Taylor and his Natal Troop leave for Matabeleland

10 24 th July 1896 - Decisive engagement at Mashayangombi's kraal led by Insp Nesbitt and De Moleyns. Mashayangombi is killed.

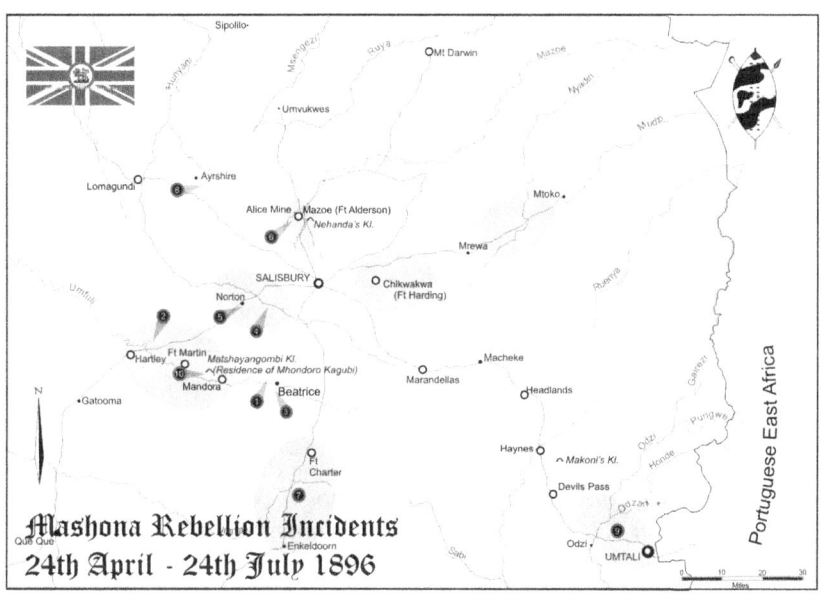

Mashona Rebellion Incidents
24th April - 24th July 1896

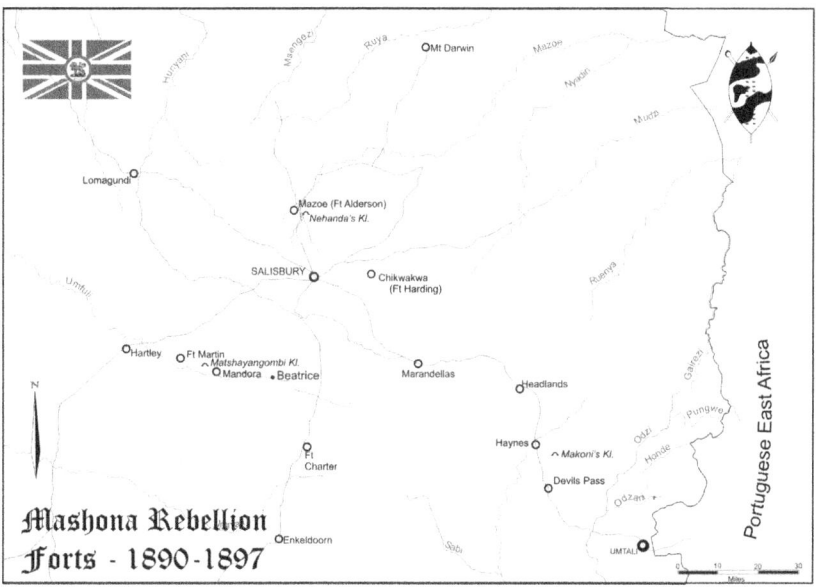

Mashona Rebellion
Forts - 1890-1897

*'...this is particularly dangerous and unpleasant work, since
the strongholds in Mashonaland consist, as a rule, of koppies
undermined in all directions with caves and crannies, in which a
very few determined men can hold their own against any number.
But Tommy Atkins [the rebels] is reported to be quite equal to the
occasion, and apparently delights in the novel form of getting killed.'*
Baden-Powell's typically upbeat way of looking at the war in Mashonaland

*'...a volunteer in Rhodesia is a man who never receives less than ten
shillings a day, plus his clothes and rations, and that some of the
officers draw as much as two pounds.'*
Lt. Colonel Alderson on the Rhodesian 'volunteers'

*'July 3. At present Chief Umtassa, in whose district we are living, is
loyal, but no Kaffir is to be relied upon; the adjoining chief, Makoni,
is in rebellion. I have fortified the government buildings and a two-
storied hotel here, and can hold my own if attacked.'*
Telegram sent from the commander at Umtali a couple of weeks
after the Mashona started rebelling

*'Even Dutchmen acknowledged that these mounted infantry could
shoot, and were astonished at the precision of the volleys which they
poured in on the enemy's positions.'*
The Times, 24 March 1897

*'Just before dawn the dynamite party was under the stockade. Behind
them was the native contingent and in the rear of them the police.
Just as the dynamite was to be fired the alarm was given by the
barking of a Kaffir-dog, and the black face of a heathen native looked
through the palisade to see what was wrong. Then began the fun.'*[1]
Times correspondent, the Honourable Hubert Howard describes a dawn attack on a
rebel stockade. Howard would be killed at Omdurman in 1898.

Chapter 16
Turning the Tide

As soon as the extent of the uprising in Mashonaland had been understood, units already in Matabeleland were quickly despatched east to deal with the new rebellion. Lt. Colonel Beal rode back with the Rhodesia Horse unit he had led into Matabeleland just a few weeks earlier. Plumer's Matabele Relief Force was also ordered to send 150 men and a Maxim, but this was soon reduced to 100 men (with no Maxim) under the command of Major Watts.[2] In addition, and as we saw in Chapter 15, Captain White's 65-strong unit of scouts (made up of Grey's and Gifford's Scouts) made an especially rapid march to Mashonaland[3] and immediately went into action to relieve the laager at Hartley.

A 70-strong troop of Natal volunteers under Captain Taylor happened to be at Fort Charter, en route to Matabeleland, when the first murders were committed. These men (and their two Maxims) were instantly diverted from their task and assigned to operations in Mashonaland.[4] The reader will recall that a detachment from this unit accompanied White's patrol to Hartley.

Elements of the imperial composite mounted infantry battalion—which we first met back in Chapter 13 and which had made it to the Cape—were quickly shipped up to Beira in Portuguese East Africa, with a plan to march into Mashonaland from that direction.[i] Commanded by Lt. Colonel Alderson, this first batch comprised the Irish and Rifle MI Companies, plus two Maxims, a pair of 7-pdrs and a small medical detachment.[5] On arrival in Beira, these were supplemented by a boat-load of troops who had been on their way to Mauritius, but who Alderson immediately commandeered for service in Mashonaland. Their timely arrival added the 43rd Company, Royal Engineers, and 50 men of the York and Lancaster Regiment to Alderson's command– an additional 111 officers and men in all.[6] These would soon be supplemented by the arrival of 150 men of the West Riding Regiment,[7] who had been shipped up from the Natal Garrison.

Getting the men and horses off at the primitive port of Beira was no easy undertaking, and the whole force still had to be transported another 40 miles up the Pungwe River in smaller craft. At Fontesvilla, the men and horses disembarked once more, and travelled up country on the narrow-gauge railway which was still under-construction. It was far from an easy route:

---

i   The reader will recall that Kruger would not permit imperial troops to cross the Republic of the Transvaal

'Their disembarkation and transport by rail was effected under great difficulties, owing to want of proper tugs, lighters, wharves, rolling stock, etc.

One lot stuck in the mud in the Pungwe River for twenty-four hours; a train ran off the line and killed several of the horses, another train collided with the wreckage, and Colonel Alderson and others on the engine had to jump for their lives.

But in spite of all obstacles the force made its way rapidly into Mashonaland.'[8]

The rather pathetic little rail line only extended as far as Chimoio—and could only take 30 men and horses at a time—so Alderson's men would have to march the final 73 miles to Umtali, with the leading elements finally arriving at the laager there on 19 July.

§

It is difficult to name a single leader of the Matabele Rebellion, and even more so in the case of the Mashona uprising. Each rebel chief operated independently and there were no major set-piece battles. Rather, various groups of insurgents were winkled out one by one in a series of fairly small actions. The Mashona rebels fought very differently from the Matabele, and showed no interest in advancing to engage the company's forces. Instead, they stuck to their traditional tactics: ambushing from cover, and firing from behind rocks and thickets. They were also patient warriors, content to lie low and wait for softer targets to present themselves. Fighting patrols sent out against the Matabele could expect a stiff fight more often than not, but many of those sent out against the Mashona rebels returned without having seen the enemy at all.[9]

The most pressing concern at this stage of the insurgency, however, was securing the supply lines. Fort Salisbury was running short, but the stocks at the Enkeldoorn and Charter laagers were severely depleted. Supplies had to be landed at Beira, brought up into Rhodesia at Umtali, and then forwarded to Salisbury for distribution. With no railway in place, this had to be done by ox wagon, and the rinderpest outbreak rendered this task almost impossible, even without rebel interference.

'Impossible' is not a word often used in the British Army, however, and with 500 mules on their way to Beira, Lt. Col. Alderson's first task was to establish control over the road between Umtali and Fort Salisbury. With the rebels cleared from the area, the mules and the few surviving oxen would be able to start pulling wagons so that a stockpile of stores could be built in the capital.[10] As the old adage suggests, wars are won by logistics–not tactics.

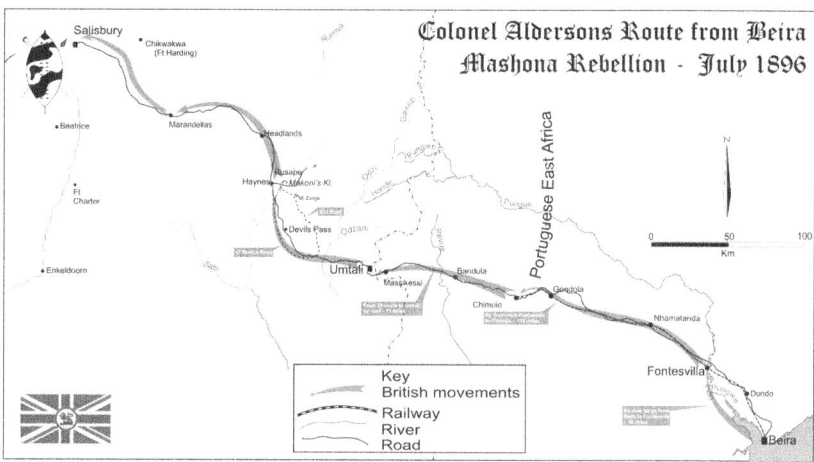

With much of his composite mounted infantry regiment still struggling up from Beira, Alderson only had 213 mounted troopers available, together with the 50 infantrymen of the York and Lancaster Regiment and small contingents of Royal Engineers and Royal Artillery— the latter manning the pair of 7-pdrs. Rather than waiting for the rest of the imperial troops to come up, however, Alderson quickly raised a volunteer force from among the men at the Umtali laager. Grandly named the 'Umtali Rifles' and commanded by Major 'Maori' Hamilton-Browne,[ii] this unit was around 130-strong. Various other gentleman adventurers and assorted merchants,[11] brave as lions but not overly enthusiastic about being subject to military discipline, also attached themselves to Alderson's column in the usual Rhodesian fashion.

Alderson's appropriation of the small York and Lancaster Regiment contingent was not well received and, when he found out, the high commissioner ordered it sent back down to Beira, and off to Mauritius as planned. As there was hesitation to march them back through Portuguese territory, Alderson instead detailed them—along with 50 men from the Umtali Rifles—to garrison Umtali, and telegraphed down to Beira for 50 of the West Riding Regiment to be rushed up to take their place. The small contingent of Yorkshiremen duly arrived in Umtali on the 27th and offensive operations could begin.[12] Hauling 45 wagons

---

ii 'Colonel' George Hamilton-Browne (1848?-1916). In an age replete with colourful characters, Hamilton-Browne was one of the most colourful of all. After emigrating to New Zealand as a young man, he claimed to have seen considerable service in the Maori Wars, and would appear to have awarded himself his nickname. 'Maori' also claimed to have hunted bushrangers in Australia, been a Papal Zouave and fought the Sioux in the American West. On the strength of this apparent wealth of experience, he was given a senior appointment in the Zulu War and another in the first Matabele War. Some of the tales he told about his early life were no doubt true, but it would later emerge that he was something of a Walter Mitty and had greatly embellished many of his stories.

laden with badly-needed supplies, Alderson's rather hotchpotch force pushed out of Umtali on 28 July, determined to find and destroy any rebel elements on or around the road to Fort Salisbury (please see Appendix 8 for details of this column).

Other than a small skirmish at Devil's Pass on the 30th, the advance proceeded without incident until 3 August, when Alderson elected to have a crack at the kraal of one of the leading rebels in the area, and indeed, the whole of Mashonaland, Chief Makoni.[13] Splitting his force, Alderson left one half to protect his camp, and led the others—two companies of mounted infantry, 60 Umtali volunteers, a Maxim, the sappers and the two 7-pdrs—out at 02h00 on the 3rd. It was the usual night march followed by dawn attack trick, and Alderson's men were in position on two sides of Makoni's kraal just before sun-up. The rebels—who had enjoyed a drunken feast the night before and must have been feeling distinctly worse for wear[14]—were rudely woken by shells being flung into the kraal by the 7-pdrs, a bombardment which continued for two whole hours as Alderson's men worked their way forward before rushing in to storm the place.[15] The fighting inside the kraal was exceptionally fierce, but Makoni's rebels were soon broken and fled for shelter in the nearby caves. Alderson did not fancy the sort of losses that sending parties into the caves would have involved, and—with the supplies running low in Salisbury—there was no time to starve them out. He briefly considered dynamite, but rejected it for reasons both moral and practical:

'Dynamite? Yes, we might frighten them with that, but the place was so big, and so rabbit warreney like, that we could not do much damage in the time we could spare. Moreover this seemed an unsoldier-like way, though perhaps the only one, of solving the problem; and at that time, when I had as yet had no experience of the treachery of the Mashona, the idea of using it was repugnant to me.'[16]

The imperial troops lost three killed—including the gallant Captain Haynes, Royal Engineers—and another three wounded.[17] Rebel losses were reckoned at around 200, of whom 60—including Makoni's principal witch-doctor and ten of his counsellors—were killed. The kraal was burned to the ground and 350 head of cattle taken.[18] A nearby loyal Mashona chief later told Alderson that Makoni had convinced himself that the imperial column was too scared to attack him, which perhaps explains the party they had been enjoying just before he did.[19]

The day after the kraal was stormed and torched, Alderson accepted the surrender of Makoni's brother, and established a fort to protect the road. This would be named 'Fort Haynes' in honour of the fallen sapper and a small West Riding Regiment contingent was detailed to man it.

On the 6th, Alderson's column met with Major Watts and his detachment of MRF, which was clearing the road from the other direction after having established a fort at Marandellas. Another fort was then built at Headlands, and 50 of the Umtali volunteers left to garrison it. The Salisbury–Umtali road had been re-opened after 46 days,[20] the telegraph line was repaired and supplies finally began to trickle north.

§

While Alderson's column was fighting its way up from Umtali, the reinforcements from Matabeleland were also active. With the arrival of these men and the Natal contingent, the company had some 600 whites and 200 loyal blacks in the Salisbury area by 22 July, and the remarkably confident decision to suspend martial law and let people return to their homes was made on the 23rd.[21] At this time, the unit of Salisbury volunteers that had been known as the Salisbury Field Force, was re-named the Salisbury Horse–though quite why the Rhodesians were so keen to keep changing the names of their units in the middle of a war is baffling, and does not make the job of a historian any easier.

Either way, two strong patrols were assembled from the forces in Salisbury at that time, and these struck out into the countryside to seek out and engage the rebels. The first of these, under Lt. Colonel Beal and comprising his unit of Rhodesia Horse which had hot-footed it back up from Bulawayo, pushed out on the 23rd, burning numerous rebel kraals and seizing several wagon-loads of grain. Only about 15 rebels were reported killed. The other force, under Commandant Smith, was made up of 'B' and 'D' Troops, Salisbury Horse, and about 150 'friendlies'. This patrol pushed out along the Umtali Road, and—again—although quantities of grain were captured, only small numbers of rebels were killed.[22]

When Lt. Colonel Alderson arrived in Fort Salisbury he took command of all the troops in Mashonaland, reporting to General Carrington who remained in Bulawayo and directed operations in Mashonaland by telegram. Though Alderson by then had over 1,500 white troops and a large, but ever changing number of loyal natives (see Appendix 9) scattered all across Mashonaland, neither rebellion had yet been defeated and Carrington's task was not an easy one. Baden-Powell described it in his colourful style:

'Sir Frederick Carrington's management of this extended force operating in a country which is equal in size to Spain, France and Italy put together, is like a man playing on a small piano to a large room full of people. Our room is over 600 miles in length, and the piano is a very small one, because the doorway (the transport and supply) is too small to admit a larger one. The piano's notes are

eight small field columns, seven laagered towns, and twenty-four
fortified posts. He plays them by telegraph from his music-stool at
Bulawayo, and has to make them reach every corner of the room.
He burns to be out himself with one or other of the columns,
but it cannot be; he has to sit here to read the music and to play
the notes accordingly, to pull the ropes, to consult with the other
heads who had to be consulted, and to be at the end of the wire
for communication with the high commissioner at the Cape.'[23]

Alderson's summary of the situation in Mashonaland was that little
had been done to the north, west, and south of Salisbury, beyond
relieving small parties of miners, prospectors, and farmers, who had
shut themselves up in laagers. The most numerous and defiant natives
were those in the Hartley district, who had made it so hot for Captain
Turner and Captain Hon. C. White's patrols. Their paramount chief was
Mashongombi (pronounced "Ma-chi-an-gombi") who was rumoured to
be harbouring many fugitive Matabele and assumed to be one of the
prime movers in the Mashona rising. It was therefore important that he
be visited as soon as possible.

Away to the north-west of Hartley was Lomaghundi's country,
where the Eyre's Farm and Ayrshire Mine murders had been committed.
Thirty miles south of Charter was a gentleman named Umtigeza, who
was reported to have said that he was only waiting for the whites to
attack him, and was not a bit afraid. There were numbers of truculent
natives under Chidamba, Amanda, and various other chiefs in the
Mazoe Valley to the west of Salisbury, and the witch Nyanda lived, and
held her court, in a large granite range in this district.

Numerous small chiefs, all of whom were hostile, had kraals along
the banks of the Hunyani and Ruya rivers, to the south-east of Salisbury.
At Chishawasha, some twenty miles north-east of Salisbury, the Jesuit
Fathers, assisted by a small guard, were laagered in their mission station,
the principal chiefs near them being Chiquaqua and Kunzi, both of whom
were hostile and bumptious. There was thus plenty of work to do.[24]

Alderson's plan was to send strong columns out into the country
and steadily smash each rebel chief in turn, kill any insurgents they
could bring to battle, and burn the kraals and supplies of those who fled
to the caves. It is difficult to see what else he could really have done,
and the scope of his operations was always limited by the supplies
available to him.[25] August thus saw fighting patrols pushed out from
Fort Salisbury in all directions, though many of these returned not
having encountered any rebels at all. Even those that did manage to
engage the Mashona could often only report having killed a dozen or
so.[26] Many kraals were burned and plenty of cattle seized, but it was
proving difficult even to find the rebels, let alone beat them.

Though Alderson bemoaned his own perilous supply situation, the rebels were infinitely worse off, with few decent rifles and pitiful ammunition stocks. While the Matabele had employed plenty of Martini Henrys, Winchesters and even magazine rifles in their rebellion, the Mashona rebels mostly used 'family guns'; old fashioned, big bore elephant guns, muskets or blunderbusses of every description, possibly just as dangerous to the user as the target. The Mashona would use pretty much anything they could squash down the barrel as ammunition–pot legs, bits of iron, telegraph wire, nails, bits of brass taps, random bits of machinery, stones, stoppers and the necks of glass bottles. One local volunteer even had to have the stopper of a Worcester sauce bottle cut out of his cheek.[27]

§

With the arrival of the reinforcements, and the Mashona having made no effort to attack the town, the residents of Salisbury began to complain, demanding that martial law be lifted and the laager broken up. Indeed, the laager had been a little pointless for a long time, with concert parties being held under lamp light in the evenings, and the Masons permitted to continue holding meetings.[28] The defence committee seems to have grown fond of their power, however, and showed no intention of relinquishing it–especially as their families were exempt from many of the more onerous rules.[29] Their determination to keep the laager in place and not give up any of their emergency powers made William Smith and his committee members, targets for derision, neatly summed up in a ditty:

'Linger, longer, laager; linger, longer, loo,
If the laager was no longer, what would Bill Smith do?
Mac will ne'er forsake it, Joe will stay there too,
Linger, longer, laager; linger, longer, loo'[30]

Before long, even some of the committee members realized the whole pantomime was serving no purpose and resigned, but the remainder stuck resolutely to their guns. On 22 July, Judge Vintcent had finally had enough and—despite protests from the remaining committee members—declared an end to martial law, broke up the laager and permitted re-occupation of Salisbury's outlying homes.[31]

§

On 30 August, another attempt was made against Makoni, who—with hundreds of his followers—was still hiding out in the caves into which he had been driven by Alderson's attack on 3 August. Led by Major

Watts, detachments of the MRF, the Umtali Rifles and the West Riding Regiment,[32] attacked and captured 11 men, and 70 women and children. For the following few days, Watts' men kept up a close siege on the caves, shooting down any rebels who tried to make a break for it. Fearing that trapped rebels would try to burst through his perimeter in the darkness, the Major recalled that 'ten men (West Riding Regiment) were stationed with fixed bayonets behind McQueen's MRF to charge any who got away.'[33]

Makoni himself tried to slip away one night but was driven back by fire from the MRF pickets. He then tried to parley, but—given his reputation for trickery and treachery—Watts refused to entertain him. In the early hours of the 3rd, Makoni tried again and was captured this time. Perhaps infuriated by it all, Watts had the rebel chief court-martialled[iii] and shot at noon on the 4th. By all accounts he was a tall, fine looking man who faced his fate calmly and with great courage. His last instruction was, 'Bury me when I am dead, or the great spirit will curse you.'[34]

The drumhead court martial saw Watts suspended by the high commissioner but he was exonerated when settlers from the Umtali area sent a message of support to the authorities[35] stating, '...the action taken in the matter was not only justifiable, but absolutely necessary. Makoni had for years past given much trouble to this part of the country himself, and had been the instigator and leader of all the surrounding chiefs. The murders which were committed in the Umtali district were traced to Makoni's people.'[36]

With tedious predictability, the modern-day liberal will no doubt seize upon the court martial as 'proof' of how callous the Rhodesians were, but it was not that simple. Watts' execution of Makoni made it safe for neighbouring chiefs to declare their loyalty and was understandably well received by settlers all over Mashonaland.[37] Makoni's two sons—aged about 11 and 12—were adopted by Watts' galloper, Captain Harding.[38] These boys—who became known as Archer and Paris—quickly became devoted to their new father, accompanying him on patrols and even into action. Indeed, poor young Paris would later be shot and killed while bringing food forward to Harding in the middle of a battle, while Archer joined the 'Black Watch' as a bugler.[39]

Watts was not alone in taking the gloves off as September went on. With the rebels retreating into caves whenever they were attacked, too many troopers were being lost in attempts to root them out. Though Alderson had earlier considered the use of dynamite 'repugnant', it was quickly becoming standard practice to[40] blast the rebels out or entomb them forever.

Despite Baden-Powell's typically up-beat claim that the Tommies delighted in this 'novel form of getting killed', the close-quarter fighting

---

iii Significantly, a Captain Pease—rather than Major Watts—presided over the court-martial, with four other officers also sitting.

in the rocks was a dangerous and deadly business and one can hardly blame Alderson and his officers for turning to dynamite. Why should they have continued to risk the lives of their own men to winkle out the rebels when they could simply blast them out without endangering themselves? While not a particularly pleasant thought to the modern mind, given the nature of the murders committed in the opening phase of the war, it is small wonder that few of the troopers felt much pity for their enemy.

§

Major Jenner, commanding elements of the imperial MI regiment and up to 2,000 'friendlies' from the Fort Victoria district,[iv] was active in the Marandellas area and had burned several rebel kraals. On 15 September, he attacked the kraal of the main trouble-maker in the area, Chief Umtigeza, and drove the rebels from it. Umtigeza and his followers fled for the safety of some nearby caves but Jenner's men carried the fight to these and the rebel chief surrendered after an hour of fierce fighting. Aside from this valuable prize, Jenner's patrol also sent large quantities of captured grain and cattle back to Fort Salisbury.[41]

The rebel cause was dealt an even more telling blow a couple of weeks later. Lt. Colonel Alderson had been planning a strike against Mashongombi—the prominent rebel leader who had been so outraged by his nephew's flogging—for some time, but it was not until 5 October that he had built sufficient supplies to have a crack at him.[42] Alderson's 350-strong column was a mix of imperial troops—the Rifle and Irish Companies of the MI having by then been reinforced by two sections of the English Company[43]—and the colonials of the Rhodesia Horse and Salisbury Rifles. A pair of Maxims and a 7-pdr provided fire support and there was a 100-strong force of 'natives'.[44] This force marched out of Salisbury with a month's worth of rations and rendezvoused with Major Jenner, who was commanding 170 troops,[v] and around 1,000 'friendlies'—at Hartley on the 10th.[45]

This combined force attacked Mashongombi's kraal and drove the rebels out after some 'hot fighting'–though only hot enough to see the imperial troops lose 5 men wounded. The following day, a strong rebel force was found at a fortified kraal on the Umfuli River and this was also stormed and burned to the ground. As usual, the rebels ran for the refuge of some nearby caves. Another kraal was attacked and

---

iv   So much for the notion that the rebellion was some sort of popular 'Chimurenga' against white rule.

v   Jenner's column comprised the Rifle Company of the Imperial Mounted Infantry, a Maxim, a 7-pdr, a troop of Natal volunteers and some scouts.

destroyed the next day, and several caves blasted with dynamite.[46]

If Alderson had thought destroying Mashongombi's kraal would end the war, he was to be disappointed. His operations had been successful, and he could claim a substantial rebel body count–but no chiefs had been captured and the vast majority of the insurgents that had fled to the caves, would simply emerge as soon as the troops left.

Establishing a permanent presence to dominate the area was deemed impossible, as there was no way the logistical set up could support such a fort. Alderson himself noted:

'The real stopper was the old question–supply. We ourselves could not provision the fort, and we knew that Salisbury, even if we sent back there, was equally powerless in this respect.'[47]

Instead, after a few more weeks in the field and after torching a few more rebel kraals, the column returned to Fort Salisbury.

Alderson was caught in a situation reflected by dozens of guerrilla wars ever since. Whenever his patrols could catch the enemy, they could defeat them–but never comprehensively so; most would simply slip away, only to pop up a little later. As we have seen, Alderson was fighting without the sort of logistical back-up that commanders in many later guerrilla wars would enjoy, and must sometimes have felt that he was fighting the country itself, rather than just the rebels: the presence of 'the fly' in the northern territories rendered mounted infantry work there all but impossible–something the rebels took advantage of, quickly retreating into such areas when threatened.[48] The rainy season started at the end of October, and made mounting offensive operations virtually impossible. This respite gave the insurgents the chance to re-group for a few months, and they took the opportunity to plant crops to sustain themselves through the following year.

§

The war in Mashonaland was far from won by the time the rains came, but the Matabele rebels had surrendered by then and both Grey and Rhodes were keen to get the imperial (and quasi-imperial) contingents out to save money. Plumer's Matabeleland Relief Force and Robertson's unit of 'Cape Boys' were both disbanded and left Rhodesia in November. The Natal troop followed shortly after and—rather remarkably—Alderson's imperial mounted infantry were all out of Rhodesia by 11 December. Though they had been in action for many weeks, Alderson's MI only lost seven men killed during their deployment[49]–though this figure does not include those members of the Umtali Rifles or the native 'friendlies' who fought alongside them in the Mashonaland Relief Force. With Alderson's

MI gone, the only imperial units left in the whole of Rhodesia were the two squadrons (nominally 200-strong) of the 7th Hussars[50] which had been based at Bulawayo since the previous November[51] and had yet to play any role in Mashonaland.

There had been more than a little tension between the imperial forces and the local Rhodesian volunteer units and the company displayed a tendency to downplay the role that Alderson's men played. It also no doubt pleased the maverick and individualistic settlers to claim that they had done all the hard work, and they could enjoy pointing out the fact that the imperial regiments had been withdrawn before the war had even been won. One history of the BSAP is particularly scathing of Alderson and the contribution of the imperial MI in general.[52] Though a natural reaction, and perhaps even an example of healthy inter-regimental rivalry, it was unfair to depreciate the efforts of the imperial soldiers: they had cleared the Umtali – Salisbury road, allowing supplies to be brought in. This action alone was worthy of credit as, without it, none of the laagers could have been held for much longer. Alderson's men had also shattered the factions of several prominent rebel leaders–though admittedly, they had failed to capture them.

For their part, the imperial officers often found the Rhodesian volunteers a little troublesome, as General Carrington remembered:

'...the local forces, although possessed of individual courage, hardihood, and aptitude for veld life, were difficult to work with. They were very independent, would not willingly do fort duty, long patrols or unpleasantly dangerous work. Their discipline, reconnaissance, and shooting were poor...'[53]

This is not a reputation that many frontier types would have been happy with. There was also the issue of terms of service: many volunteers came to the end of their stated length of service long before the rebellion had been quelled, and Alderson had been forced to reorganize his local forces as a result.

Worse still, and as we saw in the previous chapter, the men of the 'Salisbury Garrison' only signed on to defend the capital and many refused to take part in operations out of town. Alderson reorganized all the various local 'volunteer' units, forming the Rhodesia Horse into an artillery troop, a dismounted troop and a mounted troop. The Umtali Rifles would remain under the command of 'Maori' Hamilton-Browne while the Salisbury Garrison would be rebadged the 'Salisbury Rifles'. All of the some 285 volunteers signed on for another three months of service anywhere in Rhodesia.[54]

These units would not be sufficient to plug the gap left by the withdrawal of the imperial and Natal units, however, and so the Matabeleland Mounted Police and Mashonaland Mounted Police[vi] were amalgamated, reorganized and greatly expanded. Indeed, for all intents and purposes, it would be an entirely new regiment. The company would foot the bill for the police regiment, but—after the Jameson Raid debacle—would not have any control over it. This unit was originally to be called the 'Rhodesian Mounted Police' but this was quickly changed to the now famous 'British South Africa Police', a name which was first officially used on 12 December, 1896.[55] Despite all the various and rather confusing names, the new regiment could still proudly claim a lineage to the old 'British South Africa Company Police' which had escorted the pioneer column in 1896.

Reporting to Sir Richard Martin in his role as the British Government's recently appointed 'commandant general' for the region, the BSAP was made up of four divisions: a Bechuanaland Division headquartered in Mafeking, a North Zambezi Division, based up in Mount Darwin, and Divisions in Mashonaland and Matabeleland.[56] Most important to our story was obviously the Mashonaland Division, which would be under the command of Lieutenant Colonel the Honourable F.R.W. Eveleigh-de Moleyns.[vii] With the reorganization of the various local volunteer forces, the BSAP had no shortage of recruits and fifty of Alderson's imperial mounted infantry even opted to transfer into it.[viii] Raised during the pause in operations caused by the rainy season, the BSAP was quickly 600-strong in Matabeleland, whereas in Mashonaland there would be 580 white BSAP officers, backed by a 300-strong native contingent which quickly came to be known by all as the 'Black Watch'.[57] Rhodes abided by the promise he had made at the various indabas, and there were no native police in Matabeleland.

When the various forts and settlements were garrisoned, however, this left de Moleyns with just 370 men for offensive operations in Mashonaland. Indeed, even this theoretical figure is a little misleading: the native police were still considered 'undisciplined and unreliable' at that time, and many of the new BSAP recruits who had arrived from Great Britain were laid low with illness.[58] Nevertheless, when the worst of the rains began to ease up in early 1897, the men of the BSAP would get their chance to show what they could do.

---

vi   To complicate matters still further, not only did these two units share the same acronym (MMP) but both are often referred to as the Rhodesian Mounted Police in histories of the period.

vii   Frederick Rossmore Wauchope Eveleigh-de Moleyns DSO, 5th Baron Ventry (1861-1923). Born in County Kerry, Ireland, and educated at Harrow. Commissioned into the 4th Hussars in 1882. Commanded the Mashonaland Mounted Police before taking command of the Mashonaland division of the BSAP.

viii   One history of the BSAP claims that these recruits were from the Natal Troop, rather than the Imperial MI.

End Notes

1   Kane, The World's View: The Story of Southern Rhodesia, p.120
2   Plumer, An Irregular Corps in Matabeleland, p.217
3   Baden-Powell, The Matabele Campaign 1896, p.264
4   British South Africa Company, The '96 Rebellions, p.58
5   Alderson, With the Mounted Infantry and the Mashonaland Field Force 1896, p.17
6   Alderson, With the Mounted Infantry and the Mashonaland Field Force 1896, p.31
7   Alderson, With the Mounted Infantry and the Mashonaland Field Force 1896, p.59
8   Baden-Powell, The Matabele Campaign 1896, p.265
9   Keppel-Jones, Rhodes and Rhodesia, p.490
10 Keppel-Jones, Rhodes and Rhodesia, p.488
11 British South Africa Company, The '96 Rebellions, p.127
12 Alderson, With the Mounted Infantry and the Mashonaland Field Force 1896, p.67
13 Keppel-Jones, Rhodes and Rhodesia, p.490
14 Alderson, With the Mounted Infantry and the Mashonaland Field Force 1896, p.89
15 British South Africa Company, The '96 Rebellions, p.71
16 Alderson, With the Mounted Infantry and the Mashonaland Field Force 1896, p.94
17 Goodwin-Green, Raiders and Rebels in South Africa, p.81
18 Baden-Powell, The Matabele Campaign 1896, p.264
19 Alderson, With the Mounted Infantry and the Mashonaland Field Force 1896, p.98
20 British South Africa Company, The '96 Rebellions, p.72
21 British South Africa Company, The '96 Rebellions, p.70
22 British South Africa Company, The '96 Rebellions, p.125
23 Baden-Powell, The Matabele Campaign 1896, p.267
24 Alderson, With the Mounted Infantry and the Mashonaland Field Force 1896, p.130
25 Keppel-Jones, Rhodes and Rhodesia, p.491
26 British South Africa Company, The '96 Rebellions, p.128
27 Alderson, With the Mounted Infantry and the Mashonaland Field Force 1896, p.111
28 Tanser, A Scantling of Time: The Story of Salisbury, Rhodesia, 1890-1900, p.161
29 Tanser, A Scantling of Time: The Story of Salisbury, Rhodesia, 1890-1900, p.162
30 Tanser, A Scantling of Time: The Story of Salisbury, Rhodesia, 1890-1900, p.163
31 Tanser, A Scantling of Time: The Story of Salisbury, Rhodesia, 1890-1900, p.164
32 British South Africa Company, The '96 Rebellions, p.72
33 Plumer, An Irregular Corps in Matabeleland, p.233
34 Goodwin-Green, Raiders and Rebels in South Africa, p.96
35 British South Africa Company, The '96 Rebellions, p.73
36 Goodwin-Green, Raiders and Rebels in South Africa, p.98
37 Alderson, With the Mounted Infantry and the Mashonaland Field Force 1896, p.134
38 Thomson, Rhodesia and its Government, p.144
39 Thomson, Rhodesia and its Government, p.146
40 Keppel-Jones, Rhodes and Rhodesia, p.491
41 British South Africa Company, The '96 Rebellions, p.73
42 Keppel-Jones, Rhodes and Rhodesia, p.491
43 Alderson, With the Mounted Infantry and the Mashonaland Field Force 1896, p.206
44 British South Africa Company, The '96 Rebellions, p.130
45 British South Africa Company, The '96 Rebellions, p.73
46 British South Africa Company, The '96 Rebellions, p.74
47 Keppel-Jones, Rhodes and Rhodesia, p.491
48 Keppel-Jones, Rhodes and Rhodesia, p.492
49 Alderson, With the Mounted Infantry and the Mashonaland Field Force 1896, p.268
50 Keppel-Jones, Rhodes and Rhodesia, p.510
51 Barrett, The 7th (Queen's Own) Hussars, Volume 3: 1818-1914, p.174
52 Gibbs, The History of the BSAP, Vol.1, p.179
53 Keppel-Jones, Rhodes and Rhodesia, p.511
54 Alderson, With the Mounted Infantry and the Mashonaland Field Force 1896, p.142
55 Keppel-Jones, Rhodes and Rhodesia, p.512
56 Gibbs, The History of the BSAP, Vol.1, p.181
57 Gibbs, The History of the BSAP, Vol.1, p.186
58 Keppel-Jones, Rhodes and Rhodesia, p.513

*'The advance of the native contingent on the kraal was, as usual,
very funny. Once told to attack a place, or that the enemy is anywhere
near, loose off their rifles they must, up in the air, into the ground, at
every rock or boulder, and over each other's, or anyone else's, heads.
It does not matter so long as a noise is made'[1]*

*'We were now in desperate straits. Ours friendlies had proved
unreliable, my own men were down with fever, provisions were short,
and with only about 20 reliable white troops we were outnumbered
fifty to one by the hostile warriors who daily threatened attack.'[2]*

*'With the Mashonas, chiefs of a powerful kind were non-existent.
Every petty tribe acted independently, and if inclined to mischief
did so on its own initiative and in accordance with the instructions
which it happened to receive from the petty chieftain who chanced to
be at the head of it.'*

*'The natural defences were so strong that the inner stockade could
easily have been held by a dozen resolute men against any number of
assailants, but the Mashonas are not a courageous people; they can
endure heroically, but can neither defend nor attack.'[3]*

Chapter 17
After the Rains

Colonel de Moleyns' BSAP was in action shortly after New Year. The native commissioner at Fort Charter sent a telegram on 4 January 1897 to report a rebel attack on three friendly native kraals. The rebels–reported to be a mix of Matabele and Mashona–had torched these kraals, killed 16 people and carried off the usual haul of women, cattle and other loot: not something that really fits the re-invention of the uprising as some sort of independence movement, deserving of our respect and admiration.

A police patrol under a Major Gosling, BSAP, was immediately despatched to Charter to hunt down and destroy these rebels. Gosling's force was soon joined by Lt. MacAndrew and 30 'friendlies', a body of local volunteers, and the native commissioner with some native police. In all, Gosling was now in command of around 100 men who marched through the night to attack the kraals of the two rebel leaders involved, in both cases burning them down and recapturing the women. 27 rebels were reported killed in the attacks, and Gosling's command stayed in the area for a few days until he was satisfied that the rebels had been cleared.[4]

§

On 16 February, Sub-Inspector[i] Harding led an attack on Chief Gondo's rebel stronghold near Goromonzi[5]–about 25 miles to the east of Salisbury. Under increasing pressure from aggressive BSAP patrols, Gondo and his followers had withdrawn to a kopje that was riddled with caves, providing the usual protection from bombardments of police artillery. Harding had little choice but to lead an assault on the position.

Harding's force of 29 white officers and 65 of the 'Black Watch' stormed the kopje, lobbing home-made dynamite grenades into the caves. These impromptu bombs proved highly effective, and flushed the rebels out into the open where they were scythed down by the waiting Maxim gun to delighted applause and cheers from the 'Black Watch'.[6] With tedious predictability, Harding soon came under criticism but defended himself with the explanation:

'What compelled us to use dynamite was the fact that the Mashonas, when attacked, retreated at once into these caves (refusing to come

---

i   Sub-Inspector was a Police rank equivalent to an Army Lieutenant

out and surrender, even when their lives were guaranteed) and
shot down our officers and men at all times without the slightest
risk to themselves. Repeatedly I have sat for a considerable time
outside the caves, urging men, women and children to come out
to safety. I have helped many a man from a cave which was to be
blown up and not until I was convinced that only men remained
was dynamite inserted into the strongholds.
The great risk to the people who used the dynamite was that,
unless it was placed right inside, it value was negligible. To do
this, one had to go right up to the mouth of the cave, when you
would be a sure mark for any hidden armed native inside, whom
you could not see or locate.'[7]

It is difficult to see why the use of dynamite should have been
considered any less 'humane' than killing rebels by blowing them apart
with artillery or killing them with rifle or machine gun fire. Both then
and now, the usual suspects can be expected to squawk and squeal with
their trademark manufactured indignation, but why shouldn't the BSAP
have used such methods? Why should the rebels have been permitted
simply to retreat to the safety of their caves whenever threatened? Why
should the officers of the BSAP have risked the lives of their men,
sending them into the darkness of the caves to root the rebels out with
the bayonet when there was a much more logical alternative?
    Major Gosling had also been active in the few weeks since his
successful action in January and he was now leading a 70-strong BSAP
column, backed by a pair of 7-pdrs and a 30-strong native contingent.
Under their dynamic leader, the column was kept busy storming rebel
kraals and blowing up caves to the east of Salisbury. Major 'Maori'
Hamilton-Browne was equally active in the Marandellas area and also
cooperated with Gosling's operations.
    In March, Colonel de Moleyns arrived to assume personal command
of Gosling's force for another attack in the area of Makombi's kraal,
perhaps 25 miles to the north-east of Salisbury. The column had been
dubiously reinforced by another 100 unarmed friendlies, and they took
and burned various rebel kraals, destroying enormous amounts of
food supplies. The patrol then moved into the Mazoe Valley, around 25
miles north of Salisbury, and was reinforced by another 100 friendlies
sent up from the Charter region. The combined force attacked and
destroyed several fortified kraals.[8]

§

    Though successful enough, these actions followed the same pattern
as those fought in 1896: the imperial troops / BSAP would storm kraals

and kill a few rebels, but—dynamite aside—the vast majority would flee into inaccessible caves and this led to something of a stalemate. In a bid to break through, it was decided to approach Gurupila, the chief of the Matoko people, and persuade him to provide a sizable native levy. There was considerable animosity between the Matoko and the Mashona, and the native commissioner of the area, W.L. Armstrong, had recently married into the tribe[9] so the chances of support were thought to be good.

Getting to the Matoko was the first problem, however, as their lands were in the far east of Rhodesia, near the Portuguese East African border. Captain Harding commanded the BSAP patrol—comprising 20 white officers, 20 black officers and a Maxim gun—that escorted Armstrong on his mission, departing Salisbury on 4 March.[10] Harding's column was fired on 'incessantly' on their way to meet with Gurupila, but got through all right, arriving at his kraal on the 8th. The Matoko Chief immediately agreed to provide a 500-strong impi and elected to command this personally. The whole force set out on the return journey on 12 March.[11]

As Gurupila's men were 'badly armed with old muskets and assegais', it is perhaps not surprising that they panicked when attacked on the 15th while traversing a rocky pass between two rivers. 300 of the Matokos fled, but Gurupila and the others remained with the BSAP patrol and the pass was cleared of rebels. Harding had discovered that none of his men knew how to use their single Maxim, though one, Trooper Lucas was assigned to the weapon after admitting 'he was not an expert, but had driven a mowing machine'.[12] They fought off the attack, but by that time, the whites among the BSAP were suffering terribly from fever, and—about 50 miles from Salisbury—the patrol stumbled to a halt. Colonel de Moleyns himself soon arrived with reinforcements and quickly reinvigorated the column, sending the sick men off to Salisbury to recuperate while he led the others to attack various rebel positions.

When 250 of Gurupila's warriors returned to the fight, de Moleyns decided he was strong enough to have a crack at an especially formidable rebel stronghold–Shangwe Hill. This isolated peak was about 55 miles to the north-east of Salisbury and was occupied in force by the insurgents. De Moleyns invested the hill for a fortnight before storming it and killing 50 rebels. Unfortunately, Chief Gurupila was killed in the action–an event which enraged his warriors, and led to 'superstitious fears amongst the natives, who shortly afterwards exhibited signs of treachery, and at length threatened to kill Mr Armstrong and the white men of the party'.[13] Needless to say, the Matokos were released from service and headed home. Their contribution was significant, however, and de Moleyns was lavish in his praise for their efforts.

Progress might have been slow, but things were certainly moving in the right direction for the company. The reader will recall that, the previous October, Alderson had not been able to build a fort to contain Mashongombi due to supply issues. With the improving situation, however, one had since been built, and named 'Fort Martin' in honour of Sir Richard Martin.[14] Infuriated by the presence of this fort so close to his stronghold, Mashongombi led three or four hundred rebels against it on 17 March. The assault was repulsed with heavy loss after three hours of fierce fighting.[15] The BSAP commander at Fort Martin, Inspector Nesbitt—who we last met at the Mazoe Patrol—claimed that, though the fighting had been hot, they had never been in danger of being overrun, and that the position was 'impregnable'.[16] Better yet, another major rebel stronghold was stormed on 25 April, this time by a force of Umtali Rifles and 50 men of the BSAP, the whole under 'Maori' Hamilton-Browne. Unusually, the rebel chief, Svovse, was captured in the action.

§

With the arrival of the dry season, more recruits for the BSAP were able to turn up for service. 180 of these came in May, having been recruited in Great Britain and the Cape Colony. With these, and the arrival of forty Zulu recruits for the native police, de Moleyns felt confident about attacking the caves into which rebel Chief Mashanganyika[ii] had earlier retreated with his followers. A week of bitter fighting and dynamiting saw all the caves destroyed with great loss of life for the rebels.[17] The Rhodesians lost one BSAP trooper killed and two wounded.

The police then moved to attack Chief Kunzwi's kraal, about 30 miles to the east of Salisbury. This was stormed early on 19 June, and it was completely destroyed for the loss of three police killed. The official report stated, 'Large quantities of grain were captured, and Kunzwi's power was completely broken.'[18] Major Gosling, commanding the BSAP, remarked, 'From the amount of grain stored away, and the quantity of pigs, goats etc, in the stronghold [it was clear] that Kunzwi was confident of repulsing the whites, and had made ample preparations for a long stay; this opinion was confirmed by the determined resistance offered, the engagement being the most severe the police have yet taken part in.'[19]

By then, other reinforcements were arriving from Matabeleland. In late June, the two squadrons of the 7th Hussars which had been loitering at Bulawayo were finally committed to the fight in

---

ii Chief Mashanganyika was Kagubi's father-in-law

Mashonaland. It is baffling that these professional imperial cavalrymen had been left kicking their heels for so long, but worth noting that their departure from Bulawayo—coming so soon after the end of the Matabele uprising—caused protests in the town.[20] As well as the 200 Hussars, fifty more BSAP troopers, forty 'Cape Boys', a 12½-pdr and a Maxim were also sent up from Bulawayo.

With the arrival of these formidable reinforcements, it was decided to smash Mashongombi once and for all. Colonel de Moleyns—at the head of 300 BSAP troopers, three 7-pdrs and two Maxims—marched to Fort Martin, which was garrisoned by 60 BSAP troopers and a 7-pdr, and rendezvoused with the reinforcements coming up from Bulawayo.

The combined force of BSAP and Hussars attacked Mashongombi's kraal on 24 July. The outer stockades were captured quickly[21] and the chief and his followers were soon scurrying for the sanctuary of the caves in the time-honoured style. This time, however, the Rhodesians had the men and supplies to maintain a close investment and decided to wait the rebels out. A large ring of towering boulders formed a natural defensive ring around the entrances,[22] and approaching to lob dynamite grenades was a very hazardous business. Perhaps encouraged by this, Mashongombi refused calls for his surrender, but was shot dead while trying to move from one cave to another on the 25th in any case.[23] The following day, some daring fellows managed to throw dynamite into the caves, and several hundred shell-shocked rebels staggered out of the dust to surrender. It was unclear how many remained entombed in the collapsed caves. Rather remarkably, one witness reported that 'two bullets of solid gold were found after the fighting'.[24]

§

With Mashongombi finally out of the way, the rebellion was on its last legs. All agreed, however, that it would only finally be defeated when the various witch-doctors who were thought to have caused so much of the trouble had been captured or killed. To this end, strong patrols were sent out to run these last few hares to ground. One such renegade witch-doctor was hoisted by his own petard before the BSAP could get to him–the locals decided to kill him rather than providing sanctuary when he fled to another part of Mashonaland. Such was their fear of this powerful wizard that they cut him into small pieces while he was still alive.

Rhodesian victories were coming thick and fast by then. The kraal of Umzwitze, 16 miles from Fort Charter, was captured by the Hussars for the cost of three killed, and their OC, Major Ridley, badly wounded.[25] A few days later, on 21 August, Chief Zimba, of the Lo

Maghonda area, surrendered. The surrenders continued throughout August, with various rebel chiefs turning themselves in to the native commissioners at Marandellas, Charter, Hartley and Salisbury. On 2 September, Colonel de Moleyns accepted the surrender of Mangwedi and two of his subordinate chiefs.[26]

The rebellion was fizzling out to nothing by then, and by October it was thought safe for the Hussars to be sent down to Beira and the remaining volunteer formations to disband. On the 27th of that month, the infamous witch-doctor Kagubi surrendered–an event which was accepted by most to finally signal the end of the uprising. Editorial in the Rhodesian Herald declared, that with 'Kagubi the Mischievous now safe in gaol' the rebellion could be considered over.[27]

As we have seen, Kagubi—along with Mashongombi (some of whose wives the witch-doctor had found time to grab)[28]—was considered by most to be the main instigator of the uprising, and to have sparked the murders the year before, using his fellow witch-doctors to spread the rebellion across the land. Furthermore, as well as having fornicated with Mashongombi's wives, Kagubi demanded that all loot captured by his followers be brought to him–not very fitting to his latter-day reinvention as a people's revolutionary. His capture was considered important enough for the deputy commissioner at Bulawayo to have mentioned it in a letter that he sent to the high commissioner on 15 November:

'I have the honour to report for Your Excellency's information, that the detachment of the 7th Hussars having now left the country and the volunteers having been disbanded, I have directed the police in Mashonaland to resume their ordinary duties.

The natives in Mashonaland are now settling down throughout the country, and the rebellion may safely be said to have terminated.

A large number of chiefs have surrendered, including the Mandora (Kagubi, the Mashona witch doctor), and within the last four weeks 1,094 guns and rifles have been given in.

The rebellion has been one of great difficulty to deal with owing to the fact that there was no paramount chief in the country against whom a decisive blow would be struck, that operations had to be conducted against a large number of small chiefs occupying very strong positions, and that the reduction of these had little influence upon the rebels except in the immediate neighbourhood.'[29]

This largely explains why the Mashonaland rebellion lasted a year longer than the Matabele one; with no central command structure and with each rebel chief essentially fighting his own little war for his own set of reasons, each had to be picked off in turn. This also explains why, unlike the rebellion in Matabeleland which ended with indabas and peace talks, the Mashonaland insurgency simply fizzled away to nothing; the conclusion was generally accepted, either to have been the execution of Kagubi or that of Nehanda, the unpleasant old hag thought to be a witch, who, when hanged December 1897, was 'defiant, loquacious and savage to the last'.[30]

The rebellion in Mashonaland seems to have lacked any single objective. Other than the rash of brutal murders which marked the outbreak of the insurgency, there was no discernible attempt to defeat the Rhodesians, win the war and drive the whites out.

Many of the Mashona chiefs who rebelled were simply much more terrified of the Matabele than of the Rhodesians, and feared the consequences they would face if they did not rise up in support of their former terrorizers. Others were taken in by the lunatic ravings of their witch-doctors, while some had specific grievances—real or imagined—against particular native commissioners. Some seem to have pitched in, in the same way that people join in a riot: the chaos gave them a chance to settle old scores, or gather a bit of loot,[31] and hopefully get away with it–it is difficult to believe that these were thinking much further ahead than that. Others still did not actively join the rebellion but took advantage of the confusion to refuse to pay their hut-tax: something most of us would do if we thought we could, and not really indicative of anything except an understandable desire to save money. Indeed, one Mashona chief even suggested— with matchless impudence—that the government should pay him taxes in return for his loyalty.[32]

In the rush to pretend that the uprising was some sort of popular revolution against the evil white oppressors, it is normal to ignore the fact that attacks were often made against other groups of Mashonas, rather than government forces or white settlers: it is telling that just 32 members of the company police were killed in both rebellions combined.[33] The rebels in Mashonaland had no overall plan of action, no defined objectives, no command structure and made no attempts to capture towns or even to closely invest them. To pretend that the banditry of this uncoordinated, sporadic and murderous free-for-all masked a popular, over-riding—and in anyway laudable—independence movement would be stretching the facts to breaking point.

End Notes

1   Alderson, With the Mounted Infantry and the Mashonaland Field Force 1896, p.207
2   Gibbs, The History of the BSAP, Vol.1, p.197
3   Thomson, Rhodesia and its Government, p.150
4   British South Africa Company, The '96 Rebellions, p.76
5   Gibbs, The History of the BSAP, Vol.1, p.192
6   Gibbs, The History of the BSAP, Vol.1, p.192
7   Gibbs, The History of the BSAP, Vol.1, p.194
8   British South Africa Company, The '96 Rebellions, p.77
9   Keppel-Jones, Rhodes and Rhodesia, p.514
10 British South Africa Company, The '96 Rebellions, p.77
11 Keppel-Jones, Rhodes and Rhodesia, p.514
12 Gibbs, The History of the BSAP, Vol.1, p.197
13 British South Africa Company, The '96 Rebellions, p.77
14 Gibbs, The History of the BSAP, Vol.1, p.188
15 British South Africa Company, The '96 Rebellions, p.78
16 Gibbs, The History of the BSAP, Vol.1, p.203
17 Keppel-Jones, Rhodes and Rhodesia, p.515
18 British South Africa Company, The '96 Rebellions, p.78
19 Keppel-Jones, Rhodes and Rhodesia, p.515
20 Keppel-Jones, Rhodes and Rhodesia, p.515
21 Gibbs, The History of the BSAP, Vol.1, p.204
22 Gibbs, The History of the BSAP, Vol.1, p.205
23 Keppel-Jones, Rhodes and Rhodesia, p.516
24 Barrett, The 7th (Queen's Own) Hussars, Volume 3: 1818-1914, p.195
25 Thomson, Rhodesia and its Government, p.153
26 British South Africa Company, The '96 Rebellions, p.78
27 Keppel-Jones, Rhodes and Rhodesia, p.516
28 Gibbs, The History of the BSAP, Vol.1, p.187
29 British South Africa Company, The '96 Rebellions, p.155
30 Baxter, Rhodesia: Last Outpost of the British Empire, 1890-1980, p.112
31 Barrett, The 7th (Queen's Own) Hussars, Volume 3: 1818-1914, p.193
32 Thomson, Rhodesia and its Government, p.138
33 Gibbs, The History of the BSAP, Vol.1, p.207

'The struggle with the savage races was over, the dangers and trials of the pioneers were at an end, and the romance of establishing a new country lost some of its glamour. Rhodesia, at the close of the rebellions, emerged battered and depleted. Most of the cattle had been destroyed by rinderpest; there was little in the way of crops, and reserves of grain in the country were practically nil; mines which had been started had either been dismantled to barricade dwelling-houses or else had been sabotaged by the rebels. The settlers, faced with ruin, had to reorganize their devastated country.'[1]

'Generally speaking, the Rhodes game is to get rid of imperial control in the B.S.A. Co's territory. He hates it, as he hates all control.'[2]
– Lord Milner remarks on Rhodes' resistance to change after the rebellions

'They [the Mashona] say themselves that they preferred the Matabili rule to ours, because under them they were troubled but once a year, whereas now their troubles come with each day's rising sun. It is the regularity of toil, and the constant intermeddling in their lives, that they find so irksome. They would rather endure the risk of sudden onslaughts and death than the constant supervision and interference of the white man's rule.'[3]

'I am really sorry for the awful time the men have had. It couldn't be helped—the work had to be done—but I have felt for them all the same, and I confess I am proud of the way in which these mere lads responded to every call we made upon them.'[4]
– Colonel de Moleyns speaks in praise of the nascent BSAP

'What they [the Mashona] require is a firm but just rule–to be treated as children who have to be taught, but who require encouragement as well as severity to make them learn, and, above all things, justice.'[5]
– H.C. Thomson was generally critical of the company's methods, especially in respect to native labour, and spelled out his blue-print for the future.

Chapter 18
The Dust Settles

Attempts to present the rebellions as a 'first Chimurenga' or Zimbabwean War of Independence are a bizarre attempt at rebranding, even by Mugabe's lunatic standards. No one had even thought of a united nation called Zimbabwe by then. The Shona fought for the British against the Matabele in the war of 1893–just 3 years earlier, and thousands of black 'Zimbabweans' either remained neutral or fought for the empire.

Of course, these inconvenient realities do not prevent the usual suspects from dignifying the chaotic outbreak of murders by giving them the trappings of a revolution. The perennially disapproving Martin Meredith does his part to reinvent the Mashona uprising by sagely declaring, 'Within six years of the Union Jack being raised, the Shona tribes revolted against the whites on a scale which far surpassed any resistance they had previously given to the [Matabele]'.[6]

While this is all terribly damning and 'right on', it fails to mention the thousands of loyalist Mashona who fought against both the Matabele and their own rebels. What is more, Meredith's claims also completely ignore the fact that the Mashona had always resisted the violent attentions of the Matabele in their own peculiar way:

> '...these Mashona caves... are nearly always situated by the side of a stream, so there is never any lack of water, the stream generally flowing underground through the caves; and the Mashonas have always been in the habit of storing their grain in them, so that in case of an attack, they can hold out for an indefinite time. The Matabili indeed gave up trying to take them: "What is the use" they say, "of fighting against people whom you cannot see and who shoot you out of a hole in the ground, so that the bullet travels up your body and comes out of your head?"
> ... [instead, the Matabele] depended for their loot in women and cattle and grain upon the result of the first attack before the Mashonas had had time to take refuge in their caves; after that they could inflict but little damage... The Matabili raided this part of the country systematically, but they never succeeded in making the people slaves as is commonly supposed. Most of the Mashona chiefs purchased a precarious immunity from attack by the payment of a tribute, but one of two of them, like Makoni and M'tasa, did not even do that.'[7]

This is the reality overlooked (deliberately or otherwise) by Meredith.

The Matabele hordes would simply rampage into Mashonaland, grab what they could and head home. They lost many warriors in their raids and were unable to actually subdue the Mashona as such, but had no reason to. While the Matabele could simply head home with their haul of loot, this option was not available to the troopers of the BSAP–they had to storm the Mashona strongholds one-by-one.

In many ways the rebellions were, simply, a clash between the old and the new; virtually all the rebels' grievances came down to the fact that primitive Iron Age cultures had suddenly found themselves living under a 'modern' government. Simply put, many Matabele and Mashona had no interest in swapping their relatively carefree lives for one regulated by law and order, rules, work, time, and taxes.[8] They were not driven by a desire for 'independence' as such–indeed, that concept would have had no meaning to the average person; they had never been 'independent' in any sense of the word. The people of Rhodesia prior to 1890 had no democratic freedom, no civil rights and no self-determination–they simply existed under a gaggle of despotic leaders who displayed varying degrees of tyrannical savagery. To pretend that an ill-conceived, knee-jerk desire by some for a return to this murderous chaos was an 'independence struggle' is nonsense. Lobengula and a few of the Mashona chiefs whose land was situated well away from Matabeleland, might have been independent prior to 1890 (not that this benefited their people in any real way), but everyone else—even the other chiefs, Matabele or Mashona alike— lived under a regime of brutal subjugation, constantly fearing for their lives and either paying tribute or risking raids and terrible retribution.

§

It was not that they were worse off under company rule–far from it. But for undeveloped, ill-educated fellows who had previously either enjoyed a life of glorious plundering or relative ease, punctuated only by said plundering, to suddenly adapt to the rigid structures of a more modern world was asking a lot.

The company undeniably made mistakes and there were more than a few rotten apples among the settlers, but suddenly transforming primitive, uneducated tribesmen into law abiding, hard-working tax-payers was not an easy task. During a House of Commons debate on the causes of the uprising, the secretary of state for the colonies, Joe Chamberlain, stated:

> "When you say to a savage people, who have hitherto found their chief employment, occupation and profit in war, 'You shall no longer go to war; tribal war is forbidden', you have to induce them, sooner or later, to adopt the ordinary methods of earning

a livelihood by the sweat of their brow. But with a race of this kind, I doubt very much if you can do it merely by preaching. I think that something in the nature of inducement, stimulus, or pressure is absolutely necessary if you are to secure a result which is desirable in the interests of humanity and civilisation."

The clash of cultures, vastly different levels of advancement, and incongruent work ethic had other effects too; the rinderpest outbreak— and the absolutely necessary veterinary culls made in response to it—was simply not understood by the unschooled mass of either the Matabele or the Mashona, and they instead found solace in the babblings of their witch-doctors. The haughty, and once, all-conquering Matabele objected to being policed by other blacks, especially those drawn from groups they considered 'beneath them'. Worse still, though perhaps understandably, they had no interest in working for a living being content, simply to steal what they wanted from their neighbours. Even those rather lower down the totem pole who had been compelled to work for Lobengula, chaffed at the change:

'...it is a very different thing having to turn out now and again for some special purpose to being obliged to work for fixed periods. It is the regularity of work that natives cannot stand... in time they will learn the value of money. And with regard to the Matabili, it must be remembered that labour of any kind is entirely opposed to their habits; that it will take years before they can become resigned to it.'[9]

These observations will no doubt make uncomfortable reading for some sensitive souls but there is a lot of truth in them. To this day, anyone who has worked in remote locations among poorly educated people, will have seen first-hand what happens when a culture does not equate earning to working, and the result of the general feeling that work is a terrible inconvenience, rather than a necessary evil, essential to survival.

I recall working on an oil rig off Angola, in the early 2000s. There was a large gang of Angolan painters on board, and at one rig meeting, their spokesman stood up and declared, 'If there wasn't so much to paint, we could relax more.' The expat rig manager's response that they wouldn't have jobs if he didn't have painting to do was met with confusion, bewilderment and indignation from the painters.

Similarly, working in the jungles of the DRC and remote regions of the Ivory Coast, I have had to deal with strikes and mutinies by workers who were not paid overtime–even when they hadn't worked any. They in no way equated the extra money they had received the month before to the fact that they had worked longer hours on occasion–so when this overtime was not paid the following month, they convinced themselves that the wicked bosses had 'cut their wages'.

In the early 2000s, a friend in Zimbabwe whose company was facing bankruptcy, called his workers together and told them that he could either pay them a settlement and let them go, or try to keep the company going but reduce their wages. Every single one of them opted for the pay-out, so he forked out and had no choice but to start winding his company down. Later that week, when they had blown most of their pay-outs on booze and parties, it belatedly dawned on them that they would not be paid that Friday, and they all turned up and asked for their jobs back.

Still today, among a large mass of poorly educated Africans, and among people in many other places in the world, there exists little or no link between working and earning and this was also the situation the Rhodesian settlers faced in the 1890s.

This phenomenon is by no means confined to Africa. It is linked to education, development and human nature. Indeed, the welfare state established in Britain has eroded the national work ethic of a couple of generations, and created a similar culture among many, who now expect to be able to enjoy a decent life while doing absolutely nothing to pay for it. This sees the government trying to justify mass immigration by claiming immigrants are needed to fill jobs and keep the economy moving, while, at the same time, paying millions of Britons to sit idle. Any attempt to change this patently ridiculous situation would doubtless lead to mass riots and chaos – in fact, no government would dare even try it.

I played cricket in England with a fellow who had been 'on the sick' for years, but was still able to open the bowling for our 1st team. I remember him bitching and moaning about the council 'only' having paid for him and his vast family to go on holiday to Cornwall that year, whereas the year before they had enjoyed an all-expenses paid trip to Spain. If this was his reaction to finding out he was 'only' getting a gratis holiday to Cornwall, one can imagine his response–and that of the millions like him– if they were told they would actually have to work for a living.

§

It has become politically correct to overlook the fact that, in terms of development, the African tribes were many hundreds—even thousands—of years behind their European colonizers, but that is the reality, however unpleasant it is for some to admit. Luckily, the insidious forces of political correctness were not around in 1897, and a colonial administrator in Natal was able to explain this in the sort of plain terms which have become unheard-of in the thought-controlled world of today:

'The progress of any race towards civilisation in one year (if there is no retrogression) must be imperceptibly small. The races now occupying Europe required about 2,000 years to rise from barbarianism to their present status, and even superior races did not progress steadily, but had periods of relapsing. A nation advances similarly to a man ascending to the summit of a mountain. He cannot go up in a straight line, but he occasionally has to descend into a valley and then go up again. One thing is certain. Teaching will not convert a savage into a civilized being... Taken all in all, the natives have many settling qualities, and the vigour of a youthful nation. They would occasionally like to peg out a witch over an ant-heap, but I am sorry to say my ancestors have burned a witch as late as the eighteenth century.'[10]

So even if there was no way that the company could have introduced a Westminster-style, multi-party democracy in the blink of an eye, that is not to say that they could not have run their newly acquired territories better than they did between the wars. Many changes were made in the wake of the up-risings. The dreaded 'imperial factor' started playing a much greater part in running Rhodesia, and the days of Rhodes enjoying what was essentially a personal fiefdom were at an end:

'With the departure of Jameson the era of debonair amateurism in Southern Rhodesian administration came to an end. Sir William Milton, who became administrator soon after the rebellions and remained in the post until 1914, was a professional civil servant, able, dignified, public-spirited and hard-working, who provided the country with the machinery of government of a modern state and took care that it was properly staffed.'[11]

It is debateable, though, how much of this had to do with the rebellions and how much was linked to the Jameson Raid. Sir Richard Martin—old 'Whistling Dick'—had been appointed as London's Commandant General in the area before the revolts, with a specific mandate to take control of the company-funded forces. And in other ways, even without the rebellions, Rhodesia was naturally changing as more settlers arrived and the hardy—but very individualistic—pioneers became a tiny minority in the nation they had helped found.

The men joining the BSAP were also changing. The adventurous, public-schoolboy 'gentleman ranker' was becoming a thing of the past as the chance of action and glory faded, and the force morphed into a civilian one. These flamboyant, even uncontrollable, fellows were steadily replaced by 'steady, well-educated men of the artisan class' who made for 'more trustworthy police'.[12]

Despite a few hiccups, the company had been fairly popular among the early settlers–it had spent lavish sums on opening up the country, quelled the Matabele threat in 1893 and made generous and prompt payments to compensate the settlers for their losses in the rebellion. To these early Rhodesians, Rhodes was their inspiration, and Jameson their hero.[13] But with Jameson out of the picture and Rhodes soon to die, the settlers were no longer the staunch 'company men' they might once have been–and to the later arrivals, the company appeared impersonal and remote, eventually becoming an object of distrust.[14]

More surprising, perhaps, is how quickly peace returned to Rhodesia in the wake of the uprisings. Within months of the Mashonaland rebellion finally fizzling out, for example, one native commissioner's report confirmed that, 'his thorough investigation into the state of the districts' had left 'no room to doubt the perfectly pacific nature of the Mashonas'.[15] Another native commissioner recalled visiting a kraal where, in front of his assembled people, the chief had announced, 'If we hear of any man who talks of rebellion in this district, we will wring his neck for him.' At the same meeting, another senior induna, who had joined the uprising, 'stood out in front of the rest, and in a very impressive manner swore allegiance to the government. This action was quite voluntary on [his] part. He had been fooled once, but would not be again. He was an old man... [but, calling a man out of the crowd, said] "Here is my eldest son; if anything happened he would fight to the death for the government".'[16]

The prickly question of native land was addressed immediately after the war, with the imperial factor insisting that reserves be 'both suitable in quality and adequate in extent'[17] and another 1.2 million acres were added to the pre-war reserves. Many others—both Mashona and Matabele—were encouraged to live on white-owned farms, including those of Cecil Rhodes himself.

Of course, none of this is to say that all the problems disappeared after the rebellions. There was still the issue of a relatively small number of white landowners who owned huge amounts of land–but the fact that a small percentage of people own a large percentage of the land of a country is not unusual or inherently 'wrong' in any way. Indeed, in a modern society, most people do not need huge parcels of land, and farm land is bound to be held by a comparatively few individuals. Again, the 'unfairness' all comes down to a clash of the old and the new, but it would later prove to be fertile ground for exploitation by another breed of revolutionary two or three generations later.

This is not the place to get into the details of the social dynamics of post-rebellion Rhodesia, or discuss the communist-sponsored bush war of the 1960s and 70s. Suffice it to say, however, and despite the wild fantasies about wicked colonial oppression harboured by

Labouchère and every leftie ever since, it was not until 1959 (when communist rabble-rousers began to incite violent uprisings and riots) that the BSAP were again called upon to use deadly force in the line of duty[18] –a record of which they were rightly immensely proud. This puts many other countries to shame and suggests that—whatever its warts—post-rebellion Rhodesia had become a decent place in which to live–for all its people.

Indeed, in the first half of the 20th Century, Rhodesia's progress was little short of incredible, with agriculture, industry and commerce flourishing and the nation earning the sobriquet of 'the bread basket of Africa'. White Rhodesians were proud to declare themselves 'more British than the British' and fought bravely for the Motherland in the Boer War, both World Wars and Malaya. Black Rhodesians may not have enjoyed 'democracy' as we know it today, but it would have come in time and, in any case, they lived in a stable, well-run and wealthy nation, enjoying the rule of law, health and education–which was probably more important to the vast majority of them. Either way, they were much better off than they had been under Lobengula's tyranny, or than they would be under Mugabe's corrupt and chaotic dictatorship which would, to the delight of the unpatriotic meddlers of the British Labour Party, replace white rule in 1980.

Who knows what would have happened had Rhodesia been left to develop at its own pace, rather than becoming a cause célèbre for the self-loathing, guilt-ridden British Left of the 1960s and the scene of a communist-backed insurgency at the height of the Cold War.

End Notes

[1] Kane, The World's View: The Story of Southern Rhodesia, p.121
[2] Hanna, The Story of the Rhodesias and Nyasaland, p.144
[3] Thomson, Rhodesia and its Government, p.151
[4] Thomson, Rhodesia and its Government, p.159
[5] Thomson, Rhodesia and its Government, p.217
[6] Meredith, The Past is Another Country, p.20
[7] Thomson, Rhodesia and its Government, p.152
[8] Thomson, Rhodesia and its Government, p.196
[9] Thomson, Rhodesia and its Government, p.200
[10] Thomson, Rhodesia and its Government, p.218
[11] Hanna, The Story of the Rhodesias and Nyasaland, p.146
[12] Thomson, Rhodesia and its Government, p.223
[13] Hanna, The Story of the Rhodesias and Nyasaland, p.144
[14] Hanna, The Story of the Rhodesias and Nyasaland, p.146
[15] Keppel-Jones, Rhodes and Rhodesia, p.522
[16] Keppel-Jones, Rhodes and Rhodesia, p.523
[17] Keppel-Jones, Rhodes and Rhodesia, p.525
[18] Personal correspondence with Mike Edden, Rtd. Assistant Commissioner, BSAP

Appendix 1
Charter of the British
South Africa Company

VICTORIA, by the Grace of God, of the United Kingdom of Great Britain and Ireland Queen, Defender of the Faith.

To all to whom these presents shall come, Greeting.

WHEREAS a Humble Petition has been presented to Us in Our Council by the Most Noble James Duke of Abercorn, Companion of the Most Honourable Order of the Bath; the Most Noble Alexander William George Duke of Fife, Knight of the Most Ancient and Most Noble Order of the Thistle, Privy Councillor; the Right Honourable Edric Frederic Lord Gifford, V.C.; Cecil John Rhodes, of Kimberley, in the Cape Colony, Member of the Executive Council and of the House of Assembly of the Colony of the Cape of Good Hope; Alfred Beit, of 29, Holborn Viaduct, London, Merchant; Albert Henry George Grey, of Howick, Northumberland, Esquire; and George Cawston, of 18, Lennox Gardens, London, Esquire, Barrister-at-Law.

And whereas the said Petition states amongst other things :—

That the Petitioners; and others are associated for the purpose of forming a Company or Association, to be incorporated, if to Us should seem fit, for the objects in the said Petition set forth, under the corporate name of The British South Africa Company.

That the existence of a powerful British Company, controlled by those of Our subjects in whom We have confidence, and having its principal field of operations in that region of South Africa lying to the north of Bechuanaland and to the west of Portuguese East Africa, would be advantageous to the commercial and other interests of Our subjects in the United Kingdom and in Our Colonies.

That the Petitioners desire to carry into effect divers concessions and agreements which have been made by certain of the chiefs and tribes inhabiting the said region, and such other concessions agreements grants and treaties as the Petitioners may hereafter obtain within the said region or elsewhere in Africa, with the view of promoting trade commerce civilization and good government (including the regulation of liquor traffic with the natives) in the territories which are or may be comprised or referred to in such concessions agreements grants and treaties as aforesaid.

That the Petitioners believe that if the said concessions agreements grants and treaties can be carried into effect, the condition of the natives inhabiting the said territories will be materially improved and their civilization advanced, and an organization established which will tend to the suppression of the slave trade in the said territories, and to the opening up of the said territories to the immigration of Europeans, and to the lawful trade and commerce of Our subjects and of other nations.

That the success of the enterprise in which the Petitioners are engaged would be greatly advanced if it should seem fit to Us to grant them Our Royal Charter of incorporation as a British Company under the said name or title, or such other name or title, and with such powers, as to Us may seem fit for the purpose of more effectually carrying into effect the objects aforesaid.

That large sums of money have been subscribed for the purposes of the intended Company by the Petitioners and others, who are prepared also to subscribe or to procure such further sums as may hereafter be found requisite for the development of the said enterprise, in the event of Our being pleased to grant to them Our Royal Charter of incorporation as aforesaid.

Now therefore We, having taken the said Petition into Our Royal consideration in Our Council and being satisfied that the intentions of the Petitioners are praiseworthy and deserve encouragement, and that the enterprise in the Petition described may be productive of the benefits set forth therein, by Our Prerogative Royal and of Our especial grace certain knowledge and mere motion, have constituted erected and incorporated and by this Our Charter for Us and Our Heirs and Royal successors do constitute erect and incorporate into one body politic and corporate by the name of The British South Africa Company, the said James Duke of Abercorn, Alexander William George Duke of Fife, Edric Frederic Lord Gifford, Cecil John Rhodes, Alfred Beit, Albert Henry George Grey and George Cawston, and such other persons and such bodies as from time to time become and are members of the body politic and corporate by these presents constituted erected and incorporated, with perpetual succession and a common seal, with power to break alter or renew the same at discretion and with the further authorities powers and privileges conferred, and subject to the conditions imposed by this Our Charter: And We do hereby accordingly will, ordain, give, grant, constitute, appoint and declare as follows (that is to say) :—

1. The principal field of the operations of the British South Africa Company (in this Our Charter referred to as 'the Company') shall be the region of South Africa lying immediately to the north of British Bechuanaland, and to the north and west of the South African Republic, and to the west of the Portuguese Dominions.

2. The Company is hereby authorized and empowered to hold, use

and retain for the purposes of the Company and on the terms of this Our Charter, the full benefit of the concessions and agreements made as aforesaid, so far as they are valid, or any of them, and all interests, authorities and powers comprised or referred to in the said concessions and agreements. Provided always that nothing herein contained shall prejudice or affect any other valid and subsisting concessions or agreements which may have been made by any of the chiefs or tribes aforesaid, and in particular nothing herein contained shall prejudice or affect certain concessions granted in and subsequent to the year 1880 relating to the territory usually known as the district of the Tati; nor shall anything herein contained be construed as giving any jurisdiction, administrative or otherwise, within the said district of the Tati, the limits of which district are as follows, viz.: from the place where the Shasi River rises to its junction with the Tati and Ramaquaban Rivers, thence along the Ramaquaban River to where it rises, and thence along the watershed of those Rivers.

3. The Company is hereby further authorized and empowered, subject to the approval of one of Our Principal Secretaries of State (herein referred to as "Our Secretary of State") from time to time, to acquire by any concession agreement grant or treaty, all or any rights interests authorities jurisdictions and powers of any kind or nature whatever, including powers necessary for the purposes of government and the preservation of public order in or for the protection of territories, lands, or property comprised or referred to in the concessions and agreements made as aforesaid or affecting other territories, lands, or property in Africa, or the inhabitants thereof, and to hold, use and exercise such territories, lands, property, rights, interests, authorities, jurisdictions and powers respectively for the purpose of the Company, and on the terms of this Our Charter.

4. Provided that no powers of government or administration shall be exercised under or in relation to any such last-mentioned concession agreement grant or treaty, until a copy of such concession agreement grant or treaty, in such form and with such maps or particulars as Our Secretary of State approves verified as he requires, has been transmitted to him, and he has signified his approval thereof either absolutely or subject to any conditions or reservations; and provided also that no rights, interests, authorities, jurisdictions or powers of any description shall be acquired by the Company within the said district of the Tati as herein-before described, without the previous consent in writing of the owners for the time being of the Concessions above referred to relating to the said district, and the approval of Our Secretary of State.

5. The Company shall be bound by and shall fulfil all and singular the stipulations on its part contained in any such concession agreement grant or treaty as aforesaid, subject to any subsequent agreement affecting those stipulations approved by Our Secretary of State.

6. The Company shall always be and remain British in character and domicile, and shall have its principal office in Great Britain, and the Company's principal representative in South Africa and the Directors shall always be natural born British subjects, or persons who have been naturalized as British subjects by or under an Act of Parliament of Our United Kingdom; but this Article shall not disqualify any person nominated a Director by this Our Charter, or any person whose Election as a Director shall have been approved by Our Secretary of State, from acting in that capacity.

7. In case at any time any difference arises between any chief or tribe inhabiting any of the territories aforesaid and the Company, that difference shall, if Our Secretary of State so require, be submitted by the Company to him for his decision, and the Company shall act in accordance with such decision.

8. If at any time Our Secretary of State thinks fit to dissent from or object to any of the dealings of the Company with any foreign power and to make known to the Company any suggestion founded on that dissent or objection, the Company shall act in accordance with such suggestion.

9. If at any time Our Secretary of State thinks fit to object to the exercise by the Company of any authority, power, or right within any part of the territories aforesaid, on the ground of there being an adverse claim to or in respect of that part, the Company shall defer to that objection until such time as any such claim has been withdrawn or finally dealt with or settled by Our Secretary of State.

10. The Company shall to the best of its ability preserve peace and order in such ways and manners as it shall consider necessary, and may with that object make ordinances (to be approved by Our Secretary of State) and may establish and maintain a force of police.

11. The Company shall to the best of its ability discourage and, so far as may be practicable, abolish by degrees, any system of slave trade or domestic servitude in the territories aforesaid.

12. The Company shall regulate the traffic in spirits and other intoxicating liquors within the territories aforesaid, so as, as far as practicable, to prevent the sale of any spirits or other intoxicating liquor to any natives.

13. The Company as such, or its officers as such, shall not in any way

interfere with the religion of any class or tribe of the peoples of the territories aforesaid or of any of the inhabitants thereof, except so far as may be necessary in the interest of humanity, and all forms of religious worship or religious ordinances may be exercised within the said territories and no hindrance shall be offered thereto except as aforesaid.

14. In the administration of justice to the said peoples or inhabitants, careful regard shall always be had to the customs and laws of the class or tribe or nation to which the parties respectively belong, especially with respect to the holding, possession, transfer and disposition of lands and goods and testate or intestate succession thereto, and marriage divorce and legitimacy and other rights of property and personal rights, but subject to any British laws which may be in force in any of the territories aforesaid, and applicable to the peoples or inhabitants thereof.

15. If at any time Our Secretary of State thinks fit to dissent from or object to any part of the proceedings or system of the Company relative to the peoples of the territories aforesaid or to any of the inhabitants thereof, in respect of slavery or religion or the administration of justice, or any other matter, he shall make known to the Company his dissent or objection, and the Company shall act in accordance with his directions duly signified.

16. In the event of the Company acquiring any harbour or harbours, the Company shall freely afford all facilities for or to Our ships therein without payment, except reasonable charges for work done or services rendered or materials or things supplied.

17. The Company shall furnish annually to Our Secretary of State, as soon as conveniently may be after the close of the financial year, accounts of its expenditure for administrative purposes, and of all sums received by it by way of public revenue, as distinguished from its commercial profits, during the financial year, together with a report as to its public proceedings and the condition of the territories within the sphere of its operations. The Company shall also on or before the commencement of each financial year furnish to Our Secretary of State an estimate of its expenditure for administrative purposes, and of its public revenue (as above defined) for the ensuing year. The Company shall in addition from time to time furnish to Our Secretary of State any reports, accounts or information with which he may require to be furnished.

18. The several officers of the Company shall, subject to the rules of official subordination, and to any regulations that may be agreed upon, communicate freely with Our High Commissioner in South Africa, and any others Our officers, who may be stationed within any of the territories aforesaid, and shall pay due regard to any requirements,

suggestions or requests which the said High Commissioner or other officers shall make to them or any of them, and the Company shall be bound to enforce the observance of this article.

19. The Company may hoist and use on its buildings and elsewhere in the territories aforesaid, and on its vessels, such distinctive flag indicating the British character of the Company as Our Secretary of State and the Lords Commissioners of the Admiralty shall from time to time approve.

20. Nothing in this Our Charter shall be deemed to authorize the Company to set up or grant any monopoly of trade; provided that the establishment of or the grant of concessions for banks, railways, tramways, docks, telegraphs, waterworks, or other similar undertakings or the establishment of any system of patent or copyright approved by Our Secretary of State, shall not he deemed monopolies for this purpose. The Company shall not, either directly or indirectly, hinder any Company or persons who now are or concern or venture within the said District of the Tati hereinbefore described, but shall by permitting and facilitating transit by every lawful means to and from the District of the Tati across its own territories or where it has jurisdiction in that behalf and by all other reasonable and lawful means encourage, assist and protect all British subjects who now are, or hereafter may be, lawfully and peaceably engaged in the prosecution of a lawful enterprise within the said District of the Tati.

21. For the preservation of elephants and other game, the Company may make such regulations and (notwithstanding anything hereinbefore contained) may impose such licence duties on the killing or taking of elephants or other game as they may see fit: Provided that nothing in such regulations shall extend to diminish or interfere with any hunting rights which may have been or may hereafter be reserved to any native chief, or tribes by treaty, save do far as any such regulations may relate to the establishment and enforcement of a close season.

22. The Company shall be subject to and shall perform and undertake all the obligations contained in or undertaken by Ourselves under any treaty agreement or arrangement between Ourselves and any other State or Power whether already made or hereafter to be made. In all matters relating to the observance of this Article, or to the exercise within the Company's territories for the time being, of any jurisdiction exerciseable by Us under the Foreign Jurisdiction Acts, the Company shall conform to and observe and carry out all such directions as may from time to time be given in that behalf by Our Secretary of State, and the Company shall appoint all necessary officers to perform such duties, and shall

provide such Courts and other requisites as may from time to time be necessary for the administration of justice.

23. The original share capital of the Company shall be £1,000,000 divided into 1,000,000 shares of £1 each.

24. The Company is hereby further specially authorized and empowered for the purposes of this Our Charter from time to time—

(i) To issue shares of different classes or descriptions, to increase the share capital of the Company, and to borrow moneys by debentures or other obligations.

(ii) To acquire and hold, and to charter or otherwise deal with steam vessels and other vessels.

(iii) To establish or authorize banking companies and other companies, and undertakings or associations or every description, for purposes consistent with the provisions of this Our Charter.

(iv) To make and maintain roads, railways, telegraphs, harbours, and any other works which may tend to the development or improvement of the territories of the Company.

(v) To carry on mining and other industries, and to make concessions of mining, forestall or other rights.

(vi) To improve, develop, clear, plant, irrigate and cultivate any lands included within the territories of the Company.

(vii) To settle any such territories and lands as aforesaid, and to aid and promote immigration.

(viii) To grant lands, for terms of years or in perpetuity, and either absolutely, or by way of mortgage or otherwise.

(ix) To make loans or contributions of money or money's worth, for promoting any of the objects of the Company.

(x) To acquire and hold personal property.

(xi) To acquire and hold (without licence in mortmain or other authority than this Our Charter) lands in the United Kingdom, not exceeding five acres in all at any one time for the purposes or the offices and business of the Company, and (subject to any local law) lands in any of Our Colonies or Possessions and elsewhere convenient for carrying on the management of the affairs of the Company, and to dispose from time to time of any such lands when not required for that purpose.

(xii) To carry on any lawful commerce, trade, pursuit, business, operations, or dealing whatsoever in connection with the objects of the Company.

(xiii) To establish and maintain agencies in Our Colonies and Possessions, and elsewhere.

(xiv) To sue and be sued by the Company's name of incorporation, as well in Our Courts in Our United Kingdom, or in Our Courts in Our Colonies or Possessions, or in Our Courts in Foreign countries or elsewhere.

(xv) To do all lawful things incidental or conducive to the exercise or enjoyment of the rights, interests, authorities and powers of the Company in this Our Charter expressed or referred to, or any of them.

25. Within one year after the date of this Our Charter, or such extended period as may be certified by Our Secretary of State, there shall be executed by the Members or the Company for the time being a Deed of Settlement, providing so far as necessary for—

(i) The further definition of the objects and purposes or the Company.

(ii) The classes or description of shares into which the Capital of the Company is divided, and the calls to be made in respect thereof, and the terms and conditions of Membership of the Company.

(iii) The division and distribution of profits.

(iv) General Meetings of the Company; the appointment by Our Secretary of State (if so required by him) of an Official Director, and the number qualification appointment remuneration rotation removal and powers of Directors of the Company and of other officers of the Company.

(v) The registration of Members of the Company, and the transfer of shares in the capital of the Company.

(vi) The preparation of annual accounts to be submitted to the Members at a General Meeting.

(vii) The audit of those accounts by independent auditors.

(viii) The making of byelaws.

(ix) The making and using of official seals of the Company.

(x) The constitution and regulation of Committees or Local Boards of Management.

(xi) The making and execution of supplementary deeds of settlement.

(xii) The winding up (in case of need) of the Company's affairs.

(xiii) The government and regulation of the Company and of its affairs.

(xiv) Any other matters usual or proper to be provided for in respect of a chartered Company.

26. The Deed of Settlement shall, before the execution thereof, be submitted to and approved by the Lords of Our Council, and a certificate of their approval thereof, signed by the Clerk of Our Council, shall be endorsed on this Our Charter and be conclusive

evidence of such approval, and on the Deed of Settlement, and such Deed of Settlement shall take effect from the date of such approval, and shall be binding upon the Company, its members, officers and servants, and for all other purposes whatsoever.

27. The provisions of the Deed of Settlement or of any supplementary Deed for the time being in force, may be from time to time repealed, varied or added to by a supplementary Deed, made and executed in such manner as the Deed of Settlement prescribes. Provided that the provisions of any such Deed relative to the official Director shall not be repealed, varied or added to without the express approval of Our Secretary of State.

28. The Members of the Company shall be individually liable for the debts, contracts, engagements and liabilities of the Company to the extent only of the amount, if any, for the time being unpaid on the shares held by them respectively.

29. Until such Deed of Settlement as aforesaid takes effect the said James Duke of Abercorn shall be the President; the said Alexander William George Duke of Fife, shall be Vice-President and the said Edric Frederick Lord Gifford, Cecil John Rhodes, Alfred Beit, Albert Henry George Grey, and George Cawston, shall be the Directors of the Company; and may on behalf of the Company do all things necessary or proper to be done under this Our Charter by or on behalf of the Company: Provided always that notwithstanding anything contained in the Deed of Settlement of the Company, the said James Duke of Abercorn, Alexander William George Duke of Fife, and Albert Henry George Grey, shall not be subject to retire from office in accordance with its provisions but shall be and remain Directors of the Company until death, incapacity to act, or resignation, as the case may be.

30. And We do further will ordain and declare that this Our Charter shall be acknowledged by Our Governors and Our naval and military officers and Our Consuls, and Our other officers in Our Colonies and possessions, and on the high seas, and elsewhere, and they shall severally give full force and effect to this Our Charter, and shall recognise and be in all things aiding to the Company and its officers.

31. And We do further will, ordain and declare that this Our Charter shall be taken construed and adjudged in the most favourable and beneficial sense for, and to the best advantage of the Company as well in Our Courts in Our United Kingdom, and in Our Courts in Our Colonies or possessions, and in Our Courts in foreign countries or elsewhere, notwithstanding that there may appear to be in this Our Charter any non-recital, mis-recital, uncertainty or imperfection.

32. And We do further will, ordain and declare that this Our Charter shall subsist and continue valid, notwithstanding any lawful change in the name of the Company or in the Deed of Settlement thereof, such change being made with the previous approval of Our Secretary of State signified under his hand.

33. And We do further will, ordain and declare that it shall be lawful for Us Our heirs and successors, and We do hereby expressly reserve to Ourselves Our heirs and successors the right and power by writing under the Great Seal of the United Kingdom at the end of 25 years from the date of this Our Charter, and at the end of every succeeding period of ten years, to add to alter or repeal any of the provisions or this Our Charter or to enact other provisions in substitution for or in addition to any of its existing provisions. Provided that the right and power thus reserved shall be exercised only in relation to so much of this Our Charter as relates to administrative and public matters. And We do further expressly reserve to Ourselves Our heirs and successors the right to take over any buildings or works belonging to the Company and used exclusively or mainly for administrative or public purposes, on payment to the Company of such reasonable compensation as may be agreed, or as failing agreement may be settled by the Commissioners of Our Treasury. And We do further appoint, direct and declare that any such writing under the said Great Seal shall have full effect and be binding upon the Company, its members, officers and servants, and all other persons, and shall be of the same force effect and validity as if its provisions had been part of and contained in these presents.

34. Provided always and We do further declare that nothing in this Our Charter shall be deemed or taken in anywise to limit or restrict the exercise of any of Our rights or powers with reference to the protection of any territories or with reference to the government thereof should we see fit to include the same within our dominions.

35. And We do lastly will, ordain and declare without prejudice to any power to repeal this Our Charter by law belonging to Us Our heirs and successors, or to any of Our courts, ministers or officers independently of this present declaration and reservation, that in case at any time it is made to appear to us in Our Council that the Company has substalltially failed to observe and conform to the provisions of this Our Charter, or that the Company is not exercising its powers under the concessions, agreements, grants and treaties aforesaid, so as to advance the interests which the petitioners have represented to Us to be likely to be advanced by the grant of this Our Charter, it shall be lawful for us Our heirs and successors and we do hereby expressly reserve and take to

ourselves Our heirs and successors the right and power by writing
under the Great Seal of Our United Kingdom to revoke this Our
Charter, and to revoke and annul the privileges, powers, and rights
hereby granted to the Company.

In Witness whereof We have caused these Our letters to be made
Patent.

Witness Ourself at Westminster, the 29th day of October in the
fifty third year of our reign.

By warrant under the Queen's Sign Manual.

MUIR MACKENZIE.

Appendix 2
Salisbury Horse

Officer Commanding: Major P.W. Forbes
Staff:
Mr C.M. Acutt – interpreter and guide
Mr P.L. Chappé – veterinary surgeon and trumpeter
Mr J.H. Kennedy – quartermaster
Mr T.E. Tanner – orderly officer and galloper
Captain Finch and Mr J. Carden – remount officers
Captain J.A.L. Campbell – ordnance store officer
Dr H. Edgelow and Dr J. Stewart – medical officers

'A' Troop
Officer Commanding: Captain Heany
Lieutenants Bodle and Lockner
Lieutenant Tyndale-Biscoe in charge of attached Maxim detachment
One troop sergeant major, two sergeants, four corporals, one trumpeter
42 rank and file

'B' Troop
Officer Commanding: Captain Borrow
Lieutenants Snodgrass and Reid
Lieutenant Llewellyn in charge of attached Maxim detachment
One troop sergeant major, two sergeants, four corporals, one trumpeter
42 rank and file

'C' Troop
Officer Commanding: Captain Spreckley
Lieutenants Laing and Christison
One troop sergeant major, two sergeants, four corporals, one trumpeter
42 rank and file

Artillery Troop + Dismounted Section
Officer Commanding: Captain Moberley
Lieutenant Tennant in charge of the 7-pdr gun
1 x 7-pdr gun, 1 x Gardner gun, 1 x Nordenfelt gun

Colonial natives / 'Coolies' – attached to the Salisbury Horse
60 rank and file

Appendix 3
Victoria Rangers

Officer Commanding: Major Allan Wilson
Staff:
Captain Kennelly–adjutant
Lieutenants Bowen and Chalk–ADCs
Lieutenants Browne and Ware–pioneers
Captain Greenfield–quartermaster

No.1 Troop
Captain Fitzgerald
Lieutenants Harris and Hughes
c. 30 troopers

No.2 Troop
Captain Bastard
Lieutenant Sampson
c. 30 troopers

No.3 Troop
Captain Napier
Lieutenants Williams and Stoddart
c. 30 troopers

No.4 Troop
Captain Judd
Lieutenants Beal and Hofmeyr
c. 30 troopers

Infantry
Captain Delamore
Lieutenants Steer and Robinson
250 dismounted troopers

Artillery Troop
Captains Lendy and Reid
Lieutenant Rixon
Three Maxims, one 7-pdr, one 2-pdr Hotchkiss

Scouts
Captain the Honourable White
Lieutenant Dollar
Messrs Burnham, Ingram, Vavasour, Mayne and Posset

Native Contingent–attached to the Victoria Rangers
Lieutenant Brabant
400 Mashonas

Total of 414 whites, 400 Mashona warriors, 40 Mashona drivers, 172 horses, 18 wagons

Appendix 4
Shangani Patrol–Roll of Honour

Officer Commanding and CO Victoria Rangers, Major Allan Wilson. Born 1856 at Glen Urquhart, Scotland. Educated at Kirkwall Grammar School, Orkney and Milne's Institution, Fochabers. Immigrated to South Africa in 1878.

Victoria Rangers

Captain Harry Greenfield Quartermaster, Victoria Rangers. Born 1861 in Tavistock, England and educated at Tavistock Grammar School. Came to Mashonaland in 1891. Married, with 2 children.

Captain Argent Kirton
Officer-in-Charge of Transport, Victoria Rangers. Born 1857, Portsmouth, England. Immigrated to South Africa in 1873. Married with 3 children.

Captain Frederick Fitzgerald
OC No.1 Troop, Victoria Rangers. Had previously served in the BSACP at Fort Victoria.

Captain William Judd
OC No.4 Troop, Victoria Rangers. Born in the Cape Colony. Entered Mashonaland as one of the 1890 pioneers.

Lieutenant Arend Hofmeyer
No.4 Troop, Victoria Rangers. Son of a clergyman of the Dutch Reformed Church, Cape Colony.

Lieutenant George Hughes
No.1 Troop, Victoria Rangers. Educated at Methodist College, Belfast and Royal University. Entered Mashonaland as one of the 1890 pioneers.

Troop Sergeant-Major Sidney Harding
Born 1861, London. Son of Colonel Charles Harding. Educated at Felsted School and St John's College, Cambridge.

Sergeant Clifford Bradburn
Born 1868 in Birmingham, England, and educated at Queen's College. Immigrated to South Africa in 1890 and served in the Cape Mounted Rifles.

Sergeant Harold Brown
Educated at Harrow and Exeter College, Oxford. Entered Mashonaland as one of the 1890 pioneers.

Corporal Frederick Colquhoun
Born 1867 in Edinburgh, Scotland, and immigrated to South Africa in 1887. Colquhoun entered Mashonaland as one of the 1890 pioneers.

Trooper Dennis Dillon
Born 1868 in Burdwan, India. Son of the Postmaster General of Punjab. Immigrated to South Africa in 1888 and entered Mashonaland as one of the 1890 pioneers.

Trooper Harold Hellet
No details available

Trooper Alexander Robertson
No details available

Trooper John 'Jack' Robertson
Born 1867 in Pitlochry, Scotland

Trooper Edward Welby
No details available

'B' Troop, Salisbury Horse

Captain Henry Borrow, OC 'B' Troop, Salisbury Horse. Born 1865 in Cornwall, England. Entered Mashonaland as the adjutant of the 1890 pioneer column.

Sergeant William Birkley
Born in 1862 in London. Educated at Reading Grammar School. Immigrated to South Africa in 1884.

Corporal Harry Kinloch
Born 1863, Surrey, England. Educated at Harrow and Trinity College, Cambridge. Was a successful solicitor in Salisbury and a noted athlete, cricketer and champion lightweight boxer before volunteering to serve in the war.

Trooper William Abbott
Born in Cumberland, England. Immigrated to South Africa in 1889.

Trooper William Bath
Born 1856 in Middlesex, England. Immigrated to South Africa in 1876.

Trooper William Britton
Born in 1870, Essex, England

Trooper Edward Brock
No details available

Trooper L. Dewis
No details available

Trooper George Mackenzie
Born in England in 1870. Immigrated to South Africa in 1892.

Trooper Matthew Meiklejohn
Originally from the Cape Colony

Trooper Harold Money
Born in 1872 in Bengal, India. Son of Major General R.C. Money. Educated at Wellington College.

Trooper Percy Nunn
Born 1855, Bury St Edmonds, England

Trooper William Thomson
Born 1871 in Aberdeen, Scotland. Educated at Elgin Academy.

Trooper Henry Tuck
Born 1868. Entered Mashonaland as a member of the 1890 pioneer column.

Trooper Frank Vogel
Born 1870, Auckland, New Zealand. Son of the Honourable Sir Julius Vogel, KCMG. Educated at Charterhouse.

Trooper Philip de Vos
No details available

Trooper Henry Watson
No details available

Trooper Thomas Watson
Son of Colonel T.J. Watson. Educated at Wellington College.

Their remains are interred in a vault in the large Shangani Memorial at World's View in the Matapos Hills National Park, just outside Bulawayo. The impressive monument was unveiled in1904, and can still be visited today. In his unveiling speech, the then administrator of Rhodesia, Sir William Milton, paid tribute to these brave young men saying:

'England's history has ever been filled with records of the determination of her sons, through whom she has been able to extend the benign influence of her rule over vast regions and countless multitudes... Among the thousands whose great deeds have been recorded in the cause of Empire, we, the inhabitants of Rhodesia, may be proud of our fellow-citizens, who, by their deed recorded in history, have shown themselves worthy of record upon the illustrious roll of those who have deserved well of their country.'

Appendix 5
Matabeleland Relief Force

Officer Commanding: Colonel Herbert Plummer

'A' Squadron–Troops 1, 2 and 3
Captain Bowden
Lieutenants Wood, Cashel and McQueen

'B' Squadron–Troops 4, 5 and 6
Captains Straker and Satchwell
Lieutenants Constable, May, Fordham, Masterton and Williams

'C' Squadron–Troops 7, 8 and 9
Major Kershaw
Captains Fowler and Murray
Lieutenants McNichol, Forbes, Rawstone and Mathias

'D' Squadron–Troops 10 and 11
Captain Fraser
Lieutenants Tomlinson, Lees, McGeean and Heyman

'E' Squadron–Troops 12, 13 and 14
Captain Drury
Lieutenants Cazalet, Murray and Abbott

Maxim Detachment
Captain Wheeler
Lieutenants Pyke and Michell

Signalling Detachment
Captain Dent

Medical Detachment
Surgeon-Captains Michell and Lunan

c.850 officers and men (around 1,000 were on the nominal role at various stages in the campaign)

Other details
Daily Pay scales:

Captain / Inspector	17/-
Lieutenant / Sub-Inspector	13/-
Staff Sergeant	11/-
Troop Sergeant-Major	10/-
Sergeant	9/-
Corporal	8/-
Trooper	7/6

Imperial officers serving with the MRF received 15/- a day, in addition to their regimental pay

Origins of the men of the MRF

British born (having lived in the colonies less than three years)	c.300
British born (having lived in the colonies more than three years)	c.300
South African–British extraction	c.150
South African–Afrikaans	c.50
Australian	22
Canadian	5
Americans	5
German	4
Spanish	2
Others	17

Previous employment

Ex-BBP or BSACP / RMP	c.400
Farmers	c.120
Miners / Engineers	c.100
Clerks	c.100
De Beers employees	c.50
Soldiers (British Army)	c.50
Soldiers (colonial units)	c.30

The average age of the men was 25–27

Appendix 6
Imperial Composite Mounted Infantry Regiment

Commanding Officer, Captain (Brevet Lt. Colonel) E.A.H. Alderson–
2nd Royal West Kent Regiment

Adjutant
Captain A.J. Godley–1st Royal Dublin Fusiliers

No.6 Company (English)–119 officers and men
OC. Major F.S. Evans, 1st Battalion Derbyshire Regiment
4 sections, drawn from the following regiments:
2nd Norfolk Regiment
2nd Hampshire Regiment
1st South Lancashire Regiment
1st Derbyshire Regiment

No.7 Company (Rifles)–125 officers and men
OC. Captain A.V. Jenner DSO, 4th Battalion Rifle Brigade
4 sections, drawn from the following regiments:
3rd Kings Royal Rifle Corps
4th Kings Royal Rifle Corps
2nd Rifle Brigade
4th Rifle Brigade

No.9 Company (Highland)–124 officers and men
OC. Captain G.R. Tod, 1st Battalion Seaforth Highlanders
4 sections, drawn from the following regiments:
2nd Royal Highlanders (the Black Watch)
1st Seaforth Highlanders
2nd Gordon Highlanders
1st Argyll and Sutherland Highlanders

No.11 Company (Irish)–122 officers and men
OC. Captain Sir H.W. McMahon, Bart, 2nd Royal Welsh Fusiliers
4 sections, drawn from the following regiments:
1st Royal Irish Regiment
1st Royal Dublin Fusiliers
2nd Royal Irish Fusiliers
1st Royal Irish Rifles

Appendix 7
Mazoe Patrol

Settlers from the Mazoe area who gathered at the Alice Mine:
Archer Burton–store manager
John Pascoe–Salvation Army
E.T. Cass–Salvation Army (killed)
Mrs Cass
James ffolliott Darling
Mr Dickinson–justice of the peace (killed)
Mrs Dickinson
J. Fairbairn
W. Faull (killed)
T.G. Routledge–telegraph operator (killed)
J.W. Salthouse–mine manager
Mrs Salthouse
Harry Spreckley
J. Stoddart
'George'–Cape Boy

Settlers from the area who were attacked before they could get to the Alice Mine laager:
Charles Annesty–prospector (killed)
Henry Pollard–native commissioner (killed)

Initial rescue party (brought a wagon out from Salisbury to evacuate the ladies):
John Blakiston (killed)
Harold D. Zimmermann
'Hendrik'–Cape Boy

First Patrol:
Lt. Dan Judson–Rhodesia Horse
Tpr W. Carton-Coward
Tpr Charles Hendrikz
Tpr William Honey
Tpr Ernst Niebuhr
Tpr Hugh Pollet
Paymaster Captain Stamford Brown met with, and attached himself to the patrol.
Troopers Finch, Guyon, King and Mulvaney also rode out with Judson's

patrol, but were sent back before arriving at the Alice Mine due to their horses being knocked up.

Second Patrol:
Capt. Randolph C. Nesbitt–Mashonaland Mounted Police
Lt. C. McGreer (killed)
Sgt A. Nesbitt
Sgt O.H. Ogilvie
Tpr S. Arnott
Tpr H.J. Berry
Tpr T.R. Bryon
Tpr J.A. Edmunds
Tpr R. Harbord
Tpr G. Jacobs (killed)
Tpr M. McGregor
Tpr H.J. van Staaden (killed)
Tpr. O.C. Zimmermann

NB. The two Zimmermann brothers later changed their name to Rawson.

Appendix 8

Alderson's Mashonaland Relief Force

(Departed Umtali on 28 July 1896)

Commanding Officer: Captain (Brevet Lt. Colonel) E.A.H. Alderson–
2nd Royal West Kent Regiment

No.7 Company (Rifles)–125 officers and men
OC. Captain A.V. Jenner DSO, 4th Battalion Rifle Brigade
4 sections, drawn from the following regiments:
3rd Kings Royal Rifle Corps
4th Kings Royal Rifle Corps
2nd Rifle Brigade
4th Rifle Brigade

No.11 Company (Irish)–122 officers and men
OC. Captain Sir H.W. McMahon, Bart, 2nd Royal Welsh Fusiliers
4 sections, drawn from the following regiments:
1st Royal Irish Regiment
1st Royal Dublin Fusiliers
2nd Royal Irish Fusiliers
1st Royal Irish Rifles

Honey's Scouts–14 officers and men
OC. Mr Wilfred Honey

Royal Artillery Detachment–15 officers and men
OC. Lt. S.C. Townsend
2 × 7-pdrs

Umtali Rifles–75 officers and men
OC. Major 'Maori' Hamilton-Browne

West Riding Regiment Detachment–50 officers and men
OC. Lt. P. Coode

Royal Engineers Detachment–42 officers and men
OC. Captain A.E. Haynes

Medical Staff Corps–15 officers and men
OC. Surgeon-Captain F.A. Saw

Others
Mr. H.C. Deary's group of volunteers–about 10 men
Army Service Corps–2 men
2 Maxim guns
native drivers

Appendix 9

Distribution of Forces in Mashonaland–

August 20 1896–totals show officers and men

Salisbury
Staff and others	8
Imperial Mounted Infantry	52
White's Scouts (Grey's and Gifford's)	65
Rhodesia Horse	131
Salisbury Garrison	103
Salisbury Artillery	15
Natal Troop	46
'Friendlies'	98

Fort Victoria
Victoria Rifles	145
'Friendlies'	142

Enkeldoorn
Enkeldoorn Garrison	67
'Friendlies'	80

Fort Charter
Charter Garrison	42
Salisbury Artillery	11
Salisbury Garrison	59
'Friendlies'	179

Chishawasha
Salisbury Garrison	17
'Friendlies'	15

Mazoe Fort
Salisbury Garrison	30

Marandellas
Matabele Relief Force	51

Headlands
Umtali Rifles	54
'Friendlies'	40

Fort Haynes
West Riding Regiment   101
Umtali Rifles   12
Others   9

Umtali
West Riding Regiment   53
Umtali Rifles   52
Matabeleland Relief Force   50
'Friendlies'   40
Others   16

Marching from Marandellas to Salisbury
Imperial Mounted Infantry (Irish & Rifles)   172
Royal Artillery   15
Royal Engineers   42
Honey's Scouts   16
'Friendlies'   33
Others   13

Marching from Salisbury to Umtali
Volunteers under Colonel Beal   44

Marching from Umtali to Beira – leaving the theatre
York and Lancaster Regiment   51

·

Bibliography

Abercrombie, H R, 'The Secret History of South Africa', Central News Agency, Johannesburg, 1951

Alderson, E A H, 'With the Mounted Infantry and the MFF 1896', Books of Rhodesia, Bulawayo, 1971

Aston, P E, 'The Raid on the Transvaal', Dean & Son, London, 1897

Barrett, C.R.B., 'The 7th (Queen's Own) Hussars, On Campaign During The Canadian Rebellion, The Indian Mutiny, The Sudan, Matabeleland, Mashonaland and the Boer War. Volume 3: 1818-1914', Leonaur, 2008 reprint of 1914 original

Baxter, Peter, 'Rhodesia – Last Outpost of the British Empire, 1890-1980', Galago Publishing, Alberton, 2010

Blake, Robert, 'A History of Rhodesia', Eyre Methuen, London, 1977

Bower, Sir Graham, 'Secret History of the Jameson Raid and the South African Crisis', Van Riebeeck Society, 2002

Brown, William H. 'On the South African Frontier', Sampson Low Marston & Co, London, 1899

Bulpin, T V, 'Storm over the Transvaal', Howard Timmins, Cape Town, 1911

Bulpin, T V, 'To the Banks of the Zambesi', Books of Africa, Cape Town, 1968

Burnham, F R, 'Scouting on Two Continents', William Hienemann Ltd, London, 1926

Cartwright, A P, 'Gold Paved the Way', MacMillan, London, 1967

Cary, Robert, 'Charter Royal', Howard Timmins, Cape Town, 1970

Cary, Robert, 'The Pioneer Corps', Galaxie Press, Salisbury, 1974

Cary, Robert, 'A Time to Die', Howard Timmins, Cape Town, 1969

Chilvers, Hedley A, 'The Story of De Beers', Cassell & Co Ltd, London, 1939

Churchill, Sir Winston, 'My Early Life', Odhams, London, 1947

Cohen, Louis, 'Reminiscences of Johannesburg & London', Holden, London, 1924

Cohen, Louis, 'Reminiscences of Kimberley', Bennett & Co, London, 1900

Colvin, Ian, 'Cecil John Rhodes', Dodo Press, London, 2008

Colvin, Ian, 'The Life of Jameson, Vol.1 & 2', Edward Arnold & Co, London, 1922

Cooper-Chadwick, J, 'Three Years with Lobengula', Books of Rhodesia, Bulawayo, 1975

Crwys-Williams, Jennifer, 'South African Despatches', Ashanti, Johannesburg, 1989

Darter, Adrian, 'The Pioneers of Mashonaland', Simpkin, Marshall, Hamilton, Kent & Co, London, 1914

Donovan, C H W, 'With Wilson in Matabeleland', Hazell, Watson & Viney, London, 1894

Du Toit, S J, 'Rhodesia', Books of Rhodesia, Bulawayo, 1977

Duminy, A H, 'Fitzpatrick Selected Papers', McGraw-Hill, Johannesburg, 1976

Durbach, Renee, 'Kipling's South Africa', Chameleon, Cape Town, 1988

Emden, Paul, 'Randlords', Hodder & Stoughton, London, 1935

Featherstone, Donald, 'Victorian Colonial Warfare – Africa 1842-1902', Blandford, London, 1993

Fitzpatrick, Sir Percy, 'South African Memories', Cassell & Co, London, 1979

Fitzpatrick, Sir Percy, 'Through Mashonaland', Argus, Johannesburg, 1892

Fort, G Seymour, 'Dr Jameson', Hurst & Blackett, London, 1908

French, Patrick, 'Younghusband', Harper Perennial, London, 2004

Fuller, Sir T E, 'Cecil Rhodes', Longmans Green & Co, London, 1910

Gale, W D, 'One Man's Vision', Hutchinson & Co, London, 1935

Gale, W D, 'The Heritage of Rhodes', Oxford University Press, London, 1950

Garrett, F Edmund, 'The Story of an African Crisis', Archibald Constable, London, 1897

Gibbs, Peter, 'The History of the BSAP, Vol.1', British South Africa Police, Salisbury, 1972

Gibbs, Peter, 'A Flag for the Matabele', Frederick Muller, London, 1955

Glass, Stafford, 'The Matabele War', Longmans Green & Co, London, 1968
Graumann, Sir Harry, 'Rand Riches', Juta & Co, Johannesburg, 1936
Green, J E S, 'Rhodes Goes North', G. Bell & Sons, London, 1936
Grey, Albert, 'Hubert Hervey, Student and Imperialist', Edward Arnold, London, 1899
Gross, Felix, 'Rhodes of Africa', Cassell & Company, London, 1956

Hamley, Richard, 'The Regiment', Covos Day, Johannesburg, 2000
Hanna, A J, 'The Story of the Rhodesias and Nyasaland', Faber & Faber, London, 1960
Hensmen, Howard, 'History of Rhodesia', William Blackwood & Sons, London, 1900
Hind, R J, 'Harry Labouchère and the Empire', The Athlone Press, London, 1972
Hole, Hugh M, 'The Jameson Raid', Philip Alan, London, 1930
Hole, Hugh M, 'Old Rhodesian Days', Frank Cass & Co, London, 1928
Hole, Hugh M, 'Lobengula', Philip Alan, London, 1929
Hutchinson, G T, 'Frank Rhodes', BiblioBazaaar, London, 2010

'Imperialist', 'Cecil Rhodes: A Biography and an Appreciation', MacMillan & Co, London, 1897

Jackson, Stanley, 'The Great Barnato', Heinemann, London, 1970
James, Lawrence, 'The Rise & Fall of the British Empire', Abacus, London, 1995
Jeal, Tim, 'Baden-Powell', Pimlico, London, 1989
Jenkins, Roy, 'Gladstone', MacMillan, London, 1995
Johnson, Frank, 'Great Days', G Bell & Sons, London, 1940
Jollie, E T, 'The Real Rhodesia', Books of Rhodesia, Bulawayo, 1971
Jones, Neville, 'Rhodesian Genesis', Bulawayo, 1953
Jourdon, Philip, 'Cecil Rhodes', The Bodley Head, London, 1910

Kane, Nora S. 'The World's View', Cassell & Co Ltd, London, 1954
Keppel-Jones, Arthur, 'Rhodes and Rhodesia', McGill-Queens University Press, Montreal, 1983
Knight, E F, 'Rhodesia of Today', Books of Rhodesia, Bulawayo, 1975
Kotze, Sir John Gilbert, 'Memoirs & Reminiscences', Maskew Miller, Cape Town, 1934

Laurie, Charles, 'Every Man Has His Price', University Press of America, Lanham, 2008
Le Sueur, Gordon, 'Cecil Rhodes', John Murray, London, 1913
Leonard, Arthur, 'How We Made Rhodesia', Kegan Paul, Trench, Trubner & Co, London, 1896
Lewsen, Phyllis, 'Selections of the Correspondence of J. X. Merriman', various volumes, The Van Riebeeck Society, Cape Town, 1960
Longford, Elizabeth, 'Jameson's Raid', Jonathon Ball, Johannesburg, 1960

Magnus, Philip, 'Gladstone', John Murray, London, 1954
Mason, Philip, 'Birth of Dilemma', Oxford University Press, London, 1958
Mathers, E P, 'Zambesia', Books of Rhodesia, Bulawayo, 1970
Maylam, Paul, 'The Cult of Rhodes', David Philip, Cape Town, 2005
Meredith, Martin, 'Diamonds, Gold and War', Simon & Schuster, London, 2007
Meredith, Martin, 'The Past is Another Country', Andre Deutsch, London, 1979
Millais, J G, 'The Life of Frederick Courtney Selous', Longmans Green & Co, London, 1919
Millin, Sarah G. 'Rhodes', Chato & Windus, London, 1933
Morris, Donald, 'The Washing of the Spears', Pimlico, London, 1994

Nathan, Manfred, 'Paul Kruger', Knox, Durban, 1941
Norris-Newman, Charles, 'Matabeleland and How We Got It', T. Fisher Unwin, London, 1895
Nutting, Anthony, 'Scramble for Africa', Constable, London, 1970

O'Reilly, John, 'Pursuit of the King', Books of Rhodesia, Bulawayo, 1970

Pakenham, Thomas, 'The Scramble for Africa', Abacus, London, 1992
Plumer, Lt. Col. Herbert, 'An Irregular Corps in Matabeleland', Kegan Paul, Trench, Trübner & Co. Ltd, London, 1897

Radziwill, Princess Catherine, 'Cecil Rhodes', Cassell & Co, London, 1918
Roberts, Brian, 'Kimberley, Turbulent City', David Philip, Cape Town, 1976
Rose, E B, 'The Truth About The Transvaal', London, 1902
Rouillard, Nancy, 'Matabele Thompson', Faber & Faber, London, 1936

Sauer, Hans, 'Ex Africa', Geoffrey Bles, London, 1937
Selous, F C, 'Sunshine & Storm in Rhodesia', Books of Rhodesia, Bulawayo, 1968
Selous, F C, 'A Hunters Wanderings in Africa', Richard Bentley & Son, London, 1881
Shaw, Gerald, 'The Garrett Papers', Van Riebeeck Society, Cape Town, 1984
Smuts, J C, 'Jan Christian Smuts', Cassell & Co, London, 1952
Stead, William, 'Joseph Chamberlain', London, 1899
Steevens, George, 'From Cape Town to Ladysmith', William Blackwood & Sons, London, 1900
Sykes, Frank, 'With Plumer in Matabeleland', Books of Rhodesia, Bulawayo, 1972

Tabler, E C, 'Zambezia & Matabeleland in the 70's', Chatto & Windus, London, 1960
Tanner, G H, 'A Scantling of Time', Stuart Manning, Salisbury, 1965
Taylor J B, 'A Pioneer Looks Back', Hutchinson & Co, London, 1939
Taylor J B, 'Memoirs of a Randlord', Stonewall Books, Cape Town, 2003
Theal, George, 'Ethnography and Condition of South Africa before 1505', George Allen and Unwin Ltd, London, 1919
Thomson, H C, 'Rhodesia and its Government', Smith, Elder & Co, London, 1898
Thorgold, Algar, 'The Life of Henry Labouchère', Constable, London, 1913
Trollope, Anthony, 'South Africa, Vol.2', Nonsuch Publishing, Stroud, 2005
Twain, Mark, 'More Tramps Abroad', Chatto & Windus, London, 1898

van Wyk, Peter, 'Burnham', Victoria, 2003

Walker, Eric, 'Lord De Villiers & His Times', Constable, London, 1925
Warhurst, P R, 'Anglo-Portuguese Relations in South Central Africa, 1890-1900', Longmans Green & Co, London, 1962
Welsh, Frank, 'A History of South Africa', Harper Collins, London, 1998
Wheatcroft, Geoffrey, 'The RandLords', Weidenfeld & Nicolson, London, 1993
Wills, W.A, 'The Downfall of Lobengula', Books of Rhodesia, Bulawayo, 1971
Wilmot, A, 'The History of South Africa', Kegan Paul, Trench, Trubner & Co, Cape Town, 1901
Wright, H M, 'Sir James Rose Innes, Selected Correspondence', Van Riebeeck Society, Cape Town, 1972

Command Papers and Reports
C 7196 South Africa: Copies and Extracts of Further Correspondence relating to Affairs in Mashonaland, Matabeleland and the Bechuanaland Protectorate (1893)
C 7290 South Africa: Further Correspondence relating to Affairs in Mashonaland, Matabeleland and the Bechuanaland Protectorate (1894)
Major Sir John Willoughby's Report of the Battle of Changani (Nov. 1894)
Major Sir John Willoughby's Account of the Battle of Imbembizi, Fought at the Head Waters of the Bembizi River (Nov. 1893)

Periodicals and other
The Rhodesian Society, 'Rhodesiana' magazine – various
The History Society of Zimbabwe, 'Heritage' magazine – various
The Maxim Automatic Gun in Action, Naval & Military Press
The Times of London – online archives
The Cape Times – archives

Made in the USA
Monee, IL
07 July 2026

56544777R00187